Shocking Stories from the Squared Circle

SLAM! Wrestling

Also by Greg Oliver

The Pro Wrestling Hall of Fame: The Canadians

The Pro Wrestling Hall of Fame: The Tag Teams

The Pro Wrestling Hall of Fame: The Heels

*Benoit: Wrestling with the Horror
that Destroyed a Family and Crippled a Sport*

SLAM! Wrestling

Shocking Stories from the Squared Circle

Edited by

GREG OLIVER & JON WALDMAN

ECW Press

Published by ECW Press
2120 Queen Street East, Suite 200
Toronto, Ontario, Canada M4E 1E2
416.694.3348 / info@ecwpress.com

LIBRARY AND ARCHIVES CANADA CATALOGUING IN PUBLICATION

Oliver, Greg
Slam! wrestling : shocking stories from the squared circle / Greg Oliver and Jon Waldman.

ISBN 978-1-55022-884-7

1. Slam! Wrestling (Web site). 2. Wrestling. I. Waldman, Jon II. Title.

GV1195.O45 2009   796.812   C2009-902523-X

Editor for the press: Michael Holmes
Cover design: David Gee
Cover photo: Mike Mastrandrea
Typesetting: Mary Bowness
Printing: Webcom   1   2   3   4   5

Mixed Sources
Product group from well-managed
forests, and other controlled sources
www.fsc.org Cert no. SW-COC-002358
FSC   © 1996 Forest Stewardship Council

The publication of *Slam! Wrestling* has been generously supported by
the Government of Ontario through Ontario Book Publishing Tax Credit,
by the OMDC Book Fund, an initiative of the Ontario Media Development Corporation,
and by the Government of Canada through the Book Publishing Industry
Development Program (BPIDP).

Canada

PRINTED AND BOUND IN CANADA

ECW PRESS
ecwpress.com

For Bret "Hitman" Hart, whose column helped build the site's reputation, and the other columnists from the industry — Don "Cyrus" Callis, "Hotshot" Johnny Devine, and Portia Perez — who helped add to our credibility.

WWE Diva Maria Kanellis reacts to a question from Bob Kapur — knowing Bob, it was quite likely a marriage proposal.

Table of Contents

Superstars 67

The Art of Wrestling 141

After the Applause 151

WrestleMania 229

Scoops and Surprises 239

Acknowledgments

Jon would like to thank . . .

Greg for giving a scrub writer from Winnipeg a chance to write for SLAM! Wrestling in the first place. It's been a crazy 10-year journey.

Jon toils away for the good of the site.

JP, John M and Nuke for the wicked wrestling debates in the good ol' days in the Canoe office.

All current and past SLAM! Wrestling writers and readers for keeping the biz fun, especially during those really, really lame times (Katie Vick anyone?).

His wife Elana, for not only putting up with the ever-growing DVD collection, but for giving him so much support throughout the book's creation and website's management. His parents, Arthur and Denise, and sister Miriam for never questioning that there could be something to writing about wrestling for his career (okay, maybe a couple times they did, but still . . .). His parents-in-law, Irene and David, brother-in-law Jesse, buddies Michael, Steven, Mike and the rest of his family and friends for sharing in this special project. His grandfathers, Shia and Sydney, who spent many hours watching Stampede and WWF wrestling in his early years. He wishes they could be here today. His cousin, Joshua, who constantly reminds him that sometimes it's good to stop over-analyzing wrestling and just enjoy a good show.

His mentors, Sheldon Oberman, Jerry Gladman and Tim Falconer for, more than anything else, showing him that indeed, journalism is the best career out there.

Ira, Stephen, Jeff and the rest of the boys and girls at Topps for giving him the chance to live out a boyhood dream.

Michael Holmes and the ECW Press crew for everything involved with the book (especially saying "yes" to the book proposal).

All of his co-workers, past, present and future, for dealing with his wrestling chatter so kindly (or is that patronizing?).

Vince McMahon, Eric Bischoff, Paul Heyman, the Harts, Verne Gagne, the Jarretts, Tony Condello and countless other promoters who, under immense pressure, put on wrestling that has kept the ring wars fun for so many years. And all the wrestlers who have come and gone in the business through the years, who put their bodies on the line in the greatest form of entertainment of them all.

Greg would like to thank . . .

All the readers over the years, who challenged us when needed, thanked us on occasion, and sent in countless story ideas, requests, questions and more. To all the SLAM! Wrestling writers — and there have been tons of them — thanks for putting up with me through various rewrites, postponements of stories, and various other hassles. There are a few who used the clippings and experience to move on to bigger and better things, making me sad and proud at the same time.

Greg Oliver types for Mad Dog Vachon's live chat with SLAM! Wrestling at the Canoe Toronto office.

Thanks to those who helped me turn into a decent editor: At Ryerson, it was Peter Robertson; at the *Toronto Sun*, huzzahs to Ian Martin, Wayne Janes and Kathy Brooks; at Canoe.ca, it was Mike Simpson, John Sakamoto, Jim O'Leary and Art Chamberlain.

And finally, Jon Waldman, who really kept at this project while I changed dirty diapers (thanks Quinn!).

Foreword

by Scott D'Amore

Greg Oliver

Two great Canadian minds, Pat Patterson and Scott D'Amore. Next time you see Scott, ask him about Pat kicking him out of the WWE dressing room.

The first thing that comes to mind when I hear the words "SLAM! Wrestling" is a terrible picture of me. I know what you're saying: with this ugly mug, how could I ever take a good picture? Zip it!

I'm talking about that godawful picture that they have on my profile on the site. I swear that the day I die, if any newspaper actually picks up the story, right beside the obituary will be that horrible, embarrassing picture. That photo will haunt me, forever.

Here's what happened: I was backstage at a show at Medieval Times in Toronto, getting mentally ready for my match while waiting for my music to start. I had just had surgery three weeks before and I was getting in the ring to test out my knee before going on a tour of Japan.

I was about to wrestle Sabu for the first time. Oh, I should probably mention that he and I had just recently gotten back on good terms again after a bad falling-out a couple of years earlier that had him cussing whenever my name came up — so, no pressure or anything.

So there I am with all of these things racing around in my mind, trying to focus on my match, when some guy who I've never seen before comes up to me and says, "Hey, can I grab a photo?" Not knowing exactly what's

xiii

going on, I turn around and, half-heartedly, with a blank stare on my face, sort of put my fists up like I'm mock fighting.

I walked away and never thought of it again.

Now, more than a decade later, if you search for my image on the web, that's the very first thing you'll see.

So when the editors of this book asked me to write the foreword, I agreed to do it on one condition: they had to promise to destroy that picture and remove it from their site for good!

All kidding aside, when I hear the words "SLAM! Wrestling," I think of how significant it is in terms of wrestling news. Not just in Canada — though it is probably the best source for Canadian wrestling news — but around the world. Seriously, I've talked to industry people from across the globe, from Japan to Europe to Mexico, and everyone is aware of the site.

I think a lot of that has to do with the way writers cover wrestling. I'd say about 90-plus percent of what you see about it on the web is written with a very negative slant. I've never been able to understand why. If someone's a fan of something and so passionate that they watch multiple shows in a week, why, when they devote time to write about it, are they so critical of just about everything, usually just for the sake of being critical? What stands out about SLAM! Wrestling is that no matter what the story is, it's written by somebody who cares.

That's not to say that they sugarcoat things or write puff pieces — the site has covered some hard-hitting events over the years. It's just that they never come across as bitter or overly negative. What I've always liked about the site is that when they're publishing a review of a show, or an event, or a product, whether it's positive or negative, it's just about always written fairly.

And from what I've seen, that's the way they deal with the people they're writing about too. That's why it's one of a very few sites that I actually deal with. I don't want to paint everyone else with a bad brush, because there are some good people out there. But with a lot of other sites, you have to be very careful about what you say, how you word something, or else you risk being misquoted or having your words twisted and turned into something you didn't mean. When dealing with the people I deal with at SLAM! (mostly "Bloodthirsty" Bob Kapur — who eventually will be ghostwriting my book: cheap plug!), I've never felt like I had to be really careful. I've always felt I've had the chance to express my opinion and have it presented on the site honestly and accurately.

And that makes it such a valuable resource. Particularly in terms of showing Canada's place within the industry. Whether it's a story on Grand Prix Wrestling out on the East Coast, or a historical look at Stampede

Wrestling out west, or results from a Border City Wrestling show in Windsor (another cheap plug!), fans and industry people alike know that the site is the real source for Canadian wrestling news.

There's an old saying that Terry Taylor explained to me years ago: there are two ways to have the tallest building in town. The first way is to work really hard and dedicate yourself to the project and go out and build a building taller than any other. The second way is to go out and build whatever you can, and then go around and tear down every building in town taller than yours.

It seems to me that while the vast majority of wrestling news sources try to tear down everything else, SLAM! Wrestling concentrates on building a site that's the best it can be.

It's truly amazing to me that after all these years it continues to build, grow and succeed. And what's even more amazing is that it continues to build, grow and succeed, even though it's being led by that goofy-looking Greg Oliver in his ugly Christmas sweaters.

There, I'm finished.

Now take down that photo, damn it!

Scott D'Amore
(Who in a terrible oversight was left out of Greg Oliver's book *The Pro Wrestling Hall of Fame: The Canadians*.)

Abdullah the Butcher takes out his frustration on Tim Baines after learning that Baines masqueraded as Mr. X in the *Ottawa Sun* wrestling column for a while. But a hug from Kelly Kelly makes up for the pain and suffering.

A Brief History of SLAM! Wrestling

Once upon a time, in a land not so far away from here, two rabid wrestling fans came together for what would become an incredible journey.

No, that isn't a stolen tagline from *Ready to Rumble*, though perhaps if that was part of the marketing material, the forgettable WCW movie would actually have drawn a viewer or two.

Instead, this is the opening to the twisting and turning story of SLAM! Wrestling.

Indeed, as simple as it may sound, SLAM! Wrestling began because of two men — Greg Oliver and John Powell — and their unwavering fascination with the business of professional mat wars.

Back in 1996, both were in Toronto, Ontario, employed by Sun Media as part of its new internet project — CANadian Online Explorer, or www.canoe.ca. Canoe's directive, along with its subsites such as CNEWS, JAM! Showbiz and SLAM! Sports, was not only to bring headlines pulled straight from the pages of the various *Sun* newspapers, but to provide original and exclusive content.

This simple plan led to a number of specialty sections and the hiring of newshounds whose names would only appear in digital bylines. It wasn't long before Powell and Oliver, who shared a passion for the pro ranks, began to conceive of putting together a full-out wrestling website that would report on the latest happenings in the squared circle and behind the curtain.

Supported in the early days by *Sun* writers such as "Coach" Glenn Cole, who contributed wrestling articles and columns to the papers, SLAM! Wrestling began to gain a considerable audience as Powell and Oliver built an impressive array of stories that spoke to the growing internet wrestling community in a fashion unlike virtually any other website. Rather than dishing dirt with anonymous sources, SLAM! Wrestling went about its business as any other Sun Media venture would — with a traditional journalistic approach based on research, up-front interviews, facts and more than a little cheekiness.

Of course, these factors were only part of the growth of SLAM! Wrestling. What was also an integral part of the website was that it was the exclusive online home to columns by wrestlers Bret "The Hitman" Hart (from the *Calgary Sun*) and Don "Cyrus" Callis (from the *Winnipeg Sun*). This was long before MySpace and other such outlets gave wrestlers the opportunity to express their feelings and send updates to their fans with the truth of the professional ranks. It was unusual for wrestlers to have any avenue to talk about their personal thoughts beyond the walls of kayfabe (which, believe it or not, were still intact, though wobbly, when SLAM! Wrestling started).

Along with the columns and features, SLAM! Wrestling also gave readers the unprecedented opportunity to talk to the men and women in the business, as chats soon became a part of the regular schedule at the Canoe offices. Wrestlers like Roddy Piper and Ron Simmons, and outside-the-ring personalities like Barry W. Blaustein, director of *Beyond the Mat*, and Diana Hart, were guests to the SLAM! Wrestling office to sit down across virtual lines with SLAM! Wrestling's faithful to dish about the industry. With the World Wrestling Federation (WWF, now known as WWE) having a satellite office in Toronto, it all made for some natural synergy.

As time went on, Powell and Oliver were joined on the front line by a number of up-and-coming writers. John Molinaro soon became the proverbial third amigo, adding international flavor to the website with his vast knowledge of lucha libre and puroresu. Canoe staffers Alex Ristic and Stephen Laroche also contributed from the office, while outside writers like Nick Tylwalk, Chris Gramlich, Bob Kapur, Eric Benner and Jon Waldman would scribe from locations both inside Toronto and across the continent.

Yes, these were truly happy times in the land of SLAM! Wrestling, but, as was the case with so many internet ventures, the bottom fell out on Canoe.

In late 2001, just a few short weeks after the SLAM! Wrestling crew toasted what was arguably the most successful year in the fledgling site's history in a chat at the Canoe offices, SLAM! Wrestling co-founder Greg Oliver, along with other staff including Laroche and Ristic, were terminated, or in the lexicon of the just-burst tech bubble, "downsized."

The site, however, soldiered on. WrestleMania X8 was in Toronto in March 2002, and despite the loss of Oliver, the site provided the best coverage of any media, be it internet, print or broadcast.

Once the festivities of 'Mania were over, however, so too were "friendly" relations with the WWF. For reasons that would be heavily questioned (to say the least) across the internet wrestling community, WWF put a media ban in place, denying SLAM! Wrestling and other websites access to its superstars.

Needless to say, the staff was pissed off, but perhaps no one better expressed his dismay than John Molinaro. Earlier in his tenure, Molinaro had put out an editorial calling into question a similar media ban that the WWF had in place. Now, after having established a relationship with the Fed, including personal friendships, Molinaro felt slighted, and expressed his disappointment in an editorial.

Bret Hart reads through questions from SLAM! Wrestling readers at his Calgary home, just weeks after the "Montreal Screwjob."

Greg Oliver

SLAM! WRESTLING EDITORIAL: WWF MEDIA POLICY A JOKE

By JOHN MOLINARO
(March 25, 2002)

"The WWF has declared war on the media. Not the entire media, mind you. They'll gladly talk to newspapers, radio and TV stations or any news agency that doesn't regularly cover pro wrestling. But they've cut off wrestling internet sites almost entirely."
— "The WWF's war on internet sites"
(September 7, 2000)

Here we go again. In September 2000, I wrote an editorial taking the WWF to task for its archaic media policy, which prohibited any WWF performer from granting an interview with a reporter without checking with the office first.

"While the WWF claimed the policy was put in place because they viewed SLAM! Wrestling and other wrestling websites as 'competition' for WWF.com and they don't want to help supply content for their 'competitor,' the real reason was the WWF wants to manage its image and control how it's portrayed in the public eye. To that end, they've cut off contact with media agencies that could potentially hurt them."

That's what I wrote almost two years ago.

After causing a bit of a stir I was contacted by Jim Ross, the Executive Vice President of Talent Relations for the WWF (a fancy title that means he's the second most powerful man in the company behind Vince McMahon). We talked about the policy at length during several phone conversations and eventually it was scrapped.

Since then, SLAM! Wrestling has enjoyed a mutually advantageous relationship with the WWF. After ditching the policy, the WWF opened its doors to the online community, including inviting several high-profile websites to take part in the monthly TNN conference calls prior to each pay-per-view. Requests for interviews with WWF talent by SLAM! Wrestling were handled and set up in a professional, timely manner.

In addition to being on the WWF's A-list of wrestling websites, SLAM! Wrestling fostered a relationship with Jim Ross, gaining an access to him that very few other websites enjoyed. In the aftermath of my editorial, Ross invited me to call him at any time should I ever need him to comment or confirm a story I was working on. His candor in those interviews was refreshing and allowed us to write dozens of articles on the state of the WWF as viewed by one of the most powerful men in the industry.

Still, SLAM! Wrestling was not hesitant to criticize the WWF when the situation called for it. While we were critical of some of the WWF's storylines and the general direction of the company at times, we did so in a professional manner. Although he did not always agree with some of our criticisms in respective editorials and columns that we published, Ross told us that he believed we helped to set a standard of professionalism among pro wrestling websites for our "hard-hitting" coverage.

Despite being on opposite sides of the fence (being a reporter who scrutinized the WWF, our relationship was adversarial in nature), Ross paid me several personal compliments, impressed with the "diligence" and "fair manner" in which I did my job. His words, not mine.

For close to two years SLAM! Wrestling — not to mention other respected websites — went about its business covering the trials and tribulations of the WWF, thinking that as long as we continued to do so in a professional manner, we would enjoy a mutually profitable relationship.

So, you can imagine my surprise when I surfed into WWF.com last Wednesday and read their "Open Letter" to pro wrestling newsletters and internet sites.

Sadly, it now looks like we're back to square one.

I knew it was too good to last.

There's been a lot of conjecture amongst fans over what this statement actually means. SLAM! Wrestling has been inundated with emails from readers curious to find out how this will affect our coverage. I've spoken with one or two key people in the WWF's front office and I have traded "notes" with several reporters at other websites who have done their own digging.

In a nutshell, this is what we're dealing with:

- The WWF has cut off all official communication with pro wrestling websites and newsletters.
- The monthly TNN conference calls prior to each monthly pay-per-view that featured a WWF star fielding questions from reporters have been cancelled.
- The WWF will no longer grant wrestling websites or newsletters one-on-one interviews with anybody on its roster.
- Nobody in WWF front office, including Jim Ross, will comment on any news story by a pro wrestling website or newsletter.

So what's the reason behind the WWF's about-face?

According to the WWF's "Open Letter" it is the proliferation of news articles by online and newsletter reporters that make use of anonymous sources.

The "Open Letter" states the following:

"Despite our efforts to make ourselves available for official comment, it is the rare occasion when you call to confirm your facts or to get official comment before publishing information about the WWF/E. As a result, many times what you report is more rumor, innuendo and speculation than fact."

Where do I even begin to address this nonsense?

I suppose I could start by pointing out the not-so-coincidental timing of this policy. Only after the WWF milked and bilked as much coverage out of SLAM! Wrestling and every other wrestling website it could for Axxess and WrestleMania did they decide to conveniently end all communication. Such a move not only demonstrated a gross display of bad faith, but also revealed the scurrilous way the WWF does business.

I suppose I could start by pointing out the irony of how a company that professes to be a sworn enemy of censorship and staunch defenders of free speech and the First Amendment has little respect for the independence and freedom of the press.

The day before the "Open Letter" appeared on WWF.com, the WWF announced that they were heading up the Smackdown Your Vote! Campaign, a project geared at registering more voters in the United States.

"Democracy is built on a simple act: voting," said Linda McMahon, CEO of World Wrestling Federation Entertainment.

Democracy, in case Mrs. McMahon didn't know, is also built on the strength and independence of the media and the press to serve as watchdogs in order hold those in power accountable. By its actions with this policy, the WWF had made it clear that they have no respect for democracy at all.

And I suppose I could start by pointing out that while the "Open Letter" states, "it is the rare occasion when you call to confirm your facts or to get official comment before publishing information about the WWF/E," that SLAM! Wrestling and other websites and newsletters have gone to great lengths to do exactly that.

You need only look at our stories in the past on the return of Scott Hall and Kevin Nash, the signing of Jerry Lynn and Rob Van Dam or on the controversy over Big Show's racial remarks on an edition of *Raw Is War* as examples.

All of these stories, and several others that have appeared on SLAM! Wrestling, have official comment from the WWF.

So how will I start to address this policy?

How about with the WWF's laughable expectation of wrestling websites and newsletters to report as news "what is readily available to the public from our official websites and news releases."

Oh, so I get it.

The WWF would have us report press releases and news items on their website verbatim on SLAM! Wrestling without so much as questioning its authenticity and news value or having to answer any questions about it.

How the WWF is able to keep a straight face while maintaining such a ridiculous position is beyond me.

I realize the WWF is living in a "fantasy land" and is unfamiliar with how things work in the real world, so allow me to enlighten them.

Pro wrestling websites and newsletters are not here to help them promote their product and company. That's what the WWF's public relations department is for.

Our job is to report the news totally independent of the WWF's influence and authority. It is a responsibility that everybody here at SLAM! Wrestling takes very seriously and one that is shared by other websites and newsletters.

Considering the WWF currently enjoys a monopoly on the industry, that job is now more important than any other time in history.

Furthermore, unbeknownst to the WWF, the use of anonymous sources is not only perfectly legitimate, but integral to the practice of journalism.

I have read several commentaries over the past few days about WWF's unreasonable expectation for journalists to not use anonymous sources. I could easily offer my own verbose diatribe on the subject, pointing out the WWF's temerity and arrogance in actually expecting the media to bend to their whims and wishes.

Instead, I think SLAM! Wrestling contributor Nick Tylwalk said it best in his column last Friday:

> "To me, the more interesting facet of this situation — especially after reading the thoughts of the staff and readers of SLAM! Wrestling — is the WWF's notion that the normal rules of journalism don't or shouldn't apply in the world of wrestling. Since the biggest beef in the WWF.com statement seems to be the use of anonymous sources, this is the only conclusion at which I can arrive. After all, I can't think of any form of legitimate journalism that doesn't use anonymous sources to help gather information. Yet the WWF seems to think wrestling sites should report only the official company line."

A more articulate, intelligent and lucid summation of the crux of the WWF's media policy I have yet to read.

Since the "Open Letter" first appeared on WWF.com last Wednesday, I've spoken with several news editors and reporters who have been in the media for over 20 years, as well as numerous public relations people at several big companies (all of whom know nothing about wrestling and couldn't pick Ric Flair out of a lineup if their lives depended on it).

I showed them the WWF's statement and told them about the WWF's media policy and asked them for their honest feedback.

Their response?

Everybody said they had never come across any company with such a ridiculous policy.

Picture this: Bill Gates and Microsoft become irate over a series of stories that used anonymous sources appearing in the *Washington Post* over the period of one year. In his anger, not only does Gates decide to end all communication with the *Post* but also decides to cut off all communication with every single newspaper in the U.S.

Can you imagine that? Could you imagine anything more ludicrous?

And yet, that's exactly what the WWF's decision is tantamount to.

If the WWF really had a problem with wrestling websites and newsletters that they felt were irresponsible, then they should no longer deal with them.

To paint all wrestling websites and newsletters with the same brushstroke is not only negligent, but it also punishes the ones (like SLAM! Wrestling) that have been professional and responsible.

But of course, this media policy isn't about the use of anonymous sources or calling the WWF office to get official comment on stories.

As Nick so astutely pointed out, it's about the WWF and their expectation that "wrestling sites should report only the official company line."

It's about Vince McMahon and how he hates anybody that dares to question his wrestling genius.

It's about how newspapers and mainstream media sources — forever duped into reporting McMahon's revisionist version of wrestling history as fact — have been smartened up by wrestling websites and newsletters and can now see through his line of bull. (Read *Toronto Sun* reporter Perry Lefko's series of stories based on a recent interview with McMahon for evidence of that.) And it's about how McMahon, ever the corporate shyster and fixer, can no longer control and manipulate the media like he once could.

* * *

Molinaro's plea for consideration for SLAM! Wrestling to be removed from the proverbial blacklist would eventually come, but not before he and other Canoe staffers were released from their duties. Molinaro, who was in the midst of preparing his first book on pro wrestling, bid farewell to the website that he loved soon after his own notice came in early 2002.

* * *

SAYING GOODBYE TO SLAM! WRESTLING
By JOHN MOLINARO (April 23, 2002)

> *"And now, the end is here*
> *And so I face the final curtain."* — Frank Sinatra's "My Way"

Ol' Blue Eyes said it best, folks. All good things must eventually come to an end.

As some of you might have heard already, there was another round of lay-offs here at Canoe last week. In the aftermath of this latest act of corporate downsizing, several people lost their jobs. I was one of them.

After three years as a reporter and editor here at SLAM! Wrestling, I now find myself among the ranks of the unemployed. This past Friday was my last day of work, this column the last piece I will write for SLAM! Wrestling.

And so I depart, not with a bang, but with a whimper. Not exactly the way I wanted to go out, but then again, there are people in this world with far greater problems that it would be callous of me to complain.

So how shall I bid adieu?

Hmmm.

There will be no bitterness or sadness expressed in this column. No diatribe about how Vince McMahon has successfully duped fans and mainstream media agencies into accepting his revisionist version of wrestling history as fact (93,000 at WrestleMania III? Yeah, right!). No holier-than-thou rant about how Japanese wrestling, in terms of in-ring product, is superior to pro wrestling in the U.S. and Canada. No crying foul over HHH and his backstage politicking, Hogan's out-of-control ego (yet another title run, eh? Oh my) or Stephanie McMahon's laughable writing of WWF storylines (at least she isn't on TV anymore). No jokes about Kevin Nash's work rate (what work rate?). No taking pleasure in the fact that Chyna can't get a decent job in Hollywood now that she's no longer employed in the wrestling business (chuckle chuckle). No criticism of the WWF and its hypocritical media ban.

None of that.

The only thing I wish to express is my heartfelt gratitude to you, the loyal readers, and to everybody involved in SLAM! Wrestling.

These past three years at SLAM! Wrestling have been very special to me and a big reason why is the core of readers who visited the site each and every day. Not a day went by when I didn't receive a thoughtful email from a reader about the coverage found on our site. Whether it was a compliment or criticism, it was always written in the best of taste and expressed an articulate, poignant viewpoint. Time and time again, SLAM! Wrestling readers demonstrated why they are considered amongst the most passionate and intelligent wrestling fans around.

That's not to say we always saw eye to eye on the relevant wrestling issues of the day. Quite the contrary. More often than not, I expressed an opinion in a column or editorial that ruffled the feathers of more than a handful of readers out there. During his tenure as one of the senior editors of SLAM! Wrestling, Greg Oliver was besieged with a constant flow of emails from irate readers, all expressing the same thing: "How come Molinaro has to be so negative all the time?"

At the same time, others applauded my bold, straightforward and uncompromising approach, appreciative of the fact that I dared to question accepted "truths" in pro wrestling and reveal the dark underbelly of the industry. By writing in such a frank fashion and challenging wrestling's powerbrokers, a portion of SLAM! Wrestling's audience started to see that, perhaps, all is not peaches and cream, in the wonderful world of pro wrestling.

The poet Robert Frost once wrote: "Two roads diverged in a wood and I — I took the one less traveled by, and that has made all the difference." Frost's credo is how I have chosen to eke out a living as a journalist: Unflinching. Unapologetic. Uncompromising. Unwavering.

Whether you loved me or hated me, agreed with me or were staunchly opposed, thought I was a good reporter or were convinced I was a hack, hopefully, if nothing else, you respected me.

Because, truth be told, I respected all of you.

I can't even begin to tell you what an honor and pleasure it was to write for such a smart and well-read audience. Without knowing it, you inspired me to push myself every day.

Wrestling websites differ in approach and content, each one unique in its own way. What has made SLAM! Wrestling stand out over the past six years, in my view, has been the high journalistic standard it has tried to set. More than just a news board or rumors page, SLAM! Wrestling featured actual news articles and feature stories written by dedicated journalists and a network of passionate freelancers who tried to provide the most complete coverage of the wrestling industry.

Because of this editorial policy, I was allowed to pursue and write full-length stories like the life and times of "Love Machine" Art Barr; the legend of El Santo; the 25th anniversary of the Ric Flair plane crash; looking back on the career of Jumbo Tsuruta; and the tragic story of Johnny Valentine.

Stories that you wouldn't see on any other site but SLAM! Wrestling.

And for that, I am extremely proud.

I'm also proud to have helped to expand the scope of coverage found on SLAM! Wrestling by writing and reporting about the latest happenings in Japanese and Mexican wrestling. When I first started at SLAM! we offered very little coverage of the international wrestling scene, but thanks to the support of Greg Oliver and John Powell, I was encouraged to cover it by way of news articles, historical features and analytical pieces. In doing so, I received emails from readers who told me that they were going to look into purchasing videotapes of Mexican and Japanese wrestling after reading one of my articles.

A greater compliment I have never received.

But when it comes right down to it, it's the people involved that make SLAM! Wrestling what it has become.

Working alongside ex-staffers like Stephen Laroche and Alex Ristic proved a fruitful relationship as they inspired me and pushed me to do my best. Our wonderful network of freelancers added an entirely new dimension to the site. Their hard work was absolutely vital and integral to us gaining the reputation in the wrestling community that we have. I tip my cap to people like Chris "Hardcore" Gramlich, Aaron Henry, Nick Tylwalk, Bob Kapur, Yves Leroux, Donnie Abreu, Chris Schramm and Jon Waldman for their dedication. It's been a pleasure working with all of you.

A special thanks to colleagues in the wrestling media who, at one time or another, trumpeted work I had done and lauded me as someone with an actual trace of talent — go figure! People like Bill Apter, Mike Tenay and Mike Mooneyham were always very supportive of my work and made sure people knew it. A special thanks to Jeff Marek and Dan Lovranski at *Live Audio Wrestling* and Dave Meltzer of the *Wrestling Observer* who went out of their way to offer support to myself and everybody here at SLAM! Wrestling. I can't thank you enough for your help and for your friendship.

Of course, I owe the biggest thanks of all to both Greg Oliver and John Powell for helping to shape and mold a young, "wet-behind-the-ears" journalism school graduate into the poised reporter I am today. Words can't even begin to express the gratitude I feel towards both Greg and John and what they have meant to me, both personally and professionally.

Patience is indeed a virtue and over the years, Greg Oliver's was tested when it came to yours truly. Whether it was handling angry phone calls from the WWF over a scathing column I wrote, dealing with readers who complained I wrote too much about Japan and Mexico or editing yet another editorial that took Vince McMahon (a.k.a. Satan) to task, Greg never lost patience with me. It seems trite to say I learned so much working with him, but trite as it may be, it is the truth. Greg pushed me and prodded me to do better each time, challenging me to tackle a story from a different angle and taught me that sometimes less is more. If there's one person I am heavily in debt to for my writing and reporting style evolving and maturing over the past three years, it is Oliver.

As for John Powell, I learned the valuable lesson of never backing down when facing a challenge. When SLAM! Wrestling became embroiled in a war of words with Jim Ross and the WWF two years ago over its archaic media policy following an editorial I wrote, it was Powell who proved to be my closest confident. He took up the cause with me, writing his own editorial. Together, we put enough pressure on the suits in Titan Tower that shortly after the WWF opened its doors to the wrestling media. Much more than that, John has proven to be a shining example of professionalism and how to properly conduct oneself in the course of doing one's job. Thank you for showing me the way, John.

In a few months, my first book on pro wrestling (published by Stewart House Publishing) will be out and in major bookstore chains. It's safe to say that without the guidance of Greg and John that I never would have had the opportunity to tackle such a project. I am eternally grateful for everything they have done for me. Two better co-workers and friends I couldn't possibly imagine.

With my departure, the future of SLAM! Wrestling is unclear at the moment. With only John Powell left, serious decisions have to be made over the next few days. Once that is cleared up, I'm sure John will inform you of what lies ahead for the site.

And with that, I bid a fond farewell to you all and thank you for the kind (and not-so-kind) memories. SLAM! Wrestling readers wishing to drop me a line via email can reach me here.

And for anybody interested in speaking to me in person, you'll be able to find me on the corner of Bloor and Yonge Street in downtown Toronto, panhandling for spare change. I'll be the one sitting on the cold, hard pavement holding a cardboard sign that reads "WILL SLAG VINCE MCMAHON IN PRINT FOR FOOD."

Till we meet again.

"For what is a man, what has he got?
If not himself, then he has naught
To say the things he truly feels and not the words of one who kneels
The record shows I took the blows and did it my way!"

— Frank Sinatra's "My Way"

* * *

With two of the major players off the staff, SLAM! Wrestling soldiered on as best it could, but too much damage had been done. The cuts, WWF media policy and other factors led to what was undeniably one of the hardest decisions ever made by remaining producer and co-founder John Powell — to shut down SLAM! Wrestling's major coverage.

* * *

John Powell cowers in the presence of the Quebecers, Pierre Carl Ouelett and Jacques Rougeau Jr.

SO LONG BUT NOT GOODBYE

By JOHN POWELL
(May 29, 2002)

This is it. This is the last. I knew that one day I would have to write this. I just didn't think it would be so soon or under these circumstances. Funny how life goes sometimes, eh?

What you are reading is probably last piece I will ever write for SLAM! Wrestling — a site that Greg Oliver and I created six years ago and, with your support, became one of the most highly respected pro wrestling websites out there. For reasons I will explain shortly, I have decided to resign from the site as an editor and a reporter. From this day forward, I will not be a part of the daily updating of the site in any capacity. That will be SLAM!'s responsibility and I am sure they will do the best job they can.

I regret having to take my leave but there are circumstances beyond my control that have forced my hand. The most prominent reason is that two of my best friends — Greg Oliver and John Molinaro — no longer work with me here at Canoe (the Canadian Online Explorer).

As most of you are aware, SLAM! Wrestling is a part of SLAM! Sports, which in turn is the "sports section" of Canoe. SLAM! Wrestling was something we three did in our "spare time." In reality, John was a JAM! (Entertainment) editor, Greg was a part of the management team and I remain the Senior CNEWS (News) editor and part-time JAM! Showbiz reporter. Last December, Canoe laid off Greg and last month John was released from his duties along with approximately half the staff at Canoe. As you can imagine, it has been a painful and disconcerting time for all concerned. Here I am, the sole "Survivor" of SLAM! Wrestling. The kicker is there's no Mark Burnett to hand me a check for a million dollars. What a drag.

Another reason that I am taking my bow is that the current WWF product is boring me to death. At least a screen full of static has some life to it. WWF programming has none at all. Nothing the federation has done since

WrestleMania has made me stand up and take notice. Though I have been a passionate and devoted wrestling fan for 25 years, my interest fell to an all-time low right after the "Draft."

Ah, the "Draft" — another in a long line of WWF angles that has failed in every way imaginable. With 17 percent of you saying in our current poll that you've turned off the WWF completely and another 49 percent saying you don't watch as much as you used to, I can see that I am not alone in thinking that the current state of WWF programming isn't worth wasting precious time, attention or energy on either.

The WWF has now become what they've always despised. They are World Championship Wrestling: The Sequel . . . and not the good WCW from the '80s and early '90s with such stars as Cactus Jack, Sting, Arn Anderson, Rick Rude, Ricky Steamboat, Steve Austin, Ric Flair and Vader either. Ah, those were the days. It's Vince Russo–style WCW, only it is Vince McMahon driving the company into the ground this time around. As long as there's no competition for the WWF and McMahon remains at the controls, I don't see things changing anytime soon. Ratings will continue to slide. House show attendance will decrease even further. Talent will be laid off and programming will be cut. It wouldn't surprise me if *Raw* and *Smackdown* were reduced to an hour each by the end of the year. I can tell you one thing for sure — if I was a WWF mid-carder I would be actively exploring other shores or a second career because the future doesn't look too promising.

While we are on the topic, as I wrote in my editorial months ago, I still believe McMahon should promptly resign from the World Wrestling Federation. If not, he should do the next best thing, and that is quit trying to be the next Donald Trump or Ted Turner. News flash, Vince! Nobody in the general public is ever going to see you as anything more than the owner of a controversial but successful pro wrestling company no matter how many football leagues or record labels you start. It is his blessing and his curse. He should live with it and stop trying to be something he's not.

Just think of all the money Vince has wasted in his bid to "legitimize" the WWF. What he should have done is invest the money he spent on the XFL, that overpriced greasy spoon in New York and other futile projects in a national television network so his product could have a stable home. That's the Achilles' heel of the WWF. The future of the company has always rested in the hands of other network executives. All it would take for the WWF to tank is for the current television contracts not to be renewed and for no other network to be interested in WWF programming. If that ever happened, the WWF would be a shadow of its former self, relying on syndication rights, or they'd be ancient history. It's as simple as that. For all his supposed "genius," McMahon's WWF is no better off than when the first episode of *Raw* aired. Without strong ratings and the power that comes with them, it is the television networks and not Vince McMahon who still decide the fate of his company.

Anyhow, enough of that. Back to business.

There are a few people I wish to thank before I split the scene. . . .

- Former SLAM! producer and head chieftain at Canoe, Jim O'Leary. He gave Greg and I the green light to start SLAM! Wrestling all those years ago. He rarely interfered, trusted our judgment and was always extremely respectful of the site and our efforts. He helped pave the way for its success behind the scenes in so many ways. Without him, SLAM! Wrestling would still be a dream and not a reality.

- Former SLAM! producer, Dave Watkins. Just like O'Leary before him, Watkins gave us the freedom to run the site on our own and supported us through all the ups and downs.

- All of the regular contributors and "staff members" like Stephen Laroche, Aaron Henry, Nick Tylwalk, Chris Gramlich, Eric Benner, Jon Waldman, "Bloodthirsty" Bob Kapur, Pejman Ramezanpour and Donnie Abreu. Like us, they did what they did because they love wrestling. Greg, John and I will always be in debt to them for their hard work, invaluable assistance and most of all, their friendship. Hopefully, you may see many of these familiar faces when our future project is launched.

- To all the public relations people and talent over the years who've gone out of their way to accommodate and help us out.

- To all the editors, writers, photographers, reporters and ad people at Sun Media for their assistance. Shouts go out to Perry Lefko, Tim Baines, "Coach" Glenn Cole and the *Calgary Sun* for actually seeing wrestlers as newsworthy people.

- Thanks to my wife and son for their patience when Daddy had "work to do" or whenever the SLAM! Wrestling staff invaded the house on those special Sunday nights.

- My best pals and partners in crime — Greg and John. You put up with me. You backed me up. You motivated me to do things I never thought I was capable of. Wherever life takes us, I will forever be proud of the result of our teamwork. So many tales to tell, so little time. It was a wild ride that I will never forget.

- Last and by no means least, you, the readers. The decision to take my leave wasn't made in haste. Greg, John and I have put our hearts and souls into SLAM! Wrestling. It is not easy to just walk away from that. It is one of the hardest things I have ever had to do.

I am proud of what we have been able to accomplish and the work we've done. We did what we set out to do and that was to put together a wrestling site that treated the subject matter seriously and with the respect it deserved. A mainstream journalistic site that held such values as integrity, accountability and accuracy in the highest regard. I like to think we lived up to the standards we set for ourselves and that's why we were fortunate enough to garner respect from other media, the business as a whole and more important . . . you the fans. Unlike some promoters out there (that means you, Vince!) we never took your readership or your support for granted, which is why we worked on this site for six years without being paid a dime for our efforts. You are just as responsible for the achievements of SLAM! Wrestling as anyone mentioned above. Through your support, you gave us the power to live out our dreams and also to inform you as best as we could. Thanks for placing your trust in us. We hope that we didn't let you down too often.

As for me, I'll still be around at Canoe, editing the CNEWS section every day and writing movie reviews and stories for JAM! Showbiz. I will carry with me so many great memories. All the pay-per-view gatherings at my place. My chats with the Undertaker, Mick Foley and Booker T. My interview with the late, great Owen Hart just a year before he died. Buh Buh Ray Dudley for helping me cover my first ECW show when I was stopped at the door by some sort of mix-up. Chatting with Roddy Piper about our kids. My interview with Killer Kowalski in which he ripped on the Chyna book. Our battles with the WWF. Meeting Bret Hart. Email (both good and bad) from readers. The threats of being sued. It's been a blast and I don't regret a single moment.

If there is anything you should take with you from the six years we operated the site please remember:

- Wrestlers are real people. They aren't superheroes. They aren't indestructible stuntmen. They have families waiting for them at home. Friends they rarely get to see. Respect them as performers but first and foremost as people.
- Don't take what the WWF or any federation says at face value. Be critical. Use your head. Don't be a mark. If you see a yellow-feathered bird that has a beak, webbed feet and waddles around making a quacking sound, it is probably a duck no matter what Vince McMahon or anyone else tells you.
- In 1990, I sat in the 500 section of the SkyDome watching

WrestleMania VI as an unruly and appreciative fan. In 2002, I was fortunate enough to sit in a press box and cover WrestleMania X8 for SLAM! Wrestling. The moral of the story? Hard work, dedication, sacrifice and a whole lot of luck pay off if you believe in yourself and your abilities.

With that, I bid SLAM! Wrestling and you, the patient readers, a fond farewell but not goodbye as we might be seeing each other again. I look at this situation like a well-earned vacation. Until then, please continue to visit SLAM! Wrestling and take in what it has to offer and feel free to email me your thoughts and questions.

Thanks for reading our drivel. Thanks for your years of loyalty and devotion to the site. It will never be forgotten.

* * *

Though SLAM! Wrestling faded to black, the mat wars didn't completely disappear from Sun Media. Tim Baines, TJ Madigan and Don Callis continued their weekly columns and, perhaps in the harshest twist of fate imaginable, Molinaro, who had since moved on to the CBC (staying true to his international tastes by covering soccer), was brought in for an interactive chat for the release of his book, *Top 100 Pro Wrestlers of All Time*.

Molinaro wouldn't be the only SLAM! Wrestling scribe to move into the prestigious print medium, as Greg Oliver began work on his series of *Pro Wrestling Hall of Fame* books, drawing from his days with SLAM! Wrestling.

As the months went on though, a number of discussions began happening between the SLAM! Wrestling alumni. Over phone calls, MSN messages and a few bar chats, the old crew began to talk about a return. Soon, Powell, still under the employ of Canoe, began to have serious discussions with Oliver about the site returning. After negotiations and back-and-forth discussion, SLAM! Wrestling returned in full force.

It was a different setup, however, as a partner with Canoe, and not a "free time" venture. The site missed the traffic that wrestling coverage brought.

Powell reintroduced the group on March 21, 2003, just in time for WrestleMania.

THE RETURN OF SLAM! WRESTLING
By JOHN POWELL (March 21, 2003)

In a world where wrestlers retire only to reappear a month later, where

A rare gathering of SLAM! Wrestling writers at Titans in Toronto in 2004. Left to right, Steven Johnson, Bob Kapur, Yves Leroux, Chris Sokol, Greg Oliver, Corey Lacroix.

absolute fiction can become historical fact if repeated enough by a promoter, where Eric Bischoff is employed by the WWE and where the Big Show still gets a push, anything is possible.

Even the return of SLAM! Wrestling.

A short time ago, the former producers of SLAM! Wrestling got together in a downtown Toronto bar to entertain the notion of resurrecting the site through a partnership with Canoe and SLAM! Sports. The food was okay. The booze was good. The discussion was beyond excellent.

After months and months of intricate planning, discussions with our reliable team of contributors and good faith wheeling and dealing with Canoe, I am pleased to announce today that the original staff is back and to steal a line . . . you can bet that business is about to pick up. Some things may have changed since we've been gone but our commitment to providing you with accurate and responsible reporting to the best of our ability has not. We are beginning anew right where we left off.

Some thanks are in order. To my partner in crime — Greg Oliver — for his support and willingness to tackle this beast again. To Canoe head honcho Jose Leal, managing editor Tim Kraan and head marketing whiz Dave Watkins for giving us and the site a second chance. To Pejman Ramezanpour, Canoe's HTML designer, for his continued assistance and solid friendship. To our long list of invaluable contributors who are, without a doubt, the backbone of this site. You'll be seeing some familiar names returning to the site in the coming weeks, and some new faces. Take the time to email them and give them your thoughts.

Though I can't speak for anyone else, it was nice to be away from the business for a while. For me, it was a relief to send the wrestling journalist part of me away on a sabbatical of sorts and be nothing more than a regular fan again. It is not that I had forgotten about that part of me. It is just that when you are reporting on a particular "beat" like wrestling, you are always working. You can't just relax and enjoy what's before you because most of the time you are there to do a job. In stepping away from SLAM! Wrestling for almost a year, I had a lot to think about.

Briefly, here are some of the issues that I have pondered.

WWE's Internet Policy

In testing the current climate before our magnanimous return, I was stunned to learn that WWE is still shunning online wrestling reporters. Instead of forming mutually beneficial relationships with a medium that at least respects the business they are involved in, they have closed down the lines of communication and in doing so are as responsible for the unverified gossip that's out there as the people who report it.

WWE still doesn't understand that it is far more productive if they work with internet reporters rather than against them. Though it may gall them to no end, WWE will never be able to control the news media or what is written about them. From a business point of view, they should do exactly what music, book, television and movie companies do. That is, cooperate with people through an efficient, professional and proactive public relations department.

I fear though that as long as Vince McMahon is at the helm, the WWE will view the mainstream press as marks who can be easily snowed and the wrestling media as the enemy because they are better educated and can see through any bull that is propagated . . . like the "official" attendance for WrestleMania III for example.

The real WWE "attitude" has always been suspicion and paranoia. One wonders why, in a day and age where kayfabe is dead and buried, why WWE wagons remain permanently circled. Hmmm.

The resurrection of kayfabe

Speaking of kayfabe . . . when I heard that some ass clown at WWE was thinking about winding the company clock back to the 1970s, I thought it must be a joke; but after I read several WWE interviews with the mainstream media, I knew it wasn't. After all that was revealed about the business in the 1990s, how could you possibly go back to a time when wrestlers remained in character in public and never openly admitted that the tussles they have are choreographed? That's like a magician revealing how he does his tricks and then asking his fans to forget everything he just told them. It is ludicrous. It is ridiculous. There is no going back . . . not now, not ever. Anyone who attempts to is just being foolish and making others look equally so in the eyes of the media and fans alike.

The wrestling industry

It is heartening to see TNA picking up steam. Fans need a choice. Fans need an alternative to WWE. The success of TNA and other such promotions can only strengthen the business as a whole. I wish them all the best.

The WWE brand split

Another debacle by WWE. Unswayed by the mediocre television ratings and house show ticket sales since the split, WWE is still pressing ahead with the idea. Just another example of good business sense at WWE taking a backseat to someone's pride and ego. *Smackdown* vs. *Raw*? Bischoff vs. Stephanie? It is sad that so much effort is being put into an angle that fans couldn't care less about and won't warm up to . . . ever.

Enough of my blithering. There is plenty of time for that later. To those dedicated readers who continued to visit the site despite our absence, there are no words that could possibly express our appreciation. You alone kept our dream alive. For that we will always be grateful. To the new readers, welcome aboard and buckle up. It is going to be a wild and wicked ride.

To bring SLAM! Wrestling back to its former glory is going to take time. There is a ton of work that is going on behind the scenes each and every day that is not visible to you, the reader. Please be patient with us as we move forward together and complete our "house cleaning" on this musty mansion.

So go shout it from the mountaintops, through email, ICQ, news boards and text messaging that SLAM! Wrestling is back, and we will once again prove that good wrestling journalism does not have to be an oxymoron.

* * *

Indeed, SLAM! Wrestling was back. While past personalities such as John Powell, Greg Oliver, Nick Tylwalk, Bob Kapur and Jon Waldman had returned, a new breed of writers began to appear. Names like Jason Clevett, Brian Elliott, Matt Mackinder and Chris Sokol began to appear on bylines, while Mike Mastrandrea and Annette Balesteri brought an expert visual presence to the site in the form of fantastic photo galleries and insightful editorial cartoons respectively.

By 2006, SLAM! Wrestling had proved to not only survive the internet boom and bust, but was now thriving. For any internet site to reach 10 years was a huge milestone, but for the SLAM! Wrestling crew, who had been through highs and lows, the decennial mark was one to be feted, which they did in SLAM! Speaks, a roundtable sounding board that had been introduced in the new era.

SLAM! Wrestling writers Matt Mackinder (rear) and Chris Schramm (back right), and photographer Mike Mastrandrea, listen to the wisdom of Kevin Nash.

SLAM! SPEAKS: 10 YEARS OF MEMORIES

By SLAM! Wrestling Staff (November 27, 2006)

SLAM! Wrestling has been around 10 years. It's true, it's damn true.

Yes, it's hard to believe that a decade has passed since this humble little website opened its doors and ushered in an era of pro wrestling journalism that has, from the very beginning, intended to be informative, entertaining and news-breaking.

To say we've gone through a lot over the past 10 years would be an understatement. We've overcome layoffs, risen up from a blackout period and battled a (still-present?) internet media ban. We've also had the highs of having live chats with some of wrestling's greatest personalities, covered the biggest events in the industry and gained the respect of those who step between the ropes night in and night out.

Of course, along the way, each writer has had their own personal highs and lows. From road trips to rejections, the SLAM! Wrestling staff has seen it all.

Last month, after several online discussions, the SLAM! Wrestling crew decided that there was no better way to kick off our second decade in the biz than to look back at our favorite moments of the past 10 years. We certainly hope that you enjoy reading these stories of the life of SLAM! Wrestling, and take the time to follow some of the links to see just what we're talking about!

Andy McNamara

I have had an amazing time since Greg Oliver took a chance and let me join the team in August 2005. My favorite memory with SLAM! Wrestling took place during the Great Canadian Wrestling Expo in Oshawa for two days last November. Not only did I get to meet some classic wrestlers like King Kong

Bundy, Koko B. Ware, Kamala and Jim Neidhart, I also got to go out for a couple of pops with Greg and some of the indie guys at the end of the night.

But the highlight of the expo had to come when myself and photographer Josh Crocker were asked by two indie wrestlers to accompany them to the ring as their managers. To get into the ring and act as a heel manager on the outside was unreal.

Annette Balesteri

A highlight moment for me would be when Jim Ross contacted me to say he looks forward each week to my next cartoon. He also commented that he is concerned as to if or how I will draw him up at some point. I admire and respect the man, so, at some point, I will have to take up that challenge.

Bob Kapur

A definite highlight for me was interviewing Dirk Benedict for the story on the movie *Body Slam*. As a kid, I was a big fan of Mr. Benedict from his work on *Battlestar Galactica* and especially *The A-Team*, so this was a huge mark-out moment for me.

Brian Elliott

I may have made my SLAM! Wrestling debut less than a year ago, but in that time I've had the opportunity to speak to a lot of interesting people. However, it will be of little surprise to note that my conversation with Bret Hart is the highlight of my fledgling SLAM! Wrestling career. In the U.K. to promote his new DVD, I had the occasion to speak to Hart for almost 30 minutes in January 2006. Whilst he had been doing publicity work the entire previous day — and was whisked off to a television studio minutes after speaking to me — he was both humble and forthcoming, and had every ounce the class that to this day, makes him a wrestling ambassador. I'm only sorry that, in my attempts not to completely mark out, I didn't take the opportunity to truly thank him for being one of my favorite ever performers.

Chris Schramm

Looking back, I remember talking to "Superstar" Billy Graham. Graham, at the time, was writing his book (with the help of his wife). He had just started his website and I wanted to get some quick quotes about the site. It wasn't until three hours later that we were done talking that day. Graham really opened up for the first time in detail about his drug use. He did not seem to hold anything back, and he seemed to be confessing his sins to me. He also mentioned writing both Vince McMahon and Hulk Hogan, looking for their forgiveness for the past. He had not heard back from either and thought his life was ending.

Graham treated me like I was not only a reporter, but his best friend. I have met many wrestlers over the years, and even though I never met Graham in person, I had made a friend that day.

David Hillhouse

My favorite SLAM! Wrestling moment certainly comes out of the phenomenal opportunity that Greg gave me to help put together the SLAM! Wrestling Movie Database. Specifically, it felt really good to get an email from Joseph McBride, one of the writers for the vintage movie *Blood & Guts*, thanking SLAM! Wrestling for bringing some attention to the film that he watched get unceremoniously swept under the carpet and left to disappear.

It's easy to think of ourselves as SLAM! writers as fans, and we are all incredibly lucky to be able to watch, talk and write about wrestling as a (part-time) vocation. As Mr. McBride reminded me, though, it's also important to remember how we have the chance to make the people we write about feel honored for their efforts as well.

Greg Oliver

I get a real thrill from my writers when they mark out. Some examples: Steve Laroche getting Hulk Hogan on the phone (though no interview), John Molinaro with Ric Flair on Johnny Valentine (which, like the team player that he was, just got lumped into a bigger tribute piece), Jason Clevett eventually landing Bryan Danielson (a tribute to Clevett's dedication to covering Ring of Honor), Jon Waldman on Shawn Michaels, Bob Kapur landing Ed Asner to talk about *The Wrestler*. . . . As with title belts, sometimes the chase is the best part.

Fred Johns

One of the coolest memories I have comes from covering the independent scene. I was doing a piece on ECCW's TV show and had managed to get an interview with both Mauro Ranallo and the producer of the show, Kevin MacDonald, that was to take place directly after a wrestling show. The only place we could do it in any privacy was in Kevin's car. "The Stampede Kid" T.J. Wilson was getting a ride with them as well so it was the four of us crammed into this compact little sedan. It was the coolest thing because for half an hour in the pouring rain, we just sat in the car and talked about wrestling. It was, like, the ultimate indie interview — gritty, real and the conversation was so impassioned.

Jamie Kreiser

My favorite SLAM! Wrestling moment, hands down, had to be when I was fortunate enough to attend the Cauliflower Alley Club (CAC) reunion in 2005. I could easily remark how great it was to see a wrestling legend every time I turned around, but for me, I'll never forget how I got to pass Sir Oliver Humperdink potato salad. Weren't expecting that, were you? Fresh out of journalism school, I found myself sitting and having lunch, in Las Vegas of all locales, with Barry Orton, Barry's mother and sister, Ox Baker and Monsieur Humperdink. Where else do crazy scenarios like this happen except when you are chasing down a story for SLAM! Wrestling?

Jason Clevett

The World of Wheels was in Calgary and they traditionally had wrestlers do autograph signings at their events. February 2005 saw them bring both Lita and John Cena to the event. The promoter invited me to meet with both wrestlers during the weekend, and I would get the chance to speak to both of them. Cena was first up that weekend and was very happy to sit down to talk to me. We ended up being very comfortable talking and I caught him off guard by asking him about UPW and Samoa Joe. His face broke out in huge grin and he got more excited as we talked, saying, "This is awesome, you can only answer, 'How did you get into wrestling?' so many times." The interview went from just another guy with a tape recorder to something the future world champ was really enthused to talk about.

Jon Waldman

Ironically, my favorite memory is closely linked with the worst moment in my six-plus years with SLAM! Wrestling. Just a year and a bit after I said farewell to SLAM! Wrestling as a writer — before we went into a blackout period — I returned as a member of the editorial staff in the rebirth of the site. My first assignment was a story on Joe Aiello and Don "Cyrus" Callis's wrestling radio show, *No Holds Barred* (R.I.P.). Of course, all it took was one smart-ass comment about Triple H (like you'd expect any less from me) and I was live on the air; Callis ribbed me for a solid half-hour. In the process, I had the honor of re-launching the website, which was set to officially go live the next day. It was definitely a highlight of my career in journalism, period.

Matt Mackinder

Just nine months after joining SLAM! Wrestling's writing crew, I got to cover Bound For Glory in my home state of Michigan and needless to say, I was in all my glory. Just to be able to meet and talk with Kevin Nash, Rhino, A.J. Styles, Christopher Daniels, Eric Young and Brother Runt was a blast. To also meet other media members there, mention SLAM! Wrestling and have them know who we are really made me feel honored to be involved with such a tight fraternity.

Marty Goldstein

I don't know how this fits in, but my favorite SLAM! Wrestling moment was in August 2004 when I got to interview Greg Oliver in studio for my radio program, *The Great Canadian Talk Show*, in Winnipeg. My op for the series happened to be Doug McColl — a veteran of Al Tomko's promotion and numerous other indie promotions across Canada — and between the three of us and Greg's wife Meredith, it was probably the most intelligent discussion about the wrestling industry, characters and lifestyle that has ever been aired locally. Along with discussing his tag team book, Greg and I got to discuss his trip to Vegas for the Cauliflower Alley Club where he had been hanging out with some of my longtime friends including Dan Denton and Brian Howell. The feedback about that episode was as positive as any other interview I had done and if we are able to finalize the plan to soon return to the local airwaves, Greg and the stories available on SLAM! Wrestling will be at the top of the list for my first week of shows.

Mike Altamura

August 16, 2001. One of the proudest moments of my lifetime — a story I penned on Australian-based "Canadian Hellraiser" Jason Helton was published on SLAM! Wrestling. My first contribution to the website. It's a moment I'll never forget. I was a precocious 17-year-old kid and I remember feeling like a true journalist that day. See, writing for SLAM! Wrestling is an honor. Its industry credibility is second to none. Excellence in journalism, upholding journalistic integrity, this is what the website epitomizes. Regardless of pro wrestling's state, take solace in knowing that SLAM! Wrestling will consistently provide the people with unparalleled A-grade coverage of the game.

Nick Tylwalk

I've been fortunate enough to do a bunch of cool things for the site, but attending WrestleMania X-7 in Houston stands out among all of them. I had to pay for a seat in the nosebleed section of the Astrodome, though I was able to get a press pass for entry into the Fan Axxess event — as a photographer, which should be amusing to anyone who's ever seen me try to handle a camera.

In any case, when I reached the front of the line for press credentials, the PR lady looked at me, saw that I was with SLAM! Wrestling and said, "You're not Greg Oliver!" While I aspire to be recognized in my own right someday, it dawned on me that day that if the WWE knew my editor that well, I was part of something a little bigger than I suspected, and I'd be well served to stick around.

Richard Kamchen

I've only been around for a few months but my best moment goes back to the beginning of it all when Greg gave me a chance to write about the best sport in the world. I was surprised by how magnanimous most wrestlers have been in talking to me, although admittedly, there have been a couple pains. It's been everything I thought it would be and more.

Stephen Laroche

Being a fan of SLAM! Wrestling since it started in 1996, it was a pleasure to write for the site starting in August 2000. In particular, being the first wrestling writer to publish an interview with Kamala was special as he was my favorite wrestler growing up. I'll always appreciate the opportunities I had writing about wrestling for this site and offer my sincere congratulations on 10 years of setting a lofty standard for online wrestling journalism.

Tim Baines

Separating reality from "a work" isn't always the easiest thing when you're interviewing wrestlers. But this SLAM! Wrestling/Sun Media gig took me to Raleigh, North Carolina, in late March of 2005. In mid-afternoon, in a quiet RBC Center, I sat beside one of my wrestling heroes, Ric Flair. He was honest, eloquent and most important, he was Naitch, the limousine-ridin', jet-flyin', kiss-stealin', wheelin'-dealin son of a gun. It's moments like that, an hour with the Dirtiest Player in the Game, that keep this column energized.

* * *

Today, SLAM! Wrestling continues much like it did from the beginning — delivering the best coverage of professional wrestling available on the internet. From Victoria to St. John's, our neighbors to the south and our friends overseas, the staff of SLAM! Wrestling brings the wide world of the mat wars to its readers like no other entity.

We thank you for your continuing support of SLAM! Wrestling and hope you enjoy this special compilation.

Canadiana

As one might expect when you're part of a leading Canadian website, a significant amount of space on SLAM! Wrestling is dedicated to Canadians. Wherever and whenever possible, the spotlight has been turned on these rugged rasslers who grew up and trained on the frozen canvas of the Great White North.

In a way, this portion of our work has become the calling card of SLAM! Wrestling. Nowhere else on the internet are past, present and future flag bearers covered in such depth and detail as they are at SLAM! Wrestling, and there is no greater joy for any of us than to see the response we get to our unique Canadian stories.

Covering Canada's wrestling landscape has meant more than interviewing the top stars in wrestling — it's also about talking to the up-and-comers and journeymen and women on the indie wrestling scene, who toil for years as they hone their craft and grow their reputations, while also looking behind the scenes at the territories and leagues themselves.

* * *

CURSE OF STAMPEDE WRESTLING?

By TJ MADIGAN — *Calgary Sun*

Before the Calgary Flames migrated from Atlanta, before movie theater multiplexes were in every quadrant of Cowtown, before cable TV was a fixture in every home — Stampede Wrestling was arguably the most popular brand of local family entertainment.

Created by Stu Hart in the late '40s, Stampede had grown from a small-time local grappling group to a national and international wrestling phenomenon.

Thousands packed the Victoria Pavilion (and for bigger events, the Stampede

Corral) each week to watch Hart's brand of rough-and-tough grappling action. Tens of thousands more watched on TV (and tape) across Canada and around the world, as the late, great Ed Whalen served as the voice of reason amidst the mayhem.

In countries as far away as Antigua, people who couldn't point Calgary out on a map could tell you all about the Hart family, Stampede Wrestling and Stu Hart's infamous Dungeon.

While Calgary was still developing its identity, Stampede Wrestling became an undeniable part of it.

The Stampede juggernaut was finally derailed in 1984, when Vince McMahon gobbled up the local territories and took pro wrestling national.

But while many of the stars of Stampede went on to become worldwide celebrities in the WWE and WCW, tales of tragedy always seemed to out-number the stories of post-Stampede success.

To put it bluntly, a lot of bad things have happened to a lot of the big names who honed their craft in the Stampede squared circle.

Some were self-inflicted traumas. Others were unfortunate tragedies or acts of God.

Bob Leonard

The Dynamite Kid poses with his manager J.R. Foley.

Some were genuine cases of bad luck and others were probably just par for the course in a business with such a rampant drug culture.

Maybe it's unfair to call it a Stampede Wrestling curse. But looking at the men who became grappling megastars in this city during Stampede's heyday, it's hard to shake the feeling that for many of them, there should have been a better life after the ring lights went down. . . .

Dynamite Kid

Tom Billington came to Calgary from his native England in 1978 and revolution-ized North American wrestling forever.

Billed as the Dynamite Kid, Billington introduced a high-flying, high-impact style which influenced a generation of wannabe wrestlers — including Chris Benoit, who still credits Dynamite as his primary influence.

Dynamite was a Stampede Wrestling regular from 1978 to 1984, and again after his WWF run in the late '80s. He was a five-time Stampede tag champion and once held the company's highest prize, the North American heavyweight title.

But Billington paid the price for years of steroid abuse, serious injuries and surgeries.

Today, he is confined to a wheelchair, living most of his post-wrestling life as a virtual recluse in a modest U.K. home. He is partially paralyzed, suffering from a myriad of back, leg and heart problems, and is cared for by his second wife, Dot.

He will never walk again.

A bitter Billington published his autobiography in 1999.

It was a venomous no-holds-barred account of his career, his drug use and the cruel backstage bullying he was known for behind the scenes.

Owen Hart

The tragic story of Owen Hart's demise needs little explanation.

In 1999, Hart plunged from the rafters of a Kansas City sports arena when a rappelling stunt at a WWF pay-per-view went wrong.

Hart fell to his death in front of 15,000 fans, sparking a legal battle between his widow, Martha, and WWF owner Vince McMahon, which would tear the Hart family apart.

Owen, just 34 years old at the time of his tragic death, left behind his wife and two young children.

The entire city of Calgary mourned Hart's passing, recognizing him as one of the true good guys in the seedy world of sports entertainment.

Before his WWF tenure, Hart had been the headline star of Stampede Wrestling from 1986 to 1988. He won the North American heavyweight title twice in 1987, trading the belt back and forth in a feud with Makhan Singh. He also lifted the British Commonwealth mid-heavyweight belt from Gama Singh earlier that year.

Brian Pillman

In 1996, Brian Pillman narrowly escaped death after he fell asleep at the wheel of his Hummer.

Flipping the vehicle, Pillman completely shattered his ankle and spent several days in a coma before undergoing surgery to fuse his leg back together.

Miraculously, Pillman returned to wrestling as a top star in the WWF but his return would be short-lived.

On October 5, 1997, Pillman was found dead in a Minnesota hotel room.

On the eve of a big match, the 35-year-old wrestler had died of an un-detected heart condition.

Pillman had been trained by Stu Hart, turning to wrestling after a short CFL stint with the Calgary Stampeders.

Teaming with Bruce Hart to form Bad Company, Pillman won the Stampede Tag titles twice during his run with the company from 1986 to 1988.

Pillman became a top star in Stampede Wrestling, developing a high-flying style and a loose-cannon persona that made him a star around the world.

Larry Cameron

"Lethal" Larry Cameron was the last North American champion in Stampede Wrestling before the promotion folded in 1989.

A 300-pound powerhouse who got into the business at a late age, Cameron followed his run in Calgary with a wrestling tour of Australia and Europe.

But tragedy struck during a 1993 match in Bremen, Germany, when Cameron suddenly collapsed in the middle of the ring.

He had suffered a heart attack, dying in front of a German wrestling audience at age 41.

Davey Boy Smith

In 2002, Davey Boy Smith, the British Bulldog, died of a heart attack while vacationing in British Columbia.

Smith was just 39 years old when he passed away.

He had been training for a return to the ring and had recently started teaming with his son, Harry, in tag matches.

Long before he became a worldwide megastar in the WWF, Smith was a household name in Calgary.

He made the move here in the early 1980s after being discovered in the U.K. by Bruce Hart. In addition to being a Stampede headliner, Smith was married to Stu Hart's youngest daughter, Diana, from 1984 to 2000.

Bret Hart

After being manipulated out of the WWF Championship in one of the most famous real-life double-crosses in wrestling history, Bret Hart ended his 13-year WWF career on a sour note.

Hart had been with the company since Vince McMahon bought Stampede Wrestling in 1984 — the Hitman had gone from being the top star in

Calgary, a six-time North American heavyweight champion, to becoming one of the biggest wrestling stars in the world.

Things went downhill when Hart jumped ship to WCW in the late 1990s. The Hitman suffered a career-ending injury — a mule kick to the head (courtesy of Bill Goldberg) gave him a severe concussion during a 1999 pay-per-view match.

In 2002, Hart also suffered a stroke after he fell from his bicycle on a Calgary pathway. Paralysis and memory problems were some of the issues Hart battled against through months of physical therapy.

Hart has made massive strides in recovering from the symptoms of his stroke and post-concussion syndrome.

In 2006, he performed in the musical *Aladdin* across Canada and was inducted into WWE's Hall of Fame. His autobiography is expected to be released this fall.

Jimmy Caruso

Tokyo Joe in his wrestling heyday.

Tokyo Joe

Tokyo Joe Daigo was preparing to return to Japan after a successful Stampede Wrestling run in 1974.

But on a road trip to Lethbridge, Alberta, his career would be cut short when another vehicle slid on the icy roadway and smashed into the car he was traveling in.

Tokyo Joe had his leg amputated as a result of the accident, but went on to become one of the top wrestling instructors in the city, training T.J. Wilson, Harry Smith and Nattie Neidhart.

From the author: You can't write about Stampede Wrestling without pissing somebody off. Publish anything but the blandest of puff pieces, and you'll inevitably hear that some random Hart cousin or also-ran Calgary old timer has something to say about it. Just never to your face!

To spare myself the drama, I almost bailed on the assignment to do a piece on the curse of Stampede Wrestling. But when my editor told me it would not only be a SLAM! Wrestling story, it'd also be a full-page cover story for the Calgary Sun? Well, the promise of my first front page was enough to reel me in.

The list of tragedies speaks for itself, but the saddest part of this article is a detail I only noticed in hindsight.

Every person I interviewed for this story was asked if there were exceptions to the curse — and all of them mentioned one name as the single Stampede success story they could think of: Chris Benoit.

It's crazy to think that only a few weeks after those interviews took place, one of Stampede Wrestling's only happy endings would turn into its biggest tragedy.

* * *

Courtesy Vance Nevada

The crew from the 2008 Northern Death Tour.

WRESTLING'S TOUGHEST TOUR — NORTHERN MANITOBA

Performers take home golden memories from trip through tundra

By BOB HOLLIDAY
— *Winnipeg Sun*

Lance Storm has wrestled all over the world but his fondest memories are surviving the Northern Death Tour for Winnipeg promoter Tony Condello.

"It was the toughest tour I've ever done, but it has the best memories," Storm said from his home in Calgary. "Calgary can get cold, but nowhere near Oxford House after an eight-hour trip over the cracking ice of a winter road."

The former star with World Wrestling Entertainment and other pro organizations, who runs a Calgary-based training school for wannabe wrestlers, empathizes with the current crew bouncing over the frozen tundra to entertain people not used to seeing live shows.

"The worst thing is the road. You feel so isolated jammed in a van for 10 to 12 hours," said Storm. "You're like a band of gypsies. But if the people you're traveling with are good, it's the best tour you'll ever do. The crowds are really responsive."

Condello's band of merry men left Winnipeg at 5 a.m. on February 16 en route for their first stop that night in Little Grand Rapids. Other scheduled stops on the 2,000-kilometer tour were Wasagamack, Garden Hill, St. Theresa Point, God's River, God's Lake Narrows, Oxford House and Cross Lake.

Instead of hotel rooms, wrestlers sleep in the ring or on the gymnasium floor. They cook their own food in the high school cafeteria, said Condello. He chuckles at the ribs he's pulled on newcomers over the past 30 years.

"The ice was crackling so I told the guys we could break through, which we couldn't, so I tied a rope onto Scott Norton and had him walk ahead of the bus," said Condello.

Norton, a powerhouse known as "Flash" Norton, went on to a career in the defunct World Championship Wrestling and in Japan. Others who cut their wrestling teeth on the tour were WWE superstar Edge and TNA's Christian Cage and Rhino.

"I've seen people crying. They thought they were going to die, especially the year there was an early melt and water was lapping at the running board. They thought they were stuck there for another six months," said Condello.

"It's rather unsettling to see a big rig on its side and halfway through the ice," said Storm.

Condello has been on the receiving end of several ribs. On one trip Storm and another wrestler spread a trail of

Northern exposure all part of paying dues for young grapplers

So you wanna be a wrestler?

Vance Nevada supplied the talent for Tony Condello's tour through remote northern Manitoba towns.

"Ten of us drove 2,300 kilometers, nonstop from Vancouver in 25 hours to get here the day before we start a 2,000-kilometer trip," said Nevada, who grew up in the Westman area and wrestled in Winnipeg before moving west.

"Most of these guys have never been east of the Rockies. This will be a lesson for them," said the veteran of two northern tours. "You have to pay your dues."

Sharon, who goes by the stage name of Aurora, wasn't prepared for the minus 40 Celsius temperature that greeted the West Coast crew.

"I worked a year in Mexico and I'm used to 40 degrees. Not this," she said. "I'm not looking forward to the weather."

She's heard about the rigors of the trip and how traveling through the northern Manitoba terrain is like traveling through a different country.

Apparently, a demanding trip like this is just what the doctor ordered for young wrestlers.

"Doing the tour is something a Canadian independent wrestler should do. It's part of history," said Scotty Mac. "I've heard so much about it from veterans like Dr. Luther."

bread crumbs across the floor, and into the deep-sleeping Condello's moustache.

The pair let loose a Vietnamese pot-bellied pig, which followed the trail and even tried to get the final morsels from Condello's moustache.

But the tour, officially known as Wrestling with the North, is not all fun and games.

Condello and the wrestlers mingle with children and advise them to live a drug- and gang-free life.

"It's a promise I made to Grand Chief Phil Fontaine many years ago," said Condello.

* * *

Vincenzo d'Alto

Lufisto scored a victory for human rights.

FEMALE WRESTLER PINS ONTARIO ATHLETIC COMMISSION

By GENEVIEVE "LUFISTO" GOULET — Special to SLAM! Wrestling

A long battle is over for me and I'm not talking about one of my violent hardcore matches!

Recently, I got a phone call that I have been waiting for some time. A gentleman from the Ontario Human Rights Commission (OHRC) told me that I had finally won what is perhaps the most important fight of my career as a professional wrestler.

With that, it's time for a history lesson.

It was the weekend of WrestleMania 22 and yours truly was scheduled to participate in a match for a promotion right in Toronto. The match would be a hardcore, inter-gender tag team bout and it was a pretty exciting time for me back then. I was really getting a lot of bookings in Ontario and fans were really receptive to what I was doing in the ring.

But it all came to a crashing halt.

I got an email from the promoter, telling me that he couldn't book me anymore. Why you may ask? Turns out, some rival promoter in Toronto decided to file a complaint with the Ontario Athletic Commission (OAC). You see, in the province of Ontario, professional wrestling is actually regulated by the OAC, which is a branch of the Ministry of Consumer Affairs.

I didn't know it at the time, but there was a clause in the act that oversees professional wrestling, stating that a man and woman may not come into contact in the ring. Yep, that's right — in the year 2002 such a rule still existed on the books.

The commissioner, having no choice but to enforce the regulation as a result of the complaint, proceeded to contact the promoter and advise that that match I was scheduled to participate in could not happen.

To say I was slightly pissed off at that time would be an understatement. I was really upset. The simple fact that there was a regulation that basically said I couldn't do what I love to do because I'm a girl really got me down. I know some people out there don't like the idea of girls wrestling guys in the ring and I do respect those views. But this regulation was simply wrong!

What could a girl do?

The fact is lots of people in the wrestling business (in Ontario) love to complain about the OAC. Granted, I have my own opinion about whether wrestling should be regulated or not, but the fact is, the regulation in question was there and bitching about it on message boards was not going to get that rule off the books.

After consulting with some close friends of mine, I proceeded to file a complaint with the OHRC. This was the only route I could take if I wanted to fight the government.

From the first moment I spoke with a representative at the OHRC, I received nothing but unconditional support for my cause. They saw what I saw, that the regulation in question was a violation of my human rights, based on my gender. I filled out the necessary paperwork and it was time to take down that regulation.

I realized early on that this would not happen quickly. Change comes slowly in government and I had to be patient. Fortunately, I had lots of support from my fellow workers, promoters and friends in general. They really helped keep my spirit up when I thought that I would never see the light at the end of the tunnel as it were.

For a while, it seemed like there was going to be a showdown with the OAC in Toronto in the form of a hearing, but it never happened. I can only guess why; maybe the OAC realized they didn't have a chance when it came to defending such a regulation.

From there, I stayed in contact with the OHRC as they pursued the complaint for me. In the end, it came down to just one phone call. I was told that the OAC would proceed with removing the regulation once and for all.

The fight was over and I won!

Words can't describe how great it feels. To be blunt, this was my fight and I was very passionate about doing it my way. I did my homework, plotted a battle strategy and executed the plan. Mission accomplished!

For the record, I want to make it abundantly clear that in no way do I harbor any ill feelings towards the OAC or the commissioner, Ken Hayashi. I realize that back then, he was just doing his job, which is to enforce the rules and action complaints that his office receives.

For now, I'm just waiting to see when the rule will be officially removed for good. I must say, there is a part of me that is glad I went through this. I learned a lot about myself, and what I can achieve when I put my mind to something that I feel passionate about.

For those of you out there who may think you can't win against the government, think again. It's not easy and it will take time, even some of your own hard-earned money. But if you truly believe in your cause, then charge forth and fight the good fight.

To all who supported me, you will always have a special place in my heart. To all who said I couldn't win, I thank you as well. You only gave me that much more motivation to keep fighting.

And yes, to the coward that called the OAC and filed the complaint against me, I want to thank you as well. You started this saga and I'm the one who finished it. It's me who's standing in the ring of life with her arm held in the air as the winner and that's something you'll never be.

From the staff: LuFisto's complaint actually ended up being the beginning of the end of the OAC's involvement with professional wrestling, as it is no longer regulated.

* * *

D'AMORE, THE HEART AND SOUL OF BCW

By BOB KAPUR

From the writer: Besides my editors, the person that helped me the most as a SLAM! Wrestling writer is Scott D'Amore who, when I was just starting out, gave me full access to the BCW locker room.

In addition to the interviews I got from his roster, over the years his endorsement also helped me make other contacts in the business, like Jeff Jarrett and TNA's management team. Further, the look behind the curtain gave me a new perspective that (I hope) has made me a better pro wrestling journalist.

This interview took place after a BCW event in Barrie, Ontario. What I remember most is the running laugh track from Simon Diamond and Johnny Swinger who were listening in as I talked with Scott.

Border City Wrestling, an independent promotion based out of Windsor, Ontario, has earned a reputation as one of the best indie leagues going today. And not just with its loyal fan base who fill the Ciociaro Club (BCW's home arena) for every bimonthly show, but also with the many internationally known wrestlers who have performed on BCW cards.

Probably the main reason why the company has enjoyed its favorable reputation can be summed up in two words: Scotty D'Amore. D'Amore, often referred to as the cornerstone of BCW, wears many hats, plays many roles — owner, booker, trainer, wrestler — though he is quick to dismiss any thoughts that it's a solo effort.

"We have a lot of very creative people around here right now. Terry Taylor, Don (Cyrus) Callis, Johnny Swinger who's a good young mind. We have a lot of input, and I think that's one of the main reasons we have the ability to go out there and put on a solid product. One of the best things about it right now is that I don't have to make a lot of decisions anymore. I'm deeply involved, but it's not just my vision . . . it's our vision."

The vision is clear: to put on an entertaining show for the fans every time out. He tries to instill that same vision in his students, whose names make up the majority of BCW's regular roster. Speaking about his students, D'Amore loses some of his trademark gruffness, suggesting that it's that aspect of BCW that he is most proud of.

"Don't judge me by the fact that I trained Rhyno. The talent and athleticism he had, and the fact that he's such a good person, you'd have to be an idiot for him to not do well. Anybody can take a guy with star potential and do something with him. Judge us by how we deal with the guys who, at first-glance, don't have that potential."

"Tyson Dux, we put some time and effort into him. And why wouldn't you? He's a good kid, with a great effort, and he's in it for all the right reasons. He loves wrestling, he loves to perform. And look at him now, the kid is over. Another guy is Gutter. He's been wrestling for a few years, and twice a week, he still shows up at my school and trains with the students, helping them along. He loves the business, he loves working at it, he loves being part of the show. Spend some time with a guy like that, and that's what makes it worth it. He goes around, and people know who he is, and that he's a part of BCW."

Because he wants his pupils to shine, D'Amore often will step back from an active in-ring role.

Scott D'Amore, far right, with two of the TNA stars he nurtured, Robert Roode and Petey Williams.

"There are times when I don't feel like I'm sharp enough to wrestle that night. What's the point of going in there when there are five guys waiting who could do a better job? We have a lot of talented guys in this area who are hungry for ring-time. How do you look at a kid who drove in four hours in the hopes that he may get a chance to wrestle, and tell him we can't use him? He's that committed to get that chance to wrestle in front of a live crowd . . . if I can be better used someplace else, that's great."

As D'Amore puts it, he has nothing to prove and nothing to gain from denying others the chance. After all, he has wrestled across Japan, Europe and throughout North America, and spent time in all three major promotions, namely the WWF, WCW and ECW over the years.

Or, as he puts it: "For a short, fat, dumpy kid from Windsor, too short, too slow and too unathletic to get a college scholarship to play football or baseball, I think I did pretty well. I've got to see a lot."

He's seen enough of the business at least to realize that there are other ways to measure success than by in-ring records.

"Titles don't mean anything in this business. They only mean something if you make more money. If titles came with a big pay raise, then by all means, let's fight over them. Other than that, who gives a damn? Our job is to come out here and entertain."

To that end, D'Amore has constantly tried to learn from others, picking up valuable insights into how this job can be accomplished.

"I've gained knowledge [about the business] through everyone I've dealt with. I was lucky enough to train under Mickey Doyle and the late Doug Chevalier. I got to train with Al Snow, I got to train under Jody Hamilton at the Power Plant. I've had long conversations with Terry Taylor and Arn Anderson. King Kong Bundy, D-Lo Brown, Tommy Dreamer, Mikey Whipwreck, Don Callis . . . all these guys passed stuff on to me, which I take and draw upon."

Still, there are some times that even the wealth of knowledge D'Amore has accumulated cannot provide all the answers. Such was the case in October, when former WCW star Stevie Ray was not allowed to cross the border into Canada, because the company hadn't met the deadline for filing certain paperwork. Unfortunately, because of heightened security concerns (post–September 11), the wrestler was denied entrance, and the company had to run the show without one of its featured advertised headliners.

D'Amore accepts the blame for the mix-up, but hopes that they made up for it by putting on a good show nonetheless.

"Unfortunately, it happened. There were probably some people who showed up to see Stevie Ray, and were disappointed that he wasn't there. But I think we gave them a hell of a show despite that. That's what we always strive to do, put on the best product we can."

Which is, ultimately, what D'Amore wants to accomplish more than anything else.

"I think that we do a pretty good job in that when people pay to see a Border City Wrestling show, they know that they're going to see a good show. We're not perfect. We're not the biggest show in the world, we're not the next big thing. We're just a little group that's lucky enough to have a building with a great house that's a hell of a crowd to perform for."

* * *

VANCE NEVADA REFLECTS ON 10 YEARS, 1,000+ MATCHES
By JASON CLEVETT

There aren't a lot of true veterans in independent wrestling anymore. That makes it a true milestone for ECCW champion Vance Nevada to have recently wrestled in his thousandth match after more than a decade in the business.

"Mr. Beefy Goodness" Vance Nevada.

To commemorate he has released *The Best of Vance Nevada, 1993–2003*. Having traveled from coast to coast, Vance has a lot to reflect on.

"The decision to make the DVD was a combination of things. I was a big fan of keeping track of various wrestler stats when I was younger. I kept a notebook and would write down all my matches. I thought it would be interesting for people viewing the DVD to see the change in appearance, size and amount of hair," Nevada told SLAM! Wrestling.

"Anyone watching that isn't familiar with my work can chart my progress from a rookie, being led through the nose, to where I am now. As an independent wrestler, you tend to collect tapes of what you've done; I had checked my closet and had about 20 tapes. You have a lot of matches that are unmemorable but others are really worth looking at again. I've had the chance to work with a lot of awesome colorful people over the years and felt it was time to put that together and give people a look at what 10 years on the Canadian indies looks like."

The DVD also gives fans the chance to check out some of the best wrestlers this country has to offer. Young hungry athletes like Scott Savage, Scotty Mac and Adam Firestorm face off with Nevada, as well as a young Bobby Roode, who now competes in TNA. Nevada chose to use these matches as opposed to matches with former WWE stars.

"I have been very fortunate to work with some of the biggest names in the business like Honky Tonk Man, Jim Neidhart and Matt Borne. The point behind the DVD was to put matches on there that could generate interest in Canadian independents. For a guy like Mentallo, who is a workhorse and a guy I have probably wrestled a hundred times, for him to get some recognition is important. Biggie Phatz in Saskatoon is a guy who had tremendous crowd appeal but nobody outside of that city will get a chance to see him. I was really proud of that match. Indie guys deserve recognition."

That is part of what drives Vance Nevada: helping out younger talent in getting bookings and exposure. Often when booked elsewhere in the country Nevada brings other talent with him to work.

"That has really been a motivator for me. I have had a lot of problems with my neck in the past year. Some days I wake up and I am just not getting out of bed. It's cumulative injuries that a light guy endures in the wrestling business. I have no problem jumping in my car and going wherever someone wants to see me, but for me to take a long trip, like to Saskatoon. As much as I love Saskatoon and the guys, however, there isn't much more to gain professionally from going there. If I can open the door for someone on their way up to take advantage of that and use it as a building block for their own career I try to do that."

It can be frustrating to a veteran to see the state of wrestling today, and the politics and garbage that affect pro wrestling. At times, Nevada and veterans like Chi Chi Cruz feel like the business they love isn't there anymore.

"It's double-sided. Chi Chi and I actually talked about this recently; we grew up loving the wrestling business. Despite all the negatives and drawbacks and politics, we love the business for what it is and I don't think that will ever change. When you love the business that much you are always looking to work with the best people and learn, and there are fewer and fewer guys out there to learn from, which is discouraging."

At times Nevada questions why he still puts up with it.

"I ask myself why I keep going and dealing with the BS every day. It's a difficult one to answer. I have been in touch with the people in WWE when Tom Pritchard was in that role, and he was clear on what I needed to do if my goal was to get there. In reality I don't think that is going to happen — when I started 10 years ago that was the goal but now my objectives have changed. I have spent a lot of time using my name to help young guys get an opportunity. I currently have a crop of six students: Richtie Destiny, Mike Dempsey, Nate Daniels, Dave Richards, Tony Tisoy and Miss Chevius. Some trained with me and others I had an influence on that I want to make sure they take advantage of all the opportunities they can."

It's the desire to help out this younger talent that led to the birth of Just Wrestling, a promotion that runs out of Surrey, British Columbia. Bridgeview Hall is a former stomping ground of ECCW, but they gladly let Nevada take over the location and start something new.

"I noticed there were a couple of different wrestling schools pumping out students knowing full well there was nowhere to work. We have four promotions in the Vancouver area with a territory that has 50 or 60 wrestlers. New guys weren't getting any opportunities, guys fresh out of school in their first year are lucky to get four matches. When you are starting out you need to get into the ring as much as possible.

"The best advice I ever got was from [Wayne Stanton promoter of River City Wrestling in Winnipeg] who told me, 'When you are starting out in this business you want to be in front of a crowd as many times as you can and the first 100 times don't count.' I have learned to appreciate that over time. My first year I wrestled 26 matches and they were all very awful. I couldn't fathom the idea that someone was going to improve and learn the business with only four matches a year. As well, ECCW was slowing down over the summer, which meant there would be no shows. When you have seen as many different approaches to wrestling you recognize when opportunities are being missed. We saw an opportunity and that is why we formed Just Wrestling."

There are a number of things that make it difficult for independent promoters and wrestlers to earn money. Presently the wrestling business is in a slump, trickling from WWE on down.

"There really isn't a lot of cross-territory travel anymore. There used to be a lot more communication from promoters wanting to switch things up in their promotions, but now there isn't a lot of that going on. I've noticed that with WWE making fewer stops on the West Coast, it has a lot to do with over-saturation on television so people don't have to pay high prices to sit in the arena. In the independents, we are slowly starting to see those attendance numbers creep back up. It is important on the indie level to listen to your fans and what they want to see, getting them attached to the characters, then they will come back."

Another difficulty is the lack of good talent on the independent wrestling scene. Fans want to see larger-than-life characters, not 150-pound kids in tank tops that they feel they could beat up.

"It definitely hurts the business. There was a point in the '90s where the business wasn't drawing but there was a lot of interest in learning to wrestle. Wrestling schools were opening everywhere, and people not qualified to train ran a lot of them. The business now has people who are essentially backyarders walking around saying they are professionally trained. In 1993, when I broke in, it was stressed to me that if you don't have wrestling boots you simply don't wrestle. I couldn't imagine not having a pair of wrestling boots while going to the ring. The lack of attention to quality of talent on shows has hurt the business, as has the accessibility of guys who don't have a clue but work for a lot cheaper than an Eddie Watts, a Chi Chi Cruz or myself."

One promotion that did rely on out-of-province talent was Saskatoon's Pro Outlaw Wrestling. They frequently brought in talent like Juggernaut, Apocalypse and Nevada, who would drive from Vancouver with young wrestlers to the shows. He has fond memories of the city, where the chant of "Who wears short shorts? Vance wears short shorts!" was born.

"My involvement with Pro Outlaw Wrestling amounted to only about 12 appearances but has affected who I am professionally. The chant came out of nowhere. I never would have imagined that a pair of traditional trunks would generate so much heat. The creative energy in POW rubs off on everybody that works there. That ended up being the birthplace of 'Mr. Beefy Goodness.'"

POW was also where Nevada did a rare run as a good guy, at which point the chant turned into a sign of respect.

"When they first approached me about turning face I was skeptical. As much as it seemed that the people were pleased to see me, I felt like I was the guy they loved to hate. I didn't think it was going to work, and it amused me that the chant changed meaning. I couldn't be more thrilled with how that turned out."

The turn led to a lengthy feud with Wavell Starr. Nevada and "The First Nation Sensation" had a series of great matches culminating in a Singapore cane match. Nevada is happy for his former foe's OVW success.

"Wavell is an incredible talent. The first time that I saw him was on tape. When you see a lot of guys pass through the independents, someone who has a spark that you know can make it you can pick that up right away, and Wavell Starr was always one of those guys. When he was on the shelf for a year with a shoulder injury, it was frustrating for him and a lot of guys don't come back from that. To see him doing so well is awesome. The success couldn't come to a better guy."

Nevada paused to consider the milestone of 1,000 matches.

"The milestone itself was awesome. The actual thousandth match was in Portland, Oregon, against 'The Anchor' Bill Sawyer. My thousandth match might have been better suited for a different day. I love Bill, he's a great guy, but it just wasn't the match I wanted to have on that day."

It almost didn't happen. In 1999 Nevada retired from the business after being diagnosed with scoliosis.

"I did a tag match in February 1999 and during the course of the match I was taking simple bumps and there was a shooting pain in my hip. I couldn't understand what the problem was, and a specialist told me that I had a twisted spine, so my hips were uneven. When I took a bump, one hip was hitting before the other, causing inflammation. I was very lean at the time, and after six years of wrestling, a 180-pound guy takes a lot of abuse. The doctors recommended I never wrestle again.

"I took 12 weeks off and got it twisted back in the proper position. Once you are in this business if it is in your blood you can't get out. Sitting on the sidelines just killed me. After a few months I contacted Tony Condello and reffed a tour for him. Near the end of the tour they had a cancellation and threw me into a match. I wasn't 100 percent but I realized there was no way I could let the injury keep me from wrestling," he said. "Now I am a lot more conscious of the damage that wrestling does. Between massage therapy, chiropractors and physio[therapy], I pay a lot more attention to the maintenance of my body between matches."

At the time it was difficult, but reflecting back Nevada feels the negative turned into a positive as he was unhappy with the business at that time.

"I was working for Ernie Todd and the Canadian Wrestling Federation in Winnipeg. It was a very professionally stifling environment, and that combined with the injury made me say, 'I don't want to do this anymore.' The injury was the catalyst for making that decision, but the end result of not having anything to do with Ernie Todd again was positive. Even though I had wrestled six years up to that point, everything good I have done professionally has happened after I retired. It's been positive and progressed in a much bigger direction ever since."

Presently Nevada works on the West Coast, primarily for ECCW and Just Wrestling. In September 2003, he defeated Scotty Mac in a cage match to win the ECCW title; however when he started with the company he paid his dues as "The Opener."

"When I've come into a territory, promoters will look at my record and say, 'This guy has been around for awhile, we should keep him happy and push him to the top.' That was the case when I came to ECCW, they asked me right off the bat where I felt I fit in on the roster and were taken aback when I said I wanted to work the opener because nobody does. If you come into a territory and are immediately put in the main event, you have 25 guys thinking, 'Who the hell is this guy and why does he deserve to main-event when I have worked so hard to build the company.'

"I specifically told the promoter that I wanted to work the opener because I knew I would get over. I had no problem if they wanted me to lay down every night, and over the first six months I was here I think I lost to every single guy on the roster at least once, even Toga Boy who has long since quit and was terrible. In the meantime I earned a lot of respect from the guys in the locker room, so when the promoter decided to put me in a main event role the locker room didn't have a problem with it. I have no problem proving where I belong on the show."

Nevada continues the trend in independent wrestling of lengthy title reigns, having held the ECCW strap for over a year. Fellow ECCW star Major

Hardway was NWA Canadian junior champion for well over a year, while promotions like Ring of Honor and Stampede Wrestling's major titleholders have held the belts for a lengthy run as well. Nevada considers it an honor to have the belt.

"To come to the West Coast and be involved with the ECCW territory, which, like Calgary, has a rich wrestling history. This year is the hundredth year of documented wrestling in B.C. so to be the guy on top of the roster means a great deal to me. In a lot of places wrestling is an ego-driven product, and unfortunately the promoters are driving the product so they use the belt more as incentive than as a tool. Belts in wrestling aren't supposed to be rewards — they should be a tool to help you tell a story. When you see seven champions over the course of a year in Winnipeg, that doesn't go far to establish a product and who marquee players are. Also, the fact that the schedule is reduced to maybe once or twice a month affects title runs. A champion may only have 30 matches in a year. It's an introduction to your fans as to who the people are on top of your company and they respond to that."

Having accomplished so much in his career, Nevada questions what the future holds. He is still only 28 years old but is realistic in what path his career is headed.

"I would like to wrestle for a few more years, but when I hit 30 it might be time to pack it in. When I hit 30 I might say, 'Well when I hit 35 . . .' I'd like to work towards getting some publishing done. Before I got busy with wrestling I spent a lot of time chronicling Canadian wrestling history as there is very little known about it. Mainstream books and magazines limit Canadian history to Billy Watson, Gene Kiniski and Stampede Wrestling. Those three things are the biggest ever in Canadian wrestling but if that is all you have looked at then you've done the country an injustice because there has been so much wrestling here. We've contributed many people to an internationally recognized status, which has always interested me."

There are very few who truly know the history of professional wrestling in Canada. Nevada is one of those who are determined to make the current generation aware of our country's contributions to wrestling. It's been a hobby for years and will likely consume him more in future years.

"When I was breaking in, I was aware that Condello had promoted in Manitoba since 1972, so in my mind wrestling in that province started then. As I started meeting old timers at shows it generated curiosity. I spent the summer of 1994 in the archives in Winnipeg, digging up the history of wrestling there. I started digging a bit and it got bigger and bigger. Four years later I was still in the archives.

"As I would get close to finishing and waiting on some materials, I started a history of Saskatchewan because I didn't think there was much history there. I was wrong. It's insane now, I have a database of independent wrestling results from 1902 until the present. I've stemmed off into assembling individual career records for wrestlers who are really worthy of having their achievements recognized. I have been working with institutions like the Cauliflower Alley Club to make sure these wrestlers are recognized in their hall of fame. I want to generate more awareness of what Canada has done to build the wrestling industry as a whole."

* * *

Chi Chi Cruz is ready for action!

IN PRAISE OF CHI CHI CRUZ

By JASON CLEVETT

When you've had the type of career that Winnipeg's Chi Chi Cruz has had, it's hard to really put into words the life he has lived and the experiences he has had. His worldwide travels have given him such a jumble of memories that when you first ask him to talk about some of them, he can't actually give one off the top of his head.

"I've done everything under the sun; it's hard to even know where to start when asked something like that. It's mind-boggling the things that happen on the road," Cruz told SLAM! Wrestling.

He may have traveled the world, including faraway lands like Japan, Africa and Europe, but those experiences may pale in comparison to the infamous "Northern Death Tours" run by Tony Condello. Cruz has been on 14 of those tours in the past 19 years, and the duo are scheduled to be at a book signing for Greg Oliver's *The Pro Wrestling Hall of Fame: The Canadians* on Sunday, August 22 from 2–4 p.m. at Chapters on Empress in Winnipeg.

"I've seen ghosts, UFOs . . . you name it, it's happened," he said, adding, "Tony is great, a fun guy and a smart promoter. He has been doing it for something like 31 years and knows everything there is to know."

Cruz joked that, "As long as somebody remembers me I'll be happy," but he has influenced many Canadian talents. "Hotshot" Johnny Devine called Chi Chi "my hero" for some of his more amusing moments on the road, while Cruz can also take some credit for sending Wavell Starr, who has competed in Ohio Valley Wrestling as Standing Thunder, on his career path.

"Cheech made me love wrestling again to the point of wanting to get into the business after losing interest for a few years. My dad told me about a wrestling show in Regina that evening at the old auditorium and I thought why not," Starr told SLAM! Wrestling when asked about Cruz. "For the most part, the show was terrible and the 'workers' were self-taught with ridiculous physiques that did not belong in the ring. Then Cheech came out in a fancy ring robe and cut a heel promo that got the crowd worked into a frenzy. I was hooked on wrestling again and the whole outrageous atmosphere of a dark, smoke-filled arena packed with crazy fans took over. Cheech was larger than life and I specifically remember hearing the announcer call '10 minutes gone' and realizing he had only locked up once, yet the crowd had been into the whole thing. It was how I remembered wrestling to be when I was watching house shows as a kid."

Starr continued, "After I trained awhile and did a few shows for bottom of the barrel indie groups in places like Grande Cache, Alberta, and community centers in Winnipeg, I was lucky enough to have the opportunity to work with Cheech in numerous matches for Tony Condello on his northern tour. Being in the ring with a veteran like Cheech is exactly what a green piece of crap like me needed — I learned so much from him that I actually consider myself initially trained by Cheech. Any idiot can teach you how to bump, Cheech showed me how to work."

Cruz is flattered to be an influence on Starr. "Wavell is great, he has all the talent in the world and I hope he gets his break. This business is very frustrating, too much bullshit, politics and backstabbing."

"Cheech" has made friends of both sexes. "WWE talks about Owen Hart, how wonderful he was and he was a family man and really perfect. The one guy I would talk about is Chi Chi Cruz. He's a Mr. Wonderful," said retired Winnipeg woman wrestler Miss Kitty Karson. "I respect him 102 percent. Out of all the guys that I ever toured with, he was the most decent guy to tour with. And I've traveled a lot, believe me."

It can be difficult at times for a veteran like Cruz to look at the business he loves and dedicated his life to. As talented and charismatic as he is, he hasn't had some of the opportunities that others have had, and it can be frustrating. At times, Cruz contemplated throwing in the towel.

"The thought has crossed my mind but I'm too stubborn to quit," he laughed. "I don't know if that will be my downfall in the end. It does get frustrating when I see young wrestlers or promoters who think they know it all, and I can see they don't have a clue in their head about what they are talking about. I am usually pretty quiet, so I sit back and soak it in. It's depressing sometimes the way this business has gone down the toilet."

Some promoters and disgruntled wrestlers feel that Vince McMahon is entirely to blame for the slump that wrestling has fallen into. Cruz disagrees.

"I don't think Vince McMahon hurt anything by saying wrestling was entertainment; that boosted the sport as did the harder edge to the product. The problem is too many young guys having too much say in what they can do. The tendency for three million high spots with no psychology or sense, and guys having no idea how to construct a match and make it believable has hurt wrestling. The people in the crowd don't have to understand psychology — the fact that it is psychology means that it is a subconscious thing. If it doesn't make sense subconsciously they aren't going to react to it. Guys go in with all their spots worked out, and if you forget one link in the chain the whole match is screwed because of it. Taking repeated bumps, after three bumps shouldn't I be dead? It's not realistic and I think it's pathetic."

It would be great if more young guys could learn from veterans like Cruz.

"My work as a heel is most definitely based on what I learned from Cheech," said Starr. "As a matter of fact the first time I worked as a heel, I was basically imitating Cheech — the mannerisms, the attitude, how he projects himself, the way he controls the crowd and the way he controls the match, the way he sells. People used to say I even looked like Cheech," Starr continued. "Over the years I have added to this my own style and spin to develop my heel persona to what it is now, but the basics derive from what I learned from Cheech. We both like that Southern Style 'rasslin' that he was taught by Jerry 'The King' Lawler in Memphis, and I was taught by Jim Cornette at OVW. Many of our co-workers around Canada don't understand or can't grasp the simple concepts that style is based upon, so it creates another commonality between Cheech and I, as well as providing many laughs."

Cruz is a regular for the No Holds Barred promotion, and two stories stand out from those trips.

"One time on an NHB show in Winnipeg, I was working a gimmick match with a few others and Juggernaut. Juggs went to snap mare me over and I remembered seeing him do this many times before where he immediately follows with a fat guy stiff kick to the back, and a fat guy stiff kick to the chest. I was a little banged up and sold the snap mare to the floor on the outside, leaving Juggernaut alone in the ring with Crash Crimson," Starr reflected. "I couldn't help but chuckle as I looked up into the ring and saw Juggernaut looking a tad bit hot, and Crash Crimson looking the sacrificial lamb for the big stiff kicks (someone was going to take the kicks)! The look on Crash's face as he took these thunderous kicks to the body was priceless! As we drove off in the van towards Thunder Bay that night, the boys were asking me why I was such a big pussy and didn't want to sit up from the snap mare to take the stiff kicks. I replied in my best Rip Rogers impersonation (that's not all that great), 'nobody sells a goddamn snap mare anymore! Y'all are burying that move! If you grab me by the neck and drag me over, that shit hurts so I'm gonna sell it!' Cheech laughed his ass off."

As for why Cruz is Devine's hero, it stems from a visit to Thunder Bay when Cruz changed a girl's life.

"Myself, Devine, Joe E. Legend and a few other guys were in a strip club in Thunder Bay after an NHB show for Don Callis," Cruz recounted. "It was the end of the night and this stripper was onstage with bruises on her legs and rear. We thought someone was beating her or something! During the show she started slapping her ass, and she invited a couple of guys along the rail to slap her, and they tapped her like Mickey Mouse hitting Minnie. I'd had a couple of wobbly pops so I stood up and said, 'Honey I'll change your life.' She invited me over and was on all fours, lined up at chest level. It was the last song, the music died as I wound up and laid the chop of a lifetime on her ass. She went flying across the dance floor, got up with tears in her eyes, ass red and bleeding and turned and gasped, 'Thank you.' Fifteen minutes later she came out and said, 'What am I going to tell my boyfriend?'"

Legend backed up the story.

"It's 100 percent true. I was in tears laughing."

— With files from Greg Oliver

From the writer: It's easy to write a story about someone you've been a fan of for a long time. It is much, much harder to write a story on someone you only know of from reputation. The opportunity to interview Chi Chi landed in my lap during a cross-promotional show between Stampede Wrestling and the ill-fated Japanese promotion Wrestle-Aid. It was obvious from those who knew him that also wrestled that night, like Johnny Devine, that Cruz had a great deal of respect from others, which is how the basis for the story came about.

* * *

EDGE & CHRISTIAN MOCK BREAKUP RUMORS

By GREG OLIVER

Edge and Christian were best buds again on Saturday, hopping in the Toronto Molson Indy pace cars and racing around the track at Exhibition Place. They were having so much fun it was easy to forget that the seven-time WWF Tag Team champs have been bickering on screen.

"People have been saying we're going to break up for two, three years now," Edge told SLAM! Wrestling. "We've teased it before, and teased it, and that's really just to get people talking. Right now, I would see us winning an eighth tag team title, and make that record really hard to break."

When asked about the state of their friendship, which started when both were youngsters in Orangeville, Ontario, Christian pointed to Edge's E & C T-shirt as proof of their bond.

Edge jumped in with thoughts on their breakup. "We might have to do the old Rockers thing. 'You got a problem with Edge & Christian?' and rip the shirt in half. 'I don't think so!' Remember that? The old plate-glass window!"

But who ends up being Marty Jannetty to Shawn Michaels, doomed to an eternity of being in the other's shadow? "That'll probably be me because I've been holding Edge back as a huge singles star," deadpanned Christian.

"No, dude, if you go on the internet, you're the guy and I'm holding you back!" Edge retorted.

"No, no, they've been saying it for years. I've been holding you back," Christian confessed.

"Ever since you talked, they've changed their minds, brother!" Edge said, boosting his "brother's" spirits.

On the horizon is the King of the Ring pay-per-view on June 24. Both Edge and Christian are entered in the tournament, and based upon previous KOTR tournaments, a match between the two isn't out of the question. "If we did face each other, you'd get a hell of a match," Edge said. "But I'd rather face each other in the finals. Ahhh, then you've got some story!"

Saturday's Molson Indy photo opportunity was more about having fun than being WWF superstars. Both Edge and Christian took spins around the Indy track on the pace cars. The dynamic duo were the first in a series of wrestlers to take part in "WWF Invades the Molson Indy," which will also feature wrestlers Spike Dudley, Molly Holly, Tazz, Bradshaw and Faarooq in appearances before the July 15 race.

While they won't be able to attend because they will be on the road beating up their opponents, Christian, 27 — whose real name is Jay Reso — is a big fan of the race.

Edge and Christian meet their match with Molson Indy pit girls Serena, left, and Michelle.

"My father used to be a race car driver. He used to attend races quite often and I would watch them," he said.

Edge, 27 — whose real name is Adam Copeland — was decked out in his signature cool wraparound sunglasses and a T-shirt with a picture of the tag team in fighting form.

But Edge, whose flamboyant ring actions have made him a fan favorite, had a small confession to make.

"Anything that involves too much speed besides wrestling, I don't get involved in. I just get in my SUV and feel safe," Edge said.

Instead of the Indy, the two Canadians have their sights set on another pair of hosers, WWF tag team champs Chris Benoit and Chris Jericho. "I love wrestling those guys. They're awesome," Christian said. "I've always been a huge fan of both of their work. Benoit is always so intense, like he's tearing your head off, and he's hard-hitting. Jericho's the same way, he's hard-hitting and a pretty intense guy. That's the kind of match I like to have. So every time we've been in the ring with those guys, we seem to have jelled really good with them, so I look forward to doing more with them."

Edge explained that they modify their styles to fit their opponents. "We kind of struck on a good formula. When you see us wrestle the Hardys it's going to be a different match than you'll see with Benoit and Jericho. We get in there with those guys . . . it's going to be dynamic, very hard-hitting. We're beating the hell out of each other. That's just the way we like it — good ol' Canadian boys rasslin'. So it's real fun, and it's different and fresh for us, which is nice. If we could have a run against those guys for the tag straps, that would be a hell of an angle and a feud."

The other new talent starting in the WWF has them intrigued as well.

"We've cut out our teeth with Rhyno. It's fun teaming with him, but it would also be fun to get in there with him because we've both done it before and it works," Edge said, referring to their time together both in Manitoba and in Detroit. "He's a hell of a talent and a hell of a person too. Just a good guy that I'm really looking forward to getting in there with."

"I haven't seen much of Tajiri, but from what I've seen, he's been impressive," Christian said. "Spike [Dudley] is awesome. We've been in there a few times with him when he first came in, and done some pretty cool stuff with him at WrestleMania. . . . He brings a lot to the table."

Can a reunion with Kurt Angle be feasible down the road? Even after he was seemingly banished to the bottom of the barrel on last week's *Raw*, seeking help from X-Factor?

Edge thinks it's quite possible. "I think that was just for one show. Kurt's doing his own thing. The good thing with the WWF storylines is that you can always go back to that. I mean, we've had a friendship with Rhyno, we've had a friendship with Kurt, and next week you could see us in a six-man with Kurt and it would make sense because we're all still intertwined."

— With files from Carlos Corbo, *Toronto Sun*

From the staff: Edge and Christian, as it turns out, did break up, with that very King of the Ring crown helping to exacerbate their split. Neither, however, went on to become the "Marty Jannetty" of the duo. In fact, they are one of few long-standing tag teams to both come out successful, as each has held multiple singles titles, including world championships (Edge in WWE, Christian in TNA).

* * *

THE WWE TRYOUT EXPERIENCE

Wrestlers strive to fulfill a dream with WWE

By COREY DAVID LACROIX

Dangerboy Derek Wylde (left) and TJ Harley rest up after their match at the Ottawa tryout.

OTTAWA — Ten years. That's how long it has taken "Dangerboy" Derek Wylde to get to this point in his wrestling career.

Drenched in sweat, beneath the lights of Ottawa's Scotiabank Place, Wylde (real name Dennis Stewart) is catching his breath after a rigorous workout in front of World Wrestling Entertainment (WWE) representatives.

He was the first to volunteer to get in the ring for a brief wrestling match, alongside fellow Ontario indie grappler, TJ Harley. It was a chance to show what they can do in the ring.

"I've been waiting for this for a long time," said Wylde to SLAM! Wrestling. "I volunteered first because I'm confident in my abilities. Why sit around waiting?"

It's the must-have attitude if you want to make it to WWE. That and the physical conditioning to endure the demands that come with the live-action spectacle of professional wrestling.

For those who attended the tryout in the nation's capital, it was a chance to see if they have what it takes. Some, like Wylde, are active wrestlers. He and Harley knew what was coming and it showed when it came to handling the grueling regime of Hindu squats and running the stairs.

"I'm having a wicked time," said Harley (real name Mike Holt), now in his seventh year as a professional wrestler. "It's a lot of fun and I'm all smiles because this is freakin' awesome. I'm on cloud 10, maybe even 11. I've had some of my best matches with Dangerboy. Me and him have been hurting each other for a couple of years now. I was just happy to get in the ring with him here. It's probably one of my greatest moments up to this date."

"We're both personal trainers at the same gym," Wylde added. "It's funny that we ended up in the ring together because we've pushing each other every day to do more and more. He would tell me to do 500 squats in a row and I would get mad, in a good way, and do 600. I would then make him do 700."

The fact that both athletes are at this tryout is a testament to their love for the business. Wylde in particular can probably tell you of the countless faces he's seen come and go on the indie circuit. Many gave up, unwilling to continue the hardships of brutalizing their bodies for little or no pay.

Then there are those who passed Wylde by, going forward to work in the big leagues, the same place he wants to be.

"I keep going for this," Wylde says, motioning towards the ring where his fellow candidates take their turn in the ring. Draped on the perimeter of the ring is a banner that reads *Smackdown*, the weekly television show watched by millions of fans across the continent. "It's the love of wrestling. Even if I never make it, I'll still keep going for as long as my body will hold up."

But being a competent wrestler is not enough. Nor is it enough to have that Herculean physique that has become the hallmark of the WWE product. Remember, this is sports entertainment.

"I've been very lucky that when I do independents [wrestling shows], they give me a lot of mic time," said Cody Deaner, another Ontario-based grappler who was also in attendance at the tryout. "It's a big part of wrestling, obviously. We're entertainers, apart from being athletes."

In real life, his name is Chris Gray and he's been here before. In fact, he actually had the chance to wrestle at a live, televised WWE event in November of 2004. So, what happened?

"I was complimented on my wrestling abilities, but I didn't get the call. They weren't saying you're good enough to get a contract," Deaner told SLAM! Wrestling.

It was a crossroads of sorts for him. Back then, his ring persona was Cody Steele, a youthful-looking, blond-haired grappler with a toned physique. The type of look that would draw approving squeals from young girls in attendance.

But it wasn't what WWE was looking for. "Every time I come to do tryouts, I keep asking people, 'What do I got to do? Give me advice. What do I have to work on to get a contract?'" Deaner said.

The answer was to be different. For in the world of sports entertainment, having something that stands out, that certain magnetism that connects with fans subliminally, is what can make you stand out from everyone else. And if you stand out, you are an attraction and that makes money.

With that revelation, Deaner set out to do just that.

"I'm not the biggest guy in the world, so I can't show them that I'm a big monster," Deaner said. "I decided to do something that stands out. I cut my hair, grew a mustache and changed the whole gimmick."

Add in a mullet to that description and Cody Steele became Cody Deaner — the poster child for unemployed, trailer park white trash everywhere. Inspired from the Canadian cult hit film *Fubar*, it's a blatant stereotype; but it works. The gimmick has become a cult phenomenon of sorts among indie wrestling fans, his antics riling fans wherever he appears. Yes, he's different and he's getting more attention because of it.

"I Americanized it a little bit, a southern twang, so they understand a little better when I'm in the States. It's just something I've done to stand out and be different," Deaner explained.

In making the change, Deaner showed initiative in learning as much as he can about the business and a willingness to adapt. It's a proven attitude to have if you really want to be successful.

Just ask WWE star Ken Kennedy.

"I knocked on the door for about six and a half years," said Kennedy (real name Ken Anderson).

It was at the end of the tryout session that Kennedy made an appearance at ringside. Looking at the cluster of hungry faces brought back many a memory for Kennedy of his days on the indie wrestling circuit, chasing the same dream he's now fulfilling.

"Every time I would come to these tryouts I would bust my ass. I was so hungry."

Hunger, obsession, devotion; call it what you will, but it was that inner strength that drove Kennedy to work hard at his chosen vocation. In hearing Kennedy tell of his rise to success, he draws a clear map for aspiring wrestlers everywhere on what it takes to get where he is now.

"I remember wrestling a match in Milwaukee and I went up to a guy who I kinda looked up to at that time and I asked him, 'Do you think I could send a tape to WWE (then WWF) and do you think they would take a look at it?'"

"He said, 'No, you're not ready. I wouldn't send anything because you don't want to make a bad first impression.' To me, that was bullshit because if I go there and they tell me I'm the shits, then a year from now, when I send another tape, and I know I've improved, they'll see that improvement and they'll say, 'Hey, this guy can learn and we can teach him.' After I asked the guy and he told me not to, I went home and made a tape."

He sent that tape and that bold step paid off when he got a call from former WWE commentator and talent scout, Kevin Kelly. It would be the beginning of a long process of nurturing a relationship with the company.

"They brought me down to a couple of shows as an extra. Didn't do any-thing, just sat around, but I knew I was sort of in the door," said Kennedy.

"If I saw that *Raw* or *Smackdown* show was coming to Milwaukee, Chicago, Cleveland or anything within a thousand miles of my home I would drive. WWE pays the extras a little cash, so it was enough to cover my expenses. In fact, I would have done it out of my own pocket and I did many times."

It's called sacrifice and it's a huge barrier to many a wannabe wrestler. Kennedy has met his fair share of people who just don't have the will to make sacrifices, who just don't have the hunger he has. Professional wrestling is not something you can do half-assed; you have to want it because it's who you are.

"Guys come up to me all the time and say, 'Hey, should I be a wrestler?' and I say no. Nobody ever had to tell me, I never had to ask anybody. Lots of people told me not to after I told them that I was going to and I said, 'Go pound sand, I'm going to do it,'" said Kennedy.

What Kennedy did was to absorb as much information as possible on how he could improve as a performer. As much of a physical art form as wrestling is, it is also cerebral. Knowledge of the endless intricacies of a match and how to bring an audience into the choreographed drama being displayed is mastered by few.

As Kennedy was told during a past conversation with Kelly, paying your dues on the independent wrestling circuit is where the most important lessons are learned.

"One of the things Kevin Kelly told me was, 'I don't care if you're wrestling in front of five people and you're working the shittiest guy in the world, you're going to learn something in that match. Have as many matches as you can and get as many matches under your belt and always try to learn something from every match.' I still do that today."

The uncountable number of matches, the hints from experienced trainers, the networking with WWE; it all paid off when Kennedy had his tryout with the company and got his deal with Ohio Valley Wrestling (OVW), a talent development promotion based in Kentucky.

"Eventually I got to the point where I was confident and I knew what they were looking for," said Kennedy. "I had a tryout similar to this situation right here and there were a lot of people there. I was the only who knew what they were looking for. I went in there and I was hungry and aggressive."

It's a good bet that those who attended the tryouts in Ottawa will not get the call. Even so, Kennedy made it clear that those who aspire to be in WWE must continue to network with the company as much as they can.

"It's like any other business, you have to network," he said. "You can't wait for someone to knock on your door. You have to go to them [WWE] and show them that you want it."

"I see that stuff all the time. Guys will come to a tryout, they don't get asked to come back and they don't want to swallow their pride and make the phone call and say, 'Hey, can I come back?' They're like, 'Well, they know me now. If they [WWE] want me, they can call me.' Well, don't hold your breath."

Making it to the big time doesn't mean you're on easy street. As history has shown, anyone is susceptible to being released from their contract at anytime. Again, keeping a pulse on what others think about your performance may just help you avoid that unpleasant scenario.

In Kennedy's case, he goes right to the owner of WWE, Vince McMahon. "Every time I come back from a match, I look at the boss and say, 'Vince, how was that?' Some days he'll give me the thumbs up, other days he'll ream my ass out. I don't want to be stagnant. I want to go to the top."

They all want that, but the fact is, only the select few will.

With that bitter fact in mind, perhaps the most important lesson one can learn is make sure you have back-up plan if you don't make it to the WWE.

"I got my four-year degree in English-language literature and last year I just finished teacher's college," said Deaner.

He's holding back on starting a career in teaching. Just another sacrifice when it comes to chasing a dream. "I want to concentrate on this. Wrestling isn't a hobby for me. This is what I want to do for a living."

From the writer: This was a tough assignment. Not in the sense of getting a good picture or decent quotes, but in knowing that in all likelihood none of those attending the tryout would get a WWE contract. In the aftermath, that's exactly what happened. There was no mistaking the passion in the eyes of many of the tryout attendees. They were chasing a dream; you could tell they wanted it so bad. All those years of taking bumps in the ring, getting ripped-off by unscrupulous promoters, driving through blinding snow storms in a crowded car along some lonely highway . . . was it all in vain? Perhaps some felt that way. No doubt there were those at the tryout who deserved a WWE contract, who deserved to have all that hard work rewarded. But professional wrestling, as it is in life, is not fair. With that, loving this business goes a long way in swallowing that bitter pill.

* * *

CFL WRESTLED WITH WWF PROPOSAL
By PERRY LEFKO — *Toronto Sun*

From the staff: While American wrestling promoters have long harvested Canada's top competitors, at one point, one of them (guess who) was close to taking over a beloved institution. Yep, believe it or not, before the XFL was born, Vince McMahon had visions of entering into the CFL in a big way.

Almost half the teams in the Canadian Football League wanted to pursue merger talks with the World Wrestling Federation last year, but were counted out by the ruling minority.

A source told the *Toronto Sun* yesterday the Hamilton Tiger-Cats, Calgary Stampeders and Saskatchewan Roughriders wanted to continue discussions with the WWF, which aimed to take over the CFL last year.

The Montreal Alouettes reportedly took a neutral position while the Argos didn't factor because of the uncertainty of their ownership.

The source said the Edmonton Eskimos, one of the few CFL teams to make money, vehemently opposed a union with the WWF, while the B.C. Lions also rejected it.

The Winnipeg Blue Bombers' stance was unknown.

"At the end of the day we didn't have enough teams that wanted to proceed," CFL President Jeff Giles said.

A source said Giles and Chairman John Tory supported the WWF initiative, but lacked the backing of board members who wield considerable power.

Talks began in February when Giles approached the WWF about buying the Argos. The conversations escalated when the WWF proposed taking over the league.

The source said there were CFL governors and executives who feared the WWF would create its own league with or without the Canadian teams.

And, it appears that may happen.

The WWF has a major football initiative scheduled to be announced today in New York. There is speculation in the football industry that the WWF may announce the formation of an outdoor spring league next year.

Bloomberg News reported last night that the WWF plan would include an eight-game schedule for each team with games on the USA Network.

Giles said the CFL will be monitoring the announcement, which will be broadcast on satellite.

Giles said the WWF's initiative may affect the CFL and force it to escalate some of the ideas to be discussed at a strategy meeting in Edmonton in 13 days.

Giles said if the WWF decides to form its own league, it will create more demand for players and hike salaries. Moreover, the WWF might expand into Canada.

"I don't think we can take this lightly," Giles said. "We have to take it seriously."

A source slammed the CFL for failing to take advantage of the opportunity, even though the WWF reportedly failed to sweeten the deal with significant up-front money.

"They had their chance and they blew it," the source said.

STU HART, MY DAD, MY HERO

By BRET HART — *Calgary Sun*

Jim Wells, Sun Media Corp.

Stu has Bret where he wants him.

I read a folk tale about a father pursuing a son who's run far away from one world to the next. The father called to him: "Please come back!" but his son looked across the great gulf between them and shouted to him: "I can't get that far!" So his father yelled to his son, "Then just come back halfway!" But his boy replied: "I can't go back halfway!" And finally his father shouted: "Walk back as far as you can — and I will go the rest of the way!"

— Ron Hansen

People outside of my family usually think of my father as a gruff grappler famous for making the toughest of men scream for mercy.

The perception is right.

Make no mistake about it, even considering the many wrestlers of all shapes and sizes whom I've locked up with from near and far, Stu Hart is the toughest man I've ever known.

But he is also the most fair and compassionate man and an indulgent parent to 12 children. My father has iron hands that have brought down giants — but these same hands have also gently cradled wounded birds and stroked the dogs and cats that follow him from room to room.

My father is a man of gentle strength. He takes a common sense approach to life that enables him to keep a calm head when things go wrong or to unleash his harder side when he deems it necessary. It's a balance I may not have understood as a young boy but that I quickly came to respect.

I remember when I was quite young, tossing a football around in the yard with my brothers. My dad would come out and punt these perfect spirals really far. He'd tell us about when he played with the Edmonton Eskimos in 1937–38 and he put his huge, strong hands lightly over mine and showed me how to line my fingers up with the laces.

Years later, when I played defensive tackle, my dad drove me to practice every morning at 5:45 a.m. and he picked me up in the afternoons. High school football is one of my fondest memories and I used to think that was because of my triumphs on the field or with the cheerleaders. But now, being a dad myself, I realize the really special part was the time I spent with dad in his car, getting pointers and listening to the radio.

Even then, I thought it was strange lots of times when Paul Simon's song "Loves Me Like A Rock" came on, as that is the perfect subtitle for our entire relationship.

I can remember getting into one of my regular schoolyard scuffles at Wildwood elementary. I was in Grade Three and locked in a stalemate with this bigger kid when my dad arrived to pick up me and my Grade Six brother, Dean, for lunch.

Dad started driving back and forth in front of the school, honking the horn of his old, beat-up eight-door limo and Dean said we'd better hurry or Dad would kill us.

Well, I was more afraid of making my dad angry than I was of this kid, so I released a face-lock I had on him, jumped up and ran off, the whole time he and his buddies yelling "chicken."

When I got in the car, I was kind of upset, thinking I'd somehow soiled the family honor by retreating. Upon hearing Dean's assurances I was not a chicken, my dad quizzed me on what had happened.

When we got home, Dad pulled me aside and told me if I ever get in trouble, reach up and grab hold of my opponent's face, almost like I was going to kiss him, and then use my back teeth on the tip of his nose and bite the hell out of it.

After school, the big bully and I were locked in a tangle of arms and legs out by the old soccer posts when he suddenly jumped up, screaming, crying and running all the way home.

The kids who gathered around couldn't figure out what happened and I just casually said: "Aw, I guess he's chicken."

I walked away and softly said: "Thanks, Dad."

On the other hand, I remember a time when I said: "Thanks, but no thanks, Dad." I was in Grade 10 and it was the night before the city championships.

Mom got on Stu, saying things such as, "Why don't you show him some wrestling?" (Mom never really knew what went on down in the Dungeon in our basement.) I figured it can't hurt (oh, yes, it can!). He might show me that one little trick move to win.

After enduring each torturous hold, I'd explain: "But I can't do that, Dad, because I'll get disqualified."

The next day, I showed up for the city championships feeling all confident the training session would pay off. But I was so sore, I could barely raise my arms and I lost my first two matches and got eliminated.

Thanks, but no thanks — but it still meant a lot to me my dad was there to "help" me.

The next year, I was city champion when Johnny English came to town wanting to wrestle for Stampede. He had a pro championship belt from England, was about 35, fit and strong — but just too small to compete with the big-bodied men.

So, my dad calls me to the Dungeon and asks me to wrestle this guy. It reminded me of a lion that catches an antelope for the cubs to practice on. It was a pretty even match until Stu starts giving me instructions from the sidelines and, next thing you know, I was stretching this guy pretty good.

I knew Stu loved every minute of it and was proud of me. As for Johnny English, he rode off, never to be heard from again.

Then they brought in Yagi, a Japanese rookie. Stu and Mr. Hito called me to the basement (again) and asked me to wrestle the guy. I immediately said he was too big and, besides, I was 16 or 17 and he was 24.

Next thing you know, I took him down with amateur moves. Well, Yagi didn't like it one bit. Apparently, I was making him look bad but I didn't realize that because I was just doing what they'd asked.

Stu had stepped out for a few minutes and came back to see Yagi fighting really rough and dirty. He bent my fingers back and another time he bit me.

Well, Stu just grabbed this guy — enough was enough — and stretched the shit out of him. It was as scary as I can remember anyone being tortured in the Dungeon.

The guy was screaming and crying — and it was all because my dad saw him cheat and take cheap shots on me.

Then there was the night this guy tried to steal Stu's old Caddy but he couldn't get up the driveway because there was too much snow. My dad didn't even call the police — but I know the guy probably wished he had.

Stu grabbed him and stretched him — and then called his parents. Next thing you know, Stu gave him a job as an usher at the matches, which goes to show you my dad is big-hearted but just won't stand for himself or his family being treated unfairly.

I guess I knew that about my dad at an early age because, when I was 11 and watching him and Archie "The Stomper" Gouldie from the first row of a sold-out Victoria Pavilion, I didn't like how Archie was taking liberties with my father.

So when the match spilled out of the ring in front of me, I stuck out my foot and kicked Archie in the butt. I was defending my dad as he always defended me.

Years later, my dad thought I was good enough to team with him against

Stomper and John Foley. I watched from the apron as he planted a series of uppercuts on Foley and thought about how far I'd come and how proud I felt to be there as my dad's partner.

I phoned my dad the other day and he lamented that, like myself, he doesn't watch much wrestling anymore. Like me, he misses the way it used to be, when pro wrestling was an art and watches it from time to time to satisfy his curiosity.

We agreed it seems to be coming full circle, back to athleticism and telling stories with your body in the ring. We both hold our breath in relief, anticipation and hope it may yet live on for another generation.

It turns out we both enjoy Chris Benoit and Chris Jericho. We also both think highly of Kurt Angle's background as an amateur Olympic gold medalist. Stu pointed out Angle's neck and how you can just tell he's a legit tough guy.

Suddenly, Stu was talking about how he was schooled by a bunch of old shooters in Edmonton. What was it about Edmonton that attracted and/or created some of the toughest guys in the history of wrestling?

I hear a lot of them were cops. The crime rate must have been pretty darn low!

Next thing you know, Stu was talking about New York. During the Second World War, Stu was in the navy and on leave when he hitchhiked to New York City in search of Toots Mondt, a legendary wrestling promoter in the 1940s.

Stu was looking to open a door for himself so he could switch from amateur to pro wrestling, where you could earn a decent living. In those days, the business was built on shooters with the showmen rounding out the cards. Besides, there was always a local ruffian who thought he could take on the top guy and it helped to tell him he had to go through some other guy first — a shooter who would put his lights out and send him home with his tail between his legs.

In my day, the toughest guys wouldn't have been the Hogans, Dynamites, Stone Colds or the Bret Harts.

I'm sure they'd agree, nobody would want to find himself on the wrong side of "Bad News" Brown [Allen], Earthquake, Scottie Steiner, Haku, Shamrock or Goldberg — to name a few.

Stu made his way to George Brothner's gym, at 42nd and Broadway, because it had earned a storied reputation as a sparring spot for all the top shooters. (It was also a workout/hangout for all kinds of circus performers — jugglers, midgets, acrobats and boxers.)

Stu was told he could find Toots Mondt at a local coffee shop. Toots was sitting there, sipping his coffee and reading the *Daily News*, when Stu decided to walk by him — a couple of times. Toots casually mentioned to Stu: "You have a big neck. You must be a wrestler."

"Well, in fact, I am," Stu said.

"Where are you from, then?"

When Stu said he was from Edmonton, Toots continued: "You must know Jack Taylor, then?"

"Yeah, I've worked out with Jack."

To this day, Stu describes Jack Taylor as "the toughest SOB there ever was."

Toots figured anyone who had worked with Jack Taylor could work for him. Stu had a job waiting for him when he got out of the navy in 1945.

Stu met and married my mom in New York and toured the U.S. for two or three years, making enough so he was able to come to Calgary and start his own territory.

Stu wasn't afraid to lock up with anybody. I saw on the news the other day a tiger had escaped from a zoo. Lots of men with lots of guns surrounded the tiger when, all of a sudden, the trainer comes zooming to the rescue. He walks up to the cat, pats it on the head and they walk away together.

It instantly reminded me of a Stampede from days gone by when my dad wrestled a tiger. He went out of his way not to let my mom find out but, of course, it was in the paper.

Mom was surprisingly calm, saying: "That must have been interesting, Buff. Why didn't I know about that?"

Mom thought because it was a trained tiger, it was harmless. If there is such a thing as a tame tiger. Well, about six weeks later, we were all huddled around the TV watching Untamed World and the show happened to mention a tiger can decapitate a yak with one swipe of its paw. We all took a deep breath, anticipating Mom's reaction.

"Stu! What were you doing in there wrestling that tiger?"

And so began an ongoing conversation that wasn't really resolved during the following three decades of marriage. I'm not sure if that has anything to do with my dad's pet name for my mom, Tiger Bell.

To work for my dad, the audition (initiation?) was simple. First, you had to wrestle Stu and, if he thought you were tough enough, you were in.

In those days, the Canadian dollar was strong and all kinds of athletes came to Stu looking for their break into pro wrestling.

Stu especially liked training football players and amateur wrestlers.

In the late 1950s — maybe '59 — a young brute, about 23 years old from Carbon, Alberta, showed up at the matches confident he could beat Stu's top guy or anyone else. He was brawny and strong — in fact, he would have looked a lot like Bill Goldberg. This guy was rarin' to go.

Containing him was a challenge until Stu talked him down by somehow convincing him Al "Murder" Mills or Tiny Mills could have easily ripped his head off. The guy was a total mark and Stu invited him to the house to "see what he could do."

His name was Archie Gouldie and, as the Stomper, he went on to become the best "total package" Stampede Wrestling — or maybe any territory — had ever seen.

Archie scared me pale many times when I was a boy.

Meanwhile, one afternoon, in the elevator at the Hudson's Bay, a short but muscular Italian man by the name of Bruno spotted Stu.

Bruno jerked Dad by the neck, insisting Stu show him how to wrestle. Anyone who knew Stu in those days would know this wasn't a smart move. Extremely irritated, Stu invited the feisty little man to come to the house "at two o'clock tomorrow."

Bruno and Archie arrived at the same time. My almost 88-year-old father can still recall the meeting.

"I kicked the (bleep) out of both of them . . . head between the knees, hip to the head. I had Archie where he kept trying to scoot on his ass. He finally scooted in the corner until he had nowhere to go . . . gave them all the ugly stuff. . . . Everything!"

We never saw Bruno again. Archie came back the next day, a big enough man to feel humbled, and said to Stu: "Sir, I want you to teach me to wrestle."

It's nice to see some things haven't changed. The legit tough guys, such as Kurt Angle, are still on top and all the zany characters still make the shows go. My dad loved them all — the midgets, even the misfits he bailed out of jail — but his true passion is, was and always will be the shooters.

"Er, I just wanna get the stiffness out of my knees," Stu told me this week. "I don't expect to wrestle like I used to but I could still give 'em a fight."

You'll get no argument from me on that, Dad.

I started out by saying people usually think of my father as a gruff grappler famous for making people scream for mercy. In the movie *Road to Perdition*, when his father's character is scrutinized, a son replies with simple elegance, as if the very question is a non sequitur: "He was my father. Yes! And my father is my biggest hero. The only man I want to be is what my dad has been to me."

* * *

WHALEN REMEMBERS STAMPEDE

By ED WHALEN — *Calgary Sun*

A lot of people have asked me to do it and maybe I should (some day) write about my days with Stampede Wrestling.

It's a show that has followed me throughout my life and, indeed, still makes me a worldwide figure.

Let me explain that claim.

Former [Calgary] Flame Hakan Loob, now living in Sweden, recently told me, "You don't know how big a star you are in Europe."

Well, I don't know because somebody is bootlegging Stampede Wrestling (Stu Hart and yours truly get not one dime by way of residuals).

But yes, like the old cowboy ditty, "I've been everywhere." I have been everywhere — like Europe, Japan, Australia, Singapore, the jungles of Guyana, North Africa . . . the list goes on and on. In places like Rome and Beijing, there's old Eddie on the screen jabbering away in English with subtitles at the bottom of the screen.

We had relatively innocent fun with that show — innocent in contrast with the immoral overtones of the WWF today — but that's an editorial subject for another day (I fail to see how scenes like simulated oral sex on the screen have anything to do with wrestling and are of benefit to kids. However, there it was in living color, the scene performed on a bed and aired on TSN).

Don't let me get started on this subject.

I could keep going all day, but right now I'd better stop preaching. Right?

The Paris Follies of Sky High Lee

We, on Stampede Wrestling, had a lot of characters in the ring. The following couple of tales might not be humorous, but they do deal with two guys who spent time with us on the show.

How well I remember a worldwide box-office champ named Sky High Lee.

He was just about as high as the sky most of the time . . . on booze, bless him. I got to know about that part of his life in a car ride from Regina to Calgary as he happily consumed 40 ounces of rye — straight from the jug. Mind you, he never appeared to be drunk and he certainly wasn't abusive, which was a good thing.

You see, he stood something like seven-foot, eight-inches on a well distributed 450-pound frame.

Sky is gone and just before he cashed in, he starred in the *Folies Bergère* in

Ed Whalen holds the microphone for World Junior Heavyweight champion Nelson Royal.

Paris, carrying scantily clad women into a cave while chuckling with a voice that sounded like it came out of a sepulcher.

Another guy I recall was Firpo Zbysko.

He was a Polish gent who, at one time, was a world attraction. But when he continued fighting at the tender age of 70, he was relegated to the opening bout on a card. Your eyes did not deceive: 70 years old.

Dear old Firpo made only one mistake and not in the ring. He married an 18-year-old girl and was dead in two months.

Obviously, those two illustrations do not really tell you about the comical characters of the business.

But then, maybe I'll tell you about that stuff in a book. Who knows?

From the staff: Sadly, Ed Whalen never got the opportunity to publish that book on all of the comical characters in pro wrestling. In 2001, over two years after writing this article, the voice of Stampede Wrestling passed away, leaving behind family, friends, and legions of fans of his work in and around the squared circle.

Superstars

Rightly or wrongly, superstar interviews are perhaps the most enjoyable stories for SLAM! Wrestling writers.

Talk to the guys and gals who have scribed for the site and more often than not, they'll tell you that their big "mark out" moment was when they spoke, either in person or over the phone, with one of the current wrestlers. Maybe it's the "brush with greatness" factor or the simple fact that, at times, it's damn hard to get them to break kayfabe (let alone book an interview in the first place), but there's an undeniable adrenaline rush to get a few minutes with a larger-than-life hero of wrestling.

Needless to say, the reader support for these stories over the years parallels this excitement. Our highest-rated articles often come from pieces on the current talent.

Here is just a sampling of these stories.

* * *

GOING TOE-TO-TOE WITH RIC FLAIR

By TIM BAINES — *Ottawa Sun*

From the writer: Imagine sitting next to the limousine-ridin', jet-flyin', kiss-stealin', wheelin'-and-dealin' Nature Boy — in a stretch limo.

It was supposed to happen. I had been dispatched from Ottawa to interview Naitch and WWE had rented a limo so we could drive around his old stomping grounds in Raleigh, North Carolina. My plane connection from Pittsburgh was delayed a couple of times so while the limo still picked me up the airport, Naitch wasn't in it. He was getting ready for that night's Raw. But he still did the interview in the seats of the RBC Center. Ric Flair was everything I expected and more. He was honest, moved to tears by some of his memories. As the sports editor of a daily newspaper, I'm rarely in awe of an athlete; but Nature Boy was different. He was The Man. At the end of the interview, he asked if I wanted to go out after the show and be "Naturized," which would I'm sure involve hoisting a few cold beverages. Sadly, we never got together (though I have to say sitting in the hotel bar with Victoria and Lillian Garcia was an awesome consolation prize).

RALEIGH, NORTH CAROLINA — To be "The Man," you've got to beat "The Man" . . . or at least hang out with him for more than an hour right in the heart of Flair Country. The Dirtiest Player in the Game. Slick Ric. The Nature Boy. Naitch.

The bleach-blond-haired legend slides into a seat beside me in the RBC Center. North Carolina. The state where he's gained so much notoriety. So many memories.

Now 56, Flair is still stylin' and profilin'. He's still the limousine-ridin', jet-flyin', kiss-stealin', wheelin'-dealin' son of a gun. Armani suits, sequined robes worth thousands of dollars. Struttin' down the aisle.

But, for the moment, he's sitting back in his chair, offering a glimpse at what it's like to walk in his shoes.

"To be Ric Flair, the Nature Boy, to be the character is hard to describe, hard to put into words," says Richard Morgan Fliehr. "It's been outrageous, a tremendous time.

"For about 20 years of my life, Ric Flair was the same inside and outside of the ring. I lived that life. I loved that life. Every day. I couldn't get enough.

"I think I'm wrestling's Jesse James. About half the stories you hear are probably true. I had fun. There were no drugs, nothing illegal. I just wanted to be part of the party."

Flair is humble, not like the character that is so at home with a microphone, with catchphrases like: "Ric Flair is just like Space Mountain; it might be the oldest ride in the park, but it still has the longest line."

Outside the RBC Center, Mike Clark stands beside his black stretch limo. He's been a driver for Flair.

"He's larger than life. He's Ric Flair. Very flamboyant," says Clark. "Some superstars get so full of themselves, but Ric has never been anything but a gentleman."

A gentleman who has changed his lifestyle. He's toned down the nightlife. He may no longer be "The Man," but other wrestlers still put him on a pedestal.

"I grew up watching Ric and even to this day I think he's the best there has ever been," says Flair's Evolution mate Triple H.

Flair insists he's a changed man. Part Nature Boy. Part Ric Flair.

"I was so full of myself, so full of the business," says Flair. "I didn't take time to slow down and look at some of the important things in life. I was so

Ric Flair is grilled in a media scrum.

Mike Mastrandrea

wrapped up in the moment.

"Ultimately, I was selfish. I wasn't mature enough. In my eyes, family is the most important thing in life, but I don't think it was for me. I was out of control. . . . My only regrets are for the people I hurt. I was so wrapped up in my career, I sacrificed family and I wish I could have that back. But you can only say that so many times. At the end of the day, we're all close.

"Part of it is I just got older. I couldn't stay out all night. To be that character is awesome, but I've got four beautiful kids [David, Reid, Ashley and Megan] and a 10-month-old granddaughter [Morgan Lee]. I've always been pretty affectionate with kids and I love her to death."

Flair was born in Memphis, Tennessee, on February 25, 1949, adopted through the Tennessee Children's Home Society, stolen from his birth parents and put into an adoption black market. Conflicting documents say he was born Fred Phillips, Fred Demaree or Fred Stewart. He was raised by the Fliehrs — Dick, a gynecologist, and Kay, a theater writer. And he grew up a wrestling fan, admiring AWA stars like Verne Gagne, Bobo Brazil and the Crusher. He was Mad Dog Vachon's paperboy.

The Nature Boy persona started emerging long before he put on the wrestling trunks. In his book, *To Be the Man*, he says he started having sex at the age of 14.

A chance meeting with Ken Patera kick-started his wrestling career. He began in the Minnesota area, but relocated to Charlotte, North Carolina, in 1974. And the legend began. He won his first NWA title in 1981. It wouldn't be the last he'd strap across his waist. He's a 16-time, yep, 16-time world champ.

And he'd be a central figure in the Four Horsemen, along with Arn Anderson, Ole Anderson and Tully Blanchard, then later with Barry Windham replacing Ole. The Four Horsemen are the greatest faction in wrestling lore — four larger-than-life figures that lived large.

"Night after night we drew a phenomenal amount of money," says Flair. "Every night in an arena, we'd get beat, but we could draw."

And while Flair says he has no stroke in WWE's creative department, he wouldn't mind a Four Horsemen reunion of sorts.

"It would have to be Kurt Angle, Hunter [Triple H], Shawn Michaels and myself. The four best talkers they have."

And now he sits in Raleigh. Weighing and measuring his career, putting his life in perspective and talking about others who stake their claim among wrestling's giants.

"Bret Hart never drew a dime," says Flair. "He's taken the opportunity to knock everyone. But how can you knock a business that's made you $7 million? Bret's got a cult following, but he's losing that. Losing that because he just goes on and on . . . it's funny [that he knocks me] because I'm the only guy that would put him over.

"Hulk Hogan? The Hulk Hogan thing was great. He worked hard at being Hulk Hogan. I always said the difference between me and Hogan was I said yes and he said no. [Hogan wouldn't put anybody over.] I'll concede the fact that Hogan was a bigger star than me.

"But in terms of overall product, he'd wrestle a five-minute match and be back at the hotel by nine. I'd wrestle for an hour . . . and I'd give it everything I had."

"A Liar"

"Eric Bischoff? He was a liar. And that's why I beat him up. I was the one guy who punched him, but there was a line of 20 guys who wanted to do it."

"Mick Foley? He can fall off a roof, but he can't wrestle. He can entertain doing something that's insanity, not wrestling.

"The biggest problem I have with guys like Foley and Hart is they're their own biggest fans."

There have been some slumps in Flair's career too. Times when he wondered why he was still putting his limbs on the line.

"I lost a huge amount of self-confidence and a lot of self-respect in about 1997," says Flair. "I never thought I'd come back to work after WCW closed down.

"The company had been an embarrassment for two, almost three years. They let the inmates run the asylum and it was destined to fail.

"They tried to retire me. They were saying, 'He's 39 and he's too old.' I got my hair cut and they wanted to put an earring on me."

Then when he got hired by WWE, he had more doubts.

"WrestleMania in Toronto. I was operating at about 50 percent," he says. "The Undertaker carried me through the match. I was afraid I was going to fail. I had never woken up wondering whether somebody was a better wrestler than me."

Flair is having fun again. He's confident in himself, confident that he's become a better person. And confident of his role. Confidence that probably coincided with the intervention of his buddy, Hunter Hearst Helmsley, the villainous Triple H, who invited him to join Evolution with up-and-comers Randy Orton and Batista. He's stylin' and profilin' again. Once again, knowing his role.

"When we were coming in here on the flight the captain came on and said we had just flown over Atlanta, we were heading over Savannah, then going over Columbia. I turned to Shawn Michaels and said, 'Why can't the guy say we've just entered Flair Country?'"

* * *

Wooooooo! When there was such a thing as the NHL, Flair's voice boomed over the RBC Center's sound system each time the Hurricanes scored a goal. And for some Hurricanes fans, that may be the best reason to end the current NHL–NHLPA stalemate.

* * *

Wooooooo! The chant grows with each knife-edge chop Flair delivers in the ring. As a heel, he does everything he can to get the fans to hate him. But as he absorbs several body shots and does a face plant into the mat, the fans laugh. The Nature Boy is at it again. An entertainer. A crowd pleaser. An icon.

"I've been to the nuthouse, I've had a heart attack on TV, I've been buried alive in the desert and I've played musical chairs," says Flair. "There's not much I haven't done.

"I can still be very good at this; I just need to keep my head straight. Whether it's 30 years or tomorrow [that I quit], the fans know that, whether there are 200 or 20,000 watching, I've given them my best performance."

And for that we're thankful, Naitch.

* * *

EDDIE'S SET FOR HIS CANADIAN DEBUT

Guerrero thrilled with WCW role
By JOHN MOLINARO

Last New Year's Eve, Eddie Guerrero lay prone in a hospital bed, wondering if he'd ever wrestle again. He had miraculously walked away from a terrible car accident.

His thoughts turned to his family. A devoted husband and father, wrestling had allowed him to provide for his family. Now his livelihood was in jeopardy.

He was told his return would be an uphill battle. "It's not going to be easy," the doctors told him. They questioned whether or not he would make it.

But he did make it. Through hard work, determination and the power of prayer, Eddie Guerrero returned to action. And now, as a member of the Filthy Animals, he's on top of the world.

"I'm ecstatic [about the Filthy Animals]," Guerrero told SLAM! Wrestling from his home in Florida. "It's the biggest opportunity I've had in my career. I'm working with guys I really like to work with."

Part of a major program in WCW for the first time, Guerrero is quick to give credit to head writers Vince Russo and Ed Ferrera.

"What Vince and Ed bring to WCW is phenomenal," stated Guerrero. "They're really blessed in what they do. I'm very honored and grateful for the opportunity they've given me."

He's also impressed with the job they've been doing thus far.

"[With Russo and Ferrera] this is a wrestling company now," joked Guerrero. "We went from being so disorganized to everything being organized now."

Despite being kept in a mid-card position by Eric Bischoff, Guerrero has nothing but nice things to say about his former boss.

"I can't say anything bad about Eric Bischoff," admitted Guerrero. "I had problems with him here and there, but he gave me an opportunity, and he brought me in and I'm very grateful for that."

"I really didn't get a push because Eric had given so many people so much power you couldn't do anything. It was the politics of him keeping his word to other people that kept me, Chris [Benoit] and Dean [Malenko] down."

Although he's returned to his old form, Guerrero is still leery in the ring.

"I want to go out there and produce but I still don't feel 100 percent," admitted Guerrero. "I was scared to death when I came back. People are always going to be looking at you and asking, 'Does he still have it?'

"I'm dealing with a reconstructed ankle and three fractured vertebrae that I'll have for the rest of my life. I have constant pain."

Guerrero also feels a little self-imposed pressure about living up to his name. As the son of legendary wrestler Gory Guerrero and with three older brothers who wrestled, being a Guerrero isn't always the easiest thing in the

Mike Lano

Eddie Guerrero and an unmasked Rey
Mysterio during their last days in WCW.

world for Eddie.

"Having the name Guerrero opened up doors for me but at the same time I have to live up to the expectations of my brothers and my dad. It's the hardest thing because people expect you to live up to the name."

As a member of the Filthy Animals, Guerrero is one of the few Mexican wrestlers being given a push by the new booking regime. His fellow countrymen haven't been so lucky.

"They can't speak the language," conceded Guerrero. "It's hard to get a character over if you can't speak the language. Nowadays, if you're not on the mic and don't have interview time, you can't get it over.

"They're great in the ring," continued Guerrero. "I tell them all the time that no matter what [WCW] does to them backstage or in the locker room, they can't take away what they do in the ring. That's theirs. Nobody can take that from them."

Looking ahead, Guerrero is excited about being a part of this weekend's Mayhem PPV in Toronto. Guerrero has a wealth of experience competing in Mexico, Japan, Central America and several other countries around the world. Amazingly, this will be his first time wrestling in Canada.

"I'm really excited," said Guerrero. "I've been wanting to come to Canada for a long time. Especially for a pay-per-view because you get hyped up and the adrenaline gets going. It's a big deal for [Chris] Benoit as well."

"Although I'm not looking forward to the cold weather," laughed Guerrero. "I'm a Florida boy; so if it gets below 70 I start to shake."

Guerrero is also excited about the prospect of Japanese sensation and IWGP junior heavyweight champion Jushin "Thunder" Liger touring WCW next month.

"I'd love it if he came," exclaimed Guerrero. "What a worker! He's the most professional guy in the business. When I wrestled him in Japan, he taught me more about being a professional than anybody else."

The chance to square off against Liger will also make up for the fact that WCW sent Benoit and Malenko on a tour with New Japan Pro Wrestling last month, leaving Guerrero behind.

"I was real mad," kidded Guerrero. "I kept asking why did they get to go and not me?"

From the writer: I had the opportunity to interview hundreds of wrestlers during my time, but Eddie Guerrero was the only one I ever "marked out" for.

I can remember that the minute I hung up the phone after talking to him, I called up Greg Oliver in a state of euphoria and started gushing over how great it was to talk to Guerrero, how we talked about our mutual respect for Japanese and Mexican pro wrestling, and about his days in Mexico competing in a tag team with Art Barr.

Like his former tag partner, Guerrero left this world far too early.

*   *   *

Wrestling Revue

Latino Heat, before WWE copyrighted it.

GUERRERO WRESTLES WITH DEMONS

By KEN WIEBE — *Winnipeg Sun*

From the staff: Just a few years later, Eddie Guerrero was in a completely different position than when John Molinaro spoke with him. Having left WCW shortly after the Mayhem pay-per-view, he, Chris Benoit, Dean Malenko and Perry Saturn debuted in the then WWF as The Radicals. The troubles that Guerrero experienced in WCW following his car accident had stayed with him and worsened in WWE after an arm injury. His addictions later led to his dismissal from the Fed.

Guerrero would eventually return to WWE as a changed man with more focus than ever. Tagging with his nephew, Chavo Guerrero Jr., Eddie was on the cusp of superstardom, and a couple months away from winning the WWE Championship, when he sat down with Sun reporter Ken Wiebe.

Eddie Guerrero considers his lineage to be both a blessing and a burden. With a father who was a famous wrestler and promoter back in Mexico and a trio of brothers — Chavo Sr., Mando and Hector — who had success in the squared circle, it was only natural for young Eddie to make his way into the grappling business.

"It's a family thing, we're basically the Harts of Mexico," said Guerrero, referring to the Calgary-based royal family of wrestling.

Guerrero is currently one half of the WWE tag team champions with nephew Chavo Jr. The dynamic duo will defend their title on tomorrow night's *Smackdown* card at the Winnipeg Arena.

Along with the pedigree came a certain amount of pressure for Guerrero to perform as well as those who came before him.

"It's like show business, you know what I mean," said Guerrero, who is also the U.S. champ. "A lot of doors were opened up because of the family name, you might get opportunities a lot quicker than other wrestlers breaking into the business. But at the same time, you've got to live up to the name. My father and my brothers were good wrestlers."

Though he had trouble living up to the name in the early stages of his career, Guerrero has since done plenty to ensure a lasting legacy.

"In wrestling, experience has a lot to do with it and the only way to get experience is through time in the ring," said Guerrero. "I can only remember one time in my life when I didn't want anything to do with wrestling and that's because I put too much pressure on myself in my junior year of high school.

"I put the pressure on myself to always win and I got my [butt] kicked a couple of times. I didn't like it."

His passion for wrestling has long since returned, but now Guerrero is fighting another type of pressure as a recovering alcoholic who's been sober for nearly two years.

"I would love to be able to sit down for a beer with the boys, but the reality is that if I drink a beer I'm not going to stop," said Guerrero, who calls himself an extremist. "I've really accepted that fact in my life. At first, it was very hard but little by little you overcome that. Actually, I like being sober and remembering the day and what happened last week."

* * *

OWEN WANTS A REMATCH

By JOHN POWELL

From the staff: It is always fun and challenging to interview WWE superstars with the fans around. It seems to happen in Toronto a lot, with the WWE Canada offices in town, it's a chance for the company to show off a bit. The media gets a crack at the stars, and the fans get to meet their heroes. This particular interview with

Owen Hart makes his way into the WWF ring.

Hart took place at SkyDome in Toronto with fan chants ringing through the cavernous hallways.

Nugget! Nugget! Nugget!

Call him that all you want. Yell it as loud as you can. It really doesn't upset WWF superstar Owen Hart . . . or so he says.

"To me, a nugget is something you eat at McDonald's that is deep-fried chicken. The only other thing a nugget is would be something that's solid gold and you buff it up, shine it and wear it on your finger or around your neck. It doesn't bother me too much. The same people chanting it are the ones who are paying that huge salary to me," said Nation member Owen Hart as SLAM! Wrestling finally cornered the cagey veteran at SkyDome a day before he is set to square off against Ken Shamrock in a submission match on Saturday night.

Hart's long-running feud with the former Ultimate Fighting Champion picked up where brother Bret left off, climaxing in a match at the exclusive Hart family wrestling school (the Dungeon) located in the basement of the Harts' Calgary home. The match was broadcast via satellite on the Fully Loaded pay-per-view, generating critical praise from fans as an inventive and unique contest. According to Hart, Shamrock wants a rematch on American soil during the WWF's annual SummerSlam card.

The Black Hart is game if only to prove that his win wasn't a fluke.

"I thought knocking Shamrock out in the Dungeon and having him tap out would be the end of it but I guess when you lose like that then you become a cry baby and come up with excuses. I'll give him another shot if he's willing to fight me again," says Hart, indicating that it's up to Shamrock now to sign his name on the dotted line.

In the days leading up to the "Dungeon Match" it was rumored that the other Hart brothers were set to interfere on Owen's behalf. Hart says he nixed the idea firmly believing that he could take Shamrock in his own backyard without a third party entering the fray. But it wasn't easy. The Black Hart freely admits the bout took its toll on his body and the Hart's training facilities.

"In over 50 years we didn't damage the walls or ceilings and in that one match I put Shamrock's head through the ceiling and cracked the walls. It was a rough, hard-fought match and Shamrock's gotta pay for that dumbbell he dented with his head," says Hart.

Recently, it's not the self-appointed World's Most Dangerous Man who's become a thorn in Hart's side but a crafty voice impressionist mocking the Black Hart at every opportunity. Dressing up in Hart's wrestling attire and donning a false nose, Ontario-born Jason Sensation has been making Hart the laughing stock of the World Wrestling Federation through his ringside antics. Claiming to have discovered Sensation at a card held in Ottawa and alerting the WWF to the young man's unusual talents, Hart feels especially betrayed. Hart took out his frustration on a *Raw Is War* broadcast, paint-brushing Sensation as he painfully contorted him into the dreaded Sharpshooter submission hold, a brutal attack which Hart says taught the WWF court jester a lesson.

"He was becoming too much of a smart ass and needed to be smacked around," says Hart sternly. "He seems to be eating humble pie now."

Formerly a member of the Canadian flag–waving Hart Foundation, the Black Hart has since joined forces with the Nation of Domination captained by WWF Intercontinental champion, Rocky Maivia, a move which has sur-prised many of his die-hard fans. Hart explains the jump as necessary for survival upon the departure of his brother, Bret "The Hitman" Hart, and his brothers-in-law, the British Bulldog, and Jim "The Anvil" Niedhart for the Ted Turner-owned World Championship Wrestling. Being mugged by the D-Generation X gang week after week was too much to take. As his theme song decries, it was time for a change.

In his role as a Nation member, Hart thinks his years of ring savvy are rubbing off on his new teammates, leading to D-Lo Brown winning the European title and the Rock securing the Intercontinental belt. Hart has nothing but kind words for his adopted family.

"The Nation are all good guys. They are easy to get along with inside and outside the ring. There's no problems with any of them," says Hart, who appreciates the loyalty and patriotic support Canadian fans have shown him through his troubled times.

Looking ahead to the future, Hart sees his career as a pro wrestler con-tinuing for at least a few more years. Then, it might be time to walk that aisle one last time and hang up his trunks for good before his body is too dam-aged and too hurt. Still, Hart acknowledges that he might not be able to deny the passion for the sport which runs deep through his family's heritage passed down from his father, the wrestling icon — Stu Hart.

"I'd like to get out of wrestling totally when I'm done. I say that now but I'll probably end up being involved with it until I'm Ric Flair's age," con-cludes the Black Hart.

* * *

AUSTIN'S BETTER, STRONGER, NASTIER

By GLENN COLE — *Toronto Sun*

"Austin 3:16 says that I just whipped your ass."

That phrase tells you what "Stone Cold" Steve Austin generally is all about.

And his persona fits right into the louder, brasher, more risqué pro wrestling of the late '90s. It isn't the wrestling that Grandma watched on her black-and-white TV in the '50s and '60s. Nor is it the Saturday-morning wrestling of the '80s and early '90s, which often blended into the cartoons.

Some people think the World Wrestling Federation's approach is no longer family entertainment, that its television programming should be rated PG (parental guidance) because of sexual innuendo and colorful language, that its shows have become a salty soap opera for males.

Mike Lano

Steve Austin poses with his mom in 1999.

As a pickup-driving, beer-drinking, deer-hunting Texan, Austin is the right man at the right time. The WWF champion is no cookie-eating, milk-drinking, white-hat-wearing nice guy.

This six-foot-two, 33-year-old wears black boots and black trunks, tells his enemies to kiss his, uh, backside, and is the biggest hero the WWF has had since Hulk Hogan's heyday in the 1980s.

"I use a few certain words on the air, a little bit of sign language," Austin said. "In defense of myself, the things I do or say on TV are something every kid sees or hears every single day. You either know better than to do that or you don't.

"You go into sexual references or racial stuff, that's an immediate turnoff for me. I'm not into that in any shape or form. I am not on a high horse throwing rocks, because people could throw rocks at what I do."

"Austin 3:16" shocked a few people when it first came out of his mouth after he beat Bible-thumper Jake "The Snake" Roberts at the 1996 King of Ring card. It's a play on the "John 3:16" signs seen at sporting events, which refer to a scripture in the Bible stating that those who believe in Jesus Christ "should not perish, but have everlasting life."

"Austin 3:16" has become the theme for the hottest-selling merchandise in WWF history.

"It was never, ever designed to be sacrilegious, anti-religious," said Austin, the WWF champion who meets Hunter Hearst Helmsley tonight at the SkyDome with WWF owner Vince McMahon as the guest referee. McMahon's angle is to make Austin's title reign miserable.

"[Austin 3:16] is just something I said and it's stuck around. It was tongue-in-cheek," Austin said. "Some people take it seriously, others don't. It's something that has stuck with me and that doesn't bother me one bit."

Austin, whose Ringmaster character received lukewarm attention when he first arrived from the rival World Championship Wrestling faction in 1995, dropped Ted DiBiase as his manager and forged ahead with his favorite move — the Stone Cold Stunner.

A former defensive end with North Texas University, Austin relieved Shawn Michaels of the championship in March. In April, the WWF ended an 83-week losing streak in head-to-head TV ratings competition with WCW, which is owned by sports mogul Ted Turner. *Monday Night Raw*, the flagship WWF TV show, recently had a 5.7 rating on the USA Network, a record for a cable sports program. *Raw* is one of TSN's top-rated shows, outdrawing the NHL at times.

"It's hard for me to describe my success or why I have been successful," said Austin, who this month drew 250,000 viewers to TSN's *Off The Record* — the show's highest audience, almost three times its usual size.

"I guess people can identify with me because I am in real life exactly what you see on TV. I happen to turn up the volume a little more when I am playing to a bigger audience. I take pride in what I do. I have fun, but I work my butt off."

Austin souvenirs — the 3:16 T-shirts, foam fingers, caps — are sold out almost as soon as they hit the souvenir booths at WWF house shows. Austin's T-shirts, which he designs himself, have brought in far more revenue than former WWF icon Hogan did during his title reign, although the WWF did not provide exact figures.

Austin, whose real name is Steve Williams, took his wrestling moniker from the character Lee Majors used to play on the 1970s TV show, *The Six Million Dollar Man*. The show happened to be on a TV set in a southern promoter's office the day that the soon-to-be Austin arrived for a card near the start of his eight-year career. There had to be a name change because Dr. Death Steve Williams, now on the WWF's roster, had preceded Austin to the area.

Austin's stay in the WCW in the early '90s brought him some success. He won the U.S. tag team title with Brian Pillman, who died last summer at 36 of a heart attack. Pillman was a good friend to Austin, a rarity in this backstabbing business.

And Austin is realistic enough to know his success could end just as quickly as it started. It almost did when Calgary's Owen Hart put a little too much oomph when he drove Austin's head into the mat last summer.

"I couldn't move my arms or my legs (for about a minute) and it scared the hell out of me," said Austin, who thought about quadriplegic actor Christopher Reeves as he lay there on the mat. "I think I'm an extremely strong person and I have an extremely strong neck. But I realize how lucky I am to be able to move around and do the things I do."

How long will it all last? As long as Austin is physically up to it, and as long as he enjoys it.

"If it's not any fun tomorrow, then I'll find something else to do. I'm having a blast right now."

And that's the bottom line, because Stone Cold says so.

From the writer: Steve Austin was a good man. Oh, a lot of people were turned over by his attitude in ring where it was shoot first and ask questions later. That was perfect for TV. But get Austin away from the ring and the cameras and you would get a different man and new perspective on WWE's top performer at the time. There was no bull. He liked some things, some people and didn't care for others. Don't worry. Austin knew what effect he had and how important he was at the time.

* * *

THE LEGEND OF JUSHIN "THUNDER" LIGER

By JASON CLEVETT

It's hard to say what the final legacy of Jushin "Thunder" Liger will be. What men like Ric Flair are to North American wrestling, Liger is to Japanese wrestling, especially the junior heavyweight style that has grown in popularity over the past 15 years. Every high-flying wrestler today, from Rey Mysterio Jr. to A.J. Styles, owes their success in part to Liger, and today young junior heavyweights dream of stepping into the ring with him.

Born November 10, 1964, in Hiroshima, Keiichi Yamada was a lifelong wrestling fan, and an amateur standout in high school. When he applied to the New Japan dojo he was told he was too small, so he set off to Mexico to learn there. An NJPW talent scout saw him while on a tour and offered him the opportunity to join the dojo. Yamada was part of the same training camp

Mike Lano

Jushin Liger, right, ties up with the Great Sasuke.

that produced Keiji Muto, Masahiro Chono and Shinya Hashimoto before making his pro debut on March 3, 1984, against Shunji Kosugi. He worked the undercard for two years before winning New Japan's Young Lions Cup tournament on March 26, 1986. From there Yamada was sent to England before his career took a Canadian twist. He was sent to Stu Hart's Stampede Wrestling in May of 1987.

Ross Hart remembered Yamada's Calgary days. "The office was grooming him as a future junior champion there, so they wanted him to get some exposure in Stampede Wrestling. Many Japanese wrestlers had benefited so well from their training and wrestling here, such as Hiro Hase, who wrestled in the Viet Kong Express. He was here for four months and we were sad to see him go," Hart said. "Some of his best matches here were against Cuban Assassin and Jerry Morrow, as well as teaming with Mr. Hito against the Viet Kong Express. It was a good team with Hito being the ring general veteran and Yamada being the younger high-flying star. It was a nice contrast."

Today's fans may not realize it, but Liger worked very hard to have a good physique despite his small stature. It's now hidden behind a bodysuit but Yamada wore trunks in his early years.

"He had a tremendous upper body and huge neck, yet he was so acrobatic and fast-moving. He did a lot of amateur wrestling and submission wrestling and it all came together into a excellent package. He was a very humble charismatic star at that time," said Hart.

His humility appealed to the Stampede locker room. They easily took to the young highflyer.

"He was a pleasure to be around in the dressing room, very quiet and kept to himself. He was always smiling and the boys all took to him. We wished he could have stayed longer. They brought him back once specifically to wrestle Owen, as he was about to go on his first tour of New Japan. It was ironic because they had teamed up on some shows here," said Hart. "His trip here was very successful because he absorbed the North American style and performed on his own out of the shadow of other Japanese wrestlers that he likely idolized such as the Cobra, Tiger Mask, Hiro Saito or Kobashi. He had more of his own identity."

Yamada's career continues to be intertwined with the Alberta wrestling scene to this day. His battles in which he traded the IWGP junior heavyweight title with Owen Hart and Chris Benoit in Japan are legendary, while his 1992 matches in WCW against Brian Pillman were far ahead of anything seen in North America at that time. Lance Storm and Chris Jericho have both spoken fondly of Liger, and today the tradition continues — "Stampede Kid" T.J. Wilson has faced Liger in tag matches numerous times in the past two years.

"It was a mutual respect they all had for each other. Jericho and Storm came along after Liger left but they had common history of Dungeon experience," Wilson said. "It made for some interesting storylines over there as well. Since the Liger role was so successful I think they reinvented Benoit as the Pegasus Kid. Owen had fantastic matches with both of them as well."

Even in 1987, Ross Hart suspected Yamada had big things in store for him. "At that time I thought he had a great future. He reminded me a lot of Tiger Mask, who wasn't much taller than him, and El Gran Hamada," he said. "They were looking for a successor to the Cobra and Tiger Mask and when they sent him to Calgary it was a good indication that it would increase his stature considerably and give him more respect and credibility. His predecessors had been used very well when they went back to Japan and I expected no differently from them."

Within a year and a half a Japanese cartoon aired about Jushin Liger that became very popular. Yamada was repackaged in the outfit he wears to this day, debuting at the very first wrestling event at the Tokyo Dome on April 24, 1989, defeating Kuniaki Kobayashi, one of Tiger Mask's biggest rivals from his glory days in the early '80s.

As great of a wrestler as Liger is, he also has an excellent mind for the business and became the booker of the junior heavyweight division in New

Japan, creating the J-Cup and Best of the Super Junior tournaments.

"I think what gets overlooked about Liger was his strength as a booker of New Japan's junior heavyweight division," said former SLAM! Wrestling contributor John Molinaro, who lists Liger as number 36 in his book *Top 100 Pro Wrestlers of All Time*. "Liger's precision booking was masterful, and it was intricate and compelling to the point that it should be put in a wrestling textbook and studied by aspiring bookers."

Dave Meltzer, editor of the *Wrestling Observer*, newsletter agrees. "He was by far the biggest star of his division, and was so big that he could create stars with just one win over him. It wasn't going to work forever, but he had a great run with it."

Liger's selflessness helped many aspiring stars go onto greatness. The first Super J Cup was held in April of 1994 and Liger lost in the semi-finals to the Great Sasuke, who in turn lost the final bout to "Wild Pegasus" Chris Benoit. Two years later Liger did the unthinkable by putting together the J-Crown tournament in August 1996. The week-long event featured eight different junior heavyweight champions from five different promotions in Japan and Mexico during New Japan's annual G1 Climax tournament in attempt to unify the belts into one title. Liger lost in the first round to Ultimo Dragon, who lost the final match to the Great Sasuke. The belts would later appear on WCW television, as Ultimo Dragon briefly held the J-Crown in addition to the company's Cruiserweight title.

The same day as the finals, Liger announced he had a brain tumor and his career might be over. Fortunately it was benign and after an operation to remove it Liger returned, altering his style to include more mat wrestling and storytelling.

"When he picked up so many injuries from the high-flying style of his, he did a great job of changing styles and being one of the best at a new style. He understood how to get over much safer moves like the shote as opposed to crazy topes. He's probably as big a star as could have been possible for a five-foot-four, 205-pound guy who came along during the era he came along in," said Meltzer.

Liger is the creator of the shooting star press and puroresu fans speak of moves like the Ligerbomb (sit out powerbomb), Fishermanbuster and Koppou Kick with reverence. It speaks to Liger's influence that the shooting star has been used by a vast array for wrestlers such as Marc Mero, Billy Kidman, Paul London, Brock Lesnar and many others.

Liger has had limited exposure in the U.S., but his matches have all been excellent. At Clash of the Champions XIX in June 1992 he teamed with Brian Pillman to defeat Chris Benoit and Biff Wellington, all Dungeon graduates.

Three years later he defeated Benoit in the opening match of Starrcade 1995's New Japan vs. WCW World Cup of Wrestling. He returned a year later to face Rey Mysterio Jr. at the event in a Cruiserweight dream match. His last WCW appearances would be less memorable as he feuded with Juventud Guerrera, resulting in the famous and hated tequila bottle to the head loss.

It is in Japan, however, that Liger has truly shined; his matches are hot items among tape sellers and fans continue to debate his greatest matches. He has had epic battles with Ultimo Dragon, Benoit, Eddie Guerrero (wrestling under a mask as Black Tiger), El Samurai, Naoki Sano, Koji Kanemoto, Great Sasuke and Super Delfin.

Meltzer can't pick a standout bout. "It's hard to pick his best matches, because there are so many. He was the junior heavyweight star in pro wrestling in the early 1990s, and except for Satoru Sayama, I think the biggest ever. There are so many great Liger matches, from Chris Benoit to Great Sasuke to Koji Kanemoto, Shinjiro Otani, and so many others."

After 20 years in the business, Liger still is not done. He has crossed promotional boundaries working for Pro Wrestling NOAH, where he has held their junior title, and Michinoku Pro. Recently he has turned heel in Japan and dons a black outfit to represent this. Despite injuries and age, Liger is proving his longevity and shows no sign of stopping anytime soon. He has been a true pioneer and innovator for the scene and a legend no one may match. That legend will live on long after he dons the pointed red mask for the final time.

From the writer: It's an interesting challenge to write a story about someone without ever speaking to them. Wanting to create something different, I went to those who were available to me. Ross Hart from Liger's Stampede Wrestling past, T.J. Wilson, who was regularly competing in New Japan against Liger at the time, and wrestling experts Dave Meltzer and John Molinaro contributed to the piece to provide a unique look at one of Japan's greatest wrestlers. The result is something I was quite proud of. It was one of those times when I wished I didn't live in Western Canada and could have actually attended the show to see Liger himself.

* * *

ANGLE BUOYED BY NEW POPULARITY

By JON WALDMAN

As a former amateur wrestling champion and Olympic gold medalist, Kurt Angle had a tough time making a leap to the pros, but success in the World Wrestling Federation has come quickly to the "Olympic hero."

Kurt Angle dominates Steve Austin.

"There was a lot of transition and it was very difficult for me to slow down and to learn a different style, but eventually I was able to catch on and be the best I could, and I think I've done pretty well so far," he told SLAM! Wrestling during the WrestleMania X8 press conference last Monday in Toronto.

Part of the transition for Angle was adjusting to the many aspects of performing in the WWF. Angle was used to working against one opponent, whereas now there are several people he has to keep in mind while wrestling. "You're so used to competing against an opponent and focusing on that one opponent — not so many things you do in sports entertainment, which includes crowd, working with your opponent to make sure the show goes on really well," he said.

Angle is one of the fastest rising superstars in WWF history. Since joining the pro circuit in 1999, he has held the European, Intercontinental and World heavyweight championships, as well as being the 2000 King of the Ring and former WCW champion.

Angle's popularity is high across North America, in spite of his character being an American patriot. Despite being covered in the red, white and blue of the U.S.A., Angle notes that the fans react well to him north of the 49th.

"Actually, my reception is very good here in Canada," he said. "That's the one great thing about Canadian fans, or fans in the United States for that matter — it doesn't matter where you're from. It matters where you are on the card, what you're doing in the storylines."

"Fans enjoy me because I'm funny and entertaining. At least my character is," he quipped.

A lot of Angle's success can be attributed to his own enjoyment of his character. "I think he's entertaining, he's funny, and he's one of the best athletes in the World Wrestling Federation, no doubt about it," he said.

Angle, who won the gold medal in freestyle wrestling in the 220-pound class at the 1996 Olympic Summer Games, is looking forward to WrestleMania X8 in Toronto. He feels that the WWF does not do enough shows in the Ontario capital. "I don't think we're here enough," he said. "Three times a year might sound like a lot to most cities but in Toronto, Canada, they're very loyal to the World Wrestling Federation."

"Every single time we come here, it seems to be sold out. The Toronto fans really enjoy the show."

From the writer: This was the first time that I spoke with Kurt Angle. Years later, I would again get to talk with the Olympian, only that time he had just debuted with TNA. Obviously, the tones towards WWF/E were completely different, but Kurt's style wasn't — in both cases, he was a class act.

Of the two interviews, this one sticks out, perhaps for the wrong reason. The day this article was published, I was sitting at my computer, reading the story, when I got a knock on my door at Ryerson University and was told that a plane had flown into the World Trade Center. It still creeps me out to read the dateline on this story about an American hero — September 11, 2001.

* * *

DANIELSON EPITOMIZES ROH'S EVOLUTION

ROH World Champ set for big title bout Saturday
By JASON CLEVETT

On February 23, 2002, at the Murphy Rec Center in Philadelphia, a small company called Ring of Honor launched its first show, headlined by a classic match between Low Ki, "The Fallen Angel" Christopher Daniels and "American Dragon" Bryan Danielson. Four and a half years later, the company stages one of its biggest shows ever at the Manhattan Center in New York City on Saturday. The top of the card again features Danielson — now ROH world champion — defending against Pro Wrestling NOAH's KENTA.

"I am excited to wrestle at the Manhattan Center. It is a great venue and a big step forward for Ring of Honor. I am excited and nervous about wrestling KENTA. I wouldn't be nervous except for my separated shoulder, and how hard KENTA kicks. You have both nerves and excitement going through your body with a big match like that," Dragon told SLAM! Wrestling in a rare interview.

The stacked show will also feature GHC heavyweight champion Naomichi Marufuji vs. Nigel McGuinness, tag champions Austin Aries and Roderick Strong vs. Chris Hero and Claudio Castagnoli and Homicide and Samoa Joe vs. the Briscoes. As an added bonus, former WWWF champion Bruno Sammartino will be in attendance, his first New York appearance at a wrestling show in a decade.

"It is also a big step in that they are bringing Bruno Sammartino in for that show. That is a big deal because Bruno hasn't been part of wrestling for a really long time," said Danielson.

The show is special for Dragon as well because he is one of only three people on the original show that is on this one, the other two being Daniels and Jay Briscoe. Ring of Honor has come a long way from its humble beginnings.

"I have never in my life thought that far ahead to see this success. I didn't know what to expect from that first show. As an independent wrestler, you just hope the promotions keep going so you can keep wrestling for them. That is all I was hoping for," Danielson said. "At the beginning, Ring of Honor was spending a lot of money and it really didn't seem like it was making all that much money back. I remember guys like Dusty Rhodes and Abdullah the Butcher coming in, but it didn't increase the number of fans that were coming to the shows. It seemed like they were stuck at a point. Now 400 people in attendance is a low attendance show as opposed to a good one. That is really exciting to see, when you have been there from the beginning."

This is Dragon's third bout with KENTA in New York. He teamed with Samoa Joe and was pinned in a tag match to KENTA and Naomichi Marufuji at "Best in the World" in March and KENTA again pinned Danielson in a non-title three-way match that included Joe at July's "In Your Face." Despite the losses, Dragon is confident one-on-one he will beat KENTA. You can't question Danielson's toughness going into the match. On August 25 in Chicago, Danielson separated his shoulder in a match against Colt Cabana, and wrestled for another 50 minutes.

"It was about ten minutes into the match when I separated my shoulder. I don't know how I got through it," Danielson reflected. "I hate to quote movies as a source of inspiration but in *Pirates of the Caribbean*, Jack Sparrow says, 'It is either something you can do or you can't do.' When it happened, I thought, 'Either I can do this or I can't do it.' I either had to stop or keep going and really go. I made some minor adjustments and got through it and then once I got to the back it really sucked. It really wasn't that bad because of the adrenaline rush and most wrestlers learn to separate pain mentally. It sounds more impressive than it actually is, I think."

Despite the injury, Danielson is proud of the match. "I enjoyed the match with Colt even with the separated shoulder — and the shoulder is part of why I enjoyed it, because you feel a sense of accomplishment when you have gone through that and made it to 60 minutes. That last five minutes of that match you could really feel the emotions from the crowd."

Ring of Honor has established a good working relationship with Japanese promotions NOAH and Dragon Gate. Danielson successfully defended the ROH title against Marufuji at December's "Final Battle 2005."

One of the first high profile Japanese stars in ROH was in November of 2004 when the company brought in Jushin "Thunder" Liger to face Danielson.

"At the time that we brought in Liger nobody knew it would be a regular thing to bring Japanese guys over. For the Japanese wrestlers it is good for them because they come to Ring of Honor and all the magazines have photographers around ringside taking pictures of the match," he said. "ROH fans are very appreciative of the Japanese wrestlers and so it is good for them to get that superstar reaction, which makes them seem like a worldwide phenomenon in Japan. Importing Japanese talent is a good thing and will continue to happen. The cross promotions with NOAH and Dragon Gate works well — the Dragon Gate style suits Ring of Honor perfectly."

Should he successfully defend against KENTA, Danielson will celebrate a year as champion on Sunday. He defeated James (Noble) Gibson for the belt on September 17, 2005. His reign is second only to Samoa Joe's 21 months as champion.

"Winning the belt felt surreal. You live in the moment of everything and at that moment it felt like an accomplishment and still does. It is hard to project those emotions now. You grow and you develop and get used to the idea of being champion. It is a hard thing to explain to wrestling fans, it seems like only wrestlers can appreciate what they mean to you individually," he explained. "I have been really pleased with what I have been able to do so far. Holding the ROH title is tough and I feel a lot of pressure to have the best matches on the show because as the champion that is what you should be doing. When there are so many great wrestlers on the shows that is sometimes hard to achieve. It feels good that ROH has the confidence in

No one does the twist quite like Bryan Danielson.

me to put that kind of trust in me and feel that strongly."

Being part of Ring of Honor has meant a lot of growth for members of their roster. Brian "Spanky" Kendrick, Paul London, James Gibson and CM Punk have all moved on to WWE. Christopher Daniels, Low Ki (Senshi), A.J. Styles, Samoa Joe, Homicide and Austin Aries are all presently signed to TNA. Ring of Honor truly allows its roster to develop into marketable stars.

"As a wrestler, being in Ring of Honor has put me in matches with the top guys who challenge your creativity and wrestling ability," Danielson said. "As far as getting my name out there, as the company built in status by proxy everyone who wrestles for them becomes a bigger name. That factor alone is going to make fans think you are a bigger deal than you are. The same applies with TNA — a lot of guys who before TNA had a hard time getting bookings, now that they are on TV makes them seem like a bigger deal. That happens when any promotion you wrestle for achieves a mild level of success."

A new crop of wrestlers will be getting the chance to gain that experience soon. Recently, Danielson took over from Aries as head trainer of the ROH wrestling school and moved from his home in Washington State to Philadelphia. "There was hesitation on my part to take over in that I was attending college when they first asked, whereas now I am taking classes online. I had gone through two quarters of Chemistry and was getting into a really advanced course and I had to give up that last quarter — that would have been my first year-long course — to come up here. That was really my only hesitation."

There are many wrestling schools out there and it is important to carefully consider your options before choosing one. While many advocate going to schools run by veterans, there are advantages to training with young successful wrestlers as well. Dragon was trained at Shawn Michaels's wrestling academy and then trained extensively with William Regal. He brings that knowledge, along with his own success, to the school of wrestling.

"Sometimes it is better to have a guy your own age training you, but other times it is better to have a retired veteran training you. When it comes to training people, I can show the students everything I know but if they don't work hard they are never going to get anything from it," he said. "That is the same whether they are taught by me or Shawn Michaels or William Regal. There are a lot of guys who were trained by Shawn who never really did anything because they never trained hard. It was the same with Regal. I trained with him when I was in the developmental system and he offered to teach you anything he had learned and a lot of guys sat back and didn't really take advantage of it. That is the main thing with people who want to train to be wrestlers, they have got to be willing to come in and work hard."

While there is certainly influence from his trainers, Dragon prefers to let his students develop their own style as opposed to trying to be like their mentor.

"I don't know if how I train them is really different from the way I was taught. The way I train them is very similar to how Regal taught myself and Spanky. First, you show the guys the basics and then teach guys the best you can what they want to learn. A lot of the wrestlers that come to the ROH school want to learn what I can teach them, but don't want to wrestle exactly like me, and that wouldn't be wise for them to wrestle just like me. Everyone has their own interests and is going to develop their own style. Once students get their basic fundamentals down you have to teach them what they want to learn."

Ring of Honor continues to grow by leaps and bounds. They recently completed a tour of the United Kingdom and Friday's show in East Windsor, Connecticut (Danielson will not be on the card) and Saturday's Manhattan Center debut is just another step for a company that has not only survived for four and a half years but, in many ways, thrived. By offering an alternative, Danielson feels they will continue to find new fans and keep old ones.

"I believe that there is a large group of people who still would like to see wrestling, as opposed to all the skits you see on TV. Ring of Honor tries to target that market, but it is a harder core market than that. There is a lot of room in professional wrestling for a company that would just go out there and wrestle. Originally I thought that what TNA would be doing was more wrestling, but they have gotten away from a lot of that [and] into doing the WWE-esque stuff.

"There is a big market for people who just want to see wrestling. I don't even think it has to be on TV; if you have a good group of guys who can wrestle and are impressive to see in person, who people would look at and say, 'I would like to see a wrestling show where that guy is wrestling,' it will work. When people think of pure wrestling companies they think of the ROH style of wrestling, but I don't think that is necessarily the case. You can still do it with an older style of guys that isn't so big-move oriented and you are going to attract more people."

* * *

MORE TO TRISH THAN T & A

By GREG OLIVER

Rich Freeda, WWE

Posing has always come easy for Trish Stratus.

From the writer: True story, even if you don't believe it. It was just before WrestleMania 2000, and I was checking into the Anaheim Doubletree Hotel, the place all the WWF people were staying, when I noticed Trish behind me. I turned and introduced myself. "Oh my God, you're Greg Oliver. I've read your stuff for years!"

ANAHEIM — Despite her years of fitness modeling and TV appearances, Trish Stratus still got a really big kick out of appearing at Sunday's Wrestle-Mania.

"Just being there was such a thrill to me because I'm such a fan, and it's my first pay-per-view and it's WrestleMania. So put those two together and it's just amazing," she told SLAM! Wrestling after the event.

Stratus has only been with the WWF

for a couple of months now on TV. Yet, she talks like a pro, dropping words like "gimmick" and "working a program" with ease.

The Torontonian was forced to sit on the sidelines, waiting for her work visa to be processed so she could perform in the United States. Once that hurdle was cleared, she was thrust into the mix.

"As soon as the [work visa] was done, I got my gimmick and got my T & A action and away I went," she said. "We didn't build too much towards WrestleMania because, obviously, time-wise there was no time to work a program and also the main event was pretty much the big deal."

But everyone wants to know two things about Trish: What's up with the cowboy hat and cape? And Test and Prince Albert?

First, the clothing.

"The very first time they put me out, they said, 'Okay, we're going to debut you tonight. Literally, tonight. So go out and get something to wear.' So I said, 'What?!' I ran out to just get a cute outfit, skirt and top, but I didn't want to wear a typical type of outfit.

"As a wrestling fan I know that I like to associate people and characters. Like the Undertaker, you always know what he's wearing, that kind of thing," Stratus explained. "So I was trying to look for something gimmicky, and I'm actually into that kind of style, as far as the coats and stuff. I found a great hat, and I thought, 'Oh, yeah, this'll be great. I can wear this with my outfit. This can be my gimmick.' It seems to be working."

As for T & A, formerly known as Test and Albert, Stratus sees great potential in them. (And judging from their short match on *Monday Night Raw* against Road Dogg and X-Pac, the WWF seems to also.)

"I think that they have a great presence. We just recently did a house show together. It was neat, because it was really the first time that I saw them work together and when you see them together," said Stratus, "I think they've got great chemistry together, they are both really big guys and have a unique presence to them."

The duo's cooperation in the ring isn't an accident either. "They're actually close friends in real life, so it comes across, I think, in their work and teamwork."

From this point, she knows that the whole "T & A conception" needs to be explained to the fans.

"After WrestleMania, it's like January 2000. It's the beginning of the year now for the wrestling world. So now we're going to start focusing on characters and all these things. We'll probably see some vignettes, we'll see some personality between the three of us — how we're interacting, why we're together," she explained.

Stratus believes that vignettes will definitely add interest to the team. "People haven't really seen that side of Test nor Albert, or me either!"

Recently, WWF.com flew the WWF "Divas" to a sunny destination to do a swimsuit shoot. For Stratus, a veteran of the fitness magazine pages, that was old hat.

"That's the easiest part of this whole thing. You know my former career as a fitness model . . . It's funny, I say former, but I mean my 'other' career. There you go. My 'bi-career,'" Stratus explained. "So I was used to that — that was actually a comfortable environment. Doing the shoot was great, and it was a great chance to meet the girls all up close and personal, get on a personal level with all them so that we could be working under TV conditions, which is good."

Ah yes, TV. Fans who caught her debut performance on the microphone at *Raw* a while back still chuckle over how Stratus stumbled through her lines. It was not the greatest debut interview in WWF history.

"The tough part is the TV. Not the TV so much, it's the live 20,000 fans. I don't know if anyone caught my first promo on *Raw*," she said laughing. "Yeah, I was a bit stunned, to say the least. But I'll improve. I know it's in me; it's just a matter of drawing it out. Getting used to a new environment and everything. They're working with me, and I know they have confidence in my potential."

Stratus is not on the road with the WWF full-time yet, but it's coming. She's still training to be a wrestler at Sully's Gym in Toronto twice a week. "I'm really focusing on that because I think it's funny — it's one thing to have T & A, ha, ha, excuse the parody, but I want to show that I can bring more to the whole picture."

Speaking of pictures, Stratus is quite proud of her website (Trishstratus.com) and surfs the web a lot, reading what's being said about her.

* * *

GRILLING JIM ROSS IN PERSON

"Southern gentleman" answers a variety of questions
By JOHN MOLINARO

TORONTO — It's minutes after the WWF's WrestleMania X8 press conference and Jim Ross is standing all by himself.

Meanwhile his boss, the larger-than-life Vincent K. McMahon, has a herd of reporters shoving cameras, tape recorders and microphones in his face, clamoring for a quote. Ross curiously looks on as the media grills the WWF owner.

Steven Johnson

Steve Austin and Jim Ross at the 2008 Cauliflower Alley Club reunion.

I'm a mere five feet away. I seize the opportunity. I call out to Ross and he looks in my direction before heading over. I immediately introduce myself: "Hi, Jim. I'm John Molinaro from SLAM! Wrestling."

Ross's face immediately lights up and he sticks out his hand and we shake.

"Great to meet you, John. How you been? Nice to finally put a face to the name."

Funny how life turns out sometimes. A year ago, I was persona non grata by Ross after an editorial I wrote questioned the WWF's media policy. Twelve months and two dozen phone calls later, Ross greets me like an old friend he hadn't seen in years.

He may live in Connecticut, but he is, underneath it all, a southern gentleman.

With the pleasantries exchanged, I fire off a few questions for the WWF's senior vice president of Talent Relations.

You guys clearly botched the WCW invasion angle from the beginning and introduced ECW into the equation to save the storyline. Are you happy with how the angle turned out and where it's headed?

"I'm very pleased with the creative," answers Ross. "The 'Alliance' issue has been a very stimulating storyline. It has obviously piqued the enthusiasm of our viewers again. It's new, it's fresh and now it's just up to us to keep it creatively stimulating, which is always hard to do when you're doing two two-hour shows a week. It's challenging."

With the buyout of WCW and the signing of a lot of new talent, you have a lot of new faces in the company. What's the locker room atmosphere and morale like?

"It's really come together beautifully," states Ross. "I'm very proud personally of all the guys and ladies for creating a very positive environment. The new people that came in came into a positive environment and they have done nothing but add to that. And it's getting better. They're building relationships like any other co-workers in any other environment. They're building relationships and I think over the course of time it's really going to pay off because of the chemistry they're going to have."

Ross may be Vince McMahon's right-hand man and isn't without influence in the WWF power structure, but he still gets simple pleasure from doing live play-by-play on *Raw Is War*. He's asked by another reporter whether or not he's happy with the WWF's commentary teams and gives a surprisingly candid answer.

"I think we're always trying to get better and trying to improve. I enjoy working with Paul Heyman. I think he adds a unique facet to our show. J.R. and Michael Cole together sucked, which we knew, but that's the hand we had dealt at that time. Tazz is still a work in progress. The effort is there, it's just not a real easy job for someone to just go sit down and do. Certainly, Paul is doing a great job. I think we miss Jerry Lawler. He did a great job. I enjoyed working with him personally and you never know how that whole situation is going to change. [Laughing] I just hope the guy in the black hat gets to keep his spot."

What about WrestleMania X8? I ask. What does this mean for the city of Toronto in regards to its relationship with the WWF?

"It's our commitment to the fans of Toronto that the WWF considers Toronto one of our primary cities," states Ross. "The fan base here is extremely enthusiastic and loyal. I think it's a validation that Toronto, in our view, is one of the major sports cities in the world.

"I think it's a part of our commitment that Canada is extremely important to the overall success of our company," continues Ross. "By placing our biggest event of the year in Canada, I hope anyway, it indicates we're committed and we believe in our fan base here."

But why Toronto? What does it have the other cities don't?

"The city itself offers a lot of opportunity for our fans to come from around the world. I think last year we had fans from 20 or 30 countries," Ross reveals. "The SkyDome is very unique in as much as we can set a lot of folks in there. So we think the facility has some unique characteristics, the city itself does and the fact that we keep it in North America and bring it back after 12 years, we believe it's the right thing to do."

Wasn't the poor exchange between the Canadian and U.S. dollar a deterrent? Did that ever enter the decision making process?

"There's nothing we can really do about it. It's an economic issue," Ross explains. "Anybody that would have a problem with that, we're certainly going to make up for it in volume because we plan on breaking the attendance record and we'd like to certainly get close to that 70,000 mark this time, which would better what we did in the Astrodome this past year."

We're told by a WWF PR member there's only time for one last question and Ross is asked by another reporter about his general health in light of the hectic and demanding work schedule he keeps.

"I'm holding up well, thanks for asking. I think if I wasn't so passionate about my job and being around these fans and getting this adrenaline rush once or twice a week . . . it keeps you rocking and rolling. I'd like to think I'm not getting older; I'm just getting better."

Ross is quickly ushered away for a scheduled TV interview but not before he shakes my hand again, thanks me for coming out to the press conference and tells me to call him later this week when he's back in his office in Stamford.

Like I said, a true southern gentleman.

From the writer: The story was about the WrestleMania coming to Toronto, but the underlying narrative was about SLAM! Wrestling's feud with the WWF.

A year earlier, I wrote a scathing column that questioned the WWF's media policy. Jim Ross took notice and seemed to respect the stand I took, because he ended up calling me personally and SLAM! was granted unequalled access to him.

I must have called Jim's office two dozen times over the ensuing 12 months, and each time his secretary, on direct orders from Ross, always put my call through to him.

Meeting Jim in person just cemented the friendship.

* * *

RAVEN: THE SECOND COMING

Part 1

By CHRIS GRAMLICH

Scott "Raven" Levy is a survivor. He's thrived for years in the hazardous world of professional wrestling. Examples? He persevered the late 1980s and early 1990s WWF (enough said), the rigors of being ECW's top heel during their most formative and influential years, a love-hate run with WCW, a subsequently less-than-spectacular return to ECW, a return to the WWF, and above all of this, he has survived his own personal demons.

But Scott "Raven" Levy is much more than a journeyman wrestler. He has headlined, held titles and established himself wherever he has wrestled, running through a myriad of incarnations before arriving at his true calling and the persona which has garnered him the most success: the hardcore misanthropic loner known as Raven. When all is said and done, Raven's name will go down in the annals of wrestling history next to the

Terry Dart

Before he was Raven, he was Scotty Flamingo.

likes of Terry Funk and Mick Foley — hardcore competitors who helped influence professional wrestling, steering it into more violent, real and psychotic new sea.

Taking time out of his preparations for *Raw Is War* a few weeks ago, Raven was gracious enough to talk to SLAM! Wrestling about his current status in the WWF, quitting WCW, his tenures in ECW and the battles he has had with himself throughout his career.

"I wanted to come back here [the WWF] from the time I left in the first place six or seven years ago but the circumstances were just never right," commented Raven on his recent return to the WWF. "Either I wasn't available or they weren't available or they didn't want me. Whatever. It never seemed to work out. Maybe they weren't interested. I don't know. It just never came up. Eventually I was in WCW, when they were still doing quite well, but I wasn't happy because they wouldn't use me to my full potential. Eric [Bischoff] had a meeting and said if I wasn't happy that I could leave. I said alright and I left."

"I was going to try to come to the WWF then, except he [Bischoff] wouldn't let me go, he said I could come back and work for him or I could go to ECW, so I figured I'd go back and work for Paul [Heyman] for the second time. They [ECW] had just signed with TNN and I thought they were going to do things, but they didn't. Then it was just a matter of making sure they [the WWF] were interested when my contract expired and they were, so I signed," recalled Raven.

Since signing with the WWF, many are calling Raven's latest tenure his "last chance." Just like Johnny Cash says, "He's been everywhere, at least twice." Couple that with the stigma of his wilder years and it's easy to see why people might say that. Still, it seems more appropriate to see Raven's current stay in the WWF not as a final chance but a new beginning. A resurrection, if you will. Raven concurs.

"I can see that, like a phoenix rising from the flames, absolutely. I've only been here a couple months, so it's still a feeling-out process and they have so many people on the roster. It takes a little bit of time, they have their own particular style and way of doing things and even though I watch the show every week at home, it is still different when you get there. It's still a feeling-out process by both parties but it's been good here so far," he said.

Never at a loss for words, when asked what Raven can bring to the WWF that may be lacking in a federation packed to the gills with superstar caliber talent, he responds articulately, assuredly and with absolute conviction. "I think my verbal dexterity. I think my ability to garner heat, to really make people hate me or love me depending on whether I'm a babyface or a heel. I bring a three-dimensional character, which this business has always been sorely lacking in. Most people are two-dimensional. I bring a whole depth and back history to the character."

Raven paused and then continued with a chuckle, "And my high-flying ability, sometimes I fly off the bottom rope. Seriously though, I'll throw a dive over the top, here or there, I'll break it out when the situation warrants it, but I don't do it well enough or acrobatically enough to do any more than that or it would take away from when I do it."

By the same token, when asked his opinion of the current WWF product, Raven is just as forthright and adamant in his views. "I like it," he stated. "I'm an enormous mark for Triple H. I think he's the best worker I've ever seen, period, bar none."

Even better than say, a Ricky Steamboat or a Ric Flair in their prime?

"No one else can touch him," Raven proclaimed. "His work is volumes better and if you watch a lot of that stuff back then, they weren't nearly as good as you remember, they were great for their day but it doesn't hold up anywhere near the level that Hunter's does." Raven continued, switching icons but maintaining the thread. "Bret Hart always talks about 'the best there is, the best there was and best there ever will be,' and nothing against Bret because he was a hell of a talent, but he'll never be the best there ever will be because Hunter is way better than him, as good as Bret was, Hunter is that much better, absolutely.

"It's kind of like the more you know about something the more critical eye you can put to it," Raven elaborated. "I love music and I've got two months of guitar lessons under my belt, but I don't know enough about music to really have that critical an ear. If you put two drummers in a room and said pick who's who, I couldn't tell you. Whereas my roommate, who's a musician, he could hear a drum fill and tell you who's who, because the person's fingerprints are on it. The more you learn about wrestling, the more you realize that some of the stuff Hunter does, and it's just so brilliant.

"My work," Raven continued, "it's really weird, in some circles I'm considered a hell of a worker and some people, well, whatever, and some people are like, 'Yeah, he's alright.' A lot of what I do is in the same vein. It's how I make my opponents look good. Put me in a match with someone and you'd think 'Wow, what a hell of a match,' and 'Wow, Raven's opponent was phenomenal,' but a lot of the time it's me making them look good, which you don't see."

One particular example comes instantly to Raven's mind.

"One of my proudest feats was working with [Terry 'Bam Bam'] Gordy [in ECW], and Gordy had that drug overdose in Japan, his brain just wasn't the same and it was his first match back in the States in a long time. I put together a very simple match, at least it was simple for him, but to the observer it was this eventful match of, maybe not of mythic proportions, but it was a huge deal and everybody was convinced that Gordy was the old Gordy again, and then when he worked his next match and they saw that he wasn't, people realized the magic that I put forth. That's one of my proudest moments — that match, being able to get that out of him at that stage of his career.

"The stuff I do isn't the obvious, there is a lot of subtlety and there is a lot that you don't even realize I'm doing, and Hunter does that better than anyone."

Raven undoubtedly brings a unique aspect to the WWF. A character with an extensive background, an athlete just as willing to put his opponent over as himself, and a psychological aspect that hasn't been present since the calculated machinations of Jake "The Snake" Roberts or the demented rampages of Mankind — not to mention his extensive aerial skills. Nobody, not even Raven, knows what the WWF is going to do with him or his talents and this uncertainty doesn't concern him in the slightest.

"I don't know what they're going to do," claimed Raven. "It's no clearer to me than it is to the fans. I think that's fine. I think it adds a degree of spontaneity. The character can behave in a more original way than if I have time to think about it and beat it to death. I think there is more of an originality that'll come through. It would be one thing if I was involved in the writing, which I have no interest in doing, and since I'm not, I'd just as soon find out when they tell me because then there is a spontaneity that you get whereas if I knew three or four weeks in advance, I would think about it. I'd come up with 75 new ideas and change it, then I'd come up with something that I'd be set on and then I'd rethink it, analyze it to death and come up with something different. Ultimately, what I come up with first is usually the best, so when they say, 'Boom, this is what we want you to do' and how I think to portray that is usually my best call. My first instinct is usually my best."

*   *   *

RAVEN: AT PEACE WITH HIMSELF

Part 2
By CHRIS GRAMLICH

Despite constant rumors of a reformation of Raven's Flock/Nest, WWF superstar Raven is unaware whether the crowd-pleasing move will ever come to pass.

"I have no idea, I don't know anything," Raven said. "But, I'm all for it, it's fine. I like having a group of guys. What I like about it is that the finishes can be so much more complex the more people you have at your disposal to run false finishes with. So to me, I'm all for it, but by the same token, if they want me by myself that's fine."

Throughout his extensive career in professional wrestling, the dark side of Scott "Raven" Levy has become just as (in)famous as the hardcore, brawling, bleeding wrestler — a fact that neither Levy, either as himself or Raven, has ever shied away from. Be it in interviews or on national television, his drinking and addictions were highlighted frequently in ECW to develop his Raven persona. However, the Raven of today is a far cry from the disturbed, brooding nihilist of the past, at least behind scenes, if not on camera.

"I'm clean and sober. I haven't had a drink in three years and I haven't done any drugs in seven months. It's pretty easy, actually," said Raven. "I did what I wanted to do. I did enough drugs. I whored around. I did everything in life that I wanted to do and I wasn't happy. I knew it was time to make a change. Plus, I didn't want to die. I didn't want to be a casualty. It's so not cool. How cool is it to die from a drug overdose?

"Not to trivialize, but I always told all my friends that when I decided to quit, I'll quit and that'll be the end of it," continued Raven. "They were like, 'No, you can't just quit, it's not that easy.' But it is or at least it was for me. I just decided I wanted to stop doing it. Plus, not only did I quit for myself but I knew that if I was still a drug addict then the odds of me getting into

Raven as Johnny Polo, manager to the WWF's Quebecers, Jacques Rougeau and Pierre Carl Ouelett.

the WWF would be slim to none and I just didn't want to see my career end without getting my shot here."

And what of the accusations that the Raven of today has toned down because of sobriety, or that his persona no longer reflects the man? Raven will have none of it.

"Just because I'm no longer miserable and I'm no longer a drug addict doesn't mean that doesn't still inform my life, the history will always affect it," said Raven. "Now, I'm much more carefree. I'm much more at peace with myself. I don't hate myself anymore. So, in many ways I'm not that character but in many ways I'll always have that character inside of me, so I'll always be informed by it.

"The problem with drugs," Raven continued, "is that you are either one of two kinds. You can either take them or you can't, and you won't know until you take them, so there's a big risk. I always knew that I would be able to quit but I think that's very exceptional, I've never found anyone else who can go, 'I'm done and I quit,' and that was it. I don't recommend it to anyone but I don't discourage it either. I'm not going to say don't do it because I don't want to be a hypocrite. I think you need to make your own decisions but unfortunately you also have to live with them and it's not always easy."

Raven has obviously always made his own decisions and lived with them, good or bad. From walking out on a producing job in the WWF to going to WCW from ECW at arguably the height of their influence, to quitting WCW, to his years of hard living and subsequent cleanliness, still many are of the theory that his path of excess and addiction may have prevented him from becoming an star in this industry even sooner than he has.

Again, Raven will have none of it.

"Honestly, I don't think it [the addictions] affected me negatively because it never was a problem for me. I never let it affect my work and it only really became well known because I allowed it to be," he revealed. "When I was in ECW the first time, I guess it started to escalate there, but it didn't really matter. I made it part of the character because I thought it was interesting. I got to WCW and it really didn't matter because it didn't affect my position. Then I get to ECW again, by now my problem had become a 'problem,' but it still didn't affect my job. Paul E. was going to use me the same way, regardless, so it never really did affect me, honestly."

Although it may not have affected his professional life, he knew it could have if it wasn't dealt with. "It could have ended my career prematurely if I didn't quit because I wouldn't have been able to come here," stated Raven. "But, I've always been a smart man, I knew when it was time to quit, both for personal and business reasons. I think more than anything it has become a stigma, but, ultimately, even if I wouldn't have carried that stigma I wouldn't have been able to break into the 'big ten' in WCW, so I wasn't going to break in there. The stigma didn't hurt me at all in ECW, it added depth and a level of realism to it, so it didn't affect me there and now I'm back here again."

* * *

Raven cracks a smile.

RAVEN: FOREVER CONNECTED WITH ECW

Part 3

By CHRIS GRAMLICH

While it has been years since Raven's glorious run as ECW's top dog, his name still is irrevocably connected with the company. Perhaps it's because of the growth that both the wrestler and the company went through together. Perhaps it's the fact that ECW fans are loyal to a fault or perhaps it is because both the man and the company contributed to changing wrestling in the mid-1990s.

Despite the fact that it has been years since his initial departure, the subject still raises the ire of longtime ECW fans. Raven, however, sees his initial departure not as a case of leaving at the wrong time, but at the right time.

"I had done everything there was to do and I needed to make some money because I really wasn't making shit there," he said. "I was lucky enough that just as the wave started to peak I jumped on and caught the ride, but I definitely think that it was a symbiotic relationship. I did as much for them as they did for me.

"I had done everything. I had every major feud that I wanted to have. I'd done every major angle and there was no money," continued Raven. "[WCW honcho Eric] Bischoff had been wanting to bring me in off and on for the previous year. He just hadn't offered me the right amount of money and finally I said, 'This is what I want,' and he said, 'I'll give you that,' and I said alright and I came."

And while Raven is unquestionably proud of his initial ECW days, he is also a realist about the influence ECW was having and how long they had until the WWF and WCW took notice and copied their style.

"They [ECW] had reached their first pay-per-view and it had achieved everything that I wanted," said Raven. "The way I saw it was that if it was no longer going to be as influential as it was and if I wasn't going to be as influential anymore, then I at least wanted to make money if I was just going to be part of the scenery."

However, while his first run with ECW helped change wrestling, instituting the more hardcore style, pushing the limits of subject matter and crossing the lines a number of times in both regards, his return to ECW was less than the stellar impact that his first tenure had been. Raven agrees.

"I wasn't utilized and I wasn't motivated because I don't think Paul E. was that motivated. I think Paul E. had too much going on and he couldn't stay focused on the booking. When he's focused he's brilliant but he had too much going on with TNN and everything else that he couldn't stay focused, and I think it just trickled down," lamented Raven. "I wasn't used as well as I could have been or I was the first time I was there and I think I lost motivation, which is still my fault — it's still my job to keep myself motivated — but my drug problem had become worse and things had spiraled down, as they always do. I knew getting clean was on the horizon so I really wasn't too worried about it, to be honest. I kind of spent the time having fun. I really had a lot of fun when I was there in ECW, at house shows, goofing off, but now it's time to get serious again."

While it may have indeed been a long, strange trip for Scott "Raven" Levy, he has finally come full circle, emerging in the company he once left to stake his own claim as a wrestler and establishing himself as a hardcore icon in the process. After surviving the WWF, ECW twice, WCW and himself, creating a hardcore legacy and helping to pioneer the "extreme" style, his biggest challenges may be behind him. Yet, the WWF can be as unforgiving as it can be uncaring about a wrestler's past achievements and notoriety. Will Raven succeed in the WWF? All the attributes are present. Only time will truly answer the question . . . What about Raven?

From the writer: It's sometimes funny revisiting interviews years later. I recall Scott "Raven" Levy being optimistic about his run in WWE at the time, his understated pride in being clean and sober, his willingness to discuss any subject, including his demons, being a Triple H mark and the number of times I had to call him due to backstage WWE soundchecks and phone troubles to complete the interview. Years later, after a semi-successful run in TNA, Levy has all but disappeared from the mainstream radar and only the truly hardcore remember the former ECW champion who helped revolutionize the sport in the 1990s. What about Raven? Indeed.

*   *   *

BENOIT THRILLED TO BE A TEAM PLAYER

By JOHN MOLINARO

Three months ago, Chris Benoit was in Toronto wrestling Bret Hart for the WCW World heavyweight title in the main event at Mayhem.

This past Friday he returned, wrestling on the WWF's SkyDome show, putting over Rikishi Fatu in a mid-card bout.

When Benoit and pals Eddie Guerrero, Dean Malenko and Perry Saturn left WCW in late January for the greener pastures of the WWF, pundits said it would only be a matter of time before Benoit would be the breakout star of the pack and become world champion.

It hasn't happened . . . yet. In the meantime, Benoit is just content to be with an organization that values his immense skills and doesn't mind paying his dues in the WWF.

"Right now being in the WWF, it feels like a team effort," Benoit told SLAM! Wrestling backstage at the SkyDome Friday night. "Morale is great. Everybody is optimistic and positive; everyone wants to make it work. In WCW it was far from that."

Benoit and the Radicals have taken a lot of criticism from critics and members of the wrestling media. SLAM! Wrestling's own Eric Benner took the foursome to task for walking out on WCW and their contracts.

Benoit defends the decision to leave and has no moral qualms about doing so.

"In my eyes I signed my contract with Eric Bischoff. There were a number of promises and guarantees made with Eric. I trusted him, I had faith in Eric and he earned my respect. As far as I'm concerned when he left, my contract was null and void from that time on."

Benoit grew increasingly frustrated in WCW. He felt he was being held back and there was no opportunity for him to advance in the company and become a major player.

"I'm 32 years old right now. I feel I have got a lot more to offer to the business of pro wrestling than they were giving me the opportunity to offer. It constantly felt like my career was being undermined at the time from certain people who were in certain positions of power. I'm not at liberty to talk about their names right now due to legal terms."

Despite a legal gag order, Benoit has been very outspoken about one of his former co-workers in WCW, namely Hulk Hogan. Benoit penned an article on his own website, taking Hogan to task for derogatory remarks he made about Billy Kidman not being able to draw in a flea market.

Benoit feels that Hogan should be more of a locker room leader in WCW.

"Hogan, out of everyone in the business, should be the role model, should be the man everybody looks up to and respects. He should be the one setting the example.

"He's not a locker room leader. He's far from it," continued Benoit. "Your past is not your potential. I know I've said some derogatory things about him but you can change today if you want to. I was asking him [on my website] what type of legacy do you want to leave behind in the business? Fifteen years from now, if a guy asks me what it was like working with Hulk Hogan, from my experience working with him I don't have that much positive to say about him.

"The whole time I was there in WCW, I never had a conversation with Hogan that went further than, 'Hi, how are you doing?'

"I remember one time, I had a match and after the match he walked up to me, patted me on the back and said, 'Good job.' I felt so great," Benoit recalls. "Coming from him it meant so much. That night walking out of the building I remember feeling so great thinking, 'Damn, coming from him that means a lot.' I feel he should be playing more of that kind of a role to the younger guys."

When he signed with the WWF, it also ended Benoit's relationship with New Japan Pro Wrestling. Having wrestled there, off and on, for the past 13 years, Benoit knew signing with the WWF would mean he could no longer work odd dates for the Japanese promotion where he first gained international renown for his work.

He and Malenko were scheduled to take part in next month's Super J Cup, the most respected junior heavyweight tournament in the world. Benoit won the inaugural tournament in 1994 defeating the Great Sasuke in the main event, catapulting him to the top of the international wrestling world.

Still, the fact he would no longer be able to work for New Japan had little bearing on his decision to go to the WWF.

"[It wasn't a factor] because I hadn't gone that often being with WCW," stated Benoit. "They never really sent me that much. I don't look at things like, 'I could have done this, I could have done that.' I look at it like what my potential future is."

Outside of the ring, Benoit is a proud new father with the birth of his son, Daniel. It's his first child with his girlfriend, the former Nancy Sullivan, and mother and baby are doing just fine.

"Nancy's real good. She's out of the hospital now, but having a C-section takes quite a bit of time to recuperate so she's not able to lift things or do what she normally does which is frustrating."

From the writer: Chris Benoit was someone for whom I had a great deal of admiration long before I became a reporter. I always respected his work rate, the respect he had for the business and the seriousness with which he conducted himself at all times. He was, by all estimations, a model professional. Where did it all go wrong for him? I'm not sure.

I know it's insensitive to say, but I tend to remember the quiet and thoughtful Benoit I encountered countless times over the years, as opposed to the dark and destructive figure he became.

* * *

MYSTERIO HAPPY TO BE BACK IN ACTION

By GREG OLIVER

From the staff: John Molinaro wasn't the only one who had respect for Chris Benoit — the entire WWE held the Edmontonian in the same high regard. Among those closest to Benoit was Rey Mysterio. Mysterio had been away from the WWE locker room, rehabbing an injury when the Benoit double murder-suicide occurred. One of his first interviews after the tragedy was with SLAM! Wrestling.

Rey Mysterio Jr.'s return to action in World Wrestling Entertainment has been most welcome: TV ratings are up on *Smackdown* among Latino viewers, his "I Quit" bout with Chavo Guerrero Jr. last week was a wild thrill ride, and on Saturday, his appearance at a Toronto toy store drew 2,000 people. Welcome back, indeed.

Before his meet and greet at the new Toys "R" Us at the Vaughan Mills plaza in Vaughan, Ontario, just north of Toronto, Mysterio took a few minutes to talk with SLAM! Wrestling about all the things going on in his life.

Rey Mysterio gives props to a young fan at a 2007 signing in a toy store.

Having been off for three-quarters of a year, it was a joy to return to action at the last pay-per-view, SummerSlam, at the end of August, he said.

"It was definitely emotional and exciting, especially being that SummerSlam was my first big pay-per-view five years ago against Kurt Angle. Coming back brings back memories. I've never really been out on an injury as long as this one; it put me out almost nine months," Mysterio said.

He admits that he could have stayed off longer, spending more time with his wife, his ten-year-old son and his six-year-old daughter. But it was time to come back. "With my surgery, this being my fifth surgery, I wasn't ready to come back at an early stage, so I waited and I waited and I waited until the thing got better," he said. "And still, to this day, I don't feel that my knee is at 100 percent. I can't sit around all the time and just wait until it gets to 100, because it's not going to get to a 100. Once you get cut, and this being the fifth time, it's never going to be the same. So I have to learn how to suck it up and do what I do best, do what I love to do — wrestle, perform."

Some may say that he was rushed back, and even then, his return was overshadowed by the homecoming of another world champion — Triple H. Mysterio dismisses the thought that his return was dimmed by the return of "The King of Kings."

"No, I mean, there's fans for Triple H and fans for Rey Mysterio. And again, there are fans that like both of us. I think it was put in the right place, the way they advertised me, me representing Smackdown and Triple H representing Raw, was good — totally different brands, overall part of the same company."

The consummate team player, Mysterio challenges for the world heavyweight title this Sunday at Unforgiven, facing the champion Great Khali and Batista in a three-way bout. The company is once again playing Mysterio as the giant killer, a small man surrounded by giants.

With the recent suspension of ten or more WWE superstars for violations of the promotion's wellness policy, there is an opportunity for overlooked grapplers to shine, said Mysterio. "I think there is, definitely. Not necessarily smaller, but you have the Jeff Hardys, the Matt Hardys, that have never gotten the opportunity to be the heavyweight champion. There's opportunity. And I'm not saying that there's opportunity right now because there's a bunch of guys that are suspended. No. I just see the talent in the roster right now that have been around for years who I believe deserve an opportunity to take that next step up the ladder."

His return in August meant that he was away for a lot of the recent shake-ups in WWE-land, including the Chris Benoit double murder-suicide at the end of June. "The loss of Benoit really did hurt, I would have to say, the whole locker room. Firstly to me, a lot, because he was one of my road buddies. We used to travel together, work out together, so that's what hit really hard."

Morale is pretty well what it was before he left. "As far as the atmosphere in the locker room, we're up, we're up and going, man. There is nothing that can stop us from doing what we love to do. There's a couple that are suspended right now. They'll be back. Meanwhile, we keep the spirit up. We make the locker room fun."

* * *

HOMICIDE'S STYLE COMES FROM THE STREETS
By COREY DAVID LACROIX

PHILADELPHIA — At first glance, independent wrestler Homicide's appearance says one thing — street. But make no mistake, the garb and tattoos are not a gimmick, but a declaration of survival and perseverance.

"I'm an ex-gang member. I made mistakes in my life," Homicide told SLAM! Wrestling in a rare interview. "I bring my childhood to the ring, I show my character in the ring. This is what happened in my childhood, I used to be gangbanger. This is me, I'm from Brooklyn, New York."

With that kind of background, it seems only appropriate he settled on the ring name "Homicide" at the prompting of a friend while watching the television show *America's Most Wanted*. But when you sit back and speak with Homicide, what one truly understands about the Notorious 187 of professional wrestling is that he is an athlete that found his calling and went after it with passion.

Like many of his wrestling peers, the Brooklyn native got hooked on wrestling from the television set. "I've been watching wrestling since I was

Even barbed wire doesn't faze Homicide.

about five years old," he recalled. "When I turned 15, I knew I gotta do this. This is my goal, this is my life."

Unlike many active wrestlers who will account their influences with names like Flair, Hogan, Savage, Steamboat and others, Homicide will exclaim names that are foreign to most fans in North America; names like Giant Baba, Antonio Inoki and Mitsuhara Misawa — a fraternity of wrestling legends from the shores of Japan.

"I started watching Japanese wrestling in about 1988," recalled Homicide. "I just got hooked up into it. I just love the style; it's very different from the States, Germany, England and even Canada. It's a great work of art."

Setting forth on his pledge to become a professional grappler, Homicide was well ahead in achieving his goal, possessing an active sporting background.

"I played football and did some amateur wrestling, freestyle and Greco-Roman," said Homicide, noting his athletic achievements would be the pedestal for his ascent into the pro wrestling world. "You definitely got to be in good shape. Not only great shape, but you got to have a great mind when you come to the ring. You could wrestle for 20 minutes, half an hour, maybe for two hours. You definitely got to be in shape if you want to become a professional wrestler."

Having the mental toughness for the wrestling game was entrenched in his life early. "I lived in a rough neighborhood. I think I was the only person in my neighborhood out of 200 people that loved wrestling," said Homicide.

His unwavering desire to attain his goal of becoming a professional wrestler was reached on March 5, 1993, when he made his in-ring debut. But the early years of his career were not typical.

"I never had the proper training, I just trained myself," he said, noting that at the beginning, he was not getting work in independent promotions, as is the norm with the vast majority of rookies. "When I started, it was, like, in this little convenience store," Homicide recalled of his rather unique wrestling environment. "It was so crappy, so dirty, so low-down. I did this for two years."

But fortune would shine on Homicide when he attended a wrestling clinic in New Jersey, run by none other than the Raging Bull himself, Manny Fernandez. "I met Manny Fernandez and he showed me every step, psychology, how to tell a story," Homicide said, adding his praise and admiration for Fernandez and his old-school style of wrestling.

In fact, it was during his brief tutelage under Fernandez that Homicide discovered his desire to tell stories through wrestling, an act that would defy the coming evolution of professional wrestling into dialogue-driven, sports entertainment.

"I love to tell a story in my matches. It's like making a movie, that's how I like to deliver my matches," explained Homicide. "I just want to wrestle. I hate doing promos; I think I suck at promos. Like Dean Malenko: no talk, just wrestle."

As the late 1990s arrived, wrestling exploded in popularity and with it, an unprecedented time period where wrestlers could seek out high paying employment opportunities with three major promotions, the WWF/E, Ted Turner's WCW, and East Coast upstart ECW.

For Homicide though, his anonymous sojourn continued, paying his dues and absorbing as much wrestling doctrine as he could with various indie promotions. Where others would have walked away from the life of bumps, low pay and long road trips, Homicide carried on, reaching inside to find that fighting spirit to stay focused.

"I got heart. I just wanted to make it. I feel I need to accomplish something," he said.

It would be almost 10 years after he first started that fans would begin to take notice. In 2002, the Ring of Honor promotion came into existence, striving to establish a serious, athletically-based wrestling product. Among the early pioneers of the group would be none other than Homicide himself.

"I gotta thank Ring of Honor. That company gave me a chance," said Homicide, telling of how bookers from the promotion were able to see through the street gangster wrestling attire. "A lot of people say that I'm a wannabe New Jack because I look like the man. But when they see the way I've wrestled, they say, 'Okay, two different people, but the same character.'"

What fans do in fact see is a steel-eyed wrestler who brings his Japanese wrestling influence to the ring, delivering an exciting strong-style offence, topped off by his finisher, appropriately entitled "Cop Killer," his version of the Kudo driver.

That drive to execute awe-inspiring matches would manifest itself into his breakout year in 2003, with matches against the likes of Christopher Daniels, CM Punk, Samoa Joe, B.J. Whitmer, Trent Acid, Satoshi Kojima and others, in addition to a standout feud against Steve Corino, which culminated into a bloody barbed wire match finale, with Homicide coming out victorious.

There have been other accomplishments that Homicide can proudly boast about too.

Recent years have seen Homicide tour Japan with Big Japan Wrestling and more recently with Shinya Hashimoto's Zero1. For the kid who idolized Japanese pro wrestling, it has become a dream fulfilled. "It was awesome. It was always my goal to go over there."

For a while, Homicide also ran his own wrestling school, mentoring a variety of students, including indie great Low Ki. To Homicide, it seems that at times his student may have surpassed the teacher when it comes to their chosen craft. "Sometimes I need pointers myself and I'll go to him and say, 'Hey Low Ki, what's wrong with this?' We just help each other," Homicide said, confessing that his tenure as an instructor had its own special rewards. "I think it was a blessing. I just loved watching the guys learn and hope they'll achieve what they want, just like I did."

But don't think for a second that Homicide is done with reaching new plateaus of success and cementing his rightful place in professional wrestling history. "The next step up for me is going to Canada, Mexico. . . . I just want to travel all over the world and achieve my goals. I don't want to be a world champion; I don't want to be the King of the Ring. I just want to be remembered."

From the writer: Too often in the wrestling business have I seen what wrestling takes away from people — injuries that linger for a lifetime, broken relationships, financial ruin and substance addiction. In the most tragic of instances, lives are lost. Looking back on this story, it seems to me that wrestling gave life to Homicide. He could have easily ended up in prison, maybe even dead as a result of his previous gang affiliations. But he found his calling and pursued it with vigor. I hadn't intended to interview Homicide that day, but as I was wandering about the New Alhambra Arena (the infamous ECW arena) I saw Homicide and boldly asked if he'd like to sit for a talk. He did, and I'm so grateful for it. How I only wish there were more positive stories like his that could be written.

*　*　*

ON A STING AND A PRAYER

By GREG OLIVER

Wrestling Revue

A young Sting.

It's hard to imagine a movie about wrestling great Sting conceived around a kitchen table, but that's exactly how *Sting: Moment of Truth* came about.

George King, the movie's director, is married to one of Sting's agents. The Stinger — real name Steve Borden — was over at their house one day, sitting around the kitchen table.

"He started telling stories about being on the road, about the old days and what it took when you were getting $25 or $50 a night to really make it in that business. It was fascinating," King told SLAM! Wrestling. "From that conversation, about a year later, we decided to do the movie. I wrote the screenplay. The guy who was supposed to direct got another job in between, so I ended up directing the movie."

Sting had actually been flipping through various scripts that King's production company, Dove Canyon Films, had in its possession. When King had the brainwave to do a movie version of Sting's life, the wrestler brushed off the idea initially.

"At first, it was, 'Oh, no one is going to care about this,'" Sting said to SLAM! Wrestling. "He kept on me, and I thought, 'Let's try it.' So he wrote this thing and it slowly but surely began to materialize into something that seemed like it was what God wanted me to do. It was and we did."

The idea is that Sting's life is dramatized into a 96-minute feature film that gives viewers a glimpse at the story of his life, both in and out of the ring, with a dramatic turning point where he accepts Jesus Christ as his savior.

Sting had a little input into the script. "It's my life, but obviously, George took the creative liberty, license or whatever you want to call it, and just added little things here and there. I had something to say about every part of it. With me, it wasn't about the script so much as it was about the message that I'm trying to get across."

Borden started out as a weightlifter in California, as a part of Power Team U.S.A. His first wrestling work came in Jerry Jarrett's old Memphis promotion, where he teamed alongside fellow Power Team U.S.A. grad Jim Hellwig — who would later become the Ultimate Warrior — as the Blade Runners. From there, Sting went to the UWF then the NWA, which became WCW, rising into stardom with a stellar 45-minute draw against then-NWA World champion Ric Flair at the first Clash of the Champions special on TBS.

Donnie Falcate plays the young Sting in the film.

"Donnie, amazingly enough, was a long-haired guitar player who came into the audition — he's a six-foot-four, six-foot-five weightlifter — but he's in Nashville to make it in the country music business," said King. "He came in, and I looked at him, and he had the body. His read was really good. I said, 'Listen, dude, would you cut that hair?' He said, 'Sure, I'll cut my hair to be in a movie.' But I don't think he understood that I was going to cut it to about an inch above his head in a flat-top and bleach it platinum blond. I think he was a little shocked. But we did that after he signed the contract."

The film contains both vintage Sting footage (complete with WWE logo slapped onto WCW action), and new matches filmed before a TNA taping. The young Sting's matches are wrestled by neophyte Falcate, which was appropriate, explained King. "The nice thing is we got the real Sting, Steve Borden, when he was there, he choreographed (Falcate). Because it was his young career, it was real. He was teaching the moves, he taught the same way he was taught. So after a couple of weeks, he began to take the bumps, fly off the ropes. He was a real athletic kid. It really, really worked."

The real Sting takes on Jeff Jarrett and an unnamed beast in two new matches. "We shot a match that nobody's ever seen before — the Jeff Jarrett match no one had seen because that wasn't on television. The match with the Monster is about a seven-minute match, or 10-minute match in the movie," said King. "Sting got knocked out for only the second time in his career. He did this move where he flies around the guy's back and the guy smashes into the canvas. But he banged his head, and man, I thought the movie was over. Lights went out. Just for 30 seconds, then he came back and he was fine. He didn't have a concussion. It worried us. He said, 'You know, that's only happened to me one time in my whole career.'"

Both Sting and King see this as a movie that has appeal to both wrestling fans and the Christian market.

"[It's] definitely for Christians," Sting said, envisioning it as a teaching tool for youth pastors especially. "Wrestling fans, they're going to see some wrestling footage in there. Hulk Hogan, Bill Goldberg, Hall and Nash, Lex Luger, Buff Bagwell, myself, Dallas Page and I think there's some others in there as well. I put on the tights and get some new footage. I did some wrestling for the movie. But you're also going to see the man behind the mask, Steve Borden."

"It's got a far reach. The story of his career, the love story, the story of him and his wife, it's got the other stories about what happened to him when he became addicted to prescription drugs and alcohol," King said. "Then it's him finding faith in God at the end of the movie that really turns everything around.

"We've got wrestling fans, the Christian market and NASCAR, because they all go hand in hand as far as the fan base. We will be going after the same market that The Passion of The Christ went to, as well as the hardcore wrestling people."

Theatrical distribution was never really considered, said King. "We really made the movie to be a DVD. It was straight-up for home distribution. It got a few bites from people who were interested, or curious, would probably be the fair way to put it, about putting it on the big screen. But, you know, we never built it for that."

Sting recognizes that it isn't a Hollywood blockbuster that the Rock would appear in. As such, his life and career are simplified. "It's hard to capture everything. If we wanted to make a full-blown feature film, you've got a $5 million budget or something, then it wouldn't have been glossed over so much, and we would have been able to hit more. It would have not been just about the message, it would also have been more about the storyline."

There is also no doubt that Sting is curious to see how his legions of fans will react to his move. "It is a Biblical thing. God's ways, or my ways, or what I'm doing, the Bible literally says that it will be foolishness to the world out there. So I'm prepared for that," he said. "I know that there will be persecution. There will be people who think that I've lost my head and I'm involved in this religious cult. Or that I just got weak and I had to turn to God. Whatever they want to turn it into, but I have no idea. I know that's going to happen.

"But I also know that there are going to be some people that will want to know, 'Wow, he knows this God, this Jesus Christ he talks about. He's claiming through Jesus Christ and the power of Jesus Christ he was delivered from pain medication, from alcohol, from a lifestyle on the road that was pretty radical.'"

Regardless of the reaction, the man behind the paint, Steve Borden, is more content with his life than he has ever been. "Now I know what it's truly like to be a husband, a father, an example to the public out there — wrestling fans included. . . .

"There is an answer out there. We've heard about God our whole lives. I rejected God my whole life. I was one of those who thought, 'What a joke, man, I'm not going to go that route, I'm not going to live by a rule book and go through all that. I'm not going to do it.'

"But I just got to a point that every part of my life was out of control. I knew that something supernatural had to happen in order to save my life, my marriage, my family, my career; to get me off of pain medication and alcohol and the whole deal, because I never could have done it on my own."

From the writer: This is probably one of my top five favorite headlines from the site. Personally, Steve Borden is a cool, thoughtful person to talk to. I could feel the strength of his belief, yet he was never preachy. The movie is pretty ripe cheese, but it was the key to scoring the interview.

* * *

TRIPLE H ON THE COLLAPSE OF WCW AND ECW

By JOHN POWELL

Even before it was announced yesterday that the World Wrestling Federation had purchased its longtime rival World Championship Wrestling, Hunter Hearst Helmsley (Triple H) had plenty to say about why the WWF is still going strong and its competitors have tanked.

HHH had a lot to say on the sale of WCW to the WWF during a media conference call to promote WrestleMania X-7, taking place next weekend. Helmsley blamed WCW's demise on their lack of respect for the pro wrestling industry.

"As far as WCW goes, I think they lost their passion for the business. I think as a company most of their people were 'corporate people' working for Turner who were pushed down to the 'wrestling thing' and I think many of them were just nine-to-fivers that would go . . . 'Ah, I don't want to do this wrestling crap. I'd rather be doing some other thing in the company but I got stuck down here doing this,'" said Helmsley, assessing the situation that led to the WWF's takeover of WCW.

But it is not just the "suits" that Helmsley holds responsible. He points the finger at some of WCW's veteran talent who he claims did as little as they could get away with because they were guaranteed a sizable paycheck from the company no matter what kind of effort they gave. According to Triple H, that's what set the prosperous WWF apart from a continually floundering WCW.

"We [the WWF] care about putting out a great product. We care to enter-

A serious, reflective Triple H at a press conference.

tain you better than anybody else and we care to make sure that every aspect of our show is as good as we can do it," he said. "Yeah, we make mistakes. Yeah, sometimes a storyline is not where it should be, but we work to change it and we are always striving to give the best product that we can because everybody in our company, from the lowest guy on the totem pole to the top guy on the totem pole — which is Vince McMahon — everybody shares that passion about our business and that's why we are number one. That's why we will continue to be successful as other people fall."

The one legendary performer Triple H holds in high esteem for preserving through all of WCW's woes is "Nature Boy" Ric Flair. Helmsley admits that Flair isn't what he used to be in the ring. That being said, Helmsley views Flair as still incredibly fun to watch and an asset to any company he works for. He gives him full credit for remaining enthusiastic and professional.

"When I would watch their [WCW's] show sometimes over the last year one of the only things that I would find mildly entertaining was when Flair would come out because I knew he was going to cut a good promo that would make me laugh or something," Triple H said. "When I would watch him wrestle and I would think . . . 'God, that's just not the Ric Flair the way I want to remember him. . .' but I tell you what, I would still go out there and watch his matches because he would show me more passion in the 10 minutes he would wrestle than anybody else on that show. I cannot help but respect that. Ric Flair, in this day and age, still loves this business, still has a passion for this business and still wants to do it badly. I have all the respect in the world for that as opposed to guys who are in their prime and basically are just going . . . 'Well, hell. I got my money. I am going to go sit home. Why should I bust my ass? I make the same money.'"

Turning his thoughts to ECW's downfall, Helmsley commended their struggle and effort to be successful even though they were the obvious underdogs. He viewed them as a "good training ground" and a "benefit" to the industry when they were at the top of their game. Unlike WCW, it wasn't laziness or an uncaring attitude that toppled ECW. It was simply some "bad business decisions" that paved the road to ruin.

"I look at what he [Paul Heyman] did with some of the talent, and that's not to belittle anyone there, sometimes he didn't have the most talent to work with, but he made the best of it and that's genius to be able to do that," Helmsley said of the ECW owner.

Having virtually abandoned ECW as a wrestling promotion for the time being, Heyman has joined the World Wrestling Federation as a color commentator and a behind-the-scenes booker. Triple H is glad to have him aboard. The creativity and devotion he brings to the job is inspiring others and shaking up what critics have termed as a bland WWF product heading into their biggest show: WrestleMania.

"As far as him [Heyman] being here, he's great. He thinks outside the box, which is tremendous. I think he has been, and will continue to be, a huge help in this company. And the biggest thing that I like is Paul is so passionate about the business and I think that's why guys worked for him for so long when they weren't making money," remarked an excited Helmsley. "Paul is such a passionate guy that when you talk to him about wrestling you just cannot help but have that same feeling he does. He just gets you hyped up about the business and you just want to go out there and perform."

Of the talent Heyman brought along with him, Helmsley sees good things in the future for Justin Credible and Rhino.

"It is hard to say but I think Justin Credible is going to do very well. I think that Rhino is going to do very well also. He's a good guy. He'll be a player over time. There's a lot of talent out there, it is just getting it in at the right time and doing the right things with them."

JERICHO'S DAD A PROUD PAPA

By GREG OLIVER

The SPORT Collection

Ted Irvine.

From the writer: It was a spur-of-the-moment decision to track down Ted Irvine, since Jericho himself wasn't returning calls just prior to his WWF debut. The interview proved to be pretty cool, and a wholly different perspective than what readers were used to.

Everyone knows that Chris Jericho has signed with the WWF by now. Well, everyone except for his father.

Former NHLer Ted Irvine laughed when told that his son, Chris, a.k.a. Chris Jericho, was jumping to the WWF.

"I hadn't talked to him in a while, so I didn't know what was going on there," he explained, saying from his office in Winnipeg that he had been away for a week (he has since talked to his son).

On his website — www.chrisjericho.com — Jericho has posted about his jump. Most telling perhaps is his desire to follow in his father's footsteps.

"I always wanted to wrestle in Madison Square Garden, where my father fought many a battle on its famed ice," wrote Jericho, who was born Chris Irvine. "I always wanted to wrestle in the Winnipeg Arena, where I witnessed so many classic matches."

So is Dad excited about his son being able to perform in their hometown?

"Anytime anyone wrestles in their hometown, any parent is going to have to deal with the next day — what your son did or didn't do, [it] doesn't matter what age they are," Irvine said. "You're really proud of somebody in your family if they wrestle in your hometown. You're ultimate proud, but you're very sensitive also. If anyone ever says anything negative, you want to deck them!"

Sounds like more than a little of that NHL experience coming through for Irvine, who played in the big league from 1967 to 1977 with the New York Rangers, Los Angeles Kings and St. Louis Blues.

Yet, according to Dad, young Jericho wasn't much of a hockey fan.

"It was not a comfortable thing for him, the noise, it was never an important thing for him," Irvine explained. "Now he's a huge hockey fan. He plays the game in Florida, he plays it all the time and follows it. Big Gretzky fan. Now he has a better understanding of the game that we're out of it than when we were in it. But I think that's true of most kids — they'll try to do something different than their parents."

Irvine, a financial planner with Courts Financial Group since retiring from hockey, has been to see his son wrestle in locations as varied as Buffalo, Las Vegas and Fargo, North Dakota.

And he's more than a little surprised over how successful his offspring has been.

"What surprised me more than anything else about Chris was his personality — the way it comes across on the TV . . . just that professionalism, how smooth it comes to him, how easily he can rattle on off the top of his head," Irvine gushed.

"His creativity mentally doesn't surprise me. As a little guy, from the comic books, to the Dungeons & Dragons, to his music, to his rock groups, to his plays in high school, he's always had an entertainment-type mind. He has a great view of life and how to entertain people."

Dad is "ultimate proud" of his son.

"I take a lot of pride in Chris as a human being. I think Chris is an outstanding young man. That's where my pride comes from — Chris, whatever he does in life. He's got Christian beliefs, he's just a good young man, loyal to his friends, loyal to his parents."

Now that Jericho's path has been set, Irvine, like the rest of us, is looking forward to what the WWF and Vince McMahon can do with his talent.

"He's created most of the things he's done in the last couple of years," Irvine said of Jericho's in-ring antics. "It will be interesting to see where [the WWF] will take him."

It will certainly take him to Madison Square Gardens, and maybe, if the timing works out, to the Winnipeg Arena on August 21 for the next WWF show.

* * *

JERICHO STILL PUMPED FOR BOOK PROMOTION

By JASON CLEVETT

Despite being on Day 22 of a lengthy book and media tour, Chris Jericho sounds pretty happy on the phone. Reached in Seattle prior to a signing appearance, when asked if he was tired of the media interviews yet, he

Shortly after his book tour ended, Chris Jericho returned to WWE.

responded, "No, not at all, man. As long as people want to talk about my book I am happy to do it."

And talk about his book he has been. *A Lion's Tale: Around the World in Spandex* has debuted at number 22 on *The New York Times* bestseller list in part due to the massive push by Grand Central Publishing and multiple interviews by Jericho himself. Without the WWE marketing machine behind the book, this ranking is a tremendous feat.

"I think that one of the advantages of writing it outside of the WWE system [is] I could write it how I wanted it," he told SLAM! Wrestling. "I didn't want to touch on the WWE because it was my dream to get to the WWE and I got there and that's it. If I had written this book with the WWE I am sure it would have been 100 pages of international experience and 300 of WWE. That is fine, but the tale would have been lost and it would have been a constant fight. So I am really glad I did this book outside of the realm because I thought outside of the box."

Unlike many wrestling books, Jericho's story only covers his climb to WWE — a trip that took him to Mexico, Japan, Germany, ECW and WCW. It ends moments before his WWF debut, a verbal joust with the Rock.

"I didn't want to try and cram my entire career into the book. I thought there was a very interesting story of all of these places I went to internationally and originally I just wanted to write the book on that. My life is an interesting story not just as a wrestling book but as a life book, about a guy having a dream and his journey to get there. I didn't want to do anything on WCW initially — I actually just wanted to do the book on my time in Mexico as I thought that was really interesting. But then we expanded it to include my time in Japan and Germany and stop at right when I got to WCW. But then I realized that the whole story of the book was that I wanted to be in the WWE — that was my dream.

"That is what the natural progression of the story was, start in small-time Canada, tour around the world and in the end, end up in the WWE. The story can continue on from the end of the book but that is the end of the story at that point, the whole process and seeing what it was."

Many are comparing Jericho's book to Mick Foley's *Have a Nice Day*. Foley assisted Jericho in the editing process and was a huge influence on the book. Jericho takes the comparison as a compliment.

"Mick's book was the template for what you want a wrestling book to be like. I didn't want to copy his book or anything like that, but we both had an interesting, unique journey and story to tell. Mick's first book took him up to where he was at that time. The one ace in the hole I have for the sequel is I don't have to start from now, 1999 is eight years ago so I have all of those experiences. I didn't write this book for a wrestling crowd, I wrote it for everybody, about one person's journey. It is a story about how many dreams you can make come true."

Also out now is Bret Hart's book, which is similar to Jericho's in terms of the route each man took to the WWF.

"I haven't read Bret's book yet. I am reading Nikki Sixx's book right now and then Bret's book is next. I think our books are the last two books of their kind about guys coming into the business the way we did, going all these different places before we even got to the 'big time.' It's just not that way anymore and isn't going to be that way and people should enjoy the fact that these books came out at the same time because they could be the last ones of this kind."

Another similarity is that Jericho's book was written entirely by him, just like Foley's and Hart's.

"With WWE books, a lot of them aren't written by the guys themselves. Mine sounds like me because it is me 100 percent. I worked with a collaborator [Peter Thomas Fornatale] but that was more for structure, editing and as a sounding board. I knew I wanted to write this book myself; I just wasn't completely sure how to do it. I think that is part of the problem with WWE books is that the guys aren't writing them. I couldn't leave my life story up to somebody else when a) I know how to write, b) I like to write and c) I lived the damn thing so who else is going to know the nuances of what I went through other than me?

"It's an independent release from the WWE but the publishing company is one of the biggest book companies in the world. The books coming out at the same time from this company as mine are Stephen Colbert's and Rosie O'Donnell's. It was hard to tie in to what they want because I am not sure they understood what they had. My editor understood and then she got the publishing house to put its muscle behind it. My book beat Batista's book on *The New York Times* bestseller list because the story was genuine, people liked it, and the company really knew how to get the book out there and make people understand that it isn't just a wrestling book."

A large theme in the book is that of lost brothers. Jericho candidly speaks of the deaths of Art Barr, Owen Hart, Eddie Guerrero and Chris Benoit. Jericho had completed and submitted the manuscript weeks before Benoit killed his wife, child and then himself. After much soul searching, Jericho kept the book the same, and added on a foreword.

"I finished my book in May and the stuff with Chris Benoit didn't happen until June. As a result of that I went back through the book and wrote the foreword because I didn't want people who were reading the book to not understand why I was speaking so positively about Chris. So I addressed it right off the bat in the foreword and got that out of the way and allowed people to enjoy the book as it was meant to be, an inspirational and comedic book, without a black cloud hanging over it. As for Eddie, it was hard, his death, but as I look back I am just thankful that I was able to know a guy who was as cool and heartfelt and sincere as he was. He was inspirational. I dedicated the book to Eddie because he is a guy that inspired me a lot. He was a guy who really lost it all and gained it all back. It's a very interesting story, his. The really difficult one to write about was Art Barr because he was the first guy I knew that passed away. He was the first one that was a close friend that I had to deal with his passing. On that level, to go back to those times and delve into that was tough. But in writing the story of my life, I wanted to be honest and go through everything as it happened. I didn't have an agenda or want to try and stay away from anything. I wanted to tell the stories that I remember and that were relevant to the book, and that was one of the major ones for me."

Now that *A Lion's Tale* is a bestseller and has developed a large following, the obvious next step would be a sequel covering the six years in WWE and three years since leaving to focus on acting, his band Fozzy, and his appearance on *Celebrity Duets*. While a sequel is likely, don't look for it on bookshelves anytime soon.

"Now that the book is on *The New York Times* bestseller list and doing very well, I think there is a lot of interest from the publishing company and people who have read the book to do another one. I can pick up the story literally seconds after the first one ended so absolutely there will be a sequel at some point. This book took two years to write so I would say anytime within the next two years we will be having our next interview."

Part of the appeal of doing a book tour is the face-to-face interaction with fans. Whether they are emailing him through his website, telling him at signings, or during interviews with media, the general consensus is that *A Lion's Tale* is a great book.

"All across the board it has been great. I get a lot of feedback from people who take the train to work and have had people give them funny looks because they burst out laughing while reading. That is great because comedy is very hard to write to begin with, but to write it where people laugh at situations it is nice to know it is working," Jericho said, adding even fellow wrestlers love the book. "I sent the book to a couple of my friends. The funny thing about the wrestling business is when you leave your contact list kind of goes down. Everyone that has read it that is in the business seems to really enjoy it, to the point of people commenting that they were sad when it ended. I think that anybody who actually lived their dream should like this book. Even if you haven't I think you will enjoy it because the good guy ends up winning in the end."

* * *

PAST FOLLOWS SHAWN MICHAELS AROUND

The Heartbreak Kid talks about his days in wrestling
By JON WALDMAN

Shawn Michaels has been out of wrestling since 1998, but fans still talk about him and his impact on the business three years after his last fight.

"Since I have walked away, I have had more people talking about my matches, had more people comment on the influence I had on the wrestling business," he told SLAM! Wrestling at a press conference in Winnipeg on Friday to promote the WWF show in town on October 6.

"That you can't beat."

Chris Schramm

What, you don't trust me? asks Shawn Michaels . . .

Michaels, known to fans as "The Heartbreak Kid" or simply "HBK," has been described as one of the best wrestlers ever to step foot in the squared circle. His high-flying maneuvers and high-risk style brought him many accolades as an innovator of North American wrestling. Michaels is flattered by the title. "You're just trying to work hard and think of new stuff and nifty stuff, and all the sudden someone's calling you an innovator," he said.

Michaels, a former three-time WWF heavyweight champion as well as Intercontinental, European and tag team titleholder, had several highlight matches in his career, including bouts with Sid, Mankind (Mick Foley), and the first-ever Hell in a Cell match with the Undertaker. No matter his opponent, Michaels always tried to have his best performance possible. "I tried to make all of them my best match, and I hope that's why so many different individuals say, 'I had my best match with Shawn,' because I was always trying to do that with them," he said.

Michaels worked with many different wrestlers during his career, but highlights times working with friends Kevin Nash (Diesel in the WWF) and Scott Hall (Razor Ramon) in the ring. "That was a lot of fun because you're out there with your buddies," HBK said.

Michaels also enjoyed working with the late Owen Hart. He feels that working with Owen was good because the two of them were able to do a variety of things in the ring without a lot of planning. "Owen and I always had a great time because he and I pretty much could do anything."

Much of Michaels's career was spent working in programs with Bret "The Hitman" Hart. The two had several encounters throughout their careers in the WWF, including tag matches (Michaels as part of the Rockers with Marty Jannetty, Hart as part of the Hart Foundation with Jim Neidhart), and various bouts for the WWF Intercontinental title and heavyweight title, highlighted by their "Iron Man" match at WrestleMania XII.

Michaels feels that his battles with Bret throughout his career helped in his development. "Me and Bret got to do different stuff at different parts of our careers, when we were both younger and when we were both older," he said. "That was such a great learning experience and so much fun."

There were, however, stories of problems between the two. Michaels feels that the reports of locker room tension were greatly exaggerated. "The whole story behind he and I was bigger than it ever actually was."

The last match between the two was at the Survivor Series in 1997, when Vince McMahon abruptly ended the contest, handing a submission victory to Michaels without Bret giving up. The incident, dubbed the "Montreal Screwjob" has become a much talked-about part of both of their careers. While Michaels has put the incident behind him, he is still asked about it. "It was a big thing. It's always going to come up."

Michaels has not spoken with Bret since the Survivor Series, but he would welcome the opportunity to. "I'd be more than happy to sit down with the guy and talk, and I'm pretty sure he feels the same way."

Michaels had his last match against "Stone Cold" Steve Austin at Wrestle-Mania XIV. After his retirement from active ring competition, Michaels stayed involved in wrestling. He spent time as both an on-screen and off-screen personality for the WWF, and has in the past owned a wrestling school and an independent promotion, the Texas Wrestling Alliance.

Recently, however, Shawn has distanced himself from the industry. He sold his wrestling school and has not been on WWF television for quite some time. "I got out of every aspect of wrestling," he said. "I've been doing it and involved with it since I was very young, and I wanted to start new things."

Much of Michaels's time is now dedicated to his family. He spends as much time with his wife and one-and-a-half-year-old son as possible. "I have one thing I have to do and that's be good to them," he said.

The time away from the ring has allowed Michaels to look back on his career, and realize how much of a commitment he made to the business. "When you get away from it, you have a chance to gain a little perspective on life," he said. "It's very tough, demanding job you're doing every day, all the time.

"Your whole life is wrestling."

Now age 36, Michaels is still a part of the WWF, having signed a three-year contract with them in March. While he feels that he cannot work another match, he will always look back on his time in the ring fondly. "I always liked wrestling," he said. "That 20 or 30 minutes I was in the ring is what I enjoyed."

From the writer: Part of what makes this story so memorable to me is, obviously, that I got to interview one of my childhood favorites. Even when Michaels was a heel, I still enjoyed watching him in the ring.

More than that, however, the article will always remind me of one of my mentors, the late Sheldon Oberman. "Obie" was my journalism teacher in high school, and, at one point, told me to stop writing about wrestling in our school paper. Years later, this article would be my first to appear in print for a major publication (Ottawa Sun). Half as a rib, I scanned the article and sent it to Sheldon, who admitted that wrestling writing was a great foot-in-the door for me.

* * *

SPANKY EXPLAINS WWE DEPARTURE

By COREY DAVID LACROIX

PHILADELPHIA — Only those who have chased the dream of making it to the big time of professional wrestling can truly understand how arduous a journey it can be.

Now just try to imagine making that dream come true, only to make the bold decision to walk away from it.

That reality is something Brian "Spanky" Kendrick knows about first hand.

In an exclusive interview with SLAM! Wrestling at the recent Pro Wrestling WORLD-1 show in Philadelphia, Spanky sat down to talk about his controversial decision.

"I don't want to give people the impression that I hated it, or that they treated me bad or anything like that," said Spanky in reference to his tenure with World Wrestling Entertainment [WWE].

"It was a lot of fun and an honor to be there. It's just that what I wanted out of wrestling at this time, they weren't offering. I could be in Kurt Angle's spot, but it still wouldn't be what I'm looking for."

It was just this past January that Spanky, a native of Olympia, Washington, made headlines all over the wrestling news world when he parted ways with the sports entertainment giant.

As Spanky explained, his passion for professional wrestling, which guided him to WWE, was in fact what motivated him to move on from the company.

"What I'm looking for is a chance to wrestle and to wrestle for a while and to tell stories in matches; 10, 15, 20, 30 minutes, whatever it might be," he said.

Christine Coons

"Spanky" Kendrick pouts for the crowd.

"That's not really what they (WWE) specialize in. The matches are short and sweet. They're more focused on entertaining people with shenanigans, bikini contests, people getting sprayed with stuff or screwing a corpse, which is fine. It's funny stuff, it's entertaining, I guess. But I'm 24 years old and while I can still move around, it's not what I'm looking for."

Trained by WWE superstar Shawn Michaels, Spanky made his professional wrestling debut in 1999. Despite his small stature, he quickly established himself as a standout, athletically gifted talent on the independent circuit.

But Spanky will be the first to tell you that developing one's skill set for the squared circle is a constant process. Bearing this in mind, he felt that the current WWE environment would not grant him the acceleration of his already established wrestling repertoire.

"When I talked to [WWE Talent Agent] Johnny Ace about me leaving . . . he and I both agreed, that at this level, whatever my wrestling ability goes, two years from now I'll be better than I am now, but not a whole lot better because you're wrestling the same guys every night in the same style," Spanky said.

With that, Spanky contacted Zero1 American representative Steve Corino, and has already wrestled for the Japan-based promotion. Spanky made it clear that his focus will be primarily with Zero1 and only a select few independent promotions in the United States.

"Pretty much for the most part I don't plan on doing too many [independent appearances]," he said. "I really just want to focus on wrestling in Japan. I think I'll become a much better wrestler going away for a couple of years and then coming back."

Prior to his time with the WWE, Spanky had been an active member of Zero1. The road to wrestling in the Land of the Rising Sun would lead to the adoption of a rather unique in-ring identity, first proposed by Zero1 superstar Shinya Hashimoto.

"When I got there, the guy picked me up [at the airport] and in broken English pretty much told me that Hashimoto thinks I look like Leonardo DiCaprio. I was like, okay, whatever," Spanky recalled.

But what initially turned out as an unassuming comparison to a Hollywood heartthrob soon turned into a certified wrestling gimmick, whether Spanky wanted it or not.

"The reporters are there, as they always are for whoever gets off the plane, and started asking me about what I think of DiCaprio. I realized then that something is happening here."

The following day, Spanky was advised that his entrance music had already been selected for him.

"Sure enough, it was 'My Heart Will Go On' and they changed my name to Leonardo Spanky."

But rather than protest, Spanky chose to be a team player, embrace his in-ring character, and have as much fun as possible.

"That's all you can do," remarked Spanky. "Doing it in the States, I'd get killed. If they had brought me into the Fed doing that, I'd be the biggest heel in the company, and not a good kind of heel — people would just hate it.

"But over there, for whatever reason, Hashimoto knows what he's doing because it worked, so I just ran with it."

If there is anyone else aside from Spanky himself who was looking forward to his return to Japan, it is Steve Corino.

"It's awesome," said Corino, in reference to Spanky's return to the Zero1 fold. "When he first came back for his first show with Zero1, the fans gave him such a huge, great ovation. When he came back [after the match] I said welcome home and he had this big smile on his face and said, 'Yeah, I'm home.'

"Of all the people that have left Zero1 and gone on to do other things, that was the guy we missed the most," noted Corino, adding that Spanky's DiCaprio-like looks only did wonders for attracting members of the female demographic.

"He brought girls to shows," Corino pointed out bluntly. "The fans love him, the press loves him, and it's great for him to come home to Zero1."

Aside from Zero1, Spanky also had favorable recollections of his time in the upstart American-based promotion, Ring of Honor. It was there, again, that Spanky was not only given a platform to deliver stellar wrestling matches, but legitimate support as a worker, something that was not always available to him with other promotions.

"Pretty much on the indies nobody gave two shits about me, which is fine," Spanky recollected. "More than anything, it [Ring of Honor] helped me to build confidence in the ring. That someone else would believe in me."

Despite his time in WWE, where roster members receive support and direction other wrestlers can only envy, Spanky was all too aware of the current slump professional wrestling is mired in. As he explained, to endure the woes of the industry is to love what wrestlers do in the ring.

"I wasn't around six or seven years ago. When it was really booming, I'm sure there were a lot of people getting into it for the money," Spanky observed. "Right now, if you're wrestling, it's not for the money. It's because you grew up watching wrestling, it's something you wanted to do, it's something you love."

Even as far back as his time training to become a wrestler in Texas, Spanky was made all too aware of the cyclical pitfalls the wrestling business seems to fall into.

"Shawn [Michaels] said that since the beginning when I was training with him — and business was doing good then — that it goes in cycles and he knew it would go back down," Spanky said, divulging that in spite of WWE being aware of the phenomena, there remains a confidence that it is only a matter of time before business picks up.

"It's something they keep preaching, that it's a cycle business and it will pick up again. It's good to have that kind of hope in the back of your head I suppose, but if you're just wrestling because, 'Well, I know there's going to be another boom and I want to be around to cash in,' then it's ridiculous to really think like that. If that's what you're doing, is just holding on hoping some day it will pay off financially, you really are in the wrong business."

* * *

From the staff: You might have noticed a trend with the last few articles. The three previous stories all are about wrestlers who, at the time of their interviews, had left the WWF/E squared circle. All, like our next subject however, would end up returning to Vince McMahon's ring.

HOGAN READY FOR WAR WITH MICHAELS

By TIM BAINES — *Ottawa Sun*

With a few wags of the finger, a couple of shakes of the head, a couple of blocked punches, a boot to the face and a leg drop, Hulk Hogan could finally shut Shawn Michaels up at WWE's SummerSlam pay-per-view tonight.

Wrestling Revue

"Brother, where's my next payday?"

The question is: will WWE allow a 52-year-old legend to defeat a 40-year-old icon?

There's no love lost between the two, that's for sure.

"Shawn doesn't drink . . . he's found the Lord," says Hogan. "Truth be told, he still has that demon inside him. Everybody always said it was jealousy, but I'm starting to believe he really doesn't like me."

Hogan says he was a bit surprised that Michaels ripped into him recently.

"I had an idea where Shawn was going, but he went way off the script," says Hogan. "The hair raised up on the back of my neck. I thought, 'This guy really wants to get to me.'

"I really always knew he wasn't my friend, but I didn't want to believe it."

There's no question Hogan has cemented his place in wrestling history. His involvement in the early WWF days helped bring the company to where it is today. He says it's been a great ride.

Says Hogan: "It's been a great year for Hulk Hogan, but I'd give $20 million to get 20 years back."

Hogan has been accused of wielding too much influence on the outcome of his matches. But he says he's a team player, so much so that he went along with scripts even though he knew they were bad ideas.

"My first match against Ultimate Warrior . . . I was on a major roll, then the decision came down for the Ultimate Warrior to beat me. I never said no, but in my heart, I knew it was wrong. I went to do a movie and when I came back, they were begging me to take the belt back.

"In WCW, Vince Russo was trying to prove a point with the New Blood taking over from the old blood [Millionaire's Club]. So three weeks in a row, Billy Kidman beat me. It could have been a major disaster."

Hogan, who spent some of his WCW time as bad-guy Hollywood Hogan, likes to be the fan favorite.

"I always wanted to be the good guy," he says. "Being the bad guy was fun to stir the pot, but outside of the ring, as we would drive away it was tough to explain to my kids why everybody was yelling: 'Hogan, you suck!'"

Hogan says his early influences in the business included "Superstar" Billy Graham ("he had the body"), Dusty Rhodes ("he had the gift of gab") and Austin Idol ("he had the whole wrestling aura"). "I just mixed and matched everything and came up with this Hulk Hogan mainstream character," says Hogan, who says he grew up with Babe Ruth and John Wayne as his heroes.

From the staff: The match with Michaels may have been Hogan's last in WWE (as of June 2009, Hogan had not returned to the Fed), but it wasn't his swan song. He would later make a rare indie appearance, battling the Big Show (who himself would later come back to work for McMahon). Most still believe that Hogan has not wrestled in a WWE ring for the last time, and while Hogan inevitably (it seems) will return, one superstar wrestler, however, appears to have left WWE for good, and he's our next subject. . . .

*   *   *

ROCKY MAIVIA BELONGS TO THE NEXT GENERATION

By GREG OLIVER

The Rock, circa 1997, with WWF agent Gerry Brisco.

Add Rocky Maivia to the list of next-generation wrestlers competing in the WWF.

As the son of Rocky Johnson and grandson of High Chief Peter Maivia, Maivia understands what it means to be a wrestler constantly on the road, traveling from arena to arena, rarely home to visit family and friends.

As a child, he journeyed around the world with his father. "That was the only opportunity I got to spend time with him. Everywhere he went, basically I went. That was good — a great experience growing up."

Maivia thinks that many second-generation wrestlers are a step ahead of newcomers to the sport — like Canadian wrestling legend Bret "The

Hitman" Hart, whose father Stu wrestled for years, and now runs one of the best wrestling schools in the world.

Bret's been helping Maivia get to the next level in the WWF. "It's kind of like he saw some things in me that he saw in himself 20 years ago," explains Maivia. "And that's the nature of growing up in wrestling. You pick up little things without even doing them."

The six-foot-five, 275-pound Maivia faces the Sultan on Friday on the WWF's Toronto SkyDome Triple Threat card. "I expect to win. I expect everyone in Toronto to be behind me. I appreciate all the fan support," says Maivia. "But then again, I'm not taking anything away from the Sultan. As you know, regardless of what he wears, or what his deal is, he is a fantastic wrestler."

Fans may recognize the Sultan as yet another second-generation wrestler, Solafa Fatu, son of Samoan Afa.

As for the future, Maivia doesn't have a headlock on it as of yet. "I don't know where I could be. Anything could happen. I would just like to be considered in a couple of years one of the best young talents around — one of the guys that the older guys pass the torch on to."

But when asked about forming a tag team with his father's most successful partner Tony Atlas (who's still wrestling), Maivia dismisses the idea. "There's no chance of that. I'm not knocking Tony. He's a great wrestler, he done great things but I do my own thing. Rocky Maivia by himself."

From the writer: The funny part of this interview is that the press conference at Toronto's SkyDome was actually to announce the signing of Tiger Jeet Singh's son, Mick, a.k.a. Tiger Ali Singh. A young, shy Rocky was in the background, and just a nice guy to talk to. "The People's Uncle" Ricky Johnson, who lives in Toronto, is an old friend, and he swears the Rock still remembers this interview.

*   *   *

YOU DA MCMAHON!

By SCOTT ZERR — *Edmonton Sun*

Vince McMahon was never supposed to be at the helm of what has become World Wrestling Entertainment.

Back when Vince McMahon Sr. was running the Capitol Wrestling Corporation, McMahon Jr. had to plead with his father for a chance to break into the family business. After much negotiation between the two, Vince was finally allowed to promote his first event — a 1971 show in Bangor, Maine.

Oh, how far things have come since then.

Mike Mastrandrea

The two most powerful men in wrestling: Vince McMahon and his son-in-law Triple H.

McMahon is now the chairman of the board of WWE, a multi-billion-dollar corporation that emerged from the ashes of countless tiny regional promotions throughout North America to become one giant conglomerate.

An innovator in so many ways, McMahon is quite simply the man, the last man standing, when it comes to the business of wrestling.

And it almost didn't happen.

"My dad didn't want me to be in the business as a promoter, much less as a performer," McMahon said in a recent interview with the *Edmonton Sun*.

"I said, 'Pop, I want to be a performer,' and he said, 'The hell you are.'"

"I think there's no doubt my dad is looking down on me now and saying, 'What in God's name are you doing with your kids?'"

Those children — Shane and Stephanie — have stepped to the forefront of the industry, both behind the scenes and in front of the camera. Shane is president of digital media, Stephanie the director of television writing, while wife Linda is WWE's CEO.

But don't for a second believe the old man is ready to step away from the spotlight.

"I'm not interested in retiring at all," said McMahon, who will make his first in-ring appearance in Edmonton tonight on WWE's Up Close and Uncensored tour at Skyreach Centre.

"I love to do what I do. It's not work to me. There's nothing I do that I enjoy so much, so I don't know why I'd give it up. When I can't cut it, I still want us to be ahead and I'll know it's time for Stephanie and Shane to take over for me. At the same time, I feel I'm still in puberty in a lot of respects because I like to think young."

And that includes getting in the ring and mixing it up, just as he did last weekend at the Vengeance pay-per-view event in Denver, squaring off against one-legged phenom Zach Gowen, a wrestler McMahon is likely to beef with tonight.

"I had a conversation with our TV writers not that long ago. I told them that I'm turning 58 in August [on the 24th] and they said they were thinking of curtailing my on-air schedule when I reach 60. I said that was damn nice of them.

"Every time I have a match, I think it will be my last and one day it will be because I much prefer being the producer and director. I love to have my fingers in all the pots, that way I can louse up everything."

The business of wrestling — or sports entertainment as it has become known — succeeds or fails with McMahon, which is why he is forever at the forefront. He reaps the rewards of its highs, as his bank account would no doubt show, and he's the whipping boy of wrestling's passionate fans when storylines go nowhere and interest sags.

But McMahon can take the heat.

"I don't listen to critics," he declared without hesitation.

"I read the internet for a while but there was so much bunk on there, everything was so negative, that I stopped. Those people were saying that I was doing things to put somebody down and that's not what I do. I try to boost everybody because then all of us make more money.

"These small-minded people think they know who I am. I can't change them and I'm not going to try. Those types of critics are sophomoric. I am my own worst critic. I don't think I do a lot very well. I am very self-critical."

Which is why McMahon views the downturn in wrestling's popularity seriously. He pinpointed a number of factors, including the expansion of satellite television and the internet, for the drop in TV ratings and live-show attendance figures. But even in wrestling's heyday, McMahon admitted to never being satisfied by the numbers achieved.

There will surely be some changes yet. McMahon is convinced what worked in the past will breed more success.

"If you provide the highest production level, the fans will find you as long as you are distributed well," he said. "Yes, we are not where we want to be and we hope we'll get back there.

"We will always give the fans what they've never had before. They've seen a lot and it's up to us to create stuff they've never seen before."

McMahon has no serious threat to WWE's command of the business since he bought onetime rival World Championship Wrestling. The vicious rating war became a personal feud between McMahon and WCW owner Ted Turner, who snatched up WWE talent with overpriced contracts and character control. It was a battle that went WCW's way until the stars that Turner had lured away held down younger talent and ultimately ruined the show with egos run amok.

McMahon won the war of wills with Ted Turner and is the last man standing, with a complete monopoly.

That, McMahon believes, does not mean a cushy ride ahead.

"It brings with it an awesome sense of responsibility. I treasure what my forefathers have done and what every person has done in the business. There's a long list of performers and a short list of promoters who contributed mightily to the business and I owe each of them something.

"It's on our shoulders to keep the genre going. No one can match us in our longevity. My children will be the fourth generation and I'm sure there will be a fifth. This business has tremendous legs to it that no one can match."

The future seems to be a favorite topic for McMahon. Surprisingly, WWE's long-range outlook goes far beyond what many would expect, but it is tempered with a mindful short-term focus.

"We are looking at WrestleMania XXIV now," said McMahon, whose annual spectacle will return to its birthplace, New York, for its 20th showcase in April 2004.

"It's become a way of life. It's tough because things can change so much from the way shows are written out. Things can change the moment before a performer walks out.

"That keeps us on our toes all the time, but the big picture is always in the back of our heads. But in this business you have to be flexible. We combine so many forms — rock concert, comedy, drama, action-adventure — and we have the greatest athletes in the world. It is such a unique hybrid."

But as McMahon looks forward, there is one significant ghost from the past. While it may not haunt him quite in the same way it does loyal Canadian fans, McMahon still receives legitimate heat for his handling of the entire Bret Hart ordeal of 1997. Hart loyalists refuse to forgive McMahon for "screwing" him out of a championship title reign that Hart was about to surrender before leaving for WCW.

Hart was so furious he spit on McMahon and, after laying waste to the TV tables at ringside in Montreal, Hart knocked out McMahon backstage.

As he ventures back into the legend's former stomping grounds, McMahon faced the issue head-on, albeit from his own take on the often-volatile relationship between the Hitman and him.

"I would love to publicly bury the hatchet with Bret," McMahon said from his Titan Towers office in Connecticut.

"He was an enormous contributor to this business. I always said the only thing that would come between us would be Ted Turner's money and I was proven to be right.

"We had a falling-out. He might be bitter. I'm not — I don't hold grudges. Even if I did hold a grudge, all the indications are Bret will be back for one reason — because the audience wants it."

McMahon brought Hulk Hogan back and if there was ever a time to hold a grudge, that was it.

"We have a very checkered past, both business-wise and personally. But you can see I made a deal with him because the fans wanted Hulk Hogan back. With Bret it's different. I have always respected him and his family and I've kept a soft spot for Bret."

McMahon had no problem putting over a former Hart Dungeon student, Edmonton's own Chris Benoit. Though he shied away from plugging any other talent for fear some in the WWE locker room would feel snubbed, McMahon had no qualms about touting the work ethic of the Crippler.

"There's only one name that I think on the entire roster no one could legitimately be jealous of me talking about . . . Chris Benoit.

"There are few athletes in the world like him.

"He always been on the cusp of something big. He's a very unique individual. There is so much more to Benoit than the camera picks up.

"You talk with him and he is very deep. He can be moody one minute and telling jokes left and right the next.

"He is a very multi-faceted individual and in time I think that's something fans will gravitate to. In the proper forum, I think the fans will greatly appreciate who he is and what he represents and he will then break through."

From the staff: Fate would rear its head again following Scott Zerr's article, albeit in two very distinct, very different directions. Hart would indeed reconcile with McMahon and the two would go on to produce a very successful DVD chronicling the Hitman's career, and Hart would be inducted into the WWE Hall of Fame. Benoit, meanwhile, would more than live up to the promise that McMahon saw, becoming the World heavyweight champion. He would remain a fan favorite up until his suicide after killing his wife, Nancy, and son, Daniel.

ORTON TRYING TO BE A GOOD MAN, BETTER BAD GUY

By NICK TYLWALK

On WWE programming, Randy Orton plays his heel role to a tee. He's scheming, manipulative, arrogant and disrespectful, all good qualities to possess for someone playing the promotion's top villain.

Orton's track record outside the ring for the past few years made it seem quite possible some of those traits also applied to his real-life persona. There was a suspension for unprofessional conduct and stories of anger issues and trashed hotel rooms. The third-generation wrestler was beginning to look like his own worst enemy.

It may not be a coincidence though, that his current run as WWE champion coincides with reports that he has settled down — and that's in both a figurative and literal sense, as he's been married since last September and is expecting his first child in a matter of months.

Family has a way of changing one's priorities, and Orton is no different in that respect. Asked to name a current wrestler he admires a few days before WrestleMania XXIV, he skipped the usual Ric Flairs and Shawn Michaels of the world and went in a different direction.

"Right now, I look at someone like Rey Mysterio," Orton told SLAM! Wrestling and other assorted media outlets. "He's got two kids, a beautiful wife. He's a real family guy. I look at Rey out of the ring, that's how I'd like to picture myself."

Informed of those comments, Mysterio seemed touched by the show of respect.

"Coming from a third-generation wrestler like Randy Orton, when he's days from being a parent himself, it makes me proud," Mysterio said. "I'm honored that he would mention that. I know Randy very well. For him to speak on a personal level like that, I'm happy that he actually picked those words and put me in that category."

That doesn't mean fans should expect a kinder, gentler Orton at all times. He's keenly aware that perception is often reality, and that people who see him on television acquire preconceived notions of who he is as a person.

Orton is quick to dismiss the idea that he is exactly like his character, but he also says playing a heel can have its advantages at times.

The ever-modest Randy Orton strikes a pose during a WrestleMania 23 press conference.

"My character on the show is somewhat of a prick," he said. "In real life I'm not that same guy, but there's hints of that in me. If you catch me on a bad day walking through the airport, and you've got a hundred pictures you want me to sign, you might hear some four-letter word you won't normally hear coming out of my mouth. I've got a little leeway because I'm a bad guy on the show, so in real life, if I don't feel like talking to somebody, I don't have to."

His self-awareness extends to his in-ring work as well. Orton admits that he's not the flashiest worker ("I've got three moves," he quipped) but feels like his ability to tell a story and take the audience on a ride allows him to get the most out of what he's got.

It's taken a long time for him to reach the comfort level he's achieved, but he's confident now that he has a handle on what it takes to reach the top of the industry. So confident, in fact, that he doesn't mind sharing his insight with others.

According to Orton, many of his peers are missing out on chances to win over the audience because they aren't taking full advantage of the calmer moments during their matches.

"What a lot of our guys and girls throw away is the facials, the body language," Orton said. "They hurry up and get to the next thing before they should, when they should take a breather and realize there's no action, so here's a camera on me. You've got to take advantage of that. This is your money right here, this is where you're going to sell that persona, that character."

On the subject of character, Orton even had some advice for John Cena, who he's known since his days as the Prototype in Ohio Valley Wrestling at the beginning of the decade. Asked what Cena could do to win over the portion of the crowd that always seems to boo him, Orton thought maybe a bit of change would do him good.

"I started out with [Cena] and we were good friends, and he's always been that kind of white meat babyface," Orton said. "I really don't understand why they don't like him, to be honest with you. Maybe he's too much of a good guy. Maybe if he had a little bit more of an edge, that would help."

Orton kept his edge over Cena and Triple H at WrestleMania XXIV, walking out with the title belt after an opportunistic victory befitting his character. There's little doubt that victory meant a lot to him, as he says keeping up the legacy of his grandfather and dad — who appeared in the very first WrestleMania — is one of his main goals.

As he moves on to his next challenge at Backlash, the Legend Killer seems to be wiser and more mature than he was just a few years ago. He sees himself achieving success in both his personal and professional lives, and if his newfound perspective holds up, it would be easy to see him pulling it off.

"With my baby, I want to set a good example, be a good father figure," Orton said. "At the same time, when I come to work, I want to be all business."

The Art
of Wrestling

They say that a picture is worth a thousand words. Well, when you're a contributor to SLAM! Wrestling, that's definitely true.

Just as strong as our articles over the years have been the photographs and caricatures that appear on our website. Some stories just can't be told in consonants and vowels — rather, they're told in still or satirical images that have become permanent parts of our business. Often, our web stats show that they will rank up beside our news stories on hit count charts.

The same popularity extends to others around the ring, and we've been fortunate over the past few years to speak with some of the most influential people who help enhance the pro wrestling experience.

* * *

COMBAT ZONE WRESTLING: A PHOTOGRAPHER'S EYE
By MIKE MASTRANDREA

PHILADELPHIA — After 15 years of shooting wrestling from ringside, I've seen up close the risk and bumps wrestlers take — and even felt them firsthand on occasion. With such experiences, it's safe to say I even reached a comfort zone when standing so close to the action; but on Saturday, June 10, at the New Alhambra Arena in Philadelphia, that comfort zone was gone. I was shooting ringside for Combat Zone Wrestling's Strictly CZW event.

It started off as a treat, a new experience for me, shooting ringside for CZW. One of the regular fans even offered ringside security, other fans and myself some homemade cookies he brought in his Tupperware. I began to wonder, how does CZW get such a horrible reputation? After a few matches, wrestling promoter Tyrone "Maven Bentley" Scott came to ringside and suggested, "You might not want to be at ringside for this next match."

Mike Mastrandrea

Justice Pain delivers a Sitdown Slam on a table to Sabian.

Of course he was talking about the Tables, Chairs and Kaos match next on the lineup.

I happily took a spot in a hard camera position and got a great bird's eye view of the action that spilled to almost all corners of the world's most famous bingo hall. I was grateful as I couldn't have thought of a more fitting name for a match that had broken tables, busted chairs and "kaos" from the opening bell.

After intermission, I reassumed my ringside position. Things were looking good as Chris Hero and Claudio Castagnoli put on a wrestling clinic as they matched each other move for move and counter for counter.

Then it was time for the main event. The BLK OUT (Ruckus, Eddie Kingston, Joker and Sabian) vs. the Forefathers of CZW (Zandig, Justice Pain, Nick Gage and LOBO). Promoter Maven Bentley made his way to ringside again but no warning this time. I figured it would be just another tag match full of hot tags. I could not have been more wrong! I quickly realized that Bentley had some bigger things to worry about than warning some photographer, as CZW staff carried panes of glass, wood boards covered in barbed wire and thumbtacks to the ring.

Between wrestlers, security and other staff there were over a dozen people ringside so I knew this would be one of the more challenging shoots I had been involved with. But there was no time to start thinking about anything, as the main event quickly emanated from a brawl in the previous match.

As the match began it seemed the safest place to be was in the ring itself as all eight combatants spilled out all over the arena. The earlier theme of chaos was alive and well in this match as photographers were bumping into security and announcers were bumping into timekeepers all in order to avoid the wrestlers who were bumping into tables, chairs and ringside fans.

The Necro Butcher chills with a beer after the show.

There was no safe spot to stand in; at one point when the action was getting a little too close to my lens, I looked for shelter near the rampway and I still found myself dodging shattered bits of glass that flew into the air as a wrestler flew into it. Trying to avoid that area, I crossed the ringside only to step in about two dozen thumbtacks now embedded in the soles of my shoes. Even with all my experience of being at ringside, I made the rookie mistake of taking my eyes off the action. As I tried to pull some tacks out of my shoes, Zandig crashed into the ringside barricade, missing me by mere centimeters. As the match went on, the number one priority became not to get hurt and to avoid the action — forget the photos!

If my words can't help you imagine what happened, such a scene could be compared to news footage of riot and looting. It was human pinball, with bodies running around in all directions with no regard for others.

When all was said and done, I took inventory: bits of shattered glass in my hair, sweat from the wrestlers was mixed with my own, drops of blood on my shirt and dozens of thumbtacks stuck in my shoes. I could honestly admit for the first time ever in my career, I was worried. Safety was not a priority on anyone's mind, survival of the fittest was the theme of the night and you know what? I loved it! That was a true CZW experience. I wouldn't have had it any other way. My adrenaline was on overdrive, a feeling not many wrestling fans have experienced in a long while.

CZW has its critics — and many of them — but what would one expect when attending a show whose company name contains the words Combat Zone? The words Combat Zone could not be more fitting to sum up such an experience and I thank them for it.

Jim Johnston in his studio.

JIM JOHNSTON AND HIS MUSICAL WWF CAREER

By PAUL CANTIN — JAM! Showbiz

One of the hottest acts on the record charts these days is a 45-year-old resident of Connecticut who suffers from stage fright, doesn't have his picture included on his CDs and, until his latest release, never even had his name printed on the jacket.

Jim Johnston has for 15 years been cranking out the incidental music for World Wrestling Federation telecasts, but it is his four volumes of "arena entrance theme songs" that have brought him incredible success, if not celebrity.

The latest release, *World Wrestling Federation: The Music Volume 4*, entered the Canadian charts last week at number five, right up alongside Foo Fighters, Mariah Carey and Rage Against the Machine and ahead of such high profile acts as Santana, Counting Crows, Limp Bizkit and Shania Twain.

The record enjoyed similar success in the U.S. — growing evidence of the unlikely but undeniable convergence between contemporary music and wrestling.

"There's a lot of overlap in the demographics [between music and wrestling]," Johnston told JAM! from his office in Stamford, Connecticut.

"And there has been a change in how the WWF is viewed. We are less about wrestling and more like a dramatic series that appeals to a broad audience. And it is heavily musically driven, as a program. People are noticing that now."

Increasingly, wrestling is grabbing hold of the rock audience. On Friday and Saturday, MuchMusic will provide further evidence of that crossover when grapplers Chris Jericho and the Rock will drop by to serve as co-hosts (Jericho will appear November 19, 6:30–7:30 p.m. and Rock will drop in November 20, 2:30–3:30 p.m.).

MuchMusic spokeswoman Sandra Puglielli says the signs of a merger between rock and wrestling were first provided by the station's audience.

"Inevitably at our website we get references to wrestling or that certain wrestlers are cool, or there is a buzz on a certain wrestler. They will ask us: 'Did you guys here 'bout this?' It is obvious they are wonderfully popular," Puglielli says, adding anticipation for the wrestlers' appearances at MuchMusic has been intense.

The station has been bombarded with requests to attend the telecast, questions for the wrestlers and even some gifts — the kind of fervor usually reserved for only the most popular musicians.

"The response is right up there with music artists, consistent with that level of excitement. Just the way a fan reacts," Puglielli says.

Koch Records, the independent record distributor that handles the WWF releases in Canada, says *Volume 4* is their biggest seller since the techno group Prodigy's *Fat Of The Land* CD.

The previous three volumes of WWF music, which Johnston estimates have sold between three and four million copies, were credited as "various artists" projects. *Volume 4* acknowledges for the first time that, except for a few session vocalists, this is Johnston's show. His name appears on the spine of the new disc and it's his name that shows up on the charts.

"That's a big switch and a positive one," says Johnston of his new credit.

"They used to be issued like a soundtrack kind of deal. It was kind of a mutual feeling like hey . . . this album is more you than 99 percent of the albums on the *Billboard* charts. I write it all, produce it all. I play all the instruments. I engineer it. So it was like, okay. Let's get real."

A native of St. Louis but raised in Connecticut, Johnston is a self-taught musician and played in high school bands. But he didn't enjoy being onstage and gravitated to studio work. That led to scoring animation and industrial films, then promos for HBO and Showtime before meeting an art director with the WWF, who told him of a promo video that needed scoring.

"I put some music on, messed around with it," Johnston says.

The company liked what they heard and he hasn't looked back since. Theme music for the wrestling broadcasts developed into musical "bumps" to be played before and after commercial breaks, which naturally evolved into writing theme songs for each of the federation's stable of stars.

"It just so happens this is the best composing job in the universe. I am given essentially total freedom. I am trusted, which is wonderful. And I get to do an incredibly broad type of music on a daily basis," says Johnston, who estimates he writes, records, performs and engineers up to 300 pieces of music annually, working alone in his private studio.

The notion of packaging the music into CDs and selling it to the audience came by popular demand, he says.

"[The fans] really wanted to get their hands on it. . . . It finally became the obvious thing to do: we gotta release this stuff."

Deadlines are so tight for composing theme songs for the wrestlers that Johnston says he sometimes has to complete the job in a single day.

The 14 tracks on the newest WWF CD cover a broad range of music — from Chris Jericho's rap-metal "Break the Walls Down" to Mark Henry's Barry White–like "Sexual Chocolate" to the heavy-metal thunder of "Stone Cold" Steve Austin's "Oh Hell Yeah." The wrestlers don't, as a rule, sing their songs, but their characters inspire Johnston.

"The wrestlers have input to the degree that I want to make them happy. I want to write a piece of music that will pump them up, make them feel good. And it will put them in the mood of their character, like a soundtrack. I consider what I do like a live soundtrack," he says.

"I get relatively little input. I ask their size. That's important. You have got to establish a basic tempo. Like [the wrestler known as] the Big Show is a large, slow-moving guy, so you need a heavier, slow-moving piece of music, whereas a wiry guy implies something at a more frenetic tempo and pace and sound.

"I get a one- or two-sentence description of what the basic character vibe is. I just go. Sometimes I get lucky and get it right off the bat. Sometimes I tweak it a bit," he says.

"It's not just: 'Here he comes.' I want to create that vibe with the music and the light. With Stone Cold, it is glass breaking and you get that feeling: 'Here comes trouble. Who knows what is going to happen now.' It's grabbing them emotionally, immediately, taking them to new places."

In the short term, rock, rap and wrestling are about to get even closer. Johnston says in January, WWF plans to release a hip-hop remix album, with artists like Snoop Doggy Dogg remixing the wrestlers' themes, followed by a rock remix album in the spring, with Rob Zombie mentioned as one likely participant.

* * *

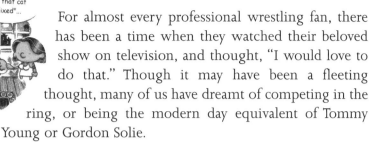

I know he's just some stray you found, but I think it's time we get that cat "fixed"...

PWI ARTIST AIMS TO BE A TOP DRAW

By BRIAN ELLIOTT

For almost every professional wrestling fan, there has been a time when they watched their beloved show on television, and thought, "I would love to do that." Though it may have been a fleeting thought, many of us have dreamt of competing in the ring, or being the modern day equivalent of Tommy Young or Gordon Solie.

There is, of course, a huge difference between "I would love to do that" and "I could do that." So when New Zealand–born Jason Conlan, *Pro Wrestling Illustrated*'s "Mister J" cartoonist, wanted to get involved in professional wrestling, he married it with his tremendous talent for art.

"My love of wrestling and drawing developed around the same time," Conlan told SLAM! Wrestling. "I was around six years old when I discovered Steve Rickard's NWA-affiliated promotion here in New Zealand. Even as early as that, I remember trying to draw Baron Von Krupp [Killer Karl Krupp], making a mistake, and throwing what I'd done away in disgust. Where was the liquid paper when I needed it then?!"

Unfortunately, Rickard's promotion — which saw legends such as Ric Flair, Harley Race, Abdullah the Butcher, and Andre the Giant come through on tours — soon lost its television deal in the country. With no outlet for his interest, it was only his discovery of the famed "Apter" magazines that maintained Conlan as a fan.

"The [Bill] Apter mags were a complete eye-opener," he said. "There were so many wrestlers, and so many promotions. There was no American wrestling on television at this point, so just about all the information I was getting was from the magazines. Even now I still mark out from time to time, when I finally get to see footage of the stories I was reading back then."

In terms of his developing artistic talents, Conlan admits to hardly being the finest student, instead preferring to plough his own working furrow. He would pay careful attention to comic book drawings, newspaper strips and political satire cartoons, all of which acted like textbooks to him.

"I found art school to be boring and expensive, which wasn't a good combination," he said. "I'd been selling cartoons since high school, and had a regular spot in the local newspaper. Looking back, having the test of my work being printed was more than I could have got out of art school."

Even though the first regular American wrestling on New Zealand television was *WWF Superstars of Wrestling* in around 1987, Conlan was always more interested in the NWA (Jim Crockett Promotions) wrestlers, perhaps because the Apter magazines had such a heavy NWA slant.

"I may have been easily led by that," he admitted. "But also, they were more interesting to draw, as they looked more like kick-your-ass wrestlers than the 'prettier' WWF performers. That's not to say that I didn't enjoy watching WWF TV, it's just that I never thought that guys like Hulk Hogan and Paul Orndorff appeared to be as tough as their NWA counterparts."

Working in a comic store while drawing part-time, Conlan's big break came when he began working for Pro Wrestling Illustrated in 1995. He had already done some wrestling magazine work, for the Wrestling Then and Now newsletter, and the Australian publication Piledriver, but PWI was what he considered to be "big time."

"I remember that I rang their office one day, out of the blue, and asked, 'How would you like a new cartoonist?' — and whomever I spoke to politely declined," Conlan explained. "Two weeks later, I tried again, and I think I actually got through to Bill Apter. I spoke to PWI backwards and forwards for two months, until I eventually got a call from Stu Saks, asking me if I would like to do a monthly cartoon, plus 30 full-page cartoons for their wrestling annual. Getting into the mag I read at high school, an international mag, and being let loose to draw whatever I wanted? It was great!"

Since then, Conlan, who works at a bookstore, has contributed to 1wrestling.com, Prowrestlingdaily.com, as well as the online version of England's Sun newspaper — the most-read daily in the country. All of these are opportunities that the 36-year-old artist is grateful to have received.

"Everyone at PWI has always been great to me. Bill helped me do some work with 1Wrestling, and Stu has invited me to work on the entire stable of PWI magazines," he said. "Getting the chance to do some work for the Sun was wonderful, but frightening as well. I had complete stage fright when I heard the number of hits their website gets. I couldn't draw anything for two whole days! I think it was just a matter of learning what I could get away with, and what I couldn't get away with. That, and working out how things would look in print."

With the aforementioned creative license that he is granted, Conlan is able to put some emphasis on the performers that he gets a particular kick out of drawing. One such wrestler is TNA star Scott Steiner, who didn't quite enjoy being drawn, as much as the artist enjoyed drawing him.

"WCW toured here towards the end of the company, so I thought that it might be nice to go and hang out with some of the guys. I sent their office some of my work, and when the tour arrived, I was told 'Scotty loved them' in a heavily sarcastic tone, and 'He's real keen to meet you' in a heavily ominous one. In other words, I was told to stay away from him. Which just meant that when I decided to draw him again, he looked even more like an overstuffed sausage!"

Sadly for Conlan, poking fun at Steiner may have to be left to another day, should he pursue his ambition to have his work commissioned by WWE. Considering that some WWE stars are also among his favorites to recreate in caricature form, it would seem to be a natural fit.

"I may joke about it somewhat, but I would really love to do a daily cartoon for WWE.com. I think it would be fantastic. When you consider that they own virtually every tape library under the sun now, I don't think I'd be stuck for ideas. Actually, I have a theory that if I draw Vince with a fang long enough, he'll hire me just to get me to stop. Hey, it's a dream!"

Conlan may consider it just a dream, but no doubt there are wrestlers at Titan Towers who would love to be drawn by Mister J. Just like the Mexican star Puma, who noted: "When I saw myself [in the *PWI* comic strip] . . . I thought I might as well just retire right there. It just doesn't get any better than that."

* * *

DRAWING INSPIRATION: SLAM! WRESTLING'S EDITORIAL CARTOONIST

By ANNETTE BALESTERI

From the staff: Annette Balesteri has been the SLAM! Wrestling editorial cartoonist for many years now. The California native has been a professional cartoonist for 24 years, drawing for local newspapers and magazines. She has picked a few of her favorite cartoons, and has shared a little about her life below. For more about Annette, see www.wrestling-caricatures.com and www.balestericartoons.com.

As a freelance cartoonist, I must draw or paint daily, and have for many years.

There is no "off season" for me — much like WWE wrestlers — which, for me, makes it all a fun challenge. Wrestling is so animated, rich with action, color, music, stories and interesting characters that are bigger than life itself.

It's a great formula for inspiration.

My ideas come from watching the shows, other SLAM! Wrestling

staff, or even readers. Sometimes the goal is to skewer, sometimes it is to poke gentle fun at something; other times, I am aiming to celebrate an accomplishment or a retirement, or share the grief of an untimely death. Unlike some newspaper cartoons, I don't think the ones I do for SLAM! Wrestling are ever bitter, mean-spirited or condescending.

I sketch and draw a cartoon idea in a Number 2 pencil on paper, then tweak

it all with shading and erasers, followed by inking in the lines. The next step is to scan it into the computer where I size it down and color it with Photoshop, adding whatever text is necessary. It's a blend of old and new media.

Away from the daily grind of drawing, some of my favorite things are teaching children under 12 drawing skills, teaching children over 12 drawing skills, chocolate and a good sappy movie with plenty of popcorn and tissues. My six granddaughters and three dogs keep my heart warm and joyous.

After the Applause

Wrestling's spotlight, no one will argue, burns as brightly as it does for any other form of entertainment. Be it a competitor, manager or broadcaster, all enjoy the warmth of this glow. The public admiration, the fan adoration, the respect of the boys and girls in the locker room all contribute to the enjoyment that is experienced and helps heal the wounds that are sustained in the ring.

Eventually though, that spotlight goes out. Some may stay on working backstage for a promotion, others will work the show circuit to meet their fans face-to-face, while others still will leave the wrestling world behind completely, almost disappearing from the landscape of the canvas.

No matter which of the above scenarios exist for the legends of the squared circle, SLAM! Wrestling has dedicated countless hours to searching for and documenting the careers of our past heroes. Each story is unique — some speak of success, others speak of tragedy. Either way, they are a testament and tribute to those who now live in the world beyond wrestling, a realm that exists after the applause.

* * *

THE OTHER ORTON

Meeting in Las Vegas leads to three-part SLAM! Wrestling epic
By JAMIE KREISER

Of course, I knew of his father and his brother. His nephew, Randy, was the first big name I ever interviewed. But all I knew of Barry Orton could be summed up in one word: scandal. After a chance meeting in Las Vegas, I was given the opportunity to delve headfirst into the enigma, the abyss that is Barry Orton.

Barry Orton as The Zodiac in Stampede Wrestling.

Brace yourselves.

I was heading to the Cauliflower Alley Club (CAC) Reunion for the first time. I had just finished journalism school and heading to Las Vegas seemed like the ultimate reward for obtaining my degree.

A few days before boarding the plane, my grandmother read my cards. An eccentric practice to some, but it was a routine within our relationship whenever we saw each other. She told me that the Vegas trip was going to change my life in ways I was not expecting, ways I was not prepared for. If she only knew . . .

* * *

It was the last day of the CAC Reunion and I remember desperately trying to keep my composure the entire time. It was so difficult not to be over-whelmed when one moment you would turn and be face-to-face with someone like Harley Race and the next moment you'd walk by Walter "Killer" Kowalski eagerly regarding the youth, knowing all too well their motivations and visions of wrestling rings dancing in their heads, partici-pating in the training sessions run by Les Thatcher.

Sin City itself had been a surreal experience for me. My entire being was buzzing from all the lights, sounds and the cheap margaritas.

I often visited the exhibition room to calm down. Amongst all the mer-chandise for sale and wrestling displays, I caught up with my good friend and fellow Canadian, Bob Leonard. As he was introducing me to female wrestling legend Penny Banner, I noticed a guy with a video camera inter-acting with a few of the wrestlers. Bob pointed at him and told me that his name was Barry Orton (actually Randal Berry Orton). Barry came by where we were standing and started filming Penny, explaining that he was making a documentary. After I introduced myself, he told me that he and a few of the wrestlers were getting together the next day and he invited me along.

It was an offer I couldn't refuse.

* * *

"Ox Baker, your limo is here!" Barry yells out his driver's side window.

We're outside the Circus Circus hotel. With the addition of Ox Baker and his wife, Peggy Ann, there are now seven of us crammed into Barry's van. It has to be a sight even to the people of Nevada. The booming Ox Baker in the passenger seat; the dignified Sir Oliver Humperdink behind him; K-9 Kohl, a manager from Tennessee, dressed all in black is next; then there's Bob Johnson, a current consultant/booker with Stampede wrestling; Peggy Ann and me, crammed in the back with my little notebook thinking nowhere in any of my journalism textbooks did it mention I would find myself in a situation like this.

We head to Barry's house, which he shares with his mother and his sister, Rhonda. The awe and bewilderment are still fresh in my eyes because Barry leans in and offers, "Relax, they're people just like you."

Feeling slightly, just slightly, more at ease, we all gather in Barry's home edit suite and watch some promos from his days at World Organized Wrestling (WOW). The tape is from the early '90s and has Barry portraying an S and M character. During one of Barry's matches, a familiar face acts as referee. It's his nephew and current WWE superstar Randy Orton. Barry relays to the group how it was one of Randy's first times in the ring. The wrestling speak soon unfolds in full force.

There's an old saying about wanting to be a fly on a wall in particular situations. For this afternoon, I was granted that privilege. I sat there amongst the boys as they gave their best Stu Hart imitations with deepest respect and fondness. Then the "biz" talk started. It began with a talk about gimmicks. A subject, I soon learned, that Barry is extremely passionate about.

Barry revealed that in his own Stampede days he was the Zodiac, a tribute to the character first portrayed by his father in the '70s in the Florida territory. The character originally came on the heels of the Zodiac Killer out in California. Barry would read all the astrology books he could get his hands on to make the character authentic. "The gimmick has to come from the heart," Barry declared.

Sir Oliver Humperdink nodded and piped in, "A gimmick won't work if you tell someone how to be."

After discussing some of their ideas for improvements and storyline suggestions for WWE, including Ox offering to portray Linda McMahon's gigolo (don't ask), it's onto relishing the days of yore. Days before the higher-flying moves, the riskier techniques of today.

Someone remarks that almost everyone is doing a power slam now.

Ox joins in the reminiscing by commenting, "I remember when Jake Roberts's DDT looked like it tore the guy's head off."

Then the gentle giant just shakes his own head.

The somber tone breaks when it is announced that lunch is ready. The forced normalcy continues and I giggle to myself thinking I just passed Sir Oliver Humperdink potato salad.

After eating, we assemble in the living room for the main event. It seems Barry has been using his creative energies outside of wrestling. He has been teaching acting classes for a few years now, enforcing a strict, organic and no-nonsense style. His current project is a film called *Tweak the Heat*.

He shows us a few clips of the film that has him involved in the directing, executive producing and even co-writing along with his friend Zoë Wild. He tells us it's about "a phenomenally intelligent New England girl" who is confronted by several obstacles in life, namely crystal meth — something I later learn Barry himself knows all too well.

The film features cameos from Sir Oliver Humperdink, Ox Baker and even Barry's brother, Bob Orton Jr.

Barry is beaming and his guests are impressed and proud of him.

At the end of the day Barry and I exchange contact information. He promises a personal interview. We hug and I thank him for his hospitality. I fly back home to Regina, Saskatchewan, wondering if I'll ever hear from him again.

* * *

On April 27, I get an email from Barry.

"I was a central figure in one of the largest and most infamous scandals in the history of professional wrestling and I am ready to break my decade-long silence, tell my side as it were. Through my eyes and with absolute responsibility and devoid of animosities. It is time."

His words were glaring at me.

Several emotions ran through my brain.

Panic.

Excitement.

Fear.

Panic.

And finally . . .

Intrigue.

I quietly cursed my grandmother's prediction.

Bob Leonard

Barry Orton.

BARRY O BREAKS HIS SILENCE

Part 2 of a SLAM! Wrestling epic

By JAMIE KREISER

Given that Barry and I reside in separate countries, our interview had to occur over the phone. Our first conversation lasted over eight hours. Barry wanted to be thorough. He wanted to do this right. A part of him wanted to be analyzed, the other wanted to be cleansed.

He starts off by saying, "I was always different."

An understatement that evokes irony, laughter and despite his protests, pity.

He tells me that wrestling didn't interest him. When Bob Orton Sr. is your father and Bob Orton Jr. is your brother, this has to be a problem. While he idolized his older brother, who is eight years his senior, and often imitated his interests, Barry's true loves were music, movies and performing.

"I can remember being five years old and hearing 'I Got You Babe' by Sonny and Cher," recalled the now 47-year-old. "I thought it was like the saddest and the most coolest thing I ever heard. It moved me to a degree. I just tapped into it."

His father was often on the road and soon so was his brother. Music was the perfect outlet for him.

"I spent a lot of time alone, so I had to keep myself entertained," he remembered. "I made believe a lot."

Then his tone softens.

"I always felt inferior and that I wasn't good enough," he confessed. "I didn't have a lot of self-esteem and I was pretty sure that I was incapable of doing anything right or well."

Those who know anything about Barry will have to shake their heads at his dark, youthful prophecy. Because for several years, it seemed Barry continued to believe in those thoughts.

And it almost destroyed him.

Barry continued pursuing music throughout his youth. He remembers his first band was called the Midget Monkees and that their playlist consisted of Monkees hits. But he wasn't one for bubblegum pop. He preferred the stylings and antics of Alice Cooper and Led Zeppelin. Barry started bands with names like Back Door, Hedonism Guru and Hedonism Twist.

He was also crazy about motion pictures, analyzing every facet about them, especially favorites like *Poltergeist* and *Tribes*. It's something he still does today. A lot of our conversation and ones that followed are spent discussing and dissecting films.

The people of Missouri, including his bandmates at the time, weren't ready for young Barry's impassioned ideas.

"No matter what I did, it wasn't cool, but I was so passionate about it," he remembered. "I was like, 'Here's what we are going to do, we're all going to wear gorilla outfits and I wrote this song.' They would conspire and kick me out of the band."

It's a common theme throughout his life and one Barry often repeats: he was always ahead of his time.

A nonconformist attitude didn't adhere with the world of academia either. According to Barry, he was asked to leave high school before he was able to finish. He kept pursuing music stardom, but when a potential record deal for his band fell through, the crestfallen 17-year-old moved to Texas to live with his sister.

While there, the two of them went down to visit their father and brother in Tampa, Florida. For the first time, Barry saw the family business in a new light.

"There was something about having that response from the crowd which is comparable to the kind of response you get from playing in a band," he divulged. "There was an energy. It was infectious. It was intoxicating." Barry expressed his interest to his father and began training in Tampa under the watchful eyes of his father, Bob Roop and Tully Blanchard, whom Barry bluntly refers to as a "dickhead."

Barry trained alongside Tito Santana and after four months he had his first match with Blanchard when Blanchard's opponent, Mike Hammer, failed to show up.

"I went out and they introduced me as Barry Orton," he recalled with a laugh. "Everyone booed. Tully was such a prick during the match, he ate me up. He gave me every bump known to man: suplexes, pile drivers, hip tosses, back drops, body slams . . . you name it. I was so nervous I couldn't see a foot in front of my face. The match went about five minutes. The ref helped me up and everyone gave me a standing ovation. They felt so bad for me."

Barry's intention was to wrestle for a couple of years, make some money and then pursue his real dreams.

But it didn't work out that way. Barry continued to wrestle in various territories throughout the late 1970s and early '80s; and when his brother ended up leaving Tampa and working for the then World Wrestling

Federation, now World Wrestling Entertainment, he got Barry booked there as well. Fans would mostly recognize him under the name Barry O, a decently built, six-foot-one quality piece of enhancement talent with a mullet.

During his career he even managed to hold a few tag titles including the International Championship Wrestling Southwestern tag team titles with his brother, Bob Jr., and the National Wrestling Alliance Americas tag team titles with Hector Guerrero. In singles competition, Barry was also the IWF heavyweight champion and the World Organized Wrestling (WOW) heavyweight champion, albeit for one day.

According to Barry, his first WWF match was a 15-minute bout with Bret "The Hitman" Hart. Barry recalls Chief Jay Strongbow exclaiming, "Goddamn, the kid can work," afterwards, but the words were lost on him.

"I was always struggling because I wanted to be a musician," he confessed. "I never saw myself as a professional wrestler. I was into the performance end, but I didn't live the lifestyle. I wasn't about being in the gym six hours a day. I was about being a rock star. Where I was gifted in the ring, I didn't do all the things you were supposed to do; and because of the fact that I didn't work out, I didn't have the looks or the body and I didn't get the opportunity, which hence frustrated me and made me continue to believe I was not worthy. I would turn to drugs and alcohol to escape and medicate."

Vices that ruined his reputation and severely altered his judgment and the course of his life.

Vices that led to straight to prison.

Barry believes that the year was 1986 and for the first time in our conversation he becomes uncomfortable, almost leery.

"I was in a car wreck and I had been drinking and someone died," he reveals carefully.

It's a topic that still troubles him. Barry, married to his first wife at the time, had been in the car with another woman. He ended up spending two weeks in the hospital. The other woman died.

According to Barry, the WWF wanted him to clear up all his legal troubles before he came back to work. In the meantime, Barry began working for Stampede Wrestling in Canada. In an homage to his father, Barry revamped the Zodiac character.

"The gimmick was kind of a cross between a vampire and the villain from *Seven*, even though *Seven* hadn't come out yet," described Barry. "Astrology had a part, witchcraft had a part, Satanism had a part. Although I never blatantly did anything Satanic, it was always innuendo. Instead of 'Hail Satan,' I would say, 'Luuuuuke!' because I thought Luke was a nickname for Lucifer. That's as far as it went. It worked really well and it was fun doing it."

Bob Johnson has been involved with Stampede Wrestling since 1979, and currently he works as a consultant. He's always been impressed with Barry's creativity and mind for the business.

"I always considered him to be the Quentin Tarantino of the wrestling business," declared Johnson in what has to be one of my favorite personal descriptions of Barry.

Johnson remembers Barry's time in Stampede with fondness, especially the way Barry raised attendance and put over then-heel Jason the Terrible (Karl Moffatt). "Barry came in and we teamed him with Jason the Terrible," explained Johnson. "Barry said, 'I have some really interesting concepts' and we were just totally blown away. He seemed to be totally creative and really understood what the word 'work' meant in the business. And connecting to the crowd, he really knew what he was doing. Jason the Terrible became a super heel, he was a bad guy already, but he became a super bad guy with the arrival of Barry Orton's Zodiac."

Johnson's favorite Zodiac moments were the infamous interviews Barry used to give.

"Barry would come in and the Zodiac character was dressed in a black mask and he has this synthesizer music and he had all kinds of graphics that had never been done on TV," he remarked. "He had this really interesting soundtrack that he did when he talked. The voice was just something really weird and different, very surreal. It was so advanced for the time and it really got over."

Johnson wasn't the only one impressed with Barry's rendition of the character. It seems Barry's own father was a fan.

"At the CAC, Bob Orton Sr. was talking to me and he said, 'Barry wasn't the original Zodiac, I was; but Barry was able to really do something with it,'" Johnson recalled.

Unfortunately, Barry's time in Stampede was cut short when it was time for him to face up to his legal responsibilities. On the advice of his lawyer, Barry decided to accept a plea, to avoid a trial and facing several years in prison.

At a mitigation hearing, he received the maximum mitigation sentence of 3.75 years.

"Had he stayed in Stampede, wrestling could have still gone full-blast here because he was bringing so many good ideas," offered Johnson. "Barry was so humble. I never saw him have false pride. And he got along with everybody. People liked him up here. To me, the dream team of the wrestling business would be some kind of combination of Bruce Hart and Barry Orton running WWE. The product would be 10 times as good as it is now."

Barry served the sentence in Arizona. He was an ideal inmate. He took the time to complete his GED and some college courses. The wildest story he has is getting a haircut from a death row inmate. He claims it's his first one. If you see the length of his hair now, he's probably telling the truth.

Barry made his first parole, being released 13 days short of two years. His wife was there for the hearing, but the marriage ended soon after. It had been too much for her. The couple's first daughter had been only a year old when Barry entered prison and their second daughter was born while he was incarcerated. She remarried and her new husband adopted the children. Barry says he wanted the best for them. He would end up marrying three more times after this, all of the relationships failing.

"What I had to deal with was all relative when you think about the victim's family," pondered Barry. "The victim is also everybody that you know. It was my wife. My kids. My mother. My father. My sister. The WWF. You feel like everything that everybody said about you all your life is true."

After his stay in prison, Barry went back to working with the WWF, albeit briefly. Times had changed.

He says he felt like his identity was slipping away.

Promoters wanted him to change his ring attire. They asked him to cut his hair.

"It wasn't even fun," Barry described. "It wasn't even enjoyable. It almost wasn't even tolerable. It just made me feel like . . . you know how it is when everyone gets together and you're having a party, hot dogs, a couple joints, beer. Everyone is having a good time, talking about what they are going to be doing with their lives, it's great. Famous scenario.

"Then there's a couple of assholes who have too many beers and they really shouldn't be there anyway. Before you know it there's all this drama. People that you love that are friends are talking about kicking each other's asses. But you are kind of stuck there because you rode with someone else. You just hate it and it breaks your heart and you just wish everyone would get along and have a good time. You're willing to sacrifice your tent and your shit if everyone would be cool. That's how it was."

It's almost heartbreaking how keen his mind is to the business. With one simple analogy, he has summed the feudal system of the wrestling business today.

I want to be neutral. I don't want to feel sorry for him especially when I know the story is going to keep shifting downwards. This is just the beginning of the downward spiral. . . .

BARRY O: SCANDAL, DRUGS, RECOVERY

Part 3 of a SLAM! Wrestling epic

By JAMIE KREISER

Mike Lano

Barry Orton with his father, Bob Orton Sr.

To ease his turmoil, Barry got lost in the old cliché of sex and drugs. But nothing worked. He was still lonely. He still felt unworthy.

Things got worse for Barry in 1992. Although no longer working for the WWF, he managed to become a key player in an infamous sex scandal involving the company.

Barry's involvement in the scandal happened years earlier in 1978. He was just 19 and wrestling with a faction of the NWA at the time. For a show in Amarillo, Barry ended up traveling with the booker, Terry Garvin.

Throughout the drive, Barry says that Garvin kept asking if he could perform oral sex on him. Barry politely kept turning him down.

"I didn't feel threatened or anything," Barry remembers. "Maybe a little uncomfortable because he was being so persistent because he did it every 30 miles and this was a six-hour trip. When we got there, it was over. I wasn't traumatized. He was so hurt or whatever that he didn't even ride back with me."

Barry didn't give the incident much thought. He says he never felt in any real danger of being harmed or sexually assaulted. Besides with his father and brother, no one would dare mess with him.

But eventually, Barry became very vocal about the incident and that decision still haunts his conscience to this day.

It seemed that the late Terry Garvin, who went on to work in the WWF front office (a job he got through friend Pat Patterson), had a penchant for trysts with young ring boys working for the company. According to the book, *Sex, Lies and Headlocks: The Real Story of Vince McMahon and World Wrestling Entertainment*, written by Shaun Assael and Mike Mooneyham, everything went awry when one ring boy, Tom Cole, refused Garvin's advances and was subsequently fired. Cole's allegations were reported by Jeff Savage in the *San Diego News Tribune* on March 11, 1992.

Once the story broke, the press was all over it. Barry says he was asked by a local radio show host if the allegations concerning Garvin could be true. Barry told him yes and then told him about his own experience with Garvin. Barry was then asked to appear on the radio show to tell his story.

"I didn't really give it a lot of thought at that point," recalled Barry. "A part of me was pissed because I thought there were boys being abused."

Barry thought he was doing the right thing. He talks about remembering another ring boy, not Cole, approaching him before the scandal broke, while Barry was still on the WWF roster. The boy confessed to Barry that Garvin was doing things that were making him uncomfortable. Barry says he gave the boy the best advice he could. Again at the time, he says it wasn't something that fazed him.

Once Barry's story was made public, the issue became even bigger.

According to Barry, he'd heard that Vince McMahon was calling him a liar so Barry went and had a lie detector test conducted. He claims he passed.

On March 13, 1992, Vince McMahon appeared on CNN's *Larry King Live* denying the allegations against Garvin. Barry called in to the show.

"My beef was, I'm not lying, I have proof," said Barry. "And I suppose from there it became personal and I got cloudy. I pushed it. From there, I was flying all over the country and doing TV shows. In retrospect it wasn't really cool. It's kind of like good intentions gone wrong. I will admit that I had a sour grape or two to grind. You wouldn't have got me to admit that then. I was also getting letters from mothers around the country saying that I was doing a great thing. I really ended up in the middle of a bunch of shit."

The pile escalated when Barry appeared on the popular talk show of the time, *Donahue*, with McMahon.

Unbeknownst to Barry the whole thing had been a sham. Everything he was trying to do had been for nothing.

Cole's brother had hired a lawyer who struck a settlement with Vince McMahon. According to Assael and Mooneyham, Cole was given a new job with the WWF and $150,000 in back pay.

But the kicker: Cole sat with Linda McMahon during the taping of the show and according to Barry if anyone not part of Team McMahon would have mentioned Cole's name, Cole was going to stand up and say that Vince was the only one who cared about him.

Mike Lano

Barry Orton carries his camera around a Cauliflower Alley Club reunion.

The incident still upsets Barry. As he tells it, Cole's brother was contacting him constantly before the talk show appearance and to have everything end up in a setup, to see it all culminate in some kid wanting a job, goes beyond angering him.

I ask Barry if he could do it all over again, would he tell anyone about the allegations?

"Absolutely not," he answers without any hesitation. "Not without knowing a hell of a lot more."

I ask him what he would like to change about the scandal.

"I'm a hell of a lot smarter now than I was then," he begins. "I was pretty gullible then because I thought people were like me and I took that for granted. I didn't realize when these people said, 'C'mon, man, you really gotta tell your story and do the right thing and come on my radio show,' they couldn't give a fuck about me or Tom Cole or anybody else. They were trying to further themselves. They smile, pat you on the back, try and give you that convicted look. They almost make you feel like if you don't do something you are responsible. If you don't come forward and say something, you are responsible for every molested child in the world. And then you want to do the right thing."

What he would also like to change about the scandal are the broken ties that resulted with Vince McMahon and Pat Patterson.

"It is important for me to express how sorry I am and how I was wrong," expressed Barry, who also intends to write apology letters to both McMahon and Patterson.

Orton says he never saw Patterson engage in any of the behavior that Garvin was accused of, but during the time of the scandal Barry remembers elaborating on incidents that occurred with Patterson (who, as it is widely known, is gay) — incidents where Patterson would tease Barry in a harmless way when he came out of the shower or on a road trip.

"When you are in the moment and people are asking you certain questions and in a certain way, I probably took it farther than it should have went," comments Barry. "I don't really remember. I know I never had anything against Pat Patterson."

In the aftermath of the scandal, Barry became an outcast in the wrestling world. To some people, he still is. Many were afraid to talk to him.

Several people in the business were told not to. Barry even started going by a different name, Barrymore Barlow.

Already relying on drugs like Valium to get through the scandal, Barry needed something stronger. Something bigger.

There seemed to be just one cure: methamphetamine.

For eight years, Barry used crystal meth.

"The way I got into it, I was bummed out at life, met this girl, went to stay with her one night and we got real freaky and I was a sexual tyrannosaurus, all day and all night," explains Barry bluntly. "Then a year later, I woke up and was like, 'Now I need this shit.' That was a long journey into the dark and the rancid and the putrid and the ridiculous and the dangerous and the deadly and the soulless."

Consumed by depression over the scandal, Barry describes his meth years as the point in his life when he fell off the world in grief.

"I laugh at everything," he remarks. "I didn't laugh for eight years."

He continues, "I swear to God that when you do meth for a long period of time, it actually replaces your soul in your body. It decides that it can't live in a place with all this shit, so your soul checks out and the souls of other dickheads jump in."

In 1999, Barry himself almost checked out.

For four days he kept a .44 Magnum in his mouth determined to kill himself. He says all he needed was one reason not to.

A friend called him on the phone and encouraged him to see a therapist. It was the reason he needed.

With the help of a therapist, whom Barry admits he still consults today, Barry beat his addictions and started experiencing life again.

Being able to have a second chance, having the ability to still be alive is not lost on Barry.

"If there was a yearbook in the wrestling business, I would have been voted most likely to OD," he comments seriously.

He also admits that whenever he hears of a wrestler who has passed away much too young, such as Curt Hennig, that he was expecting to be gone way before them.

One of the first things Barry did when he beat his addictions was focus on what he was truly supposed to be doing with his life all along. Focus on his real love: acting.

He went to New York and began studying classical theater. Barry tells me he spent a year in New York studying with Robert Patterson. We have promised each other total honesty from the beginning so I tell him I have no idea who that is.

He immediately takes offense at my lack of knowledge when it comes to theater. So he spends countless hours educating me on the subject he loves most and he also takes it upon himself to fill my email in-box immediately with information on the subject.

In his opinion my ignorance is disgraceful. By the end of yet another one of our conversations — by now there have been several — I am dizzy trying to retain everything he has taught me from the psychological perils of method acting to his beliefs that the basics are everything when it comes to acting to his theories on why Marilyn Monroe is no longer with us.

But I digress; it was during his time in New York that Barry met Zoë Wild. Wild was studying writing and, like Barry, she too had had a bout with crystal meth addiction. The two became friends and spent time taking in operas, Broadway plays and other cultural fascinations in New York.

During a bad case of writer's block, Wild called Barry up. She told him she had to write a 17-page story and that it had to be turned in by 7 a.m. the next day. She needed a last page. Barry came in and helped her out.

Barry left New York, but he never forgot the story he and Wild had written together. He called her up and asked her if she wanted to film it. Wild agreed. The story was expanded on and the script became *Tweak the Heat*. The film, a brutally honest and well-shot look at the world of crystal meth, is something that Barry has taken so seriously and is beyond proud of.

From the shocking facts given about the drug in the opening screen to the smart dialogue, Barry is hoping people will get the message.

"There's a hell of a story to be told," he says. "People should know, meth is not a glorious thing. And there is hope. People who see it realize how bad it is, but there is hope. If we save one person, we have done a hell of a thing."

Barry intends to release the film for the 2006–2007 festival season. Nancy P. Corbo plays the character Samantha in *Tweak the Heat*. She says she has known Barry for about six years. The two met in acting school.

Corbo confesses she wanted to be a part of the movie because of the script and the director, who just happens to be Barry. "He was very generous," she comments about the filming experience. "And what he did for me is one of the roles which is originally a guy, he said, 'You know what, I'm going to tweak this script, no pun intended, and Nancy, I think you would be absolutely incredible.' I told him that I would love to and he wrote a very interesting role for me."

Corbo knows Barry for his film endeavors. She admits she doesn't know him as a wrestler.

"All the years I've known him, he has seemed incredibly focused on his craft," she says. "That's why he and I really clicked. We were both really focused, really serious and willing to give up anything that we could for it."

For Corbo that meant leaving Las Vegas for Los Angeles to study acting. The initial move brought on some tough times financially for the actress. Her friend Barry noticed.

"When he saw the trouble I was going through, he obviously knew my parents didn't really understand, so he wrote this letter to them which was amazing," she explains. "It must have been a 20-page letter. He hand delivered it to them and he left. The letter just basically said, 'Your daughter is one of the best people I know. She is doing everything in her power, far more than anyone I've ever known, to do what she wants to do. She is busting her ass. She is the type of girl who could be doing anything with her life, but she chose acting.' The letter didn't preach or anything, but it was obvious I needed help."

Two days later, Corbo's father mailed her some money. She says she was very touched that Barry would take the time to help her without her knowledge.

She adds, "He is one of the few people in life that are full of passion, not just for his work, but in life. I've learned so much from him. There are times in my life where I am doing something and I will have this little voice going, 'What would Barry do?' The only thing I can say is that I hope he takes better care of himself and that he lives a lot longer than he thinks he will."

It is several months later and I still think back on my grandmother reading my cards before I ventured off to Vegas. Neither of us had any way of knowing that I would meet Barry and that he would decide I was the person worthy of sharing his story with.

I'm beyond grateful Barry trusted me. I can't even begin to tell you how many phone calls, emails, transcripts and Barry's creative writings (much appreciated by the way) that were pored over to write this story. I only hope I have done this man justice.

And only fittingly I will give him the last words, but they are not his final words. Because I truly believe we will be experiencing positive, life-altering things from this man. Brace yourselves.

"I would just like to be remembered as the guy who meant well and was plugged in. I have this ongoing thing that I was born 20 years too late and 10 years too early to really have made a difference with what I really wanted to do. The guy who would have done good if he would have had better timing; who in the end figured it out and did the best he could. I don't have much anymore, but fuck it, I'm happy. I believe in what I am doing and I believe it's good and even if I die tomorrow, these past six or seven years, I haven't had to regret waking up in the morning."

— Barry Orton

From the writer: "The other Orton" is a very personal piece for me. To prepare, I had several intense phone interviews with Barry Orton. I still remember vividly seeing the sunrise during one of our conversations.

It is also one of those pieces where fate played a huge role. Barry and I only met because he bumped into me with his camera. Writing Barry's story was also the only time in my journalism career that I was able to write about the sport I love and about a cause I'm very passionate about — educating the public about the dangers of crystal meth.

Barry and I continue to stay in touch and I consider him to be a most treasured friend.

* * *

GEORGE SCOTT: WWF'S BIGGEST BOOKER

By GREG OLIVER

From the writer: I met George Scott at the Cauliflower Alley Club reunion in 2001. We chatted a little, and he mentioned he was coming up to Hamilton later in the year, and that we should hook up. That winter, I had a lovely steak dinner with George, and his (non-wrestling) brother. Besides his in-ring career, which started in 1948, he was a key figure in wrestling history, so he had a lot to share.

Being a booker for any promotion is basically a thankless job. There's always somebody upset with the way they are being used, their payoff or their gimmick.

So George Scott was very pleased to be thanked repeatedly at a WWF house show in Tampa recently by WWF owner Vince McMahon Jr. for all his work in helping to establish the company into the powerhouse it is today.

Though he got out of the business in 1986, Scott was the booker for the WWF during all of its initial big hits — WrestleMania I and II, the first few Saturday Night's Main Event shows on NBC. His last big show with the WWF was the appropriately titled The Big Event at Toronto's Exhibition Stadium.

The irony of it, though, is that while Vince McMahon Jr. was plotting to

Courtesy George Scott

George Scott — always thinking, even in publicity photos.

take over territories across the continent, burning bridges with people his father had worked with for years, George Scott only came to work for the WWF because of his respect and friendship with Vince McMahon Sr.

Having left the Crocketts's Mid-Atlantic territory in 1982, Scott helped Jim Barnett a little with his promotion and considered buying the rights to the Oklahoma territory.

One day in 1983, he got a call from Vince McMahon Sr., with whom he used to trade talent when he ran the Carolinas. McMahon Sr. was sick in Florida, and told Scott that his son Vince Jr. needed help. "I said I'd be glad to help him," recalled Scott.

His first stop was in Atlanta, where he was to oversee the deal to replace Georgia Championship Wrestling on TBS. That deal fell apart, in part because of viewer complaints. "I don't know what the true story was," Scott said. "But I was sitting there doing nothing."

One thing led to another, and Scott starting doing the booking out of Miami for a few towns, which quickly grew into booking for the whole company.

From today's perspective of massive gates (and ticket prices), huge TV production and inflated wrestler salaries, it's hard to understand what the WWF went through. The growth was phenomenal, as was the workload.

Besides deciding who won and who lost (with a noted exception in Hulk Hogan), Scott also had to figure out what talent to bring in, negotiate salaries and plan what went into the magazines too. Everything was booked six weeks ahead. "I was in charge of everything up there."

In his typical, matter-of-fact style, Scott described how the WWF was suddenly grossing $3 million to $4 million on weekends in 1984–1985. "Things just started popping."

The money started changing the wrestlers and drugs ran rampant. "The only trouble was when I was in New York. That's when the drugs started," Scott explained. "I guess what happened was these drug dealers are coming and found out where they're staying, and said, 'Hey, try this.' They'd give it to them, and for a couple of weeks they'd be giving it all to them, then all of a sudden these guys had $500-a-day habits.

"So finally we had to go on a drug program up there, where we started drug testing."

The drug problems made planning programs difficult. "It was terrible. Doing the booking, and there'd be four to five guys who wouldn't show up for matches. It was all through drugs. We finally got it under control but it was a son of a gun doing it.

"It got to the point where we did the drug testing, and if they failed they got suspended for six weeks. When they came back, the deal was if they got caught again, they were finished. Most of them cleaned up, but a few of them didn't."

Scott's relationship with then-WWF champ Hulk Hogan deteriorated after they had a big argument backstage in Madison Square Garden about some unsavory characters hanging around. That led to Hogan going above Scott. "Hogan wasn't mine . . . I had no control over him."

George "The Animal" Steele was around the WWF in those early days, and recalled the problems between Scott and Hogan. "George Scott was a good man for the times. We were in uncharted waters and the business was changing fast. As all bookers, George had some favorites and tried to push them a little too fast. In the WWF it takes time to become a major player. That plus the Hulk had some different people in mind. Eventually those two forces came head-to-head. The Hulk had the power and there was not room for both."

Ego ran rampant at the first WrestleMania too, but not with everyone. Scott said that Cyndi Lauper was "a jewel" and remembers a drunk Billy Martin at a post-WrestleMania party claiming that he could beat up Hogan.

He did some of the initial negotiations with Mr. T, and went to Atlanta to talk to him about appearing. Things didn't go well. "What a big shot. I told him where to get off!" Eventually, it was all smoothed over.

There are two things that stand out about Mr. T's participation for Scott. For one, Mr. T ran up $22,000 in expenses during the WrestleMania I week. The other thing happened during the main event of Hogan and Mr. T against Roddy Piper and Paul Orndorff. At one point, Scott ran to ringside and pulled guest official Muhammad Ali out of the ring because Ali was to be the outside-the-ring ref, but it's off-camera.

Scott has nothing but praise for Vince McMahon Jr. "The guy's a genius," Scott said, adding that he's also a workaholic.

That workload eventually got to Scott, but not before some other triumphs.

For the initial *Saturday Night's Main Event*, he recalled working three days straight with Dick Ebersol from NBC. "Ebersol wanted to do all this goofy stuff," Scott said. "He wanted to make it like *Saturday Night Live*."

Coming from a more traditional wrestling background, Scott was opposed to the cartoony stuff. "They did a lot of stuff they didn't tell me they were doing!"

Of course, the WWF had already been doing some cartoony things on the *Tuesday Night Titans* program.

"Early on George Scott pulled me aside and told me that Vince had a tendency to go too far on the *Tuesday Night Titans* show," Steele explained. "Scott told me that Vince had high respect for me and that if things started to get too far out to just call Vince aside and tell him.

"Butcher Vachon's wedding was the first total cartoon. I called Vince aside and asked him if he was going to use that tape on the USA show. I told him if he did that he might kill wrestling. Vince said that he would find out."

The wedding was shown on TV three weeks in a row. "That is when wrestling went to the top of the charts. I knew right then that wrestling had changed so I changed," Steele said. "Vince has always been the boss but George Scott was respected as the front man. Wrestling as it was went stage left after George Scott left."

"George Scott was not the right personality, in my opinion, for that job because he was too nice of a guy. He found it very hard playing people against each other," said wrestling journalist Bill Apter. "He couldn't deal with people who said 'No.'"

Like all bookers, Apter said there were wrestlers that hated him. "A lot of guys hate a booker when they're not getting the push they think they should get. They consider it personal, but it's not."

Eventually, it wasn't the silliness that made Scott quit the WWF; it was the workload. "If I keep this up, I'm going to die," Scott recalled thinking.

After leaving the WWF in the summer of 1986, Scott went to World Class and Fritz von Erich but decided he couldn't work there. A trip to North Carolina followed, but things didn't pan out. He settled in Florida, golfs and swims quite a bit, and rents condos out.

* * *

PREACHING NOW A PART OF DIBIASE

By CHRIS SOKOL

Ted DiBiase preaches to the converted at the George Tragos/Lou Thesz Hall of Fame induction ceremony in 2007, where he received the Frank Gotch Award for contributions to society.

(vertical caption on left) Greg Oliver

Ted DiBiase may be known as "The Million Dollar Man," but to a select group he is seen as much more. He is more than a grappling great, more than another villain of the squared circle. He is a man with a message — and he wants the world to hear it.

Back in 1993, DiBiase went through a life-changing experience, where he gave his heart to the Lord and became part of a growing group of born-again Christians. The experience was so impactful that DiBiase began preaching what he was taught to others who were in the same situation he was in.

The change didn't take effect immediately DiBiase admitted, but over time he became more and more accustomed to his new lifestyle. His habits had changed, his marriage that was nearly destroyed was saved and his life was rejuvenated.

It was natural that when Summerfest 2005 rolled around a few weeks back, "The Million Dollar Man" Ted DiBiase would be on hand to share his story in front of a capacity crowd in Fernwood, New York. People from all different backgrounds and walks of life united to listen to an inspiring story, a story of a man who had it all, lost it and gained it all back.

The night started off with a parody of *The Tonight Show* with DiBiase as the main guest. DiBiase had been preaching all weekend and was ready to take a new approach. DiBiase sat down and accepted questions from fans, including ones about his "Million Dollar attire."

When the question was posed on how much the Million Dollar belt actually cost, DiBiase responded, "Forty thousand dollars. There were only three real diamonds on the belt in the back where nobody could see them," DiBiase said. "I asked them [WWF officials] why, and they told me, 'So if anyone asks if the diamonds are real, you can say "yes" and you wouldn't be lying.'"

DiBiase accepted more questions and then headed to the backstage area, where he chatted with SLAM! Wrestling. When asked what his favorite part of the weekend was, DiBiase laughingly said, "I kind of liked *The Tonight Show*."

DiBiase was genuinely excited to be able to interact with a large crowd and help them get through any difficulties that they had in life.

Once the other portions of the show were completed, DiBiase returned to the stage to tell a few more stories. DiBiase talked of a time where he and Greg "The Hammer" Valentine went and spoke to a group. There were two deaf children in attendance and they all got together and performed a miracle and were ecstatic when the girls began reacting to various sounds. It was an experience DiBiase summed up by saying, "I wouldn't have believed it had I not seen it."

DiBiase spoke of his father's death in the ring, and how his actions that nearly cost him his marriage. DiBiase was once the center of attention in the wrestling industry and unfortunately with all the fame and glory he enjoyed, also came a lot of pressure. DiBiase collapsed and let his demons get the best of him. He was drowning in a pool of his own deceit.

Once he found the errors in his ways, he once again rose to the top. Earlier this year, DiBiase was offered a contract to be a WWE road agent. DiBiase accepted and was welcomed back with open arms. The thing that shocked WWE officials the most was his change in character. DiBiase was no longer the same person — he was a man with a mission in life, a mission to help, not hurt. DiBiase had become a man that other agents could model themselves after.

Once the storytelling was done, DiBiase invited fans to accept the Lord like he had in 1993. DiBiase then said a prayer and walked over to a nearby tent to sign autographs for any and all fans who approached him. If anything at all, DiBiase left the crowd of fans thinking. He may have portrayed a dastardly demon inside the squared circle, but outside the ring, he is now a caring human being with a heart of gold and a message so powerful that people flock from everywhere to hear it.

* * *

THE WOMAN BEHIND MONSTER RIPPER AND BERTHA FAYE

By STEPHEN LAROCHE

One of the most fearsome women to ever enter a wrestling ring, Rhonda Sing, has led a long and fascinating career few North American wrestling fans are aware of.

While growing up in Calgary, Sing knew she wanted to be a wrestler from an early age and attended numerous Stampede Wrestling cards as a child.

"Stampede Wrestling was a big influence because you had it on TV Saturday mornings," she told SLAM! Wrestling. "My mom used to go and took us if we had been good through the week. She always had four ring-side tickets for about 20 years. When I was five, I wanted to be a wrestler. I was in kindergarten beating up the other kids. Everyone who knows me in my neighborhood remembers me telling them I was going to be a wrestler. It's like a lot of the wrestlers in the business now — they knew it when they were kids."

As a teenager, Sing approached members of the Hart family asking to be trained. Despite being rejected, she still dreamed of becoming a professional wrestler. A trip to Hawaii in 1978 changed her life forever as she saw Japanese women's wrestling on television.

"I was actually in Hawaii on vacation and zapping through the channels, I stumbled on Japanese women's wrestling. They were hitting each other with chairs and everything! It was an all-girl company, and I thought it was the coolest thing. It sparked my interest. This was definitely what I wanted to do," said Sing.

A friend gave 17-year-old Sing a wrestling magazine that contained contact information for Mildred Burke's training facility in Encino, California. She wrote the women's wrestling legend and sent along a biography and photo. After receiving a reply from Burke, she made a decision that changed her life.

"I cleaned out my bank account and told my parents this is what I wanted to do," she recalled. "I said to my parents, 'Give me three months, let me see if I can do this.'"

After a few weeks of training with Burke, Sing was scouted by All Japan who wanted to bring her in despite her inexperience.

"Some of the Japanese girls came to L.A. to train and scout some talent. Burke was the only U.S. trainer having women go over to Japan at the time. They were saying, 'Hey! A fat girl! We like her,'" she laughed. "That was in November, and by January I was main-eventing in Japan. I could tie my boots and do a back drop. I was pretty limited."

Her first match in Japan was with partner Mami Komeni against Beauty Pair (Jackie Sato and Maki Ueda) on January 4, 1979. She recalled it fondly, but knew how significant the win was.

"It was my first match, and I won. The Japanese girls resented it because they never had to lose. If they lost, they lost to each other. They never lost to a foreigner."

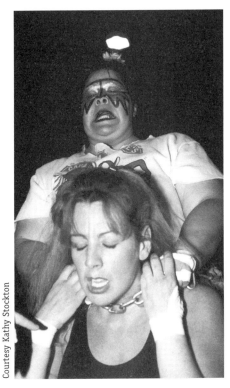

Rhonda Sing chokes KC Houston.

A combination of youth and inexperience made life in Japan somewhat difficult for Sing during her first few months there.

"They literally kicked the shit out of me," she said. "I was the first foreigner they had to lose to, and they didn't take it kindly. You were working seven, eight times a week. You had to roll out of bed and bit-by-bit get up because you were just dead."

Many of the established Japanese wrestlers were unwilling to share their experience with the young Canadian wrestler. It was not until she ran into a touring Dynamite Kid that she was able to gain a greater grasp of how to deal with her fellow wrestlers.

"It was just a matter of defending yourself and saying, 'I'm not going to take this anymore!' Once you got respect, it became very easy. They always respected you and feared you."

Sing's first run in All Japan peaked when she won their women's world title from Jackie Sato on July 31, 1979 — a little over six months after her professional debut. After losing the title to Sato six weeks later, she regained it on March 15, 1980 via countout after outside interference from the Black Pair (Mami Kumao and Yumi Ikeshita). The title was vacated in August 1980 after another epic battle with Sato.

A brief return to Calgary in the early 1980s allowed Sing the chance to finally perform in front of her hometown crowd.

"I didn't want to wrestle there until I knew I was going to be good enough," she said. "This is your hometown crowd and people you grew up with. The first time I came through, I was with a Mexican girl [Rita Moreno] that was in Japan as well. We were only going to do two weeks. Stu [Hart] liked us so much, he kept us for four. He wanted us longer, but we had to go back to Mexico."

After another stint in Japan, Sing returned to Stampede on a regular basis in late 1987 and was named their women's champion as she had defeated Wendi Richter before coming back to the territory. She held the title until September 22, 1988, losing to Chigusa Nagayo.

The camaraderie of Stampede appealed to Sing at the time, and she does not see the same level of it in today's locker rooms.

"This was one of the best territories anyone could work in," she said. "The people you met there are still your friends. Everyone had a good time. You didn't have the problems you have in the dressing room now. There was never anything that ever escalated into a major problem."

Over the next few years, Sing would once again travel throughout the world and wrestle for a number of promotions, holding several titles. She feels lucky to have been able to see many parts of the world.

"In this business you're really fortunate because it allows you to see a lot of the world you would never see," she said.

In 1995, Sing was contacted by the WWF to add depth to their fledgling women's division. However, she was repackaged as Harvey Whippleman's trailer park–dwelling girlfriend Bertha Faye. Sadly, this is how many North American fans remember her.

"It was the best and worst of times. Because I started in Japan, I had a reverse philosophy than those who start in the States, and their dream is to wrestle in Japan. Mine was to wrestle in Madison Square Garden," said Sing.

Strangely enough, Sing did have an opportunity several years before to fulfill her dream, but chose to wait.

"I had that opportunity years ago when they had Wendi Richter," she said. "Moolah called me up and said she wanted me to do a couple of pay-per-views with Wendi. The thing was, Moolah wanted half my money. Why would you take my money when you're doing nothing? I didn't even know her! You wanted to go, but you knew it was going to be a guaranteed loss."

The original plan was to be part of an angle with Bull Nakano, with whom she had many epic battles in Japan, which was meant to develop fan interest in the women's division.

"We had big heat in Japan, so this is what they wanted to do," she recalled. "Madusa was going away, and she was getting new boobs and a new nose. For three months, it was going to be Nakano and I. She was going to drop the belt to me, Madusa was going to come back after a while, we'd add a few more girls and make it a legitimate women's division. Eventually, Madusa and I would battle for the belt and it was undecided from there. I had a two-year contract, so we were going to space it out over that time."

But that isn't how it happened. Nakano was found in possession of cocaine, which prompted a change of plans. She made her WWF debut on an episode of *Monday Night Raw* participating in a sneak attack, Madusa making it appear as if they had broken her nose. Sing was not pleased with the development.

"The whole storyline went down the toilet," she said. "The only way we could save it was if we were to hurt Madusa because she was still scheduled for surgery. We had to get rid of Nakano and get me in at the same time."

Sing was also hesitant to work with Madusa after hearing numerous rumors about how she behaved behind the scenes and focused on Madison Square Garden.

"I sort of saw through her before I even worked with her," she said. "I hit Madison Square Garden in September 1995 and I didn't care after that. I went in a champion and left as champion. It was one of my better matches with her. None of the others were anything you'd write home about compared to what you could do."

During her stint with the WWF, Sing also developed a great friendship with the late Owen Hart.

"I was working in Calgary when he and [Chris] Benoit started," she recalled. "Owen really saved me when I was with the WWF. I rode with the Canadian guys, so I traveled with him a lot when I was on the shows. There's no one you'll ever be able to replace Owen with."

Despite the ridiculous antics of Whippleman and Faye, which included wearing garish outfits and hideous makeup, she did notice how his character was essentially an extension of his own personality.

"He actually did live in a trailer park. He was that guy, that's who he is. He's never bought a roll of toilet paper in his life. He'd always take it from a hotel or a truck stop."

Sing also found it incredibly difficult to adopt a new persona after spending almost all of her career as Monster Ripper.

"They put me in that character, you're not doing something you want to do. I was Monster Ripper for 15 years. It was hard to walk away from that personality."

With her character creatively restricted, Sing was also limited to what moves she could perform in the ring. She was not allowed to use an overhead press or a powerbomb as other WWF stars were utilizing them at the time.

"I couldn't do these moves because certain guys were doing it," she said. "You went in every night with one arm tied behind your back because someone else laid claim to it. I was doing these moves on a daily basis for 15 years, and now I couldn't do it. No one wanted you to look better than they did. I did power moves — that's who I was. It sort of stripped my identity. You're going to the ring skipping and blowing kisses, looking goofy. You just went to the bank and cashed your check. You felt like you were pimping yourself out. You were like a prostitute for Vince. The guys were doing it too, so you know what people will do for money."

Fan interest in women's wrestling sunk once again as the year closed, even with the addition of Japanese star Aja Kong. Sing believes there are several reasons why the women's division ultimately failed.

"There was no real storyline," she said. "There was nothing really going on. We were just there. In the background, you'd have Madusa calling Vince all the time asking why we weren't on TV. When you only have two girls, you can only do so much. She had very limited skills, she did basically the same thing all the time. I think she sort of sabotaged everything."

After a year as Bertha Faye, Sing had the WWF release her from her contract. She briefly returned to Japan, but found it difficult to adjust to a new system without guaranteed payouts.

In late 1999, she made a brief return with World Championship Wrestling and appeared on several telecasts to generate some interest in a women's division. While her stay was brief, Sing appeared to enjoy her time with the promotion.

"I like them," she said. "They're an up-front organization. When I called them, they knew what they wanted me to do. There's no secret agenda."

Women's wrestling had changed greatly in the time since Sing was last with a major North American promotion, and she was well aware of the limitations her opponents had.

"It's a different era. None of them can last as long. You used to be able to wrestle 55 minutes. These girls can't wrestle more than 10. Now they only know five holds, and that's all they have," she remarked.

However, Sing does believe it is possible for a woman to become an elite competitor if they train with organizations that allow them to develop properly.

"They all have the potential to do more. If you send any of the girls working now to Japan, they'll come back the best wrestler ever turned out. They have basic body skills, they just need the ring sense."

Despite the fact she has not wrestled in several months, Sing would not hesitate to return to another major promotion as long as she was treated properly.

"Oh yeah, you'd work for anybody," she said. "I've got no loyalty. It's whoever is going to pay me. It's always been my philosophy. As long as you pay me and treat me fairly, I'll work for you."

From the writer: When Greg Oliver asked me to interview Rhonda Sing, I was a bit apprehensive as I knew little of her work at that time outside of the Bertha Faye gimmick. After doing some research and realizing how significant her work as Monster Ripper was, I couldn't wait to speak with her. The interview was done over the phone and it proved to be one of the most insightful and interesting conversations I ever had with a wrestler. I thought about calling her again a couple of days before she died and never got around to it. That's one of my greatest regrets as a journalist and also in my personal life.

SLAM! Wrestling has captured a lot on film over the years, and here's a little sampling. Alas, many of the original photos taken with the old Apple QuickTake just didn't stand the test of time. . . .

It's a six-woman tie-up with MsChif, Cheerleader Melissa, Allison Danger, Daizee Haze, Lacey and Rain at a Ring of Honor show on Friday, March 31, 2006, in Chicago Ridge, Illinois. [Mike Mastrandrea]

Traci Brooks heads way north — to Nunavut for a Blood, Sweat & Ears tour. [Bob Kapur]

Being a part of the Sun Media chain has meant access to some of Canada's top photographers — and a little cheesecake/beefcake!

The Rock slams the Big Show and the World Champion Triple H together in March 2000 at SkyDome in Toronto.
[Ernest Doroszuk, Sun Media Corp.]

Trish Stratus and Val Venis arrive at the MuchMusic Video Awards in 2000 at SkyDome in Toronto.
[Mike Cassese, Sun Media Corp.]

"Mr. Ass" Billy Gunn is swung around at the end of a chain by "Road Dogg" Jesse James during a July 1999 dog collar match at SkyDome in Toronto. [Greig Reekie, Sun Media Corp.]

Jeff Hardy flies over Bubba Ray Dudley in March 2000 at SkyDome in Toronto. [Ernest Doroszuk, Sun Media Corp.]

Sunshine Girls and Boys

Edge shows off his clean underwear in a November 1998 Sunshine Boy shoot. [Debbie Holloway, *Toronto Sun*]

Proving anything Edge can do, he can too, Christian poses in April 1999. [Debbie Holloway, *Toronto Sun*]

Sable poses for *The Sun* in February 1999. [Craig Robertson, *Toronto Sun*]

Kelly Kelly as a Sunshine Girl in December 2008.
[Mark O'Neill, *Toronto Sun*]

The following two pages spotlight the favorite photos of Mike Mastrandrea, SLAM! Wrestling's staff photographer.

Mickie James signs an unique autograph at Toronto's Union Station on March 20, 2007, to promote WrestleMania 23. [Mike Mastrandrea]

Ultimo Dragon and his son at the WrestleFanFest show in San Francisco in October 2007.
[Mike Mastrandrea]

Kurt Angle at TNA's 2006
Bound for Glory pay-per-view
in Plymouth, Michigan.
[Mike Mastrandrea]

"Bloodthirsty" Bob Kapur interviews a bloody CZW owner John Zandig after a show.
[Mike Mastrandrea]

SLAM! Wrestling has sponsored three Titans in Toronto dinners to raise money for the Professional Wrestling Hall of Fame (www.pwhf.org). Here are some photos from the events.

Ron Doner, Rachael Dubois, "Rotten" Reggie Love and Duncan McTavish at Titans in Toronto II. [Andrea Kellaway]

Gino Brito and Paul Leduc threaten promoter Al Campbell at Titans in Toronto III. [Andrea Kellaway]

"The Wolfman" Willie Farkus takes a spin with Chris Masters at Titans in Toronto III. [Andrea Kellaway]

Editorial cartoonist Annette Balesteri shares two of her favorite creations.

"SUPERSTAR" BILLY GRAHAM: RING LEGEND

By CHRIS SCHRAMM

From the writer: "Superstar" Billy Graham's name speaks for itself, but he seemed almost as honored to speak to me as I was to speak to him. I felt like I gained a friend because we spoke for hours for three days in a row. Before he reconciled with WWE, you could feel he make some mistakes in his life and wanted to mend them. He spoke to me like a friend and not a reporter. He asked me questions, told me stories, asked for my opinion. I consider this my favorite piece ever in my career. I hope it speaks for itself.

He won the title, and he lost the title in the same manner: with his leg on the ropes. Billy Graham's WWF (then the WWWF) World heavyweight title reign might have started and ended in controversial manner, but his reign and effect in wrestling is still relevant today.

Scott Steiner, Hulk Hogan and even Minnesota Governor Jesse Ventura have mentioned Billy Graham, nicknamed Superstar, as a major influence on their wrestling personae.

He is not an evangelist, but he chose his name based on the famed religious television personality, Billy Graham.

He recently has spoken out against steroid use in sport based on his own experiences. Numerous surgeries, two artificial hips, a fused ankle and living his life in constant pain has brought him into a new knowledge of the drug he used to use to get ahead, to a drug that ultimately led him to money, fame and the world title.

Beginnings

Billy Graham, who grew up Wayne Coleman in Arizona, was not an amateur wrestler. He was a track and field star in high school and at one point was training for the 1968 Olympic Summer Games in Mexico City. He threw shotput and discus, and developed his awesome physique early in his life.

Out of high school, he had no real goals. He moved to Los Angeles, but he could never find a steady job.

"I worked as a bouncer and other odd jobs," Graham recalled for SLAM! Wrestling.

He was never a real fan of wrestling. He watched it back in the 1950s, but he never thought of getting involved in the sport.

He remembered Sky High Lee when he was growing up. Lee used to take darts to his back on television, "long before Mick Foley," Graham said.

He found out after he met his wife, Valerie, in 1976 that Lee was her second cousin.

His first connection to wrestling came, though, while he was working in

Superstar Graham has Harley Race under control.

California during late 1969. Bob Lueck, who played for the Calgary Stampeders of the Canadian Football League, asked Graham to come with him back to Calgary and give wrestling a try.

Graham had no idea who he was getting involved with when Stu Hart invited him to train in the infamous Dungeon.

"He had no fat and looked like he was holding regulation footballs in his arms," Stu Hart recalled in an interview with SLAM! Wrestling. "He was the most impressive specimen I've seen in my life."

"I felt this was for me," Graham recalled about his first days there.

Becoming the Superstar

His first gimmick was as a tough man. Coming from a weightlifting background, Graham was thrown in to challenge fans in an arm-wrestling match. Anyone who could beat Graham would win $1,000.

Graham was honored to have started with Hart, whom Graham still stays in contact with.

"I saw the bloodstains on the walls and the mats when I walked in," Graham said about his first look at the Dungeon.

Hart knew Graham had a future. "I've wrestled with a lot of strong fellows and never seen a fellow that muscular and that strong. I was impressed with his strength," Hart recalled of his brush with the future Superstar. "He was officially the strongest man in the world at the time. He could bench press 650 pounds and could lie on a bench and [lift] 350 pounds over his head. That was almost unheard of, no question about it."

When it was time for Graham to head into the ring for action, he started under his real name. It was in the summer of 1970 though that his moniker would change when he met a wrestler named Dr. Jerry Graham.

Graham, who was an established wrestler across the world, asked Coleman to become "a brother." Coleman then took the name Billy Graham based off Jerry Graham's last name and the famous evangelist Billy Graham.

The nickname Superstar came in 1972 based from the rock opera that was huge at the time, *Jesus Christ Superstar*.

Early Career

Fans watch Pat Patterson every week on WWF *Raw*, but too few know Patterson's rich wrestling history that dates back to the 1960s. Graham and Patterson teamed to defeat Ray Stevens and Peter Maivia (the Rock's grandfather) for the NWA tag team titles in July 1971 in San Francisco.

That match was the first turning point in Graham's career.

"Patterson was my mentor," Graham said about his tag team partner.

Graham learned a lot during his early days from the in-ring knowledge of stars such as Patterson, Stevens and eventually the Rock's father, Rocky Johnson.

Verne Gagne saw the power and ability of Graham and decided to bring the Superstar to work for the AWA out of Minneapolis.

"I hated working against Verne Gagne because of his old-school style of wrestling, and I was not a wrestler," Graham said about his stay with the AWA. "I was more methodical. It was physically difficult."

Graham did not complain about the crowds and money that came with his stay, but the coldness of the North really got to the Arizona native. He left the AWA for one reason — the cold.

Gagne expressed his displeasure and amazement in Graham's decision to leave. The choice was a wise one because an even bigger call came.

The WWWF

Vince McMahon Sr. called Graham up in 1975, and Graham was anxious to work for the WWWF. He was quickly accepted by the fans and by the wrestlers.

Bruno Sammartino had ruled the WWWF for 15 years, and McMahon Sr. was looking for a man to give him a run for his money. Graham was his choice.

"It was the easiest match I could have," Graham said about his legendary bouts with Sammartino. The champion's strength and similar style really helped Graham–Sammartino matches go very smoothly.

On March 30, 1977, McMahon Sr. had made the decision to give Graham the world title from Sammartino. The Baltimore crowd was split on who their favorite was, and a lot of confusion came when Graham used the ropes to pin Sammartino.

It was over. Billy Graham had become the WWWF world champion. But it was the interesting way in which the crowd reacted that made Graham an innovator. Graham had become the first major "tweener" for the WWWF, and his model was the same way in which stars like Steve Austin and Degeneration X were split. No matter how evil, how much of a rule breaker he was, the crowds were booing and cheering him at the same time.

Graham remembered getting motivation to carry this split fan reaction to a new gimmick. He wanted to have a feud with Ivan Koloff, the WWWF's biggest heel wrestler, and Graham believed that would get him over greatly with the fans. He was hoping for a long run as champion.

McMahon Sr. had a different idea though. At the same time, a young amateur wrestler was being pushed by the name of Bob Backlund. McMahon Sr. planned two years ahead to eventually give the title to Backlund.

Graham knew the day would come 10 months later to lose the title, but he had a very successful run. He sold out 19 of 20 New York City's Madison Square Garden main events he headlined, a percentage not met by any other wrestler in WWWF or WWF history.

Graham, along with many other wrestlers, was not sure if giving the title to Backlund so soon was the right decision. McMahon Sr. made what some say was a mistake. He had told Backlund and others of the decision to give Backlund the title. He could not back out.

When Graham did lose the title to Backlund eventually in early 1978, he was very discouraged with the sport. He had a bloody feud with Dusty Rhodes, but was gone soon afterwards.

"I got burnt out. I went back to Phoenix and I became a recluse," Graham said.

His absence started rumors in the *Philadelphia Enquirer* that he had passed away. Graham admitted that Rhodes started that rumor as a joke.

Graham rejoined the renamed WWF in 1982 with a new look. He had a shaved head and martial arts pants. He immediately was thrown into a feud with Backlund, but the world title that Backlund held was never to come back to him.

"I shouldn't have used that [martial arts] gimmick," Graham said.

The Graham name helped sell out arenas still, but Graham was sitting on a gimmick that was not working for him.

His personal problems with his life and steroids were the main reason for the absence of another world title reign.

Graham moved to Florida to work for Kevin Sullivan, and then moved on to work for the NWA and the Crocketts.

Onetime rival Rhodes was the booker for the NWA at the time, and he invited Graham to work for them for a while. Graham worked huge stadium shows with the group, but he never got the push he felt he deserved.

It was when he was with the NWA that he dumped the martial arts gimmicks, bleached his beard, put on the tie-dye and felt pain.

The End of a Career

"I was starting to have trouble with my hip in 1985," Graham said.

He called Vince McMahon Jr., who had taken over as the head of the WWF during Graham's absence, and offered his abilities for the WWF once again. McMahon liked the idea, and Graham was scheduled for his first match back with the WWF in Baltimore.

"I walked into the building limping," Graham said about his match back. McMahon Jr. saw this, and questioned if Graham was even in shape to wrestle. Graham said he was fine, and took some cortisone shots to get through the match.

The medicine wore off, and Graham knew it was not just a pulled muscle that was giving him pain. His hip socket was in amazing pain, forcing Graham to undergo a $30,000 operation for the hip injury. The WWF used the real surgery, which included an artificial, titanium hip placed in Graham's leg, and recovery in an angle.

Graham wanted back in the ring, mainly for the money.

"It was a big mistake," Graham admits, blaming steroids. "Steroids made you both psychologically and emotionally intense. They make you feel you can never be hurt."

Managing Don Muraco, commentating and wrestling a few matches was all that was left in wrestling for Graham.

His last match was with Butch Reed in Madison Square Garden. The sellout crowd saw a legend wrestle a bloody cage match.

Steroids

Vince McMahon Jr. promised Billy Graham that there was always a job for him with the WWF. Graham's hip surgery and 1990 ankle-fusing procedure forced Graham off the road, and it also forced Graham out of his job with the WWF.

"I became bitter at that point, and after the ankle surgery," Graham said. "I began to tell the world about the dangers of steroids, the pain, suffering I was having because of use and talking about the people who use it."

Graham started a smear campaign against the WWF. He ridiculed McMahon for allowing Dr. George T. Zahorian to sell steroids to wrestlers and would later ridicule Hulk Hogan following Hogan's infamous *Arsenio Hall Show* appearance where Hogan dismissed allegations he took steroids (a statement that Hogan would contradict in a 1994 trial).

"I was such in a state of rage," Graham said after watching Hogan's appearance. "I said, 'He is lying.'"

Steroids were part of Graham's life for over two decades. It was around 1965 that Graham was first introduced to steroids. Though the drugs were legal at the time, the dangers were not very well known. Graham knew of some dangers, but not all of the future complications were portrayed to him.

He followed with some unsuccessful lawsuits with steroids distributors and the WWF that he later called mistakes.

He has not talked to McMahon or Hogan since his campaign against them almost 10 years ago. He wrote them both letters, and he hopes his upcoming autobiography will help.

Future

"Superstar" Billy Graham made an incredible impression on the wrestling world.

"I was a prototype for Hulk and Jesse Ventura and even today Scott Steiner."

His autobiography is set to be released in November or December of this year. He is currently working on his beginnings with Pat Patterson and the NWA during 1971.

He hopes to tell it like it is. A pen and paper is all he needs. Valerie, his wife, types up the wording for the editors at the publishing company. He really enjoyed Mick Foley and Dynamite Kid's autobiographies and hopes to be as full and thorough with his book.

The internet is a great source for publicity, especially with a person trying to sell his new book. Graham was interested in creating a web page to help with the promotion of his book when he discovered a fan page. Steve Slagle's fan page is now the official website for Graham because he was so amazed by the thoroughness and look of the page.

The Official "Superstar" Billy Graham Home Page (www.SuperstarBilly

Graham.com) has everything you can possibly know about the legendary wrestler. Graham even puts his own pictures, notes, interviews (including an upcoming Terry Funk interview) and commentating (his take on Scott Steiner was recently uploaded).

Graham has had numerous surgeries in the last few years to the point where there seems no end. Two artificial hips and a fused ankle might be all Graham will take. He recently passed on the recommendation to have his other ankle fused.

Steroids may have killed his health, but his memory in wrestling will be immortal.

— With files from Nadia Moharib, *Calgary Sun*

* * *

HALL OF FAMER MAE YOUNG VOWS TO KEEP WRESTLING

By RYAN NATION

Wrestling Revue

Mae Young, many moons ago.

From the writer: This story was a result of a spur-of-the-moment phone call placed on March 22, 2008 — exactly one week before Mae Young's induction into the WWE Hall of Fame. In fact, no one was even scheduled to write the article, and my editor's response was, "Great — if unexpected — stuff!" I decided to contact her because I have always enjoyed writing stories about the legends of the industry. With cold calls like this one, it is either feast or famine. Fortunately, Mae Young and I had a nearly 30-minute, down-to-earth conversation. I just remember her responses to my questions being frank and amusing. When I asked who would be inducting her, she quipped, "I don't have the slightest idea, honey."

At 85, Johnnie Mae Young will become the oldest living female to be inducted into the WWE Hall of Fame this Saturday. However, do not expect her to slow down anytime soon.

Recently, SLAM! Wrestling caught up with Young via telephone from her home in Columbia, South Carolina, to discuss her career and upcoming induction. Young exuded a youthful vigor and enthusiasm when discussing

Andrea Kellaway

Mae Young still wowing 'em in 2006.

the business she has been a part of for so many years.

"It's the greatest thing on earth to me," said a heartfelt Young, already a member of the Pro Wrestling Hall of Fame (Class of 2004). "It's the highest spot in my life. I'm so happy about it. There's no better honor I could ever receive than from WWE because they are the greatest.

"I live to wrestle for the fans because they keep me going," continued Young. "I'm 85 years old, and I still plan on wrestling when I'm a hundred. I look forward to seeing all of the fans. When I look out from the ring and see the fans cheering, hollering, booing, whatever; it's always exciting to me."

Young was born on March 12, 1923, in Sand Springs, Oklahoma. She was an amateur wrestler for her high school wrestling team thanks in part to her sibling.

"My brother and I went to school together, and he was on the boys' amateur wrestling team," explained Young. "He taught me all of the amateur wrestling holds so I was a good wrestler. When we went to school, he would go down the street and say, 'I bet my sister could whip you.' So, I was wrestling all of my life."

Her introduction into the wide world of professional wrestling was somewhat brash, yet effective, to say the least, when she made an open challenge against the world women's champion.

"When they brought Mildred Burke to Tulsa to wrestle a girl by the name of Gladys 'Kill 'Em' Gillem, I caught a streetcar and went over and challenged Mildred Burke because she was the world's champion," recalled Young. "Billy Wolfe and Sam Avey, the promoter, told me, 'You can't wrestle the champion, there's no way.' The next day Billy Wolfe brought a girl by the name of Elvira Snodgrass and Gladys 'Kill 'Em' Gillem over to my high school.

"In the gym, I shot with Gladys and beat her within seconds," continued Young. "Then, I shot with Elvira, and I beat her in seconds. Billy Wolfe then said, 'Hell, I might make a girl wrestler out of you.' He smartened me up and said, 'You gotta go with the flow.'"

Being a female wrestler was not exactly an easy road to travel, especially considering the lack of acceptance from her male counterparts.

"Back during the time I started wrestling, they didn't like to see girls in the ring," recalled Young. "Ed 'Strangler' Lewis told me, 'Women belong in the kitchen and not in the ring. I don't like women wrestling, but if there ever was someone born to be a wrestler, you're it.' That's the greatest compliment I ever received because that was what I was born to do. That's the only thing I breathe and think about. I go to sleep thinking about wrestling. I love the business."

As mentioned in the March 6 edition of Jim Ross's Superstar of the Week blog, Young was wrestling in Memphis on December 7, 1941, when she heard Pearl Harbor had been bombed by a Japanese aircraft, which led to the United States officially entering the Second World War.

"That's right, I was there in Memphis, Tennessee when World War II broke out. That was something boy, quite an experience. Everybody was going crazy in Memphis. I went down to work for Jerry Lawler one time, and I told him, 'I wrestled here when World War II broke out.'"

Young would go on to hold the U.S. women's championship and grapple around the globe for a number of promoters while breaking down barriers for women's wrestling.

"I was one of the first girls in Canada," stated Young. "Mildred Burke and I were the first girls to work in Canada for Stu Hart. Mildred Burke and I opened up Canada for girl wrestling. That's been back around 1941 or 1942. I don't remember the exact date because it's been so many years ago, but we worked for Stu Hart in Montreal and all over Canada."

When it comes to promoters, however, Young is no stranger to working for the McMahon family. "I was the first girl to wrestle for Vince McMahon Sr. when he bought out Washington, D.C., and Joe Turner's Arena," said Young. "He and Toots Mondt promoted wrestling at the Turner Arena. I was the first girl over there to wrestle for him. At that time, Lillian Ellison started booking girls. Of course, I taught Lil to wrestle. Vince asked me, 'What do you think about Lillian Ellison and the girls?' I said, 'Vince, I think it would be the greatest thing in the world for you to get her and her girls.' Of course, Lillian would go on to become known as the Fabulous Moolah."

Young also shared her thoughts with SLAM! Wrestling about how the business has changed over the decades. "When I first started, we wrestled two out of three falls matches and to small crowds. It's no comparison to what they do today. I enjoy it more and make more money than I ever did in my life. I thank Vince McMahon [Jr.] for that because he is the one that has brought wrestling to this level. I like showmanship. There's not as much wrestling as there used to be, but it's showmanship and they have to have ability to be in there. I'm just blessed to still be a part of this business because I was in it when it was really rough and tough."

The Fabulous Moolah and Young were an inseparable duo and staple on WWE programming over the last decade until Ellison passed away on November 2, 2007.

"Lillian will be there with me although she will not be there in person; her spirit will be right beside me because her and I have always been friends, honey," explained Young. "I know that she would be happy for me to be there, and she will be right there cheering me on saying, 'Okay, do it, John!' Her and I made a pact two or three years ago that we would both be wrestling when we were a hundred years old. I am going to carry it out."

Just how serious is she about wrestling more matches? "We have a ring here, and I was just out in the ring a while ago doing a little exercise. I want to make sure I am in good shape in case I'm called to wrestle. Stephanie McMahon has promised me that when [her daughter] Aurora Rose is 17, she will challenge me for a match. I said that's the greatest thing I ever heard."

*　　*　　*

JIMMY HART AS BUSY AS EVER

By GREG OLIVER

Chris Schramm

Still shilling — that's why he's The Mouth of the South.

Jimmy Hart is running around as much, if not more, than he used to in his WWF heyday. Memphis on the weekend for the weekly TV show, Nashville on Wednesdays for the TNA PPV tapings and Thursday in Orlando for the TNA *Impact* tapings. And this Saturday, he's in Buffalo for an event at the Bisons baseball game. But he's loving it.

"I'm glad to be working. It's great," he told SLAM! Wrestling.

He has found there is a real nostalgia out there for wrestling, whether it's the baseball game this weekend, which is tied in with the Pro Wrestling Hall of Fame in Schenectady, New York, or whether it's in Memphis with *Throwback Night*.

"The past is the future. Me and Jerry Lawler were talking about that the other day," he said. "We drew 3,758 people for our show Saturday night down there. Me and Lawler tagging up after 17 years, because we were always archenemies back in the day."

Lawler and Hart took on Kamala — who had been in Hart's stable — and Cory Macklin. The promotion totally restructured their pricing plan for the evening. "We went on TV, 'We know gas prices are hard, we know it's hard for a family of four to go to baseball or basketball, but with wrestling . . .' we did that type of deal. We had $10 ringside and five-dollar general admission. Then we talked the people into doing a deal where we sold hot dogs for a dollar, Cokes a dollar and popcorn a dollar. If you do that, you're going to have a hell of a crowd." The first 1,500 fans got a commemorative program as well.

The ability to pull off such an event is only possible through good promotion through TV and by lining up a number of sponsors to help defray the expenses. "It shows that old-school stuff — having fun, having interviews and not just trying to tits and ass and fingers and drinking beer — really paid off for us."

Hart still follows all of wrestling, and has been careful not to burn bridges. Through the years, he has been involved with all aspects of wrestling, including a stint trying to run the XWF (Xtreme Wrestling Federation). He's proven invaluable to TNA (Total Nonstop Action), though he wonders why Vince McMahon and the WWE haven't come after the competition the way they did with the XWF.

"When we did the XWF, Vince took nine of our people. Jeff [Jarrett] and them are up there doing their deal, and they haven't even called about any of those guys, and they're at the same place we were, " he said.

This Saturday, Hart is slated as a guest at the Ballpark Brawl in Buffalo, along with Roddy Piper and Johnny Valiant (Hart is expected to work an angle with Dave Blezard, the morning show guy on Z103.5, for a return to the ballpark on August 14). Matches on the show include Shane Douglas vs. Chris Candido with Tammy "Sunny" Sytch, Al Snow against a competitor to be named, Hacksaw Jim Duggan vs. Greg "The Hammer" Valentine and "The Natural" Heavyweight Title Tournament featuring Ron "The Truth" Killings, Zach Gowen, Teddy Hart, Konnan, Julio Dinero, Petey Williams, Derek Wylde and a contestant to be named at the show (for more info, see www.ballparkbrawl.com).

Then on September 18, Hart is having his book launch in Toronto at a free wrestling show at the Galleria Mall (Dufferin and Dupont) as a part of another Pro Wrestling Hall of Fame–related event.

The book, entitled *The Mouth of the South: The Jimmy Hart Story*, is in its final edits before going to the printer. Hart is looking forward to promoting it, and hopes to call in lots of favors. "I can probably even get WWE to help me on that because Vince, we still have a great rapport. I'm one of the few people who never knocked him or said anything bad. Even this book coming out, I put Vince and everybody over completely, because if it hadn't been for him, you wouldn't have a home, you wouldn't have a car and half the people out there wouldn't be doing anything."

From the writer: Talking to Jimmy Hart is like standing in a whirlwind. He's just like he is on the screen — high-energy, excitable, and always promoting something. And he's a bugger to get on the phone for any length of time.

* * *

Wrestling Revue

Sam Houston shows off the Mid-Atlantic title.

SAM HOUSTON AND GRIZZLY SMITH REBUILD THEIR LIVES

Hurricane Katrina plus six months
By STEVEN JOHNSON

The first thing Sam Houston wants you to know is that he and his dad, Grizzly Smith, are safe. Forget everything that's happened to them in the last six months — the watery destruction of their home near New Orleans, the loss of their possessions, and the infection that nearly cost Grizzly his leg.

Hurricane Katrina is just a bad memory. They're safe. And that's the important thing.

"It's been real. And in a way, it's been fun. But it's not been real fun," an upbeat Houston said from his girlfriend's house near Baton Rouge, Louisiana. "We're both doing a lot better now. We're just trying to get back on our feet."

Like millions of residents along the Gulf Coast, Houston (Mike Smith), known best for his work in the WWF in the 1980s, and his father, one of wrestling's top stars in the 1960s, saw their lives turned topsy-turvy in a matter of hours last August.

Their apartment near a main highway in Metairie, Louisiana, was well west of Katrina when the Category 3 storm made landfall at daybreak on August 29. But the flooding associated with subsequent levee breeches in New Orleans dispatched waves of onrushing water that drowned their residence, and tens of thousands of other homes and businesses.

By that time, Houston already had headed to higher ground in northern Louisiana. Initially, Smith, one-half of the famed Kentuckian tag team (with Luke Brown), and a longtime backstage official in several promotions, stayed behind. Houston equipped him with a cell phone, hoping that would enable his dad, 73, to stay in contact during the storm.

But Smith balked at using the new technology, not that it would have done much good — Katrina snuffed out cellular communications in the region for days.

Even worse, the day before Katrina hit, Smith scraped his leg working at his job tending to a cemetery near the French Quarter in New Orleans. Stuck in Katrina's watery aftermath, without access to transportation or electricity, the scrape became infected and he started to develop a fever.

"He spent four days wallowing around in that nasty water and got a staph infection in his leg," Houston said. "For four days, we didn't hear from Dad and they wouldn't let anybody in the city. We were worried sick."

Finally, a female supervisor from the cemetery navigated her way through high waters to New Orleans to check on the condition of crypts that the flood washed up and out of their graves. She dropped by to check on Smith and secured a vehicle for him to drive inland.

Smith made his to way to Tangipahoa Parish, the home of Houston's girlfriend, but didn't remember the directions to her residence, or her name. On his behalf, local police officers drove around asking if anyone knew a man named Grizzly Smith. Houston's girlfriend was outside at the time, collecting ice from a Red Cross station, when she happened upon an officer and reunited Smith with his son.

"He was sitting in the police station, all disoriented because of the infection and we went up there and got him," Houston said. "After we got him, we drove him down to Texas [to his sister's house] because he didn't want to see a doctor here. That was a 20-hour trip — 10 hours up there and 10 hours back."

Grizzly Smith, complete with rope to hold up his pants.

"They almost had to take his leg off. That infection took a while to heal," Houston said.

A few weeks later, Smith landed back in the hospital to repair a hernia that he suffered trying to lift a heavy object.

When officials reopened the New Orleans area to residents, Houston and a weary but recovering Smith went back to assess the damage. Water in their apartment had crested chest-high, destroying their furniture and possessions. What little remained apparently was pilfered by looters, Houston said.

"After the storm came through, the maintenance came in and busted everybody's apartments open, and I guess they took what they wanted because we didn't have half the stuff that was supposed to be there," Houston said.

"We were able to salvage a couple of things. We were able to salvage a pair of my wrestling boots and my cowboy boots because they were on the top shelf. And I was able to salvage a couple pairs of dad's shoes. We were able to keep some of the canned goods we had in the pantry because the water didn't get that high."

Their vehicles, though, were washed away. Smith had driven his son's SUV to work at the cemetery the day before the storm. He returned home that day in a work truck to help the cemetery supervisor move some items later.

That meant Houston's SUV was parked at the cemetery. Within hours, it was consumed by 15 feet of water. Smith lost his car to the storm as well.

About a month ago, Houston bought his dad a 1996 Ford Crown Victoria, a big car for a big man. Incredibly, on his way to work at the cemetery, Smith was struck from behind twice by two different vehicles.

"It totaled the Crown Vic out, and now he's in a little, bitty Chevy Malibu, which it looks like it takes a can opener to get him out of," Houston said with a chuckle.

Despite the family's losses, Houston is grateful for what he has. He worked part-time at a construction company, and helped his father at the cemetery, which is operated by the Firemen's Charitable and Benevolent Association on a pretty, historic parcel near Canal Street. It's a 45- to 50-minute drive each way from his girlfriend's house, but Houston said the trip was well worth it one day recently.

"We'd just been cleaning the place up. And there was this woman, and I was walking by, and she was crying. I said, 'Ma'am, what's wrong?' She said, 'Who did this to this grave?'

"I said, 'Well, that's the first grave I cleaned up this morning. I pulled all the weeds and raked it and filled it back up with dirt and everything.' And she said, 'I was out here two weeks ago and the weeds were so high. My daughter's buried there, and today's her birthday.'"

Houston declined her offer of payment and promised he and his father would keep an eye on the plot. Soon thereafter, he was visited by Judge James F. McKay III, head of the association that oversees the Cypress Grove and Greenwood cemeteries. McKay told Houston that the woman had praised that "long-haired guy, that young man."

The grappler responded with a smile, and when McKay asked him why he was smiling, Houston, who passed 40 a couple of years ago, responded: "Just being called 'young'!"

"Every day is a new experience for us right now, but at least we've got a place to stay," Houston said. "You've just got to sit back and laugh about things and take it all in stride. As long as you wake up the next morning, it was a good day."

From the writer: Grizzly and Sam weren't the only members of the Smith clan affected by Katrina. Robin Smith, known as Rockin' Robin, lost her house in New Orleans. "I had about seven feet of water inside the house for two weeks," she said. She headed inland to Hammond, Louisiana, where she operates a successful real estate appraisal company.

Grizzly's health deteriorated after Katrina and he moved to Amarillo, Texas, where family members could provide around-the-clock attention. But he got a moment in the sun with a 2008 induction into the Mid-Atlantic Hall of Heroes. Sam, living and working in Louisiana, accepted the honor for him at a banquet in Charlotte, North Carolina. "My dad really wanted to be here but it wasn't one of his better days," Houston said. "From the bottom of my heart, thank you for this and for giving it to my dad."

* * *

Terry Funk, beyond middle-aged and crazy.

A HARDCORE HISTORY WITH TERRY FUNK

By CHRIS GRAMLICH

From the writer: How do you interview a legend? One of the sport's pioneers and icons? A man who not only has done it all but invented a great deal of it along the way? With a great deal of anxiety, in my experience. I can still remember the night Greg Oliver and I went to meet Terry Funk in a sports bar on the outskirts of Toronto. While the name of the venue escapes me, I remember the Funkster being eager to watch a returning Mike Tyson later that night on pay-per-view. I remember being too nervous myself to eat anything and the hours of stunning, captivating wrestling history an affable and soft-spoken Funk graced us with. Unquestionably one of my best interview experiences ever.

Terry Funk is a man riddled with contradictions. A polite, soft-spoken, middle-aged Texan, who after 30 years in the wrestling business is as likely to apologize for cussing or spitting tobacco as he is liable to split another wrestler's head open with a broken bottle. Therein lies the walking, talking paradox that is Terry Funk.

Not only is Funk "middle-aged and crazy" in the ring, outside of the ring he is as equally unstable as evidenced by his favorite era of wrestling, one which nearly cost him his life.

"I loved the era of the riots. In Puerto Rico there'd be riots where I'd have to fight my way to the back, San Antonio, the Dallas/South Houston area. It was absurd. They would have to stop the matches because too many people would be hitting the ring. In Kentucky I can remember when they took forty guns off of people coming to the show. I've had guns pulled on me and knifes too," said "Terrible" Terry, as he is called.

"Corpus Christi is where I got stuck with a knife in the neck. Fortunately, it wasn't that big a blade. It went all the way into the hilt and I thought it

Terry Funk shares his thoughts with ringsiders during his 1989 WCW run.

was a dart or something, so I left it in. When I got to the back and saw it was a knife my eyes got as big as saucers when I realized what it was and that someone had tried to kill me."

While most people would view a riot and attempted homicide as signs of taking things way too far, Funk derives another interpretation from them.

"The riots were a form of flattery. The greatest thing [for a heel wrestler] is to do your job so well that someone wants to kill you. What could be more wonderful? People who have done terrible things to me and wanted me to charge them, well I wouldn't. I mean, do I want to put someone in jail because I convinced him or her that I needed to die? I did it to them. That's how I look at it and that may be sick but it's also beautiful," said Funk, in town for the Apocalypse Wrestling Federation's Scar Wars event which featured the legendary "Funker" battling Abdullah the Butcher in the main event.

SLAM! Wrestling's Greg Oliver and I were fortunate enough to have the chance to sit down and talk with the hardcore institution over dinner and few would argue that anyone has done a better job in professional wrestling than Terry Funk. However, doing your job well in the world of wrestling sometimes means losing, and Toronto is where Terry Funk lost one of his most prestigious titles to the equally infamous Harley Race.

February 6, 1977 — a date, match and opponent Funk remembers well.

"Sure, Toronto has special memories, some that I'm not that especially fond of. That was the end of my NWA reign as the heavyweight champion against Harley. I always had respect for Harley because he came up through the school of hard knocks. He started out being a driver for Happy Humphrey and he would do the carnivals and work his way up from them. He was a self-educated person and a man who did well in this profession and as champion after he won the belt from me."

It is obvious from the respect in Funk's voice for people like Harley Race, Lou Thesz and Mike DiBiase, that Funk appreciates tradition. Yet, unlike many, Funk has kept up with the times, practically inventing the hardcore style of wrestling that is so popular now. Still, Terry can remember when wrestling was more of a family affair.

"It was a wonderful thing as I grew up and when I started, I think I caught the tail end of it. When my father started back in the 1940s, everyone had their own trailer and what a wrestler wanted to do [if he had children] was get into an area [promotion or territory] where he could stay for at least the school year for the children's sake. It seemed like all the wrestlers lived in trailer courts and all the kids became buddies. It was a great time," said Funk, who was also fortunate to wrestle alongside his brother, Dory Funk Jr., on many occasions.

"There wasn't wrestling on Sunday or even Saturday. You didn't fly any-where. You only worked five days a week and you went where you could drive. On the weekend someone was always barbecuing and would invite everyone over and it was very family-oriented. Divorce was something which didn't plague our profession like it does now."

But in Terry's opinion, wrestling, like all sports, has changed with the times. Whether these changes are for the better or worse has yet to be seen.

"Wrestling has definitely changed a great deal since when I started in the business. I think not only in wrestling but in all sports that the athletes are greedy right now and I can understand that. Not being greedy for the sake of being greedy but because the salaries in all sports have escalated so much that it really tends to make a mockery of a fella who fixes a toilet or drives a cab for a living. It really doesn't make much sense to pay one person more for a night or a year than another will make in a lifetime. I can't really com-prehend that."

* * *

LARRY HENNIG ONE TOUGH GUY

By GREG OLIVER

They don't come much tougher than Larry "The Axe" Hennig. Yet, when he learned of his induction into the George Tragos/Lou Thesz Professional Wrestling Hall of Fame, his eyes teared up. Not that he would say such a thing.

Instead, it was his wife of 50 years, Irene, who told SLAM! Wrestling that "The Axe" was more like his old "Pretty Boy" persona when he was told of

Larry "The Axe" is ready for action.

the honor in July by Mike Chapman, executive director of Iowa's International Wrestling Institute and Museum.

"We were down in Newton, Iowa. It was a very, very hot day. From the hotel we were staying, we could walk over to the museum. So instead of walking around to the front door, we were going to take a shortcut through the basement," recalled Irene Hennig. "That's where we ran into Mike Chapman. He said, 'Can I talk to you a minute?' He took us aside and he looked me in the face, and he said, 'Irene, I just want you to know that you're standing next to next year's Hall of Famer.' Of course, I looked at Larry, and I put my hands to my face. My eyes welled up, and his welled up. It was just awesome. We were just overcome with happiness."

Like a true championship tag team partner, Larry also said the honor in the plural — "We're thrilled. We're overwhelmed" — a credit to his wife.

Besides the support of his "Battle-Axe" Irene (as Bobby Heenan dubbed Irene Hennig in his autobiography), how did Hennig get to this point? After all, he's entering the Hall of Fame with a pretty well-regarded Class of 2006: Dory Funk Sr., Bret Hart, Mike DiBiase, Tom Jenkins and Bob Roop.

A 1954 high school state champion in Robbinsdale, Minnesota, Hennig accepted a scholarship to the University of Minnesota to wrestle and play football. However, real life would interfere.

"I was married when I was 19," Hennig said. "The red, white and blue, the college, I had to bypass that. I went a year and a half there to college on my scholarship, but I just couldn't maintain because we had a young family started. We had to do it the old-fashioned way and get a job."

The Hennigs started Larry Hennig Realty & Auction Co. Inc., a company that survived the wrestling years and is still going strong. But Larry also learned the pro business under Joe Pazandak, and entered Verne Gagne's AWA (American Wrestling Association) promotion for further schooling. He was a quick study, and after refereeing and prelims, he would become a tag team specialist, winning the AWA tag titles with Duke Hoffman (Bob Leipler) and then teaming with "Handsome" Harley Race, taking the belts four times.

Hennig and Race had met in Texas. "Harley came in here as just a young kid to Minnesota. Harley's about seven or eight years younger than I am," said Hennig. "Harley came to Minnesota and wrestled on TV. They just threw us in one day together and all of a sudden, it was unbelievable. We were a good team because we didn't do the same things. I was more surface transportation and he was more air express. It worked out real good for us."

In the book *The Pro Wrestling Hall of Fame: The Tag Teams*, Race talked about the team, ranked in the Top 20 of all time. "If you go in there with the attitude of being a team, and leaving your ego and all that stuff out of the ring, you can become a hell of a team, and I think Larry and I were one of the better ones. . . . Had he not gotten hurt, who knows?" Race speculated. "We might have stayed together."

Ah yes, the injury. Hennig's blown knee was one of the more famous in-ring incidents in wrestling history.

In his autobiography, *King of the Ring*, Race described the match in Winnipeg in 1967.

"During a match on November 1," Race wrote, "Larry was lifting his opponent, a 260-pound John Powers, when another wrestler bounced off the referee and into Larry's legs, bending them inward. As Hennig lowered Powers, one of his knees bent the wrong way at nearly a 90-degree angle, tearing the cartilage and tendons in his leg. As I watched, I knew in an instant that our on-again, off-again two-year title run was off again. It would be the last time we would own the title."

Race's description only scratches the surface though. Hennig said that he didn't want to go to the hospital in Winnipeg, and rode in the back of the car with Harley driving all the way back home. "I gutted that thing out. It's a 500-mile trip back to Minneapolis," said Hennig. "The next morning, the doctor put me in the hospital, ready for surgery. That was on a Friday. Saturday they had the Amphitheater running in Chicago and Verne came to the hospital and said, 'Larry, you've got to do me a favor. You've got to go to Chicago. You've got to make an appearance there. We've got to do something with the belts.'"

Business was going well, so Hennig agreed, and was taken to a plane in a wheelchair to go to Chicago. At the arena, he was suited up — his leg was taped, he was given crutches and he leaned on Harley on the way to the ring. "They got me up on the apron and boom, boom, boom, the whole deal anyway. We lost the title there."

Hennig turned around and went back to Minneapolis for the surgery. "I got back to the hospital at one o'clock in the morning, and they couldn't

Larry Hennig with his son Curt's widow Leonice upon Mr. Perfect's induction into the Tragos/Thesz Hall of Fame in 2007, making them the first father-son inductees.

operate on Sunday so they operated on Monday. Verne made the payoff . . . and he gave me $50 more than he gave me the week before."

The poor payoff is just one of the Axe's beefs with Gagne. But he acknowledges it demonstrates his toughness. "Who [else] would do that? Ride all night in a car, go to a hospital, they put me in there and prepped me for surgery. Guy said, 'Where you going?' I said, 'I'm going to Chicago to wrestle.' I told the guy in the bed next to me. Of course, they thought that was a big joke."

Hennig took 18 months off to heal, and the knee still bothers him today. At the 2005 Cauliflower Alley Club banquet, Hennig led a prayer: "Oh Lord, oh Lord, send us down a good knee doctor."

After coming back to wrestling, he worked a little differently as a singles wrestler, morphing into "The Axe." On numerous occasions, he would head east to New York's WWWF to challenge for Bruno Sammartino's world title.

As his career in the ring wound down in the 1980s, Hennig's son, Curt, was beginning to wrestle. It was among his favorite memories, teaming with his son, even winning the Pacific Northwest tag titles together in 1982. Larry Hennig retired from wrestling in 1985, but unlike many of his peers, he had something to fall back on — his real estate business.

"It was hard to balance, but it was certainly worth it now," said Hennig. "With the exposure that I had through wrestling, it's still opening doors for me in Minnesota. It turned out to be a two-bladed sword for me. It worked then, and it's still working now."

Being well known in the area only gets one so far, he said. "It's a foot in the door. . . . I always had my own company, I've always been a broker; I've never been an agent. . . . After you get your foot in the door, you've got to perform. When you take on a client, you're representing them and if you've got a seller, you're representing them. You've got to get the job done in order to be successful. If you're not selling and delivering sales, and getting a good reputation, it doesn't work."

So we're back to his reputation, a big part of the reason he is joining other legends like Race, Frank Gotch and George Hackenschmidt without major amateur credentials in the George Tragos/Lou Thesz Professional Wrestling Hall of Fame.

"I could hold my own with anybody; I really felt that because I had the basic knowledge and the stuff I picked up from guys like Lou Thesz and Joe Pazandak, some of the old hookers. I didn't have to take the backseat to nobody," said Hennig. "Win, lose or draw, if they wanted to fuck with me, they knew they were going to have a problem. Make it simple. There were 10 tough guys in the world, and I get nine Christmas cards every year."

The Hall of Fame induction makes up for a lot of the pain and sacrifices. "It's magnificent and I'm overwhelmed. I'm delighted, and it's the best thing that could happen after all these years, these hills and valleys — I lost my son, my leg, my limbs. The traveling and the hard times. I kept my nose to the grindstone, and at the same time, kept a good public image through my business. So when I went out on top, I didn't come back and end up in the bars. I don't drink and I don't smoke, and I kept myself in pretty good shape."

* * *

VOLKOFF'S THEME SONG: "I AM A REAL AMERICAN"

By STEVEN JOHNSON

It was 1968 in Eastern Europe, and Soviet tanks were crushing the Prague Spring Reform movement. Individual freedom was virtually unknown. Repression against students and dissidents everywhere was commonplace, and advocates of democratization landed in jail, if they lived at all.

Josip Nikolai Peruzovic, an elite teenage weightlifter and wrestler of

Wrestling Revue

Nikolai Volkoff in a custom T-shirt.

Russian and Croatian blood, had seen enough. So the young man made a fateful and solitary decision. When his Yugoslavian weightlifting team prepared to return home after an international competition in Austria, Peruzovic balked.

And then he was gone for good.

Thirty-five years later, Peruzovic is telling this story softly, in heavily accented English — how he left Yugoslavia and his family to defect to the West without benefit of the English language or money. He speaks matter-of-factly as he describes the conditions that caused him to flee, and only at one point does a trace of anger creep into his voice.

"Those communist bastards," he said. "I hated them."

Even in the bizarre world of professional wrestling, it sounds curious to hear a bitter denunciation of communism from Peruzovic, better known to the wrestling community as Nikolai Volkoff.

As a monstrous villain from Russia, Volkoff was a headliner against the likes of Bruno Sammartino, Gorilla Monsoon and Hulk Hogan in the WWWF and elsewhere for most of the 1970s and 1980s.

To his legions of friends and family though, Volkoff is neither monstrous nor a villain. Nor is he from Russia, though he speaks the language and his mother is Russian.

In fact, he was just an immigrant hoping to turn his amateur wrestling background into work when he landed in Calgary after his defection to train with the legendary Stu Hart.

At 300-plus pounds of rock-hard muscle, Volkoff had size, athletic ability and great bloodlines — he was trained by his grandfather, a onetime bodyguard for Austrian monarch Franz Josef.

But he had no real expectations and his cover story, to protect his parents from possible harassment at home, was that he was merely traveling and would return to defend his country's honor in event of a war.

Creating a unique blend of his Russian character and American pride in 2003.

"I was just so happy to get out from there," said Volkoff, who chose Canada as his destination because it processed immigrants quickly. "Here, with freedom, you can say what you think. There, they go behind your back, and the next thing you know, you're going to Siberia to cool off for the rest of your life."

Working with Hart, Volkoff quickly caught the attention of Newton Tattrie, a.k.a. Geeto Mongol, who wanted a partner for a tag team idea that occurred to him while he was browsing through books at a Calgary library.

With their partially shaved heads and fearsome visage, the Mongols — Volkoff was called "Bepo," a term of endearment from his mother — were an instant in-ring success.

The food and the language — that was another matter.

"Man, I could not eat any food," he recalled. "Chicken, meat, oh, it tasted terrible. Where I came from, it's all natural food — you kill a cow and eat the same day because there was no refrigeration. It's all nice and fresh. When I came here, I could not eat."

And what he could take in was severely limited by the communications barrier.

During their time in Montreal, Geeto, his restaurant interpreter, had to leave his young charge alone for a few days. Before he left, he taught him "When you're hungry, 'apple pie and coffee,'" and that's what Bepo ordered for several meals.

After a few days, he grew weary of the same bland diet and spotted a woman nearby eating a tasty hamburger steak. Bepo looked at the waitress and pointed to the woman and her meal.

"What is it you want, then?" the waitress asked.

He kept pointing, grunting, and gesticulating towards the steak to no avail. Finally, he abandoned hope. "Apple pie and coffee," he told the waitress.

After prepping in Montreal, the Mongols invaded the WWWF in 1970 after a carefully planned, three-month program of television exposure. "He caught on pretty quick. He was a good athlete and he was in good shape. He was very easy to train," Geeto said.

The Mongols captured the International tag championship, the highest WWWF tag belts at the time, from Victor Rivera and Tony Marino in June 1970. They held them for a solid year, an eternity by today's standards, and enjoyed another four-month reign in the late summer of 1971.

With that success as a Mongol, Bepo understandably recoiled at being packaged as a ruthless, methodical Soviet destruction machine when the Volkoff persona arose in 1974.

But the legendary Freddie Blassie, who was retiring to become a manager, persuaded him that aggrandizing the Soviet system could actually serve Volkoff's anti-Soviet ends.

"He told me, 'The more you say about that, people are going to hate you more.' I said, 'But I hate communism.'"

Responded Blassie: "Then if you hate communism, that's how you destroy it. Tell people how good it is over there, so they know you're lying."

Volkoff followed his manager's advice and became the wrestling caricature of a Soviet tool for more than 15 years.

"If you say something truthful, there is no heat. Nobody cares," he said. "But if you say, 'In Russia, people buy cars only until the style wears out, then they drive it right to the junkyard to be melted down for military purposes,' then people know you are lying. Then you get the heat and the people say, 'That is ridiculous!'"

In March 1974 Volkoff established himself as a major player for years to come when he battled to a one-hour draw with WWWF champion Bruno Sammartino at Madison Square Garden.

The match set a gate record for the famous arena and the duo continued their feud up and down the East Coast for years. Blessed with long fingers and a vise-like grip, Volkoff could crush an apple with one hand — on televised interviews, he said the apple represented what he planned to do to Sammartino.

In reality, his admiration for Sammartino knows no bounds. "He was the greatest," Volkoff said. "He was the greatest wrestler who ever lived."

Volkoff also had successful runs in the Southern U.S. and Japan, holding the NWA Mid-Atlantic tag title with Chris Markoff and the NWA Georgia heavyweight title.

In 1983–84, he started using an ingenious gimmick developed by promoter Bill Watts. Before his matches, Volkoff insisted fans stand and respectfully observe the singing of the Soviet national anthem.

When he re-entered the WWF in 1984, frequently teaming with the Iron Sheik, a former WWF champion, Volkoff continued to belt out the Soviet anthem before each match.

With Blassie earnestly standing by, hand on heart, and the hated Iron Sheik in the ring, Volkoff's vocals attracted enough debris from irate fans that Monsoon once commented, "There's no need for a food drive when this guy starts to sing."

"Oh, the heat that drew," Volkoff remembered. "It was unbelievable. People hated me and they hated Russia. So that worked."

At WrestleMania I in 1985, Volkoff teamed with the Iron Sheik to beat Barry Windham and Mike Rotundo for the tag team championship he had first held with Geeto 15 years before.

He later paired with Boris Zhukov as the Bolsheviks, a thoroughly despicable pair of Soviet sympathizers who were a fixture on television, pay-per-views and house shows from 1987 to 1990.

On a televised *Superstars of Wrestling* show in the spring of 1990, Zhukov entered the ring first and delivered an indifferent version of the Soviet anthem. As Volkoff grabbed the microphone, he pledged to show Zhukov how to sing properly.

To stunned fans, Volkoff launched into a stirring rendition of "The Star Spangled Banner" to wild applause, setting up a feud with Zhukov and cementing one of the most memorable turns in years.

Ironically, political developments in Eastern Europe, which once sent Volkoff fleeing for the West, facilitated his transition to wrestling hero.

The Berlin Wall fell in 1989. Reformers in Poland and Czechoslovakia drove Communist leaders from power. The Balkan Republics started to declare their independence from Russia and, in 1991, Soviet communism collapsed.

And Volkoff joyously ended his days as a staunch Russian heel.

"When Russia fell down, I said, 'That is enough for me. There's no more reason for me to be a bad guy. I don't have a reason to be a bad guy.' Communism was gone and I was so happy," he said.

Volkoff did a final stint with the WWF in 1994–95 as part of "Million Dollar Man" Ted DiBiase's stable, but still occasionally wrestles on weekends. He also has started his own one-man show onstage called *An Evening with Nikolai Volkoff*, sharing the story of his escape from communism. He also performs magic tricks and sings.

As his career wound down, he became one civil servant that no one wanted to anger, as a code enforcement inspector in Baltimore County. He lives on a sprawling, 50-acre farm near Baltimore with Lynn, his wife of 33 years, and looks back fondly on his long and amazing journey.

"When Russia was in power, I did everything I could to make them look bad. Then one day, Russia was gone, and I said, 'My job is done.'"

THE SNAKE BITES BACK AT *BEYOND THE MAT*

By STEPHEN LAROCHE

Jake "The Snake" Roberts slithers at ringside.

Mike Lano

From the writer: This was the first piece I wrote for SLAM! *Wrestling and it was hot on the heels of the celebrated* Beyond the Mat *documentary. The opportunity to interview one of the greatest promo men in wrestling history was incredible but there was some sadness to it all that day as well. When Jake walked into the arena before the show, it was like stepping into the documentary itself since he looked a lot older and worse for wear. I'll never forget the disappointed look on his face when he saw a small child holding up a sign that said "Jake's A Drunk" . . . it just goes to show that the jeers of wrestling fans can often hit home.*

Professional wrestling legend Jake "The Snake" Roberts has lashed out against the makers of *Beyond the Mat*, a documentary featuring a side of sports entertainment many fans do not have a chance to see.

Roberts, born Aurelian Smith, was on tour with the Hardcore Wrestling Federation and took time to speak with SLAM! Wrestling at their Maximum Insanity event in Belleville, Ontario, about his career and the documentary, in which he was featured prominently.

According to Roberts and his business partner Valerie Burnham, the documentary was to be a tool helping children see the darker side of professional wrestling. The theatrical release did not sit well with them, as they were not compensated.

"I was approached and told it was going to help children and I was lied to," said Roberts. "I was used . . . again."

Director Barry Blaustein categorically refutes Roberts's charges. "I never said to Jake this was intended for kids," responded Blaustein over the phone from his Los Angeles office.

At one time, Roberts was on top of the wrestling world. During the late '80s, he worked close to 300 nights a year for the World Wrestling Federation. The loneliness of the road and alienation from family took a toll on him personally and professionally, culminating with an ongoing battle with alcohol and drugs. *Beyond the Mat* makes note of these battles and features compelling and disturbing images, including Roberts dealing with his personal demons by smoking crack in a hotel room after a reunion with his daughter, Brandy.

Roberts did not appear pleased with the end result or with the actions of Blaustein. "Blaustein did a lot of lying — you need to know that," he said.

However, Roberts did note one thing would make the project worthwhile in his eyes. "If one kid is helped, then it was worth it," he said.

Blaustein is dumbfounded by Roberts's accusations. "I have no idea what he's talking about," answered Blaustein. "I know I did not mislead him or anyone else in the making of this film. I'm sorry he feels this way."

Blaustein isn't quite sure why Roberts is making these accusations. "I don't know why. Jake's looking for publicity for himself, maybe. I don't know. He has problems with reality. I wish Jake all the best."

Burnham noted a fact presented at the end of the documentary is not accurate as Roberts had been in contact with his daughter during the time between its filming and release.

Blaustein argues otherwise.

"My source is the daughter who I think has a better understanding of reality than Jake," stated Blaustein. "He contacted his daughter a week before the film premiered. I called the daughter when the film was edited — before a film comes out, it has to be completed a month before it gets to the theaters so you can make prints and everything. And up to that point, which was a year and a half, two-year period, the daughter said she had not spoken to him, that Jake only called as the movie was about to come out."

At present, Burnham is working with Roberts on putting together his autobiography, entitled *The Life and Death of Jake "The Snake" Roberts*. She expects it to be published next year.

Roberts's personal demons, which many wrestling fans know him best for, may not be his true legacy. He has worked with some of the greatest names in wrestling, from Andre the Giant to "Stone Cold" Steve Austin and helped to preserve and jumpstart the careers of other wrestlers.

During his series of matches against Andre in 1989, many televised and arena bouts were incredibly short and alluded to his opponent's alleged fear of snakes. In reality, the late wrestling legend was battling a variety of ailments including a bad back. While reminiscing about this period, Roberts noted that in wrestling, "you never expose a man's weakness."

When Roberts returned to the World Wrestling Federation in 1996, he inadvertently helped to jumpstart the renaissance of professional wrestling. At the time, he was in a feud with Austin and using religion as a central theme during his interviews. An infamous retort by the younger star of

"Austin 3:16 says I just kicked your ass," after a match created a catchphrase, sold untold amounts of merchandise and boosted television ratings to new heights. When looking back on the time, Roberts believes his responsibility was to teach Austin.

"I started it because I wanted to," he said. "He [Austin] was just the Ringmaster then, so it was to teach."

This teaching role appears to be a running theme throughout his career.

When asked about several other superstars of the period, including Rick Rude, Randy Savage and Ricky Steamboat, Roberts believes his role was to prepare them for greater things. "The reason I worked with them was to teach them and get them ready for [Hulk] Hogan," he said.

When asked if he would consider working with any of the "big three," Roberts appeared confident about their interest in him but uninterested in a return to the spotlight at this time.

"If I wanted to," he said. "I could if I wanted to now."

— With files from John Molinaro

* * *

Roger Baker

Bruno Sammartino strikes a pose in a dressing room at Buffalo's War Memorial Auditorium.

SAMMARTINO: MCMAHON IS "A SICK-MINDED IDIOT"

By MATT MACKINDER

From the writer: Meeting Bruno Sammartino was a thrill and an even bigger one to do it on a professional level. We were backstage at a Ring of Honor show in Detroit during WrestleMania 23 weekend and I remember several times during the interview thinking, "Wow. I'm one-on-one with Bruno freaking Sammartino. How awesome is this?" Just knowing the man's career history and what he did for the business and to be talking to him and hearing him rip the absolute hell out of Vince McMahon was an incredible moment in my career. When I left the backstage area, another SLAM! Wrestling writer, Jason Clevett, was waiting and said, "Dude, you're glowing." That pretty much sums up my 20-minute chat with the Living Legend.

Bruno Sammartino during a Ring of Honor appearance in Detroit WrestleMania weekend 2007.

You'd think a wrestling legend like Bruno Sammartino would love to chat about the business and note how far it's come since his heyday.

Think again, people.

The Living Legend sat down with SLAM! Wrestling while he was in town to take in a Ring of Honor show in Detroit recently and had some rather intriguing things to say about the business, especially former employer Vince McMahon Jr.

Sammartino has a legacy in WWE that, sadly, will probably be overcome someday and forgotten; but that's alright with him. He said he rarely follows the industry anymore and for good reason.

"What's this I hear that Vince has a club where guys have to kiss his butt?" asked Sammartino, still looking fit at the age of 71. "Come on. That's just ridiculous. I can't believe that's the state of the business nowadays and I can't believe that's what people watch for. Cable companies should be ashamed for even showing that garbage on television in the first place."

At his prime in the 1960s and 1970s, Sammartino had two WWWF title reigns totaling 12 years. One was from 1963–1971 and the other from 1973–1977. It's rare in this day in age for a wrestler to hold a world title more than a few months. Sammartino attributed his success to McMahon — Vince McMahon Sr.

"It was great working for Vince Sr.," stated Sammartino emphatically. "There's no comparison between Senior and Junior. Nowadays, Vince [Jr.] makes the wrestlers depend on him. Back in my day, Vince Sr. depended on me. We didn't have pay-per-view or WrestleMania, but we would sell out [Madison Square] Garden, no problem, 12 to 15 times a year and all we had back then were house shows. Vince depended on me. When he would want to bring in a new wrestler for a program with me, he'd run it by me first and if I liked the idea, we'd go with it. If not, then we'd come up with something else.

"Junior, he just doesn't care. He'll do whatever he wants. He's just a sick-minded idiot. I mean, who else books a match where you wrestle God? How low can you go? It's disgusting."

Ironically, Sammartino's appearance in Detroit was on the eve of the WWE Hall of Fame induction ceremony. Sammartino is not a member, won't be a member, and has no idea what the Hall of Fame even is.

"They've called plenty of times," Sammartino admitted. "I turn them down every time. What's the point to a Hall of Fame? Is it a building I can actually go to? No. Give me a break. If I gave in and was inducted, what would that say about me? It would make me a hypocrite and then Vince would turn right around and sell DVDs about me and my career and make more money.

"Look at a guy like Pete Rose. Why is he in the Hall of Fame? It's a sham." Sammartino was then told why "Charlie Hustle" was in the Hall.

"Because a real wrestler piledrove him?" Sammartino asked. "Please. That makes him Hall of Fame material?"

Sammartino then learned NFL legend William "Refrigerator" Perry, who competed in the WrestleMania II battle royal alongside Sammartino, was also a member of the WWE's hallowed hall.

Sammartino merely rolled his eyes.

He knows he's not alone.

With McMahon Jr. now a world champion, having put the ECW title on himself at Backlash on April 29, many fans and observers have continued to walk away from pro wrestling much like Sammartino did many years ago. Sammartino says McMahon has an ego problem.

"People would always tell me that if I didn't like the product to stop being involved," noted Sammartino. "So I have, for the most part. If I do watch a show nowadays, they say it's a sellout, but you block off a third of the arena for lighting and what not, plus you tarp off another section and what do you have left? We turned people away back when I wrestled. We drew the fans for the pure wrestling, not for the sex and vulgarity that Vince throws at you now.

"It's just ridiculous."

* * *

Greg Oliver

Brad Rheingans during his brief WWF run.

OLYMPIC BOYCOTT STILL HAUNTS RHEINGANS

By GREG OLIVER

Brad Rheingans knew he was in over his head. Just a short while into his pro career, after the disappointment of the 1980 U.S. Olympic boycott, he found himself in Anchorage, Alaska, harnessed in for the dreaded Alaskan sled dog match. Across the ring was an aging, but still dangerous, "Big Thunder" Gene Kiniski.

"It was early in my career, and I was nervous anyway. Everyone's telling me about this Gene Kiniski that would just as soon give you a knuckle sandwich as shake your hand," Rheingans told SLAM! Wrestling recently.

For the Alaskan sled dog match, each wrestler gets tied up in leather just like a sled dog would be, and then the combatants are attached by a five-foot long strap.

"I'm used to armdrags and bodylocks and headlocks and leapfrogs, and all of a sudden, I'm wrapped up in leather goods here," he laughed. But Kiniski, in his first meeting with Rheingans, was a true professional. "Gene came through with flying colors. He's the one that had all the experience."

Rheingans was recently reunited with Kiniski at the induction ceremonies for the George Tragos/Lou Thesz Professional Wrestling Hall of Fame in Newton, Iowa, where both were a part of the Class of 2004.

Museum director Mike Chapman can rhyme off Rheingans's accomplishments with ease. "Eight national titles, two Olympic teams, third in the world, Pan-American Games champion, 14 years of wrestling pro, AWA tag team champion. All that, and still a booker in Japan," he reported.

But Rheingans isn't really the type of guy to get all worked up in his feats. He's an admitted loner, who found success in one of the most solitary of sports out there — amateur wrestling.

A native of Appleton, Minnesota, a small Midwestern town located in western Minnesota just 20 or so miles from South Dakota, Rheingans credits his brother, Bruce, both for tough love and eventually convincing him to truly give himself to the amateur game.

"The biggest influence on me getting into amateur wrestling was my brother. He was two years older than me and he was wrestling. When he came home, I had no clue about wrestling at all," Rheingans said. "My brother would come home after his wrestling practices and he'd work me over on the living room rug. I'd pretty much come away with knee burns, burns on my forehead. I vowed that I was never going to do that, never get into wrestling because I couldn't stand it. I had no control over what was going to happen. My brother had the experience. Shoot, I knew I was stronger than him but he just knew too much. I was kind of disillusioned there on the living room carpet.

"One day, my brother came up to me and told me, 'You know, if you really want to find out what you are made out of, you'd better go out for wrestling. You're going to develop your own character and you're going to find out what you are really capable of doing when you're out there by yourself.'"

It turned out to be true. While Rheingans excelled at football in high school, where he was co-captain of his 1970 high school football team and voted MVP, he did even better in discus and shotput, and, of course, wrestling.

"In a team sport, you can always blame somebody else, whereas in a wrestling match, you're the only one out there either to fail or succeed," he said.

To this day, nothing he did on the mat or in the pro ring compares with his first state title in high school. "The most exciting time in my amateur career was when I went from Appleton, which is basically way out in the middle of nowhere, and I went to Minneapolis and I won my first state title.

"When you're in high school, you're thinking, 'God, the state tournament. Wow, that's everybody in the state.' I didn't start wrestling until I was a sophomore in high school, then the next year I won the state and the next year I won the state. But that first time, that was exciting."

His success in high school led him to North Dakota State University, where he was a four-time NCAA All American and NCAA Division II champion. One of his coaches at NDSU, Jim Duschen, convinced him to give Greco-Roman wrestling a shot and therefore open up the Olympics as a possibility.

Rheingans had to go to the Minnesota Wrestling Club for training. "I was starting all over again. All of a sudden, here's people flying through the air, getting gutwrenched across the mat. That wasn't something that I was used to, but I knew I wanted to do it because it was a physical sport, and I liked

Greg Oliver

Brad Rheingans and Baron von Raschke in 2008.

things that were physical. It was always a challenge to do something different," he said.

The head of the Minnesota Amateur Wrestling Club was Alan Rice, who was also the U.S. Olympic coach in 1972. He brought in other top amateurs from Poland, Russia and elsewhere to compete and train. "You couldn't help but get better because all of a sudden you're training with the best people," Rheingans said.

After making it through the tough Olympic trials, he made the squad for the 1976 Olympic Summer Games in Montreal. Rheingans finished fourth at 220 pounds in Greco-Roman. "I actually beat the guy who took the bronze medal [Andrzej Skrzydlewski of Poland]. I beat him in the third round."

Under today's scoring system, Rheingans would have been in the gold medal match. His fourth place finish doesn't haunt him at all. He can't say that for 1980, however.

"It haunts me that I didn't get a chance to do it in '80. That was my peak. I had knee surgery right after the world championships in '79, which I did win a bronze, then I got the knee surgery and my knee was just like day and night. I was ready," he said. "Ironically, the two that took second [Roman Bierla, Poland] and third [Vasile Andrei, Romania] I'd beat the year before in the world championships, then they got second and third in the Olympics and the Bulgarian [Georgi Raikov] won it."

At the time, Rheingans agreed with U.S. President Jimmy Carter's decision to boycott the Games in Moscow as a protest of the Soviet invasion of Afghanistan. "I thought it would bring world peace. I was going along with Jimmy Carter. . . . If something like that would have made a difference in world peace, I'm for it, no matter what. Everybody should be for it if it's going to make a difference. . . . The war just escalated, the embargo went on, the farmers suffered, the athletes suffered. It didn't do anything. So I was a little disappointed, but I wasn't the only one."

Rheingans got one more crack at the Olympics, this time as an assistant coach in 1984 at the Los Angeles Games.

Back in 1976, he met the man who would set his future in motion as a pro wrestler, Verne Gagne. It just happened that Rheingans had been a fan of pro wrestling growing up, idolizing those who had legit backgrounds like Gagne, Mad Dog Vachon and Baron von Raschke.

"I met Verne Gagne up in Montreal. He was up there watching the Olympics. I met with him afterwards. He was very nice, very respectful. We had a talk and he asked if I'd ever considered pro, and I told him that's what I really wanted to do. But I told him that I still wanted to go and win a medal. I had a chance to go pro in '76, but I thought, 'Doggone, I came so close to getting a medal in Montreal. I want to be the first American to win a medal in the Olympics,'" Rheingans said.

Gagne and Rheingans stayed in touch over the next four years, and Gagne gave money to support the Olympic wrestling program and would have the team on his *AWA Wrestling* program.

After the boycott in 1980, Rheingans decided to make the jump and put about a month into training with an old college teammate in New York — Bob Backlund. "Bob was a good friend of mine. He was actually a senior at North Dakota State when I was a freshman. So I got to know him pretty well. At the time, he was WWWF champion. He kind of broke me in there for about a month. I didn't wrestle any matches; I just went through the training. Then I came back through Minnesota and went through Verne's camp for about two or three more months. After that I had my first match."

Rheingans worked for the AWA for about five years, his biggest claim to fame being a part of the Olympians tag team with Ken Patera that claimed the tag team title. "Anytime you win one of the belts, that's the pinnacle."

He learned a lot during his career from Gagne, Tito Santana and Rick Martel. Others like Baron von Raschke and Mad Dog Vachon, even if their styles hardly meshed with his clean-cut, All-American persona, helped too. "They all had a different perspective because they all had different gimmicks; they all had a different presentation in the ring. Obviously Mad Dog wasn't going to go out and start shooting fireman's carries and body blocks."

After his AWA run, he went up to the WWF as a favor to his friend, Hulk Hogan. "When I went up to WWF, I was going in there to do a camp for Hulk Hogan. That was the whole purpose for me going up. He wanted to do this dream camp, this Hulk Hogan's Dream Camp and he wanted me to run it. He said, 'Well, c'mon in. Vince will keep you busy, he'll keep you on the payroll and you'll wrestle some matches and when the time is right, we'll do this camp.' After about six or seven months, Vince sent me a nice letter and said, 'We just don't have time to do that right now. We're involved with this other stuff, WrestleMania. If and when we do it, you're going to be a big part of it.'"

The experience of planning the camp, even if it didn't come to pass, would help Rheingans down the road. He had broken his wrist near the end of his WWF stint, and took some much-needed time away from the ring.

Then Antonio Inoki and New Japan Pro Wrestling came calling. Inoki had big plans for a Russia vs. Japan vs. U.S.A. concept, made up of pros who had amateur backgrounds, and he wanted Rheingans to be a part of it.

"I started wrestling for Inoki, spent quite a few tours over there and wrestled continuously. We did that thing with some of the amateur wrestlers from Japan and Russia, some of the world champions from Russia, we worked with them and trained them," he said. "Then my knee — my knees were bad anyway. They'd been banged up so many times. All of a sudden, I just couldn't take it anymore. I told Inoki and Saito, my knees, they're way overdue. So I had my first knee replaced in 1995 [right] and I had my second [left] one in 1997."

Since then, Rheingans had a shoulder (1998) and hip (1999) replaced. "Basically, I'm Titanium Man!" he quipped.

Rheingans was smart with his money, and invested well. Now, at 50, he says he's about 85 percent retired, planning on more fishing and hunting in his native state.

He has been running the World Wide School of Professional Wrestling in Hamel, Minnesota, as a place for real prospects to try to make it. Rick Steiner, the Nasty Boys, the Beverly Brothers, Big Van Vader, Scott Norton and Brock Lesnar are all graduates of his training.

After his knee replacement surgery, he was kept on by New Japan as a booking agent, and has been with them now for 17 years. Rheingans was the guy who put together the business plan between WCW and New Japan and brought them together; for about six years, he'd be the guy calling the WCW offices to arrange a wrestler's participation in a New Japan tour.

Rheingans is pretty content with the way it all worked out. Capping it off with his recent induction into the George Tragos/Lou Thesz Professional Wrestling Hall of Fame seems to fit. "It's the biggest honor you can have, it's the highest honor," he said. "It's not just about the awards, or the medals or ribbons and championships and that stuff, it's about what you've acquired from these people in terms of stories that have inspired your life or motivated you."

* * *

FOR BACKLUND, IT'S STILL ABOUT MOTIVATION

By STEVEN JOHNSON

Terry Dart

WWWF champion Bob Backlund.

PRINCETON, NEW JERSEY — The alarm clock that sits beside Bob Backlund's bed at his home in Glastonbury, Connecticut, is set to sound at 6:15 every morning. But it never gets a chance to awaken its owner.

A few minutes before the appointed hour, Backlund reaches out with his beefy hand, the same one that was raised in victory time after time before millions of wrestling fans, and flicks off the switch. He does not need an alarm to remind him that dawn has broken. He is ready to meet the day.

By his own admission, Backlund, now 50, would not have done that just a few years ago. The alarm would have sounded, his eyes would have been bleary, and he would have spent another day in the futile search of personal fulfillment.

For, by then nearly two decades removed from his six-year run as world champion, there were no crowds, no cheers, nothing to get the adrenaline pumping again. There was no motivation for the ultimate self-motivated man.

"I had been struggling. I couldn't find a business that was rewarding enough to the point that I would be excited to get up in the morning," Backlund said at a reunion of wrestling champions in New Jersey last weekend.

A little more polished as Mr. Bob Backlund in 2008.

"In 2001, I got into the mortgage business. And that's when I got excited about life again," he said. "I start my day very positive because I'm alive. I think it's very easy, once God gave you another day . . . you've got to be happy. There's ups and downs in life, but always keep a smile. I think it's healthy for you."

Today, Backlund looks very much like he did in his prime as a star in amateur and professional wrestling. The crow's-feet around the eyes are more noticeable, but his grip is as powerful as a vise. He maintains an insatiable commitment to physical fitness and radiates the wide-eyed naiveté of someone whose harshest invective is "jeepers." Put him in a white, picket-fenced house in Pleasantville, and he'd be a perfect fit.

It's not an affectation. Backlund's rise from an impoverished childhood in Minnesota to the top ranks of pro wrestling is a story befitting an "All-American boy," which is the way he was portrayed — accurately — during his time in the ring. But his life also is the story of motivation lost and motivation found.

"I learned some things along the way," he said. "If something happens to you, negative, you can't blame it on other people. You've got to turn around and look at yourself first. And you've always got to find something positive out of the negative."

Growing up in Princeton, Minnesota, Backlund's family lived on a farm with no outdoor plumbing, no electricity, and no television until he was about 16 — about 1970, long after such amenities had become run-of-the-mill for most families. "We were poor," Backlund said.

The farm boy started wrestling in eighth grade, and not necessarily on the mat. He said he got into more than his share of scraps. He didn't take learning seriously. Teachers did not like to see him come to school.

Only through his athletic ability was he able to slide through high school and to North Dakota State, where he played football and wrestled. He won the NCAA Division II wrestling championship at 190 pounds in 1971, and was inducted into the school's Hall of Fame in 1983.

The motivation was on the field and on the mat, but even today, Backlund said his degree in physical education is "just a piece of paper" because he didn't work hard enough to gain the knowledge to back it up.

"I confess I was lazy academically because I wasn't motivated. You have to want to learn," Backlund said. Before he dies, he wants to be able to read 5,000 words a minute. "In college, it was maybe 50 words a minute."

Turning pro in 1973, Backlund headed to Baton Rouge, Louisiana, full of big ideas about money and championships. The money wasn't there, and the room he booked for himself at a hotel went unused. He slept in the "voluminous" trunk of his car to save a few dollars.

But things moved quickly. He did well in Florida and St. Louis, two key National Wrestling Alliance territories, and was summoned to New York to meet Vincent J. McMahon, the father of the current WWE empire.

With no more than a handshake in 1978, Backlund embarked on a run that took him to the top of the federation. "Vince Sr. was a wonderful boss. We shook hands in 1978 and promised each other that our words meant something. And I'm proud of my word too."

Backlund drew well as WWWF champion against the likes of Ken Patera, Don Muraco, Pat Patterson and even Harley Race, with whom he had NWA-WWWF title unification bouts. But Vincent K. McMahon gradually took over the business from his father with a very different view of the future of pro wrestling.

And Goody Two-Shoes Bob Backlund, who was regularly taking time to work with children's groups, was not part of it.

The day after Christmas 1983, Backlund lost his title to the Iron Sheik, who promptly lost it to Hulk Hogan. McMahon wanted Backlund to dye his red hair and become a bad guy. For someone whose wrestling persona matched his real life persona, the idea of caricature was anathema to Backlund.

"That's when I was into doing the stuff with the kids and I took it very seriously. That's when I had to make a decision. I had a daughter who was six years old too. I didn't want to be doing certain things on television," Backlund said.

"Having this relationship with Vince McMahon Jr. was a lot different than the father. We had differences. His dad liked a man who would stand up for his word. [The younger McMahon] didn't like a guy who would say no."

Perhaps more surprisingly, Backlund said, in retrospect, that he was not as good a champion as he could have been.

"I don't know if I was even a 'good' good guy," Backlund admitted. "I don't think I was, really. I don't think I was as 'over' as I could have been."

Part of that might have been his personality; Backlund acknowledged that he was something of a "loner" and a bit standoffish in the wrestling fraternity. "I was very sort of outside the business, almost. I'm not sure why, but when I look back, I wasn't really 'in' like I should have been."

Race, who has known Backlund from the outset of this career, attributed that to the fact that, as WWWF champion, Backlund was locked into the northeastern United States. He seldom wrestled in front of fans in other parts of the country, so there was no way he could gain their allegiances.

"This man was, at one point in time, as good as there's ever been inside a wrestling ring. His problem was he was never allowed to venture out to other venues," Race explained.

In 1993, Backlund, 43, took another stab at the WWF. He started with the same "Howdy Doody" image, but quickly shifted into a more memorable — and, he maintains — enjoyable character.

"Mr. Bob Backlund" was a heel alarmed by the deterioration of standards and morals in and out of wrestling. He used ten-dollar words and railed in indignation against the business. To "procure his signature" — Backlund-speak for an autograph — fans had to recite the names of the presidents in order.

The incredible thing is that persona was not far from Backlund either. As he sees it, he didn't change. Wrestling did.

"It was just as rewarding, being a bad guy," he said. "I think it was one of the best experiences I've ever had in my life, being a bad guy. I learned more being a bad guy in two years, about life, about people, than I did my whole career trying to be a good guy."

In November 1994, he beat Bret Hart in an "I Quit" match at Survivor Series to win the WWF world title. This time, he was the transitional champion, as he lost the belt in a matter of seconds three days later to Kevin "Diesel" Nash.

For a variety of reasons, WWF business immediately went into a slump. Backlund was not part of it. Judging by crowd reactions, he predicted to McMahon that fans would change his "Mr. Bob Backlund" character into a good guy.

"The bigger bad guy you are, the bigger babyface you'll be. And I went to McMahon and said, 'You know what? One of your worst nightmares is going to happen. I'm going to be your biggest babyface someday.'

"I was gone three days later."

Backlund made sporadic appearances in the late 1990s as he sought a new direction for his life. In 2000, he ran for Congress as a Republican in Connecticut's heavily Democratic First District; Backlund garnered 30 percent of the vote. He enjoyed the experience, which was a logical follow-up to a brief WWF "Backlund for President" angle.

"The reason I ran for Congress is I was looking for something. I didn't win. I had a great time doing it. I had a theory that if you could get all the people that knew me in Hartford [Connecticut], we'd win."

But too many people don't vote, Backlund said. "I learned if we all voted, we'd control government, but it [voting participation] is under 50 percent."

Backlund has made few wrestling-related appearances in recent years. There was some confusion about his presence in New Jersey last weekend as he interpreted his two-hour commitment to include speaking, meeting with fans, and signing autographs. In fact, the signings portion was to last two hours.

Promoter Terence Brennan said he wasn't sure about the source of the problem, but that everyone who purchased tickets got to meet Backlund.

Still, Backlund is booked for a few more shows, and it's a sure bet with the same message that has brought him to this station in life.

"If you have a negative attitude, bad things come into your world. It attracts more negativism. Positive mental attitude brings more happiness," he said. "I'm not an expert speaker, but I enjoy telling my story."

* * *

BREAKING KAYFABE WITH KAMALA

Jim Harris: The man behind the Ugandan Giant
By STEPHEN LAROCHE

From the writer: I spent months tracking Kamala down for his first-ever interview out of character and it was worth the effort since we became friends as well. He was my favorite wrestler as a child and it took a lot of convincing to gain his trust to speak about his amazing career. There was a lot of reader feedback over this article and I hope it opened the eyes of some fans who don't realize how hard he worked to get the gimmick over and also how unfairly he had been treated by the industry at times. It's easily my favorite article that I wrote for SLAM! Wrestling.

When longtime wrestling fans hear the name Kamala, it often conjures up images of the wild, untamed savage who terrorized his opponents in and

Andrea Kellaway

Kamala poses for a portrait.

out of wrestling rings throughout the world.

However, the man behind the makeup couldn't be more different from the character he portrayed for nearly 20 years.

James Harris, born May 28, 1950, in Senatobia, Mississippi, has kept a relatively low profile in the wrestling world since his last major run with World Championship Wrestling in 1995 as part of the Faces of Fear. Since then, he has worked with independent federations sporadically.

"1993 was the last time I worked with the WWF," Harris told SLAM! Wrestling. "I came home and went back to doing what I did before I started wrestling, which was driving trucks. That's when my good friend [Hulk] Hogan gave me a call and asked if I wanted to come into WCW. I went down for three months, and they didn't give me a contract or anything, and I wanted to start a deal. That was in 1995. That was the last time I worked until April 1 at WrestleMania [in Houston]."

Harris realizes it has been a long time since most fans have seen him in the ring, and explained his decision to appear in the gimmick battle royal.

"I know it was a big span there," he said. "Howard Finkel, one of the agents for the WWF, called and asked if I was interested. I said, 'Why not, I'll give it a try.' It was just for the one-time shot though."

Interestingly enough, Harris never appeared at a WrestleMania event during his three stints with the company. He was to appear at WrestleMania IX against Bam Bam Bigelow, but the match was canceled prior to the show.

"As long as I worked with the WWF, I was never in a WrestleMania. I don't know how to describe it. I was glad to be a part of it for once, even though it's after I'm over the hill," he joked. "I was glad to be a part of it and glad they thought enough of me to ask me to be a part of it."

Debuted in 1978

Harris's wrestling career began in 1978 when he made his debut in Greenwood, Mississippi. He wrestled throughout the South under a variety of aliases, most notably as Sugar Bear Harris. In the early stages of his career, he briefly held the Tri-State version of the NWA United States tag team titles with Oki Shikina in October 1979. Additionally, Harris was set up with his first of many managers, Percy Pringle, better known today as Paul Bearer. With little experience under his belt, he decided that in order to further his career he would wrestle in Europe.

"During that time I really didn't have a name and it was hard to get in any-where," he explained. "I was in Germany one year, and the English promoter was there and he was interested in me coming to England the next year."

While wrestling in England in 1981, Harris began developing a new character — the Mississippi Mauler. This persona planted the seeds for later things, he explained.

"I only did that when I was living in London. A lot of people don't know I was painting my face and stuff like that before I came back to the United States. I have pictures of that too. It was painted just a little different from the way the Kamala image is."

Kreation

Upon returning to the United States, Harris soon found himself looking for work in the wrestling business once again. As fate would have it, a trip to the Mid-South Coliseum in Memphis would change the path of his wrestling career forever.

"When I first came to Memphis after I moved back from England, I went to see a friend of mine about getting some wrestling tights and things from him because my gear hadn't arrived," he said. "When I walked in, Jerry Lawler and the other wrestlers saw me, but they didn't remember me. I wrestled there before, but I had a hat on my head as Sugar Bear Harris. They asked me if I was looking for a job, and I said no. So they asked, 'Do you want to work?' and I said yes, but my ankle was broken but it was healing real well. He [Lawler] said, 'Well, I tell you what, why don't you give me your phone number and go back home and don't let the fans see you.'

"It was a real bad house out there that night, really bad. I went back home that night, it was a Monday night, and on that Wednesday they called me to put this Kamala gimmick together. They had live TV in Memphis then, so they showed I was going to wrestle Lawler, with that broken ankle, that Monday night and the house was sold out. When they showed that little gimmick of me in the jungle, it was sold out."

The video promoting Harris's new character was shot in Lawler's backyard. Billed as Kamala the Ugandan Giant, a former bodyguard of Idi Amin, the character played into the American public's distrust of the Ugandan dictator.

"They had never seen anything like that before," he said. "I think I was one of the first to paint my face except Kabuki. They were just amazed by something like me. They didn't know I was a homeboy from right here in Memphis. I've got family there, and they didn't even know it. It didn't take them long to figure out who it was."

The creation of the Kamala character cannot be credited to one person, Harris explained. "Jerry Lawler helped," he said. "Who really came up with it was myself and a guy who's no longer in the business, he used to wrestle as the Great Mephisto. When I was in England, I used to call him and tell him I was going to Africa, which I did go quite a few times, and he told me to get a gimmick and come back to the States and make a whole lot of money. So Lawler and I both came up with Kamala."

After several epic battles with Lawler and briefly holding the Southern heavyweight title, Harris began moving around to several different territories with his "handler," Friday, originally portrayed by Buddy Wayne.

"I can't remember whose idea it was at the time, but it was because of my size and they were going with bigger guys at the time," Wayne told SLAM! Wrestling. "They basically had no use for me and they came up with the idea."

Wayne recalled the impact Kamala had on wrestling fans during the three years they worked together throughout the South and how he felt about the character.

"At the time, you never saw anything like it. With the video of him coming out of the jungle, they were ahead of their time back then. At first I thought it was kind of goofy, I mean, who's going to believe this? He was in character so well that for some reason you started to believe it. At first I was very apprehensive, but I needed to keep working."

While in the role of Friday, Wayne had a bit of a scare during one of Harris's matches with Lawler.

"Lawler threw fire one time and it hit me in the face. He threw it at Kamala, and he ducked. I had the mask on, but you could feel the flames burning and it singed my eyebrows."

Wayne — who described Harris as professional, well liked and a hard worker — gave his impressions of his traveling partner.

"He was very laid-back, very easygoing. Kind of like a country boy," he said. "That's how he came across to me. He had a good business head."

One of the strangest feuds in wrestling history also occurred during

Harris's time in Memphis. To shake things up, longtime wrestler Stan "Plowboy" Frazier (later known as the WWF's Uncle Elmer) was put in makeup, called himself Kamala II and attacked him after a match. The 600-pounder came into the ring and delivered a crushing leg drop, and in the process, turned Kamala into a babyface for a brief period.

Harris also began to live his public life as Kamala to keep up the image of the character to the fans.

"I worked my gimmick," he said. "People never did see me without my gimmick on. When I walked through the streets every day I wore a long green dress-like thing. I always had my manager with me and I wouldn't speak English to anybody. It was a hard gimmick, but it was a good gimmick."

After working in Memphis, Harris began shuffling between territories in order to keep the gimmick fresh. He seemed to enjoy his time in Mid-South the most as wrestling was beginning to pick up interest on a national level.

"I went to Bill Watts's territory, that was the best territory I had ever been in, including the WWF," he said. "I made the most money with Mid-South. I know that's kind of hard to believe, but that's the way it was."

Andre

With his six-foot-seven-inch frame, it was only a matter of time before Harris would take on the biggest of them all, Andre the Giant.

"I was working with the Dog, the Junkyard Dog, and we worked a little gimmick where I beat him. Bill Watts was a smart promoter. After I beat all the guys, then they would bring in Andre the Giant."

Harris recalled his matches with Andre, and said there were initially some problems between the two of them in the ring.

"It just drew," he said. "Everywhere was sold out. Everywhere. My first match with Andre the Giant was in 1983, and we got into a little fight the first match. I mean, a real fight! I drove him back into the corner, and I had his lip bleeding. I nailed him because he called me an SOB. And when I did that, he called me a dumb SOB and I laid into him. People couldn't believe it. The fans didn't know what was going on."

Despite the brief conflict, the two began to work well together in the ring throughout the South and Andre invited Harris to New York to work with the World Wrestling Federation.

"After that, I had no more problems with Andre," said Harris. "He respected me, and I wrestled him in Mid-South. Then I went on to World Class out of Dallas with the Von Erichs, and he came down and we did the same thing there. He said to me, 'When you finish up, I want you to come to New York.' So Andre was responsible for me coming to New York. We did real good after that. Andre and I worked really well together."

The Chicken

Now with manager Fred Blassie, Kamala began to terrorize the WWF's top stars and ended his feud with Andre in a steel cage match. As the WWF was expanding its reach to the public, on a talk show–styled program called *Tuesday Night Titans*, Kamala ate a live chicken on television. In actuality, the animal was not harmed due to creative video editing. Harris's wide-eyed stare at the camera with feathers in his beard combined with Vince McMahon's appalled reaction produced one of the most notable moments in WWF history.

"We did that in Baltimore because they had a thing called *Tuesday Night Titans*," he recalled. "They brought me up, and I didn't know what we were going to do. They had the chicken there and they told me they wanted to show on TV that I actually ate the chicken. But we made it look good."

After leaving the burgeoning New York territory, Harris appeared with a number of promotions throughout North America, including the Quebec-based IWA. Managed by Eddie "The Brain" Creatchman, Canadian fans were treated to numerous appearances by Kamala on television. Harris enjoyed his time in the Montreal area, and, when told during the interview, was unaware of his former manager's death.

"I really enjoyed that. I'm sorry to hear about that too," he said. "I think I worked with him just the one time, I don't remember who I wrestled against, but I remember him.

"I used to love coming to Montreal. There's a place there, I can't remember the name, where I used to get smoked turkey and smoked duck. I used to get the whole duck. It was nice."

Working with Hulk

However, the WWF would soon come calling again. This time, Harris was to be groomed for some of the biggest matches of his career against the then-unstoppable Hulk Hogan. He noted how much he enjoyed working with Hogan, and also how he was mistreated by the company.

"Hogan's a sweetheart," he said. "I never worked with many world champions, and he was the only guy that I felt comfortable working with. I could just do what I wanted. We'd still have good matches, I always wanted to have good matches, but he was the easiest guy to work with. More comfortable than Andre, even after he and I had our little run-in. I looked forward to working with him. I didn't make a lot of money, but the money was always there. Vince just wouldn't pay me. I almost needed a second job when I worked for Vince."

Hogan often spoke with Harris during their time working together during one of the biggest feuds of 1986. They had several big matches, including a steel cage bout at Maple Leaf Gardens.

"He used to call me off to the side and say, 'Look man, we put those butts on the seats.' He said, 'Get your money. Get your money because I'm getting mine,'" Harris said. "I went to Vince and had a meeting with him. Vince told me, 'If you think you can get more money somewhere else, then you're welcome to go.' That's why I left so many times."

It was also during this run that a young wrestler billed as Jack Foley took on Kamala in a typical squash. Now better known as Mick Foley, he did his first stretcher job in a match recently shown on the *WWF Classics* program in Britain.

After the program with Hogan, Harris was shuffled to the side and partnered with Sika, who were both managed by the Wizard (Curtis Iaukea). A short while later, Iaukea left and Mr. Fuji took over as manager. During the second run, Steve Lombardi took on the role as Kim Chee, a role he has used ever since whenever necessary. They briefly feuded with Jim Powers and Paul Roma before Harris left once again. He noted that he enjoyed working with Sika, and considers him a pal.

"Sika and I were real good friends," he said. "He and his brother, Afa, and his other brother took me to the Samoan Islands. Oh man, we had a good time. They took care of me like a brother. I hear a lot from Afa, but I don't hear that much from Sika, but he tells me he's doing really good down in Florida."

SLAM! Wrestling recently spoke with Sika, who currently trains young wrestlers, to get his memories of working with Harris.

"Jim Harris is one of the best business people I've run into," he said. "We worked very hard for Vince. He's a good man, a good friend."

After working in Texas for World Class and feuding with the Von Erichs, Harris kept a relatively low profile in the wrestling world until 1992.

"I did a lot of independent shows and went overseas," he said. "It didn't really take a whole lot for me to live. I never had a house payment and I don't live a big, extravagant life. I don't live a high life. I'm just an old country boy and that's about it."

While working for the USWA in the early '90s, Harris feuded with Lawler and Koko B. Ware and held the promotion's championship on three occasions. It was also during this time that Harris considered suing for merchandising money he felt was owed to him by the WWF for items such as action figures using his image.

"Vince called me himself to come back in 1992," he said. "I know the reason for it. He never did say it, but it was because I had contacted a lawyer and was going to sue Vince for merchandising. From 1987, when the first doll was out, to 1992 when the second doll came out I might have made $30,000 out of all those years. After I had contacted the lawyer, I wanted to see all the sales and proof. That's when Vince called me up and asked me about coming back to the WWF. After I went back, my lawyer called me and said, 'I see you're back in the WWF, I guess you want to discontinue,' and I said, 'Yeah, we might as well.'"

With the decision to return, Harris was thrust into a feud with the Ultimate Warrior.

"I really liked the start of it," he recalled. "I had a little run with the Ultimate Warrior. The Ultimate Warrior had limousines everywhere he went, and it was paid for by the WWF. Steve Lombardi, myself, and Harvey Whippleman had to split a rental car and a motel room. That's how bad it was. Even the Ultimate Warrior told me one time, and I don't know how he knew, he said, 'Kamala, I know you aren't making much money. I just don't see how you can do it. Anytime we're booked against each other and we're on the same flight, just hop in the limousine with me. Hell, I don't have to pay for it — the WWF's paying for it. Just jump in with me.' I take my hat off to him."

After the Warrior's departure from the WWF, Harris began a program with one of wrestling's then-rising stars, the Undertaker. The response from fans was often lukewarm, and they fought in front of 80,000 fans at Wembley Stadium for the SummerSlam pay-per-view.

"That was my first big match against the Undertaker," he said. "It was alright. I had some pretty fair matches with the Undertaker, but we just didn't have matches like Hogan and I would have. The response wasn't as great."

While the event was successful, Harris believes he was not properly compensated for his participation.

"Another thing I heard was that it grossed $40 million," he said. "The Undertaker made half-a-million dollars, I heard. I made $13,000. It was terrible. I never saw the Undertaker's check, and didn't dare ask him how much he made. One night I was in Nassau Coliseum, Steve Lombardi went in the dressing room and Pat [Patterson] had left his briefcase open. Steve was browsing through it and we saw the pay book. I know what I made, it said 'Kamala, James Harris, $13,000.' Then I saw 'Undertaker, SummerSlam, a half-million dollars.' It was a big difference, man. It was terrible."

Casket Match

The feud continued to simmer throughout the fall and culminated at Survivor Series with the first-ever casket match. Harris was more than apprehensive about the match.

"I'm afraid of dead people and I'm afraid of caskets," he said. "All of it was an act, but I'm really afraid of a casket. When we did the casket match, I was a little leery about going in it, but that was the plan and I went in anyway. If you notice, during that match I looked at it a lot myself. I didn't like it at all. But once I got in there, I was so tired and so hot I thought I was going to pass out. I just stayed as calm as I could and I was alright."

In the weeks following the match, an angle was played out where Kamala would be mistreated by Kim Chee and manager Harvey Whippleman. Eventually, Kamala would turn on them and align himself with Reverend Slick (Kenneth Johnson) who would attempt to civilize the once-untamable Ugandan Giant. Kamala's ring mannerisms changed greatly, and this is especially evident on the commercial videotape *Invasion of the Bodyslammers*, where he appears in a bizarre match with Doink the Clown, a battle royal and is taught how to bowl. Harris was displeased about the face turn, but realized he truly had no say in the matter if he wanted to continue working with the WWF.

"It was all done by Vince," he said. "Vince would call me and ask me what I'd like to change and what I'd like to do. The only thing you could say is, 'Yes, I'll do it,' because if you said no, then you're fired anyway. So we didn't have much of choice. I didn't like it at all, especially when they turned me babyface," he said. "I didn't like it, but I couldn't leave because the little money I was making, Vince was taking 15 percent of it out. He told me if I happened to leave before the contract was up, my money was gone. I don't know if they did that to anybody else back then or not."

Despite the mistreatment by the WWF, Harris does not have any regrets.

"No, as far as being a part of the biggest organization in the world, I'm proud to tell people I worked for the WWF," he said. "The only regrets I have is that I didn't get paid. Most of the guys I worked with throughout my run with the WWF are all wealthy guys. They're all good guys, they're doing good. I'm the only one who had to file bankruptcy. I have a home, my home is paid for, I did pay cash for it, but it didn't come through the WWF. It came through Bill Watts. I ended up having to drive a truck and all that kind of stuff. I've never been a drunk or a drug user or have any bad habits, so I didn't throw any money away. I just didn't make any."

* * *

A PENNY FOR BANNER'S THOUGHTS

By GREG OLIVER

Wrestling Revue

The beautiful Penny Banner.

You'd think that a book about a poor girl from St. Louis who stumbles onto a career in pro wrestling, dates Elvis Presley, survives an abusive marriage and eventually becomes a senior Olympian would be a cinch to capture a publisher's attention. Or a movie producer's. But no.

After two years of writing her autobiography with *Charlotte Observer* writer Gerry Hostetler, Penny Banner worked fruitlessly to find a publisher, and eventually they decided to self-publish the book, *Banner Days*.

It was an eye-opening experience for Banner in many ways, a self-exploration and self-evaluation.

"When I got into this thing, I realized the dangers I had gone through and how lucky I was," Banner told SLAM! Wrestling. "Then the hardest part was when I went through my husband, the years of marriage. That was really, really hard. I think that took me six months to get through those 35 years. Believe me, those 35 years are kind of skipped as they were. But I didn't want to say it in a mean way or a bad way. I just wanted to look at it as an onlooker. But yet, it really led me down a lot of paths that made my life interesting and happy. It kind of tells a story that, no matter what happens to you, you can always find something good."

Banner had heard again and again from people that she should write her life story. According to Banner, Kay Flair (Ric Flair's mother) was interested in helping her out, but the timing wasn't right. It was *Charleston Post & Courier* wrestling writer Mike Mooneyham that finally convinced Banner that it should be done.

But it was a chance reconnection with Hostetler that brought it all together.

Banner and her husband, wrestler Johnny Weaver, moved to Charlotte in 1962, and went out for dinner with Billy Two Rivers and met Gerry there too. They went out nighclubbing afterwards.

A couple of years ago, they reconnected again after an obituary that Hostetler was working on at the Charlotte newspaper.

Banner recalled the conversation. "'Do we know each other?' Then [Gerry] recalled the incident when we went out to the lounge. Then we met. Her life's changed. . . . Of course, I'm divorced now."

"At lunch one day, I said, 'You ought to write a book,'" said Hostetler. "[Banner] said she didn't know anyone who could help her. I just looked at her and raised my hand."

It was a different relationship than many writers and subjects, said Hostetler. "After a bump at the start, when I thought I would do the interviewing and writing, I was extremely surprised that Penny was so well organized. She did the actual writing; my part was suggesting form and rewriting and recasting a great many sentences. And there was a lot of explaining about why my sentences were better and why certain techniques were needed. I told her, 'You're the rassler, I'm the editor. I won't rassle if you won't edit.'"

Hostetler was amazed at the stories Banner told and could not imagine anyone doing those things for a living — especially a woman.

"I wanted to write a book about girl wrestling, and how it was for girl wrestling. When I started, there were maybe 49 girls," Banner said.

Almost right from the start, she was matched up against June Byers for the women's title. "With me being a fresh 19-year-old, fresh and strong, powerful. Of course, June Byers had 10 years experience on me and I didn't know that. But the promoter, Billy Wolfe, June Byers had already been around the country with these other girls, but when I came along it was different. Then one promoter heard about the matches we had, then the next promoter heard. They all wanted to see the matches that she and I were having. Now, they might have called them matches, but I don't call them matches. I purely got the dookie knocked right out of me in each match. But it made me good."

Banner Days will be an interesting read for non-wrestling fans too. Banner, born Mary Ann Kostecki, came out of St. Louis and stumbled into pro wrestling because she had a bit of training in judo, which she had started to prepare for an overzealous beau. Later, she really did date Elvis Presley, and after her wrestling career, she worked in real estate and kept in shape to compete as a senior Olympian as a swimmer and tossing the discus.

"It's the time of segregation, and so much where you don't give a woman the same opportunity as you give a man. It tells about those times. Our payoffs weren't the same as men," added Banner. "But the young fan today, they don't care about that. If you're a fan of wrestling today, you're probably not going to buy my book. That's as plain as I can think."

Banner doesn't want to rule out today's fan completely, however. "For today's fan, they just might want to know what opened the door for what's going on today. But for me, you can't even compare what's going on today with my day. They might want to know what wrestling is."

Her own eyes were opened over the last number of years, both through the writings of Mooneyham and by reading other books by wrestlers.

"When I read some of the things that [Mooneyham] had put in the paper, I found out the answers to the questions that I asked myself all the years that I traveled from one state to another state in a week. Girl wrestling is not like men wrestling. It's as plain as that, and that's all there is," Banner said. "Today, I don't know what goes on today, but back in 1954 when I began wrestling, there were cities and states that didn't allow women wrestling because they thought we were lewd. Then there were girls wrestling who would break an ankle the first week, and they stopped, went home. Got their nose broke, got their jaw broke in the ring, and stopped and they went home. Then there were those that were the athletes that got by and didn't leave. They had other reasons. Some of them had the same reasons as the girls do today, which is money, travel and fame. But none of that appealed to me."

Other mysteries were revealed as well. "I always wondered why I would go to a territory, and then a month later, two months later or three months later, the same guys would be in the territory, still. How come those guys get to stay in the territory so long? And my book says that in my time, there was no time for any programming, planning, doing these things that these books are saying that the men have written."

In the end, *Banner Days* is more of a story of a life than a story of a wrestler.

"Penny is an amazing, resilient person. She went through experiences that would have crushed a lesser woman and came out all the better for them. You might expect a certain coarseness in a lady wrestler, but there is none in Penny," said Hostetler. "My biggest surprise was her lack of using any foul language either in person or in the book. I would have expected some of that, but she didn't use any curse words. If some are in the book — I put them there for emphasis. The book is so good that it doesn't need to rely on shock value."

From the writer: Penny always thanked me for this article, but she just hated the review that Rod Desnomie wrote on SLAM! On more than one occasion, she asked me to remove the review, which I politely declined.

WrestleMania

It's been called the "granddaddy of them all," the "showcase of the immortals" and the "Super Bowl of wrestling"; and while most hype that surrounds the squared circle is pure, unadulterated hyperbole, no one will argue that WrestleMania is the single biggest event on the calendar for wrestling fans young and old.

The same anticipation can be found on the story schedule for the SLAM! Wrestling staff. Virtually from the time one ends, the planning for next year's coverage begins. Our writers and photographers have traveled across the continent and have been live at almost every 'Mania over the past decade, something that virtually no other media entity, be it mainstream or wrestling-specific, can lay claim to.

* * *

BEHIND THE CREATION OF WRESTLEMANIA

By GREG OLIVER

We're just hours away from the Colossal Tussle XIX and the wrestling world is abuzz. Wait a minute. Colossal Tussle?

According to George Scott, who was the booker for the first two WrestleManias, that was the name that was almost used.

About six months before the March 31, 1985, mega-event, Scott remembers a meeting in Vince McMahon's office. The gatherings there were sometimes free-flowing idea sessions, and office staff who were wrestling fans often were invited to participate. On this occasion, everyone was brainstorming a name for a big event that would further marry pro wrestling with mainstream culture. Someone piped up with the name "Mania," and Scott remembers immediately saying, "WrestleMania." Later, "The Colossal Tussle"

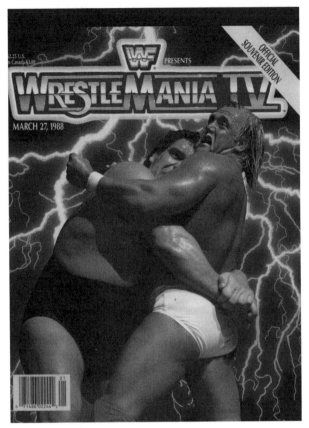

The program for the fourth WrestleMania.

came up and won McMahon's vote.

A final decision was not made that day. The next morning, Scott further argued against the Colossal Tussle, doing funny voices to mock the way the words rolled together. Eventually, McMahon relented to Scott, who had been involved in wrestling since 1948.

In Basil DeVito's WWE-produced *WrestleMania: The Official Insider's Story*, the close-call on a bad name isn't mentioned. "Credit for the name, incidentally, is generally given to Howard Finkel, known to many fans as one of the World Wrestling Entertainment's announcers. Howard is the unofficial company historian and fact-finder and the nuggets he unearths are affectionately called 'Finkel Facts,'" DeVito wrote. "It's sort of a Finkel Fact about Finkel that in a legendary meeting in the winter of 1985, while a roomful of staffers were trying to think of a name for their big closed-circuit event, Howard Finkel blurted out . . . 'There's Beatlemania, right? Why not WrestleMania?' And that was that. WrestleMania was born."

It's just part of the fascinating stories you get when you talk to some of the people, like Scott, who were involved backstage at the early WrestleManias. The stories don't always match the official company line.

Jim Barnett was a longtime promoter in Chicago, then Australia, then Atlanta, who joined the WWF in 1983 as senior vice president and stuck around until 1987.

How did WrestleMania come about? "They got the idea in 1985 when they were on a trip, a vacation for a week in Martinique, maybe it was St.

Marten. They came back and said they'd like to do this big show in Madison Square Garden with talent-like people to ring the bell, referee, all kinds of celebrities," Barnett said.

In the following years, Barnett was one of the key people in the WWF and for the WrestleManias. "Vince got the locations, but I worked real hard on it. It was a five, or 10-people show and I did a lot of work on it," he said. "The third show was in Pontiac, and I worked very hard on that. I got the biggest bonus of anyone for that show. I left their employment later and went to work for Jim Crockett."

George Scott is quick to credit his hardworking staff for the success of the WWF in the early days of national expansion. "I had some great guys working with me," he said.

Terry Garvin was his assistant, and Barnett and Rex Jones were all part of his team. To Scott, Howard Finkel is "a genius" who has a great memory — "Unreal. I couldn't believe it."

Scott's memories of the first WrestleMania are almost exclusively about what happened backstage before and afterwards. It was Scott who was sent to Atlanta to talk to Mr. T about appearing. "What a big shot. I told him where to get off!" Scott laughed.

Obviously, things were worked out in the subsequent weeks. According to Scott, a native of Hamilton, Ontario, Mr. T had $22,000 in expenses during the WrestleMania I week.

Backstage at the event, it was chaotic. "I remember Vince McMahon at WrestleMania I where I had to grab him by the shoulders and say, 'Stop. You're driving us nuts. Go in your office,'" recalled Roddy Piper. "Some guy's taking pictures of my feet. Get this guy out of here! Guy's name was Andy Warhol. I'd never heard of him. Liberace with the Rockettes. What's wrong with this picture? Little Richard . . . Dr. Ruth Westheimer."

Out in the arena, things weren't all that different. When Muhammad Ali started shadowboxing in the ring as the special referee for the main event, Scott ran to ringside, grabbed his ankle and got him to calm down, all off camera.

In the end, it was a special time where all the elements lined up properly. "I think that we were all lucky to be there. Timing is everything. In my opinion, WrestleMania was not as premeditated as people believe today," Roddy Piper told SLAM! Wrestling in a chat a few years back.

George Scott agrees. He recalled a conversation with Vince McMahon after WrestleMania. McMahon told him later that, "If we had not been successful at it, we would not have been in business."

WWF LOOKING FORWARD TO WRESTLEMANIA X8

By STEPHEN LAROCHE

TORONTO — Finally, WrestleMania has come back to Toronto!

After a 12-year absence, WrestleMania, the Super Bowl of professional wrestling, will return to Toronto on March 17, 2002, when it attempts to blow the roof off the SkyDome.

Thousands and thousands of rabid wrestling fans descended on sun-drenched Nathan Phillips Square at city hall for the official announcement. Stars like the Rock, "Stone Cold" Steve Austin, Canada's own Chris Jericho, and a host of other dignitaries, including WWF owner Vince McMahon himself, joined Toronto mayor Mel Lastman and Ontario premier Mike Harris in welcoming the WWF with open arms.

Lastman, who has never attended a live WWF event, appeared excited about the prospect of attending *Raw Is War* later today.

"I'm going tonight for the first time," he said. "I've never seen wrestling before."

While he may be surprised by what he witnesses at the Air Canada Centre, Lastman won't be surprised by the impact WrestleMania will have on the city.

"It's gonna be great," he said. "It'll be great for our economy. There's so many layoffs and there's going to be a lot more coming and this is going to bring a lot of money into Toronto. It's going to bring a lot of tourists in. It's going to keep our hotel industry growing. It's going to keep our restaurants going. And it's going to help the SickKids Hospital. This is great for Toronto."

The most venomous reception of the day was reserved for Harris. Chants of "asshole" and "Harris sucks" were louder than his speech, riddled with clichés and incorrect catchphrases to the hostile crowd. Harris didn't appear to be rattled by the catcalls.

"I think it's great," he said. "This is a great event for Toronto. Fans cheer, fans boo . . . I think we all agree this kind of entertainment is fun, it's exciting, it's professional and it's great for everybody and that's why we're happy to be here."

There was a great deal of speculation as to why the WWF chose Toronto as the site for WrestleMania. One rumored reason was the weak Canadian dollar, a theory that McMahon refuted.

"That's not that much of an issue. When you're putting on an event like WrestleMania, you do it for a lot of reasons, not just financial ones," McMahon said. "You're looking for that enthusiasm, you want that enthusiasm to come across television to a worldwide television audience and that

"Stone Cold" Steve Austin at the podium announcing WrestleMania X8 for Toronto.

was another reason why we chose Toronto, because of the fans."

WWF senior vice president of Talent Relations Jim Ross, acting as emcee for the proceedings, also agreed with McMahon and has high hopes for the event drawing a large number of people.

"There's nothing we can do about it. It's just one of those issues where it's just an economic issue," he said. "We're going to certainly make up for that in volume because we plan on breaking the attendance record and we'd like to get as close as we can to the 70,000 mark this time, which would surpass what we did in the Astrodome this past year."

Toronto has built a reputation for itself amongst the higher-ups within the WWF, and Ross noted that the dedication of fans enhances it.

"It's our commitment to the fans of Toronto that the WWF considers Toronto one of our primary cities," he said. "The fan base here is extremely enthusiastic and loyal. I think it's a validation that Toronto, in our view, is one of the major sports cities in the world."

Ross also believes fans will flock to Toronto for a variety of reasons to make WrestleMania a truly international event.

"The city itself offers a lot of opportunity for our fans to come from around the world. I think last year we had fans from 20 or 30 countries. The SkyDome is very unique in as much as we can set a lot of folks in there. So we think the facility has some unique characteristics, the city itself does and the fact that we keep it in North America and bring it back after twelve years, we believe it's the right thing to do."

McMahon appeared to appreciate the efforts made by both Lastman and Harris to secure WrestleMania, but noted the dedication of Canadian wrestling fans sealed the deal.

"There were so many cities actually clamoring for this event in terms of economic impact. It's extraordinary for any city, be it in the United States or in Canada. The elected officials here in Toronto and in the province, quite frankly, did everything they possibly could to attract the World Wrestling Federation to Toronto for WrestleMania. But the biggest reason why we were here is the fans in Toronto. They are, as you can tell, pretty souped up about the WWF."

Souped up they were. Fans were excited, if not ecstatic, about the announcement. Almost as excited as the WWF stars themselves.

Dwayne Johnson, otherwise known to millions of wrestling fans as the Rock, spoke candidly about his ties to the city and hinted that he has an idea who his opponent will be at WrestleMania.

"I'm really excited obviously, I've got a lot of ties here in Canada, especially in Toronto. My dad's from Toronto, and I can't wait . . . The last WrestleMania I think was WrestleMania VI. I think Hogan and the Ultimate Warrior, now it's going to be the Rock and whoever. It's going to be fantastic no matter who I work in the ring against. I've got a feeling who it might be."

Austin, the current WWF champion, stayed in character when asked about how he feels about the annual pay-per-view event coming to Toronto.

"I don't feel too good about it. I'd just as soon see it in the United States," he said. "But we're here tonight, we're here tomorrow and we're going to be here at WrestleMania. I go wherever they send me. I don't really like Canada, I'll tell you that much."

However, he briefly stepped out of character to reflect upon what the WrestleMania experience means to him.

"I'm looking forward to it. Last year in Houston, Texas, in the Astrodome we had the biggest gate in the history of that building. As far as being in the ring it was the best night of my career and I got to go against the Rock and it was a hell of a match. It was a great atmosphere. I've wrestled in the SkyDome many times and it's a great building. We've had some great events there and we've had a lot of people but it hasn't been sold out. I anticipate it'll be 100 percent sold out. I want it to be better than the Astrodome. If the people show up on fire and we do a hell of a job in the ring, it's going to be an experience not to miss. I'm looking forward to wrestling in a sold-out SkyDome."

McMahon, Austin's perennial nemesis, believes the SkyDome will not only sell out but also set a new attendance record for the stadium.

"I believe so," he said. "We probably can. It depends upon the size of our set and things of that nature. Whatever capacity we can possibly put in there, I'm sure we'll fill it."

Winnipeg native Chris Jericho offered his thoughts on how much he is looking forward to appearing at a Canadian-based WrestleMania after seeing two of the largest events in WWF history on video several years ago.

"When I was a kid I watched WrestleMania in 1990, and I watched the Big Event at the CNE," he said. "I always wanted to be a part of Wrestle-Mania, I always wanted to be part of the WWF and I always wanted to do it in Canada. It's going to be a great kind of homecoming."

Toronto resident Trish Stratus is looking forward to the opportunity of performing in front of her hometown crowd.

"I'm excited," she said. "I think it's a great chance to show everyone what I do and they get to see me strut my stuff. It's wonderful. I love it."

When asked if she was nervous about the possibility of being seen by friends and family at the largest event of the year, Stratus remained cool.

"I always try to deliver my best stuff out there but it's extra special. Mom'll be out there and you want to do your best. It's exciting."

Olympic gold medallist Kurt Angle believes the 18th edition of WrestleMania will be the best yet for several reasons.

"I predict that it will probably be one of the best WrestleManias of all time, not because it's in Toronto, and not because we're guaranteeing this great WrestleMania, but because we have the most blessed and gifted athletes in the history of the World Wrestling Federation right now."

Even though he has never appeared in the ring at WrestleMania, WCW mainstay Booker T believes Toronto wrestling fans are in for a treat.

"It's a great feeling," he said. "The fans right now are very happy. Everybody is excited, not only about [WrestleMania] but about the big show coming up tonight and *Smackdown* tomorrow. So it's going to be great. It's a lovely time right now."

Toronto has had a long-standing appreciation for professional wrestling dating back to the 1930s. Whether the event was in Maple Leaf Gardens, SkyDome or the Air Canada Centre, fans have attended the events in large numbers. The Rock appreciates the dedication that the fans have shown over the years.

"I'm not just saying this because I'm here in Toronto," he said. "I can honestly say that not only in Toronto but all across Canada because we're not here every single week. In Canada they [the fans] always give so much passion and energy, especially in the ACC where acoustically it sounds fantastic. I can't wait, it's going to be great.

"That live audience vibe, I feed off that, so that's something I look forward to tonight, that's something I look forward to tomorrow for *Smackdown*, and definitely for SkyDome for WrestleMania."

Angle also has an appreciation for the warm reception of the WWF superstars by Toronto fans.

"Every single time we come here, it seems to be sold out," he said. "The Toronto fans really enjoy the show. I don't think we're here enough. Three times a year might sound like a lot to most cities, but in Toronto, Canada, they're very loyal to the World Wrestling Federation."

— With files from John Molinaro, Greg Oliver and Jon Waldman

* * *

Mike Lano

Randy Savage does his patriotric part.

MACHO MAN'S 'MANIA MEMORIES

By BRIAN FRITZ — Special to SLAM! Wrestling

For the last two decades, one special night each year has captured the grandness of professional wrestling. Combining spectacular action and breathtaking drama along with the glitz and glamour of sports entertainment, World Wrestling Entertainment's WrestleMania has become the premiere wrestling event around the world since 1985.

While hundreds of superstars have graced the WrestleMania stage, only a handful have been able to leave an indelible mark on the business with their majestic performances. Perhaps no other superstar has performed at a higher WrestleMania level than former WWE champion "Macho Man" Randy Savage. Recently, he shared some of his greatest memories about being a part of the granddaddy of them all with SLAM! Wrestling.

Savage, real name Randy Poffo, brought a look and charisma to the World Wrestling Federation that few had seen before. He paraded out to the ring with long, thin hair and star-glittered robes that exemplified his grandeur. He sported a dark pair of sunglasses that, once removed, revealed his wide-eyed, crazy look as he pointed his index finger in the air.

He combined a unique wrestling style with those characteristics, featuring high-flying moves and a jaw-dropping elbow off the top rope for a finisher. Plus, it never hurt to have a beautiful woman, Elizabeth, accompany him to the ring when it came to garnering the fans' attention.

Savage used that package to catapult himself into a major wrestling star in the 1980s and 1990s which included him winning the WWF championship on two different occasions, the WWF Intercontinental title once and becoming World Championship Wrestling World heavyweight champion three times. But to Savage, working at WrestleMania was the highlight of his career.

"WrestleMania is the show," pronounced Savage. "It's the Super Bowl. It's the World Series. No doubt about it."

All together, Savage has appeared on eight different WrestleMania shows, wrestling an astonishing 11 matches in total including four times in one night.

On two separate occasions, Savage was able to capture the WWF title at WrestleMania, once from Ric Flair at WrestleMania VIII, the other four years earlier at WrestleMania IV in a tournament. Originally, he was not scheduled to win the title until other circumstances unfolded leading up to the big show.

"It actually started when they wanted to get the belt off [Hulk] Hogan," Savage explained. "I guess he didn't want to lose it so they put it up in a tournament. Right before it, there was an Intercontinental title match between me and the [champion] Honky Tonk Man. You know, Honky just had this attitude that he didn't want to lose. So, I went and did the business move and Honky Tonk Man kept his cracker jack title. Then what happened was Vince did make the change from [Ted] DiBiase to me at WrestleMania so it worked out better for me."

WrestleMania IV would prove to be a memorable night for the Macho Man as he won his first WWF championship, but he had to work a record four matches before the night was over, competing with Butch Reed, Greg Valentine and One Man Gang before defeating DiBiase in the tournament final. If that wasn't tough enough, there were others trying to impede his path to the top that night.

"I kept going back in my dressing room after every match and changing outfits. One of the people who didn't like me locked me in my own dressing room before the fourth match, hoping that I couldn't get out of there. But I busted that door down because I had so much enthusiasm in me. I think I could have gone through two of them. Just making it harder for me, well, the harder the conflicts the more glorious the triumph. It made it even more worthwhile."

For the next year, Macho Madness ruled the WWF, leading up to a showdown at WrestleMania V: The MegaPowers Explode where he dropped the title to his real-life nemesis Hogan. While the two have never seen eye to eye on many things, Savage did enjoy working in the ring with the Hulkster.

"Well, Hulk Hogan and me have personal differences," said Savage. "At the same time, in the ring we had good chemistry, good entertainment value for the fans."

After his year-long run at the top, Savage's career took a downswing as he was dropped to mid-card level, being paired with Sensational Sherri. When WrestleMania VI rolled around, Hogan was still in the main event but Savage teamed with his valet to square off against a polka-dot-wearing, comedic Dusty Rhodes and his female partner Sapphire. It was something that Savage was not used to.

"In a way, that was way different than what I was used to," he said. "It just takes a matter of time. If someone tries to hold me down, that's fine for a little while but then they usually get tired. They punch themselves out and I rise to the top. Everything is a test. Any obstacle in front me just makes me stronger."

While he would go on to face the Ultimate Warrior the following year at WrestleMania VII and regain the WWF championship from Flair at WrestleMania VIII, the match that most people remember involving Savage goes back to WrestleMania III when he went toe-to-toe against Ricky "The Dragon" Steamboat in a classic that is still talked about to this day.

"It's really flattering that people still talk about it," said Savage. "I think Ricky and myself were primed and peaked and everything just worked. We have good chemistry in the ring and it all flowed together. The entertainment of the fans had a definite hum right there because there were 93,000 plus people in the arena and you could hear them all. It was just incredible. I'll never forget that."

Of all the accomplishments that Savage achieved throughout his career, he still appreciates each and every moment he was a part of the biggest stage of them all, WrestleMania. "Vince McMahon gave me a break a long time ago. The first time I got called into New York I told him, 'Thank you for the opportunity,' and I still mean it," said Savage. "That's all he guarantees people is an opportunity. When you get the ball, you've got to run with it. That's all I needed. He gave me that opportunity and I'll be forever grateful to him."

Scoops and Surprises

As any journalist would tell you, the best stories are, at times, the unexpected ones. You might, for example, be going to a simple press conference and before you know it, a gentleman is down on one knee proposing to his longtime girlfriend.

Think that didn't happen? That we'd make such a story up? Well, it happened. While the crew was at the WrestleMania X8 press conference, expecting that the big story of the day would be the official announcement of the über show's return to Toronto, Ken Pauze became just as prominent a headline-grabber as Vince McMahon, as he asked longtime girlfriend Lesley Smith to marry him. Thankfully, she said yes.

This wasn't even the only wedding proposal the SLAM! Wrestling crew has witnessed, among the many times where our reporters have found stories that either came out of nowhere or emanated from well outside the squared circle. Here are a few of our favorite scoops and surprises.

* * *

THE PLANE CRASH THAT CHANGED WRESTLING

It's been 25 years since Valentine, Flair, Woods, Crockett went down
By JOHN MOLINARO

From the writer: Growing up as a wrestling fan, I knew about the famous plane crash in the Mid-Atlantic, but I always heard conflicting stories about what happened. That's what drove me to write about the 25th anniversary — I wanted to clear up any confusion and talk to the main principals involved, so I could write a definitive account of what really occurred. I talked to David Crockett and Tim Woods, and they told me horrifying details of what it was like just before the plane crashed. It took me more than a month to do the interviews, but it was worth it because I think of all the articles I wrote for SLAM! Wrestling, this is the one I'm most proud of.

It was supposed to be a routine flight.

On October 4, 1975, a twin-engine Cessna 310 plane carrying a promoter and four wrestlers took off from Charlotte for Wilmington, North Carolina. En route to an evening show at the outdoor Legion Stadium, the passengers were counting on a restful flight. It turned out to be something quite different.

As they approached the Wilmington Airport runway the plane ran out of gas, cutting across several treetops and a utility pole before crashing to the ground. And with that the lives of promoter David Crockett and wrestlers Tim Woods, Bobby Bruggers, then-U.S. heavyweight champion Johnny Valentine and a 24-year-old upstart named Ric Flair were inextricably changed forever.

It is remembered as one of the most historic plane crashes in wrestling lore. It was the talk of the industry for years. The landscape of Mid-Atlantic Championship wrestling, the cornerstone of the National Wrestling Alliance (NWA) was forever changed. Two careers were ended as a result of the crash, and another one, that of Flair's, was almost stricken down before it ever really got started.

Twenty-five years later, Crockett, vice president of production for WCW, remembers the terror and fear that overcame him as the plane started to nose-dive.

"At the time I was scared to death," Crockett recently told SLAM! Wrestling from his office at WCW headquarters in Atlanta. "I just remember as we started going across Cape Fear River, the engine started to fail. I remember leaning over trying to control my breathing. My wife had had our first child two weeks before, so I was trying to do Lamaze so I wouldn't get the wind knocked out of me and pass out, because I knew if I passed out I'd be deader than a doornail. I remember thinking I've got all these wrestlers in front of me, if we crash in this water, I'll never get past them and get out. There'd be no way."

Tim Woods, who wrestled under a mask at the time as the original Mr. Wrestling, remembered a conversation he had with Austin Idol, a plane crash survivor himself from a few years earlier.

"Austin Idol did not have his shoes on in the plane," recalled Woods from his Charlotte home. "And it tore the bottoms of his feet down to the bone and he nearly never wrestled again. When Austin Idol told me about that that was the first thing that went through my mind. I didn't have my shoes on either. . . . The pilot had a big briefcase with some airplane manuals in it. I grabbed that and put it under my feet because I didn't have time to get my shoes on.

"I knew we were going down, there was no question of that," continued

Johnny Valentine tried to stay involved in wrestling after the crash; here, he seconds Dale Valentine (Buddy Roberts).

Woods. "We just dropped like a rock. The controls leveled the plane out and that was about it. I knew that I wasn't going to die but I figured we'd all get hurt, it was just a matter of how badly."

Even though he knew they were going to crash, Johnny Valentine believed he would come out unscathed.

"All the time when they were going down, he said he knew he wasn't going to be hurt," said Valentine's wife Sharon. "He said he felt like he was indestructible. He said they were in trouble but that he was going to be all right. He kept telling them that."

The crash came about as a result of human error. The pilot, Vietnam veteran Joseph Michael Farkas, had trouble getting the plane off the ground in Charlotte because of the bulk of the wrestlers. He did not distribute the weight of the passengers in the plane properly and decided to dump fuel from the gas tank to lighten the load.

Valentine was the first to notice that the plane had run out of gas.

"John got to looking over at the gauge and said, 'Gee, we're out of gas.' And the pilot said, 'Don't worry about that, my wing tanks are full,'" explained Sharon Valentine. "When they started sputtering and spinning the pilot panicked and started screaming. John reached over and slapped him to try and bring him to. Had the guy not panicked, they could have landed safely."

"It was a beautiful day. There weren't any headwinds or rough air . . . he dumped fuel," recounted Crockett. "[The plane] was overweight. Luckily for me, because I probably would not be here today, is that I should have been sitting where John Valentine was sitting because of the weight factor. The weight was distributed wrong and the pilot had to dump fuel to take off. None of us knew he had dumped fuel [before taking off]."

As the plane began to drop, several thoughts raced through Crockett's mind.

"I kept on wondering why were we trying to get to Wilmington, why couldn't we land in some place like Fayetteville [North Carolina] or Florence [South Carolina] instead of still trying to go all the way to Wilmington. There

Ric Flair and Rip Hawk, from 1974.

was this luggage compartment behind me and I sort of remembered that the plane had this plastic bubble back there. I was scared enough and thought that if I survive hitting the water I'll bust through the luggage door somehow.

"At some point when I was leaning forward, praying hard, I thought I saw a light and heard a buzzer going off," continued Crockett. "This crash was after the Eastern Airlines crash here in Charlotte where they just flew the plane right into the ground and the FAA were talking about installing devices on planes that they were flying too close to the ground to let [the pilot] know. I was thinking maybe [that buzzer] was it. That's the last thing I remember."

After leveling off at 4,000 feet, the plane began to sink. It was a close call and Crockett said the pilot almost landed the plane safely.

"We crashed about 100 yards short of the runway. We just missed a water tower from the prison camp, which is there at the end of the runway. [The pilot] stalled it and hit a tree and luckily we didn't flip and turn upside down. We hit another tree and bounced off and nose-dived into a railroad embankment. If we had gotten past the trees we would have made the clearing right before the runway."

"When we finally hit the ground, [the pilot] stalled the plane," recalled

Woods. "By doing that, he got our speed down as low as possible. We were still between 85 and 100 miles when we hit the ground but we didn't slide that far. That was a real jolt. We kind of came down and it spanked us. That's where we had the back injuries and it threw everybody forward."

To this day, Crockett's memories of the crash are foggy. He has relied on the recollections of his wife, Wendy, and the other passengers to fill in the gaps in his memory.

"Talking to Valentine, he was conscious the whole time, he said, 'David, be glad that you don't remember.' All the seats except mine broke loose and went forward."

Contrary to media reports at the time, none of the six passengers were thrown from the plane. Woods says all six passengers were pinned inside, struggling to survive. "I think I was the only guy who didn't get knocked out. I was sitting right behind the pilot. All the seats broke loose. What happened was our forward motion took all the seats up in such a way that they were cascading one on top of the other. David was immediately behind me. It wasn't long. The rescue squad was there and took everybody out through the back baggage compartment door out the back of the plane."

All six were admitted to New Hanover County Hospital in Wilmington. All of them suffered a litany of serious injuries. After two months of fighting for his life, the pilot died in the hospital. He was 28.

Crockett, who felt the effects of the crash for six months after it happened, suffered trauma to his head and sustained other injuries.

"They stitched me up in my mouth, and I didn't realize that I had dislocated my shoulder. They tried to give me crutches to walk out of the hospital but my right arm wasn't working so they checked that and found out I had a dislocated shoulder. I was always complaining that whenever they put water or anything in my mouth I would scream bloody murder. When my wife got me back to Charlotte I was still complaining about it. I didn't want to eat or drink anything because it was hurting. She took me to our dentist, and he . . . looked inside and he said, 'Well, I can understand that, he's shattered two teeth and the nerves are just sitting there exposed.'"

Ironically, Crockett wasn't even supposed to be on the plane.

"I wasn't supposed to be flying that day, my brother Jimmy was. He called up and said he was feeling really bad with the flu. This was a Sunday event in Wilmington so I said I'd go because it was only a 45-minute plane ride."

Although Crockett will get on a plane today, he's still a little leery of flying.

"I'm still today very aware of what goes on in an airplane. I sleep on planes now, but if there's a smell or sound or motion I shoot straight up. I'm very aware."

Chris Swisher Collection

Flair poses post-crash.

Both Bruggers and Valentine sustained broken backs. After spending 10 days in the Wilmington hospital, they were flown by chartered plane to a hospital in Houston where they underwent back surgery. A steel rod was later inserted into Bruggers's spinal column and he was released from the hospital three weeks later. Although he could have continued on in his career, he never wrestled again.

Crockett's head crashed through the seat in front of him, cracking and bruising Tim Woods's ribs. Woods also suffered a concussion and a slight compression fracture in his back, but was the first to be released from the hospital the next day.

"I wanted to get out of there just as quickly as I could," commented Woods on his quick exit. "My wife was going crazy, we had two small children at home and she didn't know what to think. I was insistent on getting up and keeping moving. I got up and literally I had to have a person under each arm to get me to a commercial airline plane out of Wilmington to fly back to Charlotte. So I got in the plane and the plane landed in Charlotte . . . don't you know the brakes failed when we were on the end of the runway. This is the next day and I'm thinking, 'Holy cow! What's going to happen next?'"

It was Valentine who suffered the worst fate. Having broken his back in the crash, a bone fracture wedged itself into his spinal column, forcing his back to be reattached with a clamp. Valentine was paralyzed for life. His career came to a tragic end and he never wrestled again.

Valentine was the U.S. heavyweight champion and top star for Jim Crockett Promotions and was scheduled to face then–NWA world heavyweight champion Dory Funk Jr. the following week at the Greensboro Coliseum. Considered one of the best workers in the country at the time, Valentine's injury and forced retirement were a devastating loss to the wrestling community.

"I was a big fan of Johnny Valentine when I was growing up, watching wrestling in the '60s," said Bill Apter, editor of *WOW* wrestling magazine. "And this was a very sad end to one of the most magnificent careers in the business. Especially being based in New York when I was growing up, he was either in the semi-final or the final match at Madison Square Garden for so many years. For me, the worst thing that came out of that whole plane crash was the end of Johnny Valentine. I remember him the most from that."

To this day, it's Valentine's toughness that his colleagues remember the most.

"Valentine was known to be as tough a human being as probably there was around," opined Woods. "He'd beat your brains out. He was tough, physically tough. I won't say he had the finesse of some of these other wrestlers, but I mean when it came to physical ability, my God, that guy was tough. We went back and forth with the U.S. heavyweight title for some time. We wrestled each other all over the place. I always enjoyed wrestling him because it always seemed like I learned something. John was a master. Never been another like him, I doubt that there ever will be."

Ironically, had it not been for a simple twist of fate, it could have been Flair's career that ended, not Valentine's.

"I talked to Johnny Valentine about the crash and Johnny was next to the pilot, he was up front in the plane," informed Mike Mooneyham. A reporter and columnist with the *Charleston Post and Courier* (South Carolina) since 1979, Mooneyham is among the top wrestling historians in the U.S. "Flair was supposed to have been in [Valentine's] seat. He [originally was] in that seat next to the pilot but Johnny said he was kind of scared to be up there. He said Flair kept whining until Johnny said, 'You get in the back, I'll sit up here in the front.' So really it could have changed the future of wrestling."

Looking back at this cruel twist of fate, Valentine's wife insists that Johnny bears no grudge against Flair for changing seats with him.

"It's okay that it happened. That's fate. Neither John nor I feel bad about the fact that had Ric still been sitting there, he'd be in this shape. John's never shown any animosity or anything about that."

Although he saved his money during his career, the cost of medical care drained Valentine's savings completely, leaving him totally broke. Since the crash, he has had to live largely on the assistance of Social Security.

Still, Sharon Valentine insists that the crash didn't make her husband a bitter man.

"John never got angry. The only time I ever heard him get angry was when people say something derogatory against the business. He said there's no respect left amongst each other in those in the business. That angers him.

Tim Woods took one for the Crockett team.

No one has any respect for protecting the business or for each other. He said it used to be a brotherhood of respect among all and it's no longer there."

If there are any hard feelings about the crash, they're harbored by Sharon.

"John never heard from the Crocketts. He made them millions and millions of dollars. He blew [the territory] wide open. He never got nothing from them. Not talking about money, we're just talkin' about coming to see how their star is, and the guy who's doing the booking and taking care of things. Nothing."

That's not the way David Crockett saw it, and he said that he did get to see Valentine. "I saw John later, when I went to Houston," Crockett said. "As a matter of fact, he was managing some wrestler in crutches and braces. I don't remember who it was. They were trying to make him another Johnny

Valentine, which you couldn't do."

Sharon also categorizes Flair's actions and attitude towards Valentine as "callous" and "cold," claiming her husband never heard from Flair after the crash.

"For Ric to hardly talk to him and ignore him, that's hard for me to swallow."

Valentine stayed involved in the sport, helping to train wrestlers from the backyard in his home. Last year, he and Sharon were invited up to New York where WCW held a special banquet and affair for the ailing star.

"They did a three-day honorary thing for John up there, big dinner and party and stuff," described Sharon. "One of the WCW wrestlers came up to John and said, 'Mr. Valentine, I heard years ago when you hit somebody you could hear it back in the parking lot. How'd you do that?' And before he could open his mouth John reached up and grabbed him by the hair of the head, jerked him face forward and put that big arm of his across his back and just drilled him to he floor. He really showed him how he did it. And then John looked at him and said, 'There's no room in this business for wussies, boy.'"

Fate was kind to Ric Flair as, had he not been in that front seat, it's possible that it would have been his career and not Valentine's that came to an end. Nevertheless, Flair too suffered a broken back as a result of the crash and received a devastating prognosis from the doctors.

"They originally told him he probably wouldn't wrestle again because he had broken his back in three places," said Mooneyham. "And then they said the recovery time was probably going to be a year at the minimum, but he beat the odds and is still going today. He was remarkably resilient. He bounced right back, doctors were fairly negative in the beginning. He always knew he was going to be back. It was just another injury to overcome."

Prior to the crash, Flair was being groomed by the Crocketts to be the promotion's top star. He also had long-term aspirations of becoming the NWA world champion and knew that a prolonged stay on the sidelines would hurt his career.

"He wanted to get back because he was really making some big inroads at the time," offered Mooneyham. "He didn't want to lose any time because he had some pretty hot feuds going on. He wanted to get back in and start his feud with Wahoo [McDaniel]."

In a sign of just how much wrestling has changed in 25 years, Mooneyham recalled how the hospital staff was legitimately worried when McDaniel showed up at the hospital.

"Wahoo was one of the first guys to visit him in the hospital and of course the hospital attendants were startled when [they saw Wahoo]. They tried to restrain him," Mooneyham relayed. "They believed it was a real feud and that Wahoo was trying to break into the hospital to get at Ric because

Wahoo was barging right through the [security] in his style and they thought they might have to call the police on him."

Despite the prognostications of doctors, Flair returned to the ring just four months later, in February 1976, and started his legendary feud with McDaniel. On May 24 in Charlotte, Flair defeated Wahoo in a hair vs. title match to win the Mid-Atlantic heavyweight championship.

Flair was back in the game and everybody knew that nothing could stop him this time.

"He was pretty much destined for stardom," opined Mooneyham. "Everybody in the office was very high on him and everybody I remember talking to at the time knew that he was going to be world champion, it was just a matter of when. He was really itching to get back and that was an era where unless you were really bent in half, you didn't miss any ring-time. You knew you didn't miss time unless you absolutely had to."

Prior to Flair's return, things did not look good for the Crocketts. With their two top stars sidelined, Mooneyham says business took a turn for the worse.

"It was almost catastrophic because Valentine was 'The Man' back then. What it effectively did was take the two biggest stars in that promotion out of the loop and paralyzed the promotion for several months."

News of the crash was covered by major newspapers and media outlets throughout the Southeast, including a front-page story the next day in the *Charlotte Observer*.

"We based our [reportage on] *Associated Press* wire service reports that came into the office," remembered Roger Mikeal, the reporter who covered the story for the *Observer*. "That [crash] happened out of eastern Carolina and we covered it out of Charlotte. I never went down there to the site [of the crash]."

This was 1975. Wrestling was still a "closed" business. The internet was decades away. Fans back then were not as "wise" to the business as they are today. It's easy to assume that the Crocketts went to great lengths to "kay-fabe" people so as not to have it come out that Tim Woods, a babyface, was riding in a plane with Johnny Valentine, a hated heel and his scheduled opponent that evening in Wilmington.

Crockett insisted there was no "cover-up."

"That didn't really come into play because of the severity of the accident. No one really brought that up. People were more concerned with the accident and the people being hurt."

Mooneyham remembered it differently.

"They sweated that one because it was so kayfabe back then and they didn't want anybody to know that heels and babyfaces were on the plane together flying to a show. In fact, the newspaper reports had Tim Woods's real name on there because the promoters didn't want the people to know that Tim Woods was on a plane with Ric Flair and Johnny Valentine, whom he feuded with. [The *Charlotte Observer* and the *Greensboro Daily News*] reports came out with a guy named George Burrell Woodin [Woods's real name], a promoter . . . I think they listed him on the police reports as a promoter. (The Crocketts) gave them that information. They were very protective of any kind of fraternization between bad guys and good guys."

Tim Woods confirms Mooneyham's version of the events, stating he went to great lengths in helping the Crocketts to kayfabe their audience.

"I was wrestling under the mask at the time and George Woodin is my real name. When we went down they started taking information at the hospital. I gave them my real name. They didn't recognize my real name. We told them I was a promoter. . . . You always hear stories today about wrestlers riding together and everything else, which just didn't happen back then. In this case, we were coming in from different places and Valentine was my foe that evening. That's why we [gave them the name] George Woodin [so] that nobody would recognize."

As word began to leak that the masked Mr. Wrestling was on the same plane with Johnny Valentine, Woods appeared on TV and at house shows days after being released from the hospital so as to give the impression that everything was normal and that he was not involved in the crash.

"This was important because I was under the mask . . . I made appearances. I went to the towns. I never missed a beat. The first match I wrestled was maybe two weeks later against 'Superstar' Billy Graham in Richmond, Virginia. The pain was just excruciating."

As for that evening's show, the Crocketts were left scrambling for an explanation to offer the live audience.

"The show started on time and the ring announcer came into the ring," remembered Mooneyham. "He announced to the crowd that there was an airplane crash and that Valentine and Flair were injured and he told the fans that Tim Woods was lost and he couldn't make it on time [laughs]. They were still trying to kayfabe people. They didn't want people to know Tim Woods was on the plane with those guys."

A horrific crash like this puts things in their proper perspective. It underlines what's truly important in this life: family and friends. If any good came of this crash, it's that it helped to strengthen the bonds of friendship and reinforced the value of life itself.

"I remember that I would not shut up until they put me in the same room as Ric at the hospital," said Crockett. "I had a head injury and Ric had a back injury so they put us on different floors. I raised holy hell saying I wasn't going to go anywhere and I wanted to be in the same room as my friend. I think [the crash] brought us closer together. We're still close. We don't see each other as much because I'm management and he's all around. But occasionally we get together socially and remember the good old days."

— With files from Greg Oliver

CONFESSIONS OF A CANADIAN TITLE JUNKIE

By GRIFF HENDERSON — Special to SLAM! Wrestling

Andrea Kellaway

Griff Henderson with slightly less than 10 pounds of gold.

While some might call my connection with the old Canadian title an obsession, I prefer to call it a quest . . . a quest for what is in my opinion, the Holy Grail of Professional Wrestling. Here's my story.

Toronto, Ontario: Spring 1981 was when I was first bitten by the wrestling bug. Introduced to it by my schoolyard friends, I would spend countless hours in front of the television watching AWA All-Star, World Championship Wrestling, Mid-Atlantic Wrestling, Vancouver's All-Star Wrestling, and my personal favorite, Maple Leaf Wrestling.

I was in love. I instantly became smitten with the squared circle, collecting hundreds of "Apter" magazines, imitating my new idols during recess and dreaming of one day walking the ramp at Maple Leaf Gardens as my alter ego the 'Nomad of the North' Wildcat Williams. While other kids were playing hockey and softball, I was planted firmly in front of the tube, wrists wrapped in sports tape, wearing my Speedo "wrestling trunks" and cheering on "Rowdy" Roddy Piper, Ric Flair and "The Boogie-Woogie Man" Handsome Jimmy Valiant.

My first Maple Leaf Gardens card was in July 1981. That night, something caught my attention for the first time — the championship title. Not just any "strap" but the Canadian heavyweight wrestling championship. Angelo "King Kong" Mosca battled the hideous Mr. Fuji in a Texas death match. As Mosca walked down the ramp, the glare from the lights shining on the illustrious belt was blinding. I was awestruck. I couldn't get over how awesome it looked. The eagle with its wings spread looking so majestic on the leather strap. I decided right then and there that I would one day become the Canadian heavyweight wrestling champion. Wildcat Williams could not take the title from King Kong Mosca because there was no way two "good guys" could wrestle each other, but being only 11 at the time, I figured I could cross that bridge when I got there.

In 1984, Vince McMahon's monopoly of the wrestling industry continued and consequently Maple Leaf Wrestling as we knew and loved it closed up shop, rendering the Canadian title defunct.

Then 1988 rolled around. After a couple of years of working like a dog at my after-school job and saving every penny, my dreams of mat stardom were shattered following a difference of opinion between me and my would-be tag team partner. That disagreement caused the cancellation of our fall enrollment at the Hart Brothers Calgary wrestling school. A few months later, I discovered the world of radio and the rest as they say is history.

The thing is, my dream of wrestling never really died, it just sort of transformed: living vicariously checking out indie shows while enjoying a successful career "on-the-air."

In 2002 I decided to see what I missed out on. I met with Ron Hutchison and Rod Boudreau and the gang at Toronto's AWF. A couple of "bad bumps" and a torn rectos muscle later, I quickly came to the realization that things happen for a reason.

During my involvement with the AWF, I discovered that their AWF title was actually, in fact, the old Canadian TV title out of the long defunct Maple Leaf promotion. It was the closest I had ever come to a "real" wrestling belt and I have to say, for an "old-school mark" like myself, it was awe-inspiring. It immediately brought to mind the simple question: What ever happened to the Canadian heavyweight title belt?

Still being fairly immersed in the wrestling business from a hobby standpoint, I knew of a guy in Tennessee named Dave Millican who is a belt-maker and a collector of vintage ring-used belts. I sent Dave an email asking if he knew the whereabouts of the Canadian title. He said he didn't know where it ended up, so I pretty much came to the conclusion that it was probably hanging in Angelo Mosca's basement or in Jack Tunney's garage.

About a year later I stumbled across a great old-school wrestling chat site, called the Kayfabe Memories message board, that just so happened to have a chat page devoted to the Maple Leaf Wrestling territory. Just for the hell of it, I posted an inquiry hoping that someone may know what ever happened to the "10 pounds of gold." Lo and behold, the same Dave Millican, who a year earlier didn't know of its whereabouts, responded to my post claiming he owned one of the old Canadian titles. He emailed me a picture and after all this time — SUCCESS — it was the belt I was looking for.

I immediately pleaded with Dave to sell me this prized possession, basically telling him the story you've read here. It was not to be. He told me he'd only had it in his possession for a few months, having obtained it from an independent wrestling promoter in Maryland. As the story goes, this promoter had the belt for some time and was still using it in-ring. He had received several offers from nostalgists to purchase it. Millican was finally able to persuade the promoter to swap the piece of Toronto wrestling history in exchange for three new belts. Although I gave Dave my sob story and offered him "the world," Dave said he had absolutely no interest in parting with his recent acquisition. He did however tell me he planned to restore the belt and if time permitted sometime in the future, he might possibly consider making and selling me a replica. He took my email and said if he ever became desperate, he would contact me, but not to hold my breath.

A few months went by and I have to tell you, I was putting myself through hell. Knowing full well it would probably never be mine, yet I couldn't stop thinking about it.

Then one Monday morning, I arrived at the MIX radio station in Toronto to do the morning show with Carla Collins and, as I did to start every morning, I checked my Hotmail account. To my utter delight I read the name Dave Millican in my inbox. Before I even opened the email I knew what it was about. Dave had just purchased one of the NWA tag titles and was in need of some cash. Although he didn't necessarily want to part with the Canadian title, he knew by selling it to me it would be appreciated and in good hands. In essence, the belt was "going home."

After much scraping and skimping and a couple of meetings with my bank manager, the day finally arrived. When FedEx arrived at my door, I felt like I had just pinned Angelo Mosca. Now, after all these years, I was the Canadian heavyweight wrestling champion! (What a mark, eh?!)

A wise man was quoted as saying to me, "You've been through enough . . . that you've done more to earn that belt than any of the 'champions' that wore it . . . LOL."

End of story right? Not exactly.

For my new quest, I'm frantically looking for pictures or images of the 10 different Canadian champions pictured wearing the belt. They are Dino

Bravo, Greg Valentine, Dewey Robertson, Iron Sheik, Angelo Mosca, John Studd, Sergeant Slaughter, Mr. Fuji, Ivan Koloff and Angelo Mosca Jr. Anyone with photos, magazine or *Stranglehold* program images they're willing to sell or make copies of please contact me at mayorgriff@hotmail.com. The toughest ones to find seem to be Valentine, Fuji, Koloff and especially Mosca Jr. In fact, I've been in touch with Big Ang and even he doesn't seem to have a picture of Junior with the belt. I'm also researching the history of the belt and its travels since Maple Leaf Wrestling closed up shop. Any information or assistance would be greatly appreciated.

Special thanks to Andrew Calvert, Mike Cannon, Terry Harris and SLAM! Wrestling's Greg Oliver, for their help in my obsessive pursuits.

From the staff: Griff has since sold the belt, tapping out to financial issues.

* * *

ADRIAN STREET PROPOSES TO MISS LINDA

By GREG OLIVER

Greg Oliver

The bride, groom and . . . mortician? Miss Linda, Paul Bearer and Adrian Street on the day Adrian proposed.

LAS VEGAS — In the make-believe world of pro wrestling, reality can often seem out of place. But Friday night, "The Exotic One" Adrian Street stunned a captive audience by proposing to his companion of 35 years, Miss Linda.

In front of a room of friends at a Baloney Blowout during the annual Cauliflower Alley Club reunion at the Riviera Hotel & Casino in Las Vegas, Street talked a little about his childhood before popping the question.

As a teen in England in a family of coalminers, Street was into body-building, but recalled buying a wrestling magazine for a friend who was a wrestling fan; "I happened to notice a boxing and wrestling magazine in the store. I bought that for my friend Peter," Street said, starting to choke up. "I took that book home, and damn was I hooked, damn was I hooked. My heroes were Buddy Rogers, the Stanlee Brothers, the Tolos Brothers, the Grahams, Killer Kowalski, Yukon Eric, Antonino Rocca and my favorite of all time, Don Leo Jonathan. You guys, you rescued me. In my life — I've never met some of you — but you meant SO much to me, so much to me. You gave meaning to my life."

Street left home at 16, not wanting to work in the coal mine and became a pro wrestler in 1957, as Kid Tarzan Jonathan, in tribute to his hero.

Looking around at the gathered crowd, including former world champions and stars of tomorrow, Street, wearing a ladies' white wig to cover his bald head after a bout with cancer, tearfully choked out the question. "I would say that it doesn't get better than this, but there's one thing that can top this, my friend, my love [Linda] marrying me."

After establishing that Linda did indeed say yes, it was announced that Don Leo Jonathan would be the best man. Father Jason "Wolfman" Sanderson will marry them Saturday.

Before leaving the podium, the cross-dressing Street joked, "I don't want any cracks about same-sex marriages!"

After meal of cold cuts and salads ended, Miss Linda — looking the same as she had for years heading to the ring with Adrian Street (minus the big boots) — talked to SLAM! Wrestling.

"It was quite a shock. . . . We sort of never really thought about [getting married] very seriously," she said. "It'll be really nice to do it, to do the deed."

Linda was not sure what she was going to wear, let alone what someone with such exotic tastes as her fiancé would wear. "He brought a fancy suit with him, one with peacocks down the side!" And like her longtime partner, she too was quick with a flash of wit. "What about a pre-nup?"

Earlier in the evening, Nick Bockwinkel laid it on the line, instructing the hundreds in attendance to try to appreciate today's wrestling and wrestlers.

"I see high risk moves that they couldn't have bribed me to do," Bockwinkel said. "They're on the front line today . . . we should welcome them."

In another few years, he said, today's stars from TNA and WWE will be welcome at the Cauliflower Alley Club reunions. A second-generation star himself, Bockwinkel heaped praise on wrestling families like the Guerreros (with Mando Guerrero in attendance), and the Ortons, saying how the talent ramped up from Bob Orton Sr. (who was in at the CAC in the afternoon) to Bob Orton Jr. to current WWE star Randy Orton.

Saturday night is the 40th annual CAC banquet, honoring the likes of Terry Funk, Jack Brisco, Les Thatcher and Ernie Ladd.

From the writer: A right place at the right time story, for sure. But what I remember most isn't the proposal — it was the wedding, which happened the next night, before the Cauliflower Alley Club banquet. Someone decided to do the wedding earlier than originally planned, so many of Adrian and Linda's friends actually missed the ceremony.

ASNER AND GAGNE RECALL *THE WRESTLER*

By BOB KAPUR

Wrestling Revue

From the writer: I think the Movie Database is a great example of SLAM! Wrestling's unique nature. When it was started, our editors challenged us to get unique stories from the people involved in making the movie — wrestlers, or otherwise — as opposed to simply writing a standard movie review. Interviewing Ed Asner was a real thrill for me. I'm a complete TV junkie, so getting the chance to talk to him was as big a mark-out moment as when I got to meet my wrestling heroes like Terry Funk, Jimmy Snuka and Bruno Sammartino.

A wrestling promoter turns his back on the company's aging champion, and instead puts all of his promotional power behind a young up-and-comer.

Sounds like a storyline that one might see on *Raw* or *Smackdown*, doesn't it? But it's also the plot of *The Wrestler*, a movie that some historians call one of the best movies ever made about the sport. SLAM! Wrestling talked with two of the movie's stars — wrestling legend Verne Gagne and TV icon Ed (Lou Grant) Asner, to discuss this one-of-a-kind film.

Released in 1974, and currently available on video and DVD, *The Wrestler* tells the story of wrestling promoter Frank Bass and the struggle he has in trying to wrest the title away from the company's champion, Mike Bullard, played by Gagne. Bass, portrayed by Asner, would prefer that Billy Taylor (real-life British wrestler Billy Robinson) wear the belt and represent his company in the upcoming "Super Bowl of Wrestling," a tournament pitting the champions of the various regional promotions against one another.

Of course, this wouldn't be a problem in real life — after all, the promoter could simply write an angle where Bullard drops the belt to the youngster. However, the movie was made during the time when the industry was still very protective of its scripted nature. So rather than expose the secret world behind the scenes, the movie depicts the "kayfabe" world of wrestling. In other words: the events going on are real. So when Bullard ducks the match against

Taylor by claiming he's injured, there's little that Bass can initially do about it. Ultimately, he makes the match, but only after pulling a power play on Bullard; he embarrasses him on TV by calling him a cowardly champion and threatening to strip him of the title. Bullard agrees to go through with the match, even though everyone doubts he can beat Taylor.

The climax of the film comes when the two finally square off in the ring. The match goes on for a little while before Bullard goes for his big finishing move, the flying dropkick, which should put Taylor away for good. The camera zooms in for a close-up on the bottom of Bullard's boot, which is heading straight for Taylor's face . . . and then the film comes to an abrupt stop, making it one of the most open-ended movies since Butch and Sundance jumped off the cliff. The viewer has to guess what happens next. Does Bullard land the kick and go on to win the match? Or does the young lion Taylor retire the wily veteran and bring some new blood to the "Super Bowl"? Though neither Asner nor Gagne had the answer to that question, both of them had other memories about the making of the film.

For Gagne, the experience was both positive and negative. As executive producer, he took on a lot of the risks associated with making the film, despite not necessarily understanding the intricacies of the Hollywood machine.

"Nobody had [done a movie] on wrestling in quite a while," Gagne recalls. "So I thought it might be a good idea. We had enough TV exposure around the country that we could plug it. I put the most money [into the movie] than anybody — I had a little over 50 percent of it. Financially, it wasn't my biggest success . . . I never saw any money out of the thing."

Still, despite the financial results, Gagne did achieve one of his goals — raising awareness and appreciation of the sport generally. Throughout the movie, wrestling and wrestlers are held in the highest esteem. In one scene, a newspaper reporter dismisses the in-ring death of a wrestler as unimportant, telling Bass that wrestling belongs in the theater pages and not the sports section. Bass passionately defends wrestling, detailing the history of the sport, and lists the names of real-life wrestlers who died in the ring, arguing that they deserve tribute as well. "You don't want to write about the sport," Bass tells him, "because you don't understand it."

Asner himself left the movie with a newfound understanding and respect for wrestling — and the wrestlers he got to work with.

"They were wonderful guys," he recalls. "Kind and considerate, very professional. And what struck me is that they were such superb athletes. I had some muscle back then, but I was around all these guys who could swat me around like a fly."

The movie was filmed in Gagne's stomping grounds of Minnesota, and includes cameo appearances by several Hall of Famers who were in the territory at the time. Historians will be interested in seeing Dusty Rhodes and Dick Murdoch (the two get into a bar brawl in one of the movie's funnier moments), as well as Larry "Pretty Boy" Hennig, Wahoo McDaniel, and Jim Brunzell during their younger years. It was a hectic time for all of the wrestlers involved, Gagne remembers.

"During the filming, we were also wrestling and jumping all around the country, coming back the same night to Minnesota, and going to work on the movie the next morning. It was a lot of hard work, doing the movie and trying to keep the wrestling business going at the same time. We were really juggling things in the air."

Gagne credits Asner a lot in helping him keep things on track on the set, often working with the wrestlers on honing their acting skills, and generally helping them adapt to life on a movie set.

Not that Asner had a great deal of experience himself in that arena. Though he was one of TV's most recognized stars, starring in *The Mary Tyler Moore Show*, *The Wrestler* was one of Asner's first movie roles. Not really a wrestling fan — though, as a kid, he did go to some matches with his father — his interest in making the movie was more for building his resumé.

"I was relatively new to TV, and was eager to make a name for myself in the movies. The offer came around, it seemed like a decent enough role, a decent enough script, so I went for it," Anser says.

He is quick to return Gagne's compliments, maintaining that it was the talent and professionalism of the wrestlers that made the shoot go smoothly.

"The wrestlers didn't have Hollywood experience, but they still held their own. They played roles they were comfortable in. They did stuff they knew, and stuff they could do, and they did it well."

Of course, it wasn't all routine for the wrestlers. The filming sometimes required them to "break kayfabe" during a match — again, something that was not normally done in that era.

George Schire, longtime Minnesota superfan, was lucky enough to be in attendance to witness some of that occur. "I was at the match tapings at the old St. Paul Auditorium in 1973," he reminisces. "They would fill the auditorium with artificial smoke, to make it look like a typical smoke-filled wrestling arena. When they were filming the Gagne vs. Nick Bockwinkel match, Verne hit Nick with a dropkick that really connected, and just about knocked his head off. They had to stop filming for a bit until Nick was okay. Then, when it was time for Verne to put his sleeper hold on Nick, Bockwinkel told the crowd that that would be the only time he would ever sit down for Gagne. It was also fun to see what they did with the death scene match, when Ray Stevens killed Jack Cutter [played by Joe Scarpello] with his 'Bombs Away' jump off the top rope. They had to redo the scene about three times to finally get it the way they liked it."

Although this experience gave Schire, and the other fans in attendance that night, a small peek through the veil of wrestling, Gagne didn't really "smarten up" Asner about the business, nor did any of the wrestlers. Asner confirms this, noting that the wrestlers were overall very good about protecting the industry.

"It was unbelievable," he says. "It's like a secret world, a very closed society. They have their own code, a language like carny speak, and they would resort to using that at times. I found it very intriguing. It really was a fascinating world to be in."

It's a world that Asner won't rule out visiting again if, he says, the script and the role are interesting. But it's safe to assume that if he does, it won't be in the Frank Bass role. Indeed, we may never know what happened to Bass and Bullard after the cameras stopped rolling — since, according to Gagne, there are no plans to do a sequel.

For some people, this news may not be too disappointing; for example, Marc Thibideau, who panned the movie in a 1975 issue of *Wrestling Monthly*. "Anyone wishing to see it," he wrote at the time, "should not expect a cinematic gem. The plot lacks in excitement and imagination [and] often lags, hindered by an inane script."

However, other critics like Andy Bator, whose review appeared alongside Thibideau's, were able to appreciate the film regardless of some of those flaws. "There is a little bit for everyone here," according to Bator. "[The movie is] some good clean fun."

Where both writers did agree was in their praise of the performances put on by the wrestlers in the movie. Thibideau was particularly impressed by Billy Robinson. "Not only does [Robinson] provide spectacular action in the ring, he shows excellent acting talents," according to Thibideau. "[He] really shines and brings out much of what wrestling is all about."

As well, both writers did acknowledge that the movie was useful in introducing wrestling to a brand-new, mainstream audience. Bator credited the film with, "[depicting a] side of wrestling no one knows about."

Thibideau himself expressed hope that the movie would be only the first step in that direction. "Perhaps now the Hollywood moguls will realize the vast potential inherent to the oldest and most exciting sports spectacle."

Thirty years later, it's difficult to say what impact, if any, *The Wrestler* really did make on the professional wrestling industry. But for Gagne and Asner, it doesn't really matter; for them, their memories are what count.

The Wrestler was directed by Jim Westman and runs 95 minutes long. The DVD edition (full-screen) includes limited extra material — a biography on Verne Gagne and Ed Asner, and a short interactive quiz about the events in the movie.

* * *

The People's Eyebrow is raised.

THE ROCK KNOWS HIS ROLE

By GLENN COLE — Toronto Sun

Four years ago, a young man stood in the corner of a SkyDome press box.

No one had talked to him for a while. It was understandable as Vince McMahon, the head of the World Wrestling Federation, was the center of attention.

The young man was the new kid in the WWF, which at the time was struggling, getting beaten badly in the U.S. television ratings by the rival World Championship Wrestling.

Yesterday, that young man was back in town. And you couldn't get near him for the crowds.

The Rock has the city of Toronto in his hands. In fact, he has all of the wrestling fans in North America in his hands.

If there were any doubts about the Rock's popularity, they were erased yesterday. Several hundred fans were in a downtown movie theater for his news conference. And there was a long lineup outside a nearby bookstore where the Rock was signing copies of his book The Rock Says . . .

Give the man credit. He knows what he is doing, both in the ring and out of it. In his early WWF career, there were those who felt he was a mid-carder and would be nothing more than that. Well, look at him now.

He has grown so much in popularity that NBC's Saturday Night Live has engaged him to be the host of their popular program two weeks from tonight. The only other wrestler hired to be a guest host of the show was Hulk Hogan many years ago.

With his work ethic, and the fact that "Stone Cold" Steve Austin is on the sidelines recovering from neck surgery, there is little doubt that the Rock, who will appear in a movie called *The Mummy II*, is the number-one attraction the WWF has.

"We're in the business of entertaining," said the Rock, who took questions from both the media and fans in the movie theater before leaving to sign books.

"Characters like the Rock, Stone Cold, Triple H (Hunter Hearst Helmsley) and Mick Foley . . . there is a lot of crossover appeal there."

Entertainer

"Of course, there is the fact that there's no longer people pulling the wool over anybody's eyes. What we do is sports entertainment. It is choreographed. It is predetermined. Getting over that stereotypical bump, we as entertainers are able to put out an entertaining product," Rock said.

Originally, the word was that the Rock would answer questions only about his book, which vaulted to number one on best-seller lists after only four days on the market. But he relented. He smoothly answered questions from the media about his book and WWF happenings. Then he entertained queries from the fans who had welcomed him with a "Rocky, Rocky, Rocky" chant.

There has been divided opinion about the book, which itself almost seems split in two.

The first part deals with the growing and maturing of Dwayne Johnson, the Rock's alter ego. The second part deals with the character of the Rock and how it has developed quickly into one of the most popular in wrestling history.

He has taken a bit of heat for writing the second half of the book "in character."

"I think when you look at the character of the Rock, his first and foremost purpose is to entertain the fans like nobody else can," the Rock said. "The feeling I got going from Dwayne to the Rock (in the book) and speaking in the third person was that it was just entertainment."

Come to think of it, that is what the Rock was doing most of yesterday.

The man knows his role and he doesn't have to wait in a corner to see if someone wants to talk to him.

Everyone wants a piece of the Rock.

From the writer: It was strange looking back at that interview with the Rock, especially considering what he was on the popularity charts just a few months earlier. Give the Rock credit. He worked on his act and very quickly advanced to the top. He was always athletic and that gave him an edge over some of the less-than-ready-to-compete men of the day. He would get that look in is his eyes. He was ready to put you down. As an interview, he was a treat. He always had something to say, whether it was in character or out.

* * *

BEARING IT ALL FOR GINGER —
THE STUPIDEST THING I'VE EVER DONE

By JEFF MORRIS — Special to SLAM! Wrestling

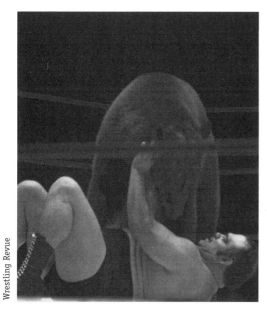

Wrestling Revue

Jesse "Bull" Ortega is pinned by a bear.

What's the stupidest thing you've ever done in your life? I'm sure you have one. If not, then I've got more than enough for both of us. Next week marks the 25th anniversary of the absolute epic moment of stupidity in my life. It was more than stupid. It was stupid-and-a-half.

In the summer of 1981 a just-a-bit-seedier-than-a-carny guy came through the doors of the *Prescott Journal* in Prescott, Ontario, where I was enslaved as a summer student at a buck-fifty an hour. God bless you, Dad. I know he's smiling and looking down at me saying, "Yeah, son, but that was 1981 money . . ."

The poster said that "Big Time Wrestling" was coming to the Prescott Community Centre, now the Leo Boivin Arena. All of the big names were coming. Whipper Watson Junior, the Sheik, a couple of fat, bald, hairy Slavic dudes, and the headliner, Ginger the Wrestling Bear.

So Steve Bonisteel, our editor, tag-teamed with Bruce Hayes, and they tapped right into my unstable craving for making a complete idiot of myself in public.

"Come on, Jeff, you always said you liked George Plimpton," said Steve.

"Yeah," Bruce jumped in. "I bet George Plimpton never wrestled a real bear before."

Within seconds Steve was on the phone with the Big Time Wrestling promoter/poster guy/bus driver/janitor/surgeon. He hung up the phone and had a big smile and this Chucky-becomes-an-editor look on his face.

"It's all set up," he beamed. "You will be the volunteer from the audience to fight Ginger."

What have I done now? Ohhhhh crap!

Wednesday night arrived — those six days went quickly — and the Leo was filled to the rafters with the townsfolk of Prescott. Remember, this was before specialty channels. You had to actually leave your home to see a good sociological train wreck, like the one I was about to be. I was destined to become an urban legend that night, shredded to death by this huge, ugly, smelly, shaggy, beast being swarmed by flies. Did I say huge?

So I'm there in the ring, wondering why I can't swallow, hoping I don't soil myself in front of the whole town, looking at this thing. The bear's trainer, a slightly bigger and smellier and shaggier man than Ginger, and who was likely a retired wrestling bear himself, approached me gruffly.

"She's de-clawed, but she can still hurt you so be careful. Don't go near her head because the muzzle isn't fastened, it just slips on. Don't pull her hair — that makes her mad. When you're ready, just walk into her. When I give her a signal, she will pin you. Just let her and you will be okay."

Walk into her? For all the times I fought through ADD in my life, this was the one moment I wish I actually hadn't been paying attention.

So I "walked into Ginger," and the huge, hairy trainer holding Ginger on a chain made this primal sound and the beast rose majestically onto its hind legs, scaring away the hundred or so flies buzzing around its face, and thudded its enormous paws onto my not-so-big-after-all shoulders.

Standing up, Ginger was almost eight feet tall. I reached up and put my arms on the bear's shoulders, and we looked like two kids slow-dancing at their first sixth grade sock hop. Actually, that was slightly more frightening than wrestling a bear.

Then, without warning, the big hairy man gave a signal, and in a flash, I was flat on my back, looking at the light fixtures, while Ginger started to climb on top of me for the pin.

Realizing my moment of glory was nearly over and I had yet to make a worthy spectacle or idiot of myself, I panicked. You see, I was a wrestling fan, and I knew what to do. I was near the ropes at the side of the ring, and I quickly rolled onto my side and started pounding the mat, feigning agony, just like wrestlers and soccer players do on TV. My leg was also on the bottom rope, which nullifies the pin. Those are the rules in wrestling. I mean real wrestling, not that crappy, boring kind they do in high school and the Olympics.

So I got up, and figuring this would be the only time I would ever be in a wrestling ring in my life, I started running around and bouncing off the ropes, stopping occasionally to flex my disproportionately chickenlike arms.

I went back and forth, and Ginger was getting a little worked up and the big hairy man started yelling at me to stop.

Ginger was trying to follow me around and was getting tangled in the chain and was getting upset and confused. The trainer looked at me, with foam leaking out of the corner of his mouth and yellowing, angry eyes with Wal-Mart Lab red-eye.

"What do you think this is, a comedy show?" he barked. Evidently, he didn't get the memo. He dug his heels in and fought in waterski position to try and control the bear, but I didn't care. I was driven by adrenaline from the roar of the crowd, even if they were all laughing at me, not with me.

Even my mild-mannered and very proper grandfather was standing along the boards of the arena pounding the glass with his fists while laughing uncontrollably at me.

Eventually, the bear trainer calmed me down enough so that I could grapple with Ginger a bit more, though I'm sure he let the bear take a few liberties with me. She seemed a lot rougher and more aggressive the second time around and swatted me around pretty good.

He gave the signal again, and wham, I was down. This time, I let the beast pin me, not wanting to freak it out. The fact that Ginger was rubbing her head against my side, trying to slip the muzzle off, while I lay on my back with a tree-trunk-size leg and paw on me kind of added to the "thrill" of the experience.

I immediately thought of all those stories you read, you know, "Camper mauled to death by bear." I lay there, helpless, thinking of how much fun the Journal staff could have if Ginger would have worked the muzzle off and went Siegfried and Roy on my throat.

Ginger took on more comers that night. Bill Martineau gave it a try, and then Steve Dring, a brilliant soccer player, got in and lasted several minutes with Ginger before he was finally pinned.

Ginger's Only Loss

Over the years, throughout the 1980s, Ginger took on thousands of bozos like me in small towns across North America.

But one of those bozos, a larger-than-life animated character named Barry "Bear" Vinson of Sparta, Tennessee, actually beat Ginger in the ring. In over 10,000 matches, Ginger lost only once. Bear Vinson, now 46, put the smackdown on Ginger back in 1980.

"There was this elderly gentleman with Ginger as a sideshow at the local fair," said the Bear with his thick, southern drawl from his home in Tennessee. "People were lined up to rassle that thing, and my friend said to me 'Bear, y'all gotta get in there and rassle that bear.' I just looked at him and said, 'I ain't gonna rassle no dang bear.'"

Bear Vinson was no ordinary 20-year-old. Nicknamed the Hulk, he was a big, strapping lad who played offensive line at Tennessee Tech. He bench-pressed 575 pounds and he could squat 1,400 pounds. In the days before steroid use, these numbers were staggering. Bear was also undefeated at the state level as an arm wrestler. If anyone could take out Ginger, it was Bear.

"I watched that dang bear for three days," said Bear. "I studied it and I watched it, and then I figured I would give it a try, but figured I'd change things up. You know, surprise her."

It was old timers' day at the fair that day, and Bear was wearing overalls. The trainer had been smashing watermelons on the ground for Ginger to eat, and Bear noticed how slick the floor was and that Ginger's opponents couldn't get any footing — not that it would matter.

"Instead of just climbing through the ropes, I dove through them, right into the ring," said Bear, who I could tell was wishing he could demonstrate it even though we were talking on the phone. "She came right at me and was swinging her big arms. Even though she was de-clawed, she slashed my chest pretty good. But out of sheer terror, I just did what we were trained to do in football. Keep your feet shoulder-width apart, and keep them moving. I tried not to get too close to her where she could hurt me and get an advantage."

Bear managed to get Ginger on all fours, and then he pounced on her back. Ginger started swiping her big paws at his feet, but he kept backpedaling away from her swats.

Bear got Ginger up and then went at her feet. Somehow, he managed to flip Ginger over his back, and the great Alaskan bear landed with a thud.

"She fell, but she got up swinging at me," Bear explained. "And I did the same thing and she flipped over me again."

Ginger got up and just walked over to her corner and sat down. "She wouldn't get back up," said Bear. "The trainer came up to me and said he wouldn't allow me to rassle her no more. I said to him don't worry, 'cause I don't wanna rassle no dang bear no more. I figured it's just one of them things you get to tell your kids about some day."

Bear's legend grew in Sparta, but outside of the town, many doubted his 725-pound tale. Even his ex-wife, a doctor, had her doubts, until a client came in who happened to be from Sparta. When the girl found out that her doctor was married to Bear, the story was confirmed.

"She came home and said 'I thought you was just jokin', but this girl came in and she didn't know me from diddly, and she said it was true.' In Sparta, that's how I got my nickname, Bear. That and the fact I was 14 pounds, nine ounces when I was born."

Ouch.

Bear became a computer teacher and has been a motivational speaker, and his story of defeating Ginger the Wrestling Bear is one of his favorite ones to tell.

"You always have to believe in yourself and stay positive," he said. "You're dealt a hand of cards every day and you just gotta put your poker face on and do the best you can.

"I walked in there believin' I could beat Ginger, and I sized her up and went in with a plan. It just shows that you can do anything you put your mind to in this world."

After talking to Bear, I thought about my experience in the ring with Ginger. I didn't have a plan. Well, I kind of had a plan, but it was more to act like an idiot than to actually wrestle the bear. Then the plan became not to get killed.

And I don't think a plan would have done much for me. But it worked for Bear Vinson — a man who earned his nickname the hard way. I guess, in some sort of twisted Freudian way, I overcame a big fear of bears by actually wrestling one.

But as for my other big phobia? There's no bloody way I'll ever get into the ring and wrestle a clown.

* * *

FOR THE LOVE OF THE BUSINESS

By RICHARD KAMCHEN

"Why the hell am I doing this to myself?"

That has to be the question many wrestlers, especially those struggling to reach greater heights by way of the independent circuit, habitually ask themselves.

Of the thousands who try, only a select few make it to the big stage, and fewer still become main-eventers there.

Many of the would-be wrestling stars of tomorrow are first drawn to the spectacle known as professional wrestling as children, watching their favorite stars hammer each other into oblivion on TV. The obsession eventually grows to the point where they think that they too could get into the squared circle and entertain fans around the globe.

But most discover the road to stardom is a grueling one to journey, especially during the early days of punishing training and subsequent arduous road tours.

"They see wrestling on their TV every week and it seems thrilling, but they don't realize that there is a ton of time away from home, family and friends," said Winnipeg, Manitoba's Chi Chi Cruz (a.k.a. Corey Peloquin), a 20-year veteran of the business.

TV has a tendency to show only the glamour of the sport, not the travails that led to the glory.

"Lumber" Jack Johnson (a.k.a. Jason Collier) was once evicted from his apartment when he could not pay the rent. But refusing to give up on his dream of becoming a wrestler, the Nova Scotia-born Johnson slept at Toronto's Pearson Airport and showered at a gas station while still attending training sessions.

"That lasted two-and-a-half months 'til the classes ended. Then I was on the first bus back home to Cape Breton," Johnson said, adding that once he arrived home, he had to go through another wrestling school to pick up some work. After completing numerous other training schools, he went on to wrestle for MainStream Wrestling in Canada's East Coast.

Scotty Mac, who wrestles for British Columbia promotion Extreme Canadian Championship Wrestling, revealed the highly educational nature of his initial workouts.

"After my first training session, I remember getting a ride home with my girlfriend at the time, and I had to pull over and throw up. When I woke up the next morning, I had a hard time getting out of bed," said Scotty Mac, who requested his true identity remain anonymous.

"Kowboy" Mike Hughes (a.k.a. "Hangman" Hughes) remembered touring with Atlantic Grand Prix Wrestling after 10 one-hour sessions with René Dupre, his father Emile Dupre and Hubert Gallant, and facing a less than magnanimous opponent during his first match.

"I was put in the ring with Bobby Bass and all he did was squash me and take advantage of me. He was a real ass and the Cuban Assassin came to my aid," said the six-foot-five, 260-pound native of Stratford, Prince Edward Island.

Hughes added Assassin thereafter became something of a mentor to him, teaching and helping build his confidence: "I owe the Cuban everything; he taught me how to be a pro."

Luckily for Kingman/Brody Steele (a.k.a. Peter Smith), a six-foot-six, 300-pound "monster," his immense size precluded abuse.

"I was first trained by Emile Dupre then went to Calgary and furthered my training with Leo Burke. I could have kicked any trainer's ass in the world before I got trained, shoot, so that was never a concern of mine," said the Cole Harbour, Nova Scotia resident.

Stu Hart once lamented the state of today's wrestling schools, calling them, "dancing schools," and other wrestlers have echoed his sentiment about unqualified trainers too.

"These 'schools' are killing the business," said Kingman.

Winnipeg's Rawskillz (a.k.a. Bryce Ridgen), without naming names, said there are a couple of organizations in Winnipeg that run schools with trainers that are not properly trained themselves. "It's a dangerous sport when guys don't know what they're doing."

Cruz agreed: "Always be careful of trainers who never did a thing in their careers, because really, what can they truly teach you?"

The tours can be just as devastating as the training, and perhaps more so. Just ask anyone who has competed in and completed famed Winnipeg promoter Tony Condello's annual Northern Tours.

"If you can survive those you can survive any promotion," Condello said, noting the inherent dangers of these freezing winter excursions into northern Manitoba Aboriginal reservations. "If you don't know your way, you're not going to make it back."

The veteran of 30 such tours (which Don Callis dubbed "Death Tours"), said a lot of guys have backed out of the trips after being unable to cope with the adversities.

Death Tours represent a mental as well as physical test, as wrestlers endure temperatures that can dip to 50 degrees below zero Celsius, and multi-hour drives across frozen lakes and tundra. Conditions improve little once arriving at a destination, as the talent is forced to sleep on mats on gym floors, wrestle every night and cook for themselves because of few, if any, available restaurants.

Bringing food along is a must, unless a performer is willing to pay about four times the typical cost of provisions, Condello said (the exorbitant cost is due to the challenge of transporting food to these northern hamlets).

Some of the notables who have survived the tour include Edge, Christian Cage, Rhino, Chris Jericho, Test, Lance Storm, and Cruz.

"If you aren't sure you want to be a wrestler, you'll know after living through one of those tours," said Cruz, who has been on every Death Tour since 1990, save maybe two or three. "Most guys don't realize the tremendous amount of time it takes to travel between shows and how boring it is to deal with."

Traveling from one destination to another (not including harrying circuits into the wilds of Canada's North), can also be a heavy financial burden for wrestlers as many must pay their own way.

"Young guys have to pay for it more because they need the experience and if they are unknown, then who is going to pay to see them? You spend your career building your name and your worth," said Cruz, who at this stage of his career can get promoters to pay for his transportation.

Rawskillz works only in Winnipeg partly because of the expense in moving province to province.

"It costs a lot to get your name out there," he said, adding he also stays close to home because he is attending university to earn an Education degree.

Those who withstand the training and begin traveling the indie circuit soon discover wrestling is not necessarily the gateway to riches.

"My first match, I got an envelope with $10 in it," said Scotty Mac.

Although his pay has since improved, he still needs the income from a second job to live on his own. Complicating matters is every job he takes outside of wrestling must accommodate bookings he gets. "Wrestling is my number one priority," Mac says.

"It's really tough to be able to stay on top of bills, rent, gym membership, food and all the other necessities in life and still keep the drive and desire to keep on going in the business that is going to make you or break you," added Johnson.

Rawskillz said there is not much money to be made for the typical indie wrestler, with guys averaging $20 a match. If traveling, some guys can makes upwards of $100 a card, but that is not the norm, he said.

When Rawskillz first started out, his goal was to one day go an entire year making a living from wrestling, but that never panned out.

"There's a lot of talented wrestlers out there. You've got to totally dedicate yourself," Rawskillz said.

Cruz said he has made a living exclusively wrestling at many points in his career, but emphasized holding down a back-up job is a smart move to ensure one's bills get paid. Even now, Cruz said he works security at a Ramada Inn in Edmonton, Alberta.

The business can also put great strain on personal relationships.

"A lot of times my girlfriends don't like my wrestling character. And they don't understand why they can't come on tours," said Scotty Mac.

"I wrestled 32 matches from April 21 to May 18, 2006, mostly against former ECW star 'High Flying' Chris Hamrick," said Johnson. "Wrestling a schedule like [that] really takes a toll on your mind, thinking about your wife and child at home, and your body, from night after night of bumping, lack of sleep and traveling sometimes nine hours to the next town. But in the end it's worth it."

Working regularly in Europe among other places since 2002 has often kept Kingman away from home: "I am lucky to have an understanding wife. I've been gone for months at a time very many times."

"You sacrifice so much that it becomes hard to explain," said Cruz. "I have left friends, family, and girls I loved behind in order to make a name for myself in wrestling."

But those vying for the top are willing to sacrifice almost if not everything, including their health, to perpetuate their careers.

"I was on the road 157 nights straight my first tour. I wrestled through a lot of injuries including a torn quad and never complained," Hughes said.

He said Cuban Assassin took a picture of his torn quad and displayed it on the refrigerator in his apartment. When another wrestler griped about a pain in his shoulder, Assassin pointed to the picture and said, "That kid hasn't complained once. What's wrong with you again?"

The most ambitious of wrestlers accept and endure their assorted trials and tribulations to attain their ultimate goal, which most commonly is getting a job with WWE or with a Japanese promotion.

"I would love to work for WWE but living in Prince Edward Island doesn't give me a lot of exposure or access to tryouts," said Hughes. "They don't come to you like other sports recruiting, you have to go to them. TNA is also very appealing to me. I've worked with a lot of their guys in Puerto Rico and the talent kept asking me, 'Why don't you come to TNA?' So who knows?" Hughes also wrestled with New Japan Pro Wrestling in 2005 and has plans to return.

"I've had hundreds of matches, but in terms of WWE, they're a step above everyone else," said Scotty Mac, who attended a WWE training camp in Louisville, Kentucky, last year and called it a humbling experience. "They even teach the basics differently. There is so much to learn. Even guys who've been wrestling for years and years, they don't know as much as they think they do.

"There's a reason they're [WWE] in the spot they are. They set the standard. WWE's the place to be in."

Although many Canadian wrestlers applied to attend the September WWE tryout in Ottawa, Kingman felt such events were a waste of time.

"WWE tryouts are a joke. They want you or they don't," Kingman said. "I work as often as I like for All Star Wrestling in the U.K., and subcontract myself to other one-off groups while I'm there."

Cruz thought the tryouts made it easier for wrestlers to get a chance to catch WWE's eye, but admitted he is not actively pursuing a spot in that organization.

"I am not giving up hope either, I have merely readjusted my goals," said Cruz, whose current goal is to get a TV show idea, a wrestling-based comedy, filmed and produced. "I am happy helping young guys develop their talent too. I help the younger wrestlers in Monster Pro Wrestling and Power Zone Wrestling and it is nice to be appreciated."

Rawskillz also is no longer looking at making his future all about wrestling. "It is so physically demanding and the reality of it is not a lot of guys will make it. It's sort of a weird dynamic. I'm realistic about it — I do it for fun. . . . When the match is over and I'm proud of it, it's like a piece of art."

Still, Rawskillz said he aspires to one day wrestle in Japan, saying he preferred the style there over that of WWE because the Japanese matches focus more on competition and sport than "wacky storylines."

Rawskillz felt WWE did not put much stock in a wrestler's experience and pedigree, instead placing much greater emphasis on those who completed its own training camps. With fewer performers working their way up through the ranks, there is little to differentiate the newer talent, he said.

"Most of today's stars don't have the charisma that was there before," Cruz added. "I think it's due to pushing guys before they are ready. They can do the moves, but that connection with the crowd is absent."

Hughes agreed, pointing out a lot of "cookie-cutter wrestlers" lack a feel for the crowd or their craft. "In this business, I feel the best way to learn is working as many different people and styles as possible in as many different countries as possible. In Europe and Japan the style is technical and stiff, in Puerto Rico it's brawling and violent with some lucha libre. . . . In this business you never stop learning.

"When Undertaker, Flair, Benoit, Booker T, Finlay and Regal are gone that's the end of the great workers — the end of the old-schoolers," Hughes said.

Many bemoan the loss of the "old-school" mentality in wrestling and feel it is sorely missed.

"Emile paid me well for a green guy but I paid my dues and earned every penny," said Hughes. "I worked twice a night, set up and tore down the ring, etcetera. I was brought in properly and learned to respect the business."

Cruz said the scene has changed a great deal, where many of the young guys want to perform all their "cool spots" every match, which often comes at the expense of telling a good story in the ring.

Traditionalist Condello, however, revealed some things never change, and stressed wrestlers still need to remember five basic rules if they want to make it: Listen, mind your own business, don't complain, show respect ("Yes sir, no sir"), and be on time.

"Otherwise, the business will chew you up and spit you out."

* * *

TURNED OFF BY NAKED WOMEN WRESTLING

By BOB KAPUR

Say what you will about Carmen Electra's Naked Women's Wrestling League, but they have absolutely nothing to hide. Unlike some other wrestling companies that merely tease their fans by having their women appear in scanty outfits but never deliver the goods, NWWL strips itself of any false pretenses and gives the audience the real deal. You want to see naked women wrestling? Brother, you've come to the right place.

The right place on Monday night was the Docks nightclub in Toronto, where the NWWL taped its next pay-per-view show in front of an invitation-only audience of hundreds of (mostly male) fans. And what a show it was.

Model/actress/next Mrs. Bob Kapur, Carmen Electra, kicked off the show, whipping the crowd into a frenzy with her poignant question, "Do you guys want to see some naked women?!" (Psst . . . Carmen, honey? Did you really expect them to say no? I mean, jeez, it's not like they thought they were there for the church social. The sign says Naked Women's Wrestling . . . not too many ways to take that. What's that? Your head hurts now? That's okay, you just lean it on my shoulder . . . that's right . . .)

But, what's this? That's Jimmy "Mouth of the South" Hart. He's not a naked woman! What is this, some kind of bait and switch?! Oh, no, wait, Jimmy has just confirmed it. There will indeed be naked women wrestling in a little while. First, though, there will be four matches featuring women in bikinis. Okay, nearly naked women, that'll work.

Though "work" is probably not the best term when describing the actual wrestling that went on. Flair-Steamboat this wasn't. However, to be fair, the buxom beauties with names like Trish the Dish, Ninja Chops, Cleopatra and Josieann the Pussycat did seem to try hard. And what they lacked in psychology, they certainly made up for in spirit . . . and nakedness . . . well, near-nakedness for now.

Lots of hair whips were employed, along with the occasional body slam. And, presumably to accentuate the near-nakedness, lots of back bridges and arches, chest chops, and roll-up pinfall finishes. (An aside: The NWWL hired

Toronto trainer Ron Hutchison to train the girls a little in the finer points of wrestling, much like he helped Trish Stratus, Traci Brooks and Gail Kim.)

The highlight of these matches had to have been Mandy Weaver, a stunning competitor whose previous claim to fame was that she played one of the Mary Annes on the quasi-reality show *The Real Gilligan's Island*. She seemed very energetic and honestly excited to be participating — reminiscent of Christy Hemme when she was still in WWE. But, enough about that . . . let's get to the naked wrestling!

Finally, after a brief intermission, Carmen introduced a couple of clothed (boo) women, and the clothed (yay) Jimmy Hart who introduced the clothed (boo) April Hunter. I didn't really pay attention to this, since nobody was naked. And then, it began, with a rematch between the two competitors who wrestled in the first bikini match of the night. And they wrestled the exact same match — the same hair whips, the same chest chops and the same back bridges and arches, even leading to the same roll-up pinfall finish. But this time . . . it was naked.

But you want to know the strange thing? Naked Women Wrestling isn't as great an idea as it may seem like on paper. Let me explain. Did you ever see that episode of *Seinfeld* where Jerry's girlfriend kept walking around naked? George thought that this was a great thing, but Jerry, surprisingly, wasn't too thrilled with the situation. He went on to explain the difference between "good naked" and "bad naked," citing the difference between a woman brushing her hair (good naked) and a woman straining to open a jar of pickles (bad naked). Naked Women Wrestling: bad naked.

The powerful spotlight flooding the ring seemed to magnify every muscle ripple, every jiggle, every bounce — and for reasons I can't fully articulate, this just wasn't appealing. In fact, it was actually kind of disturbing. Now, don't get me wrong; I like naked women as much as the next guy. But some activities are better left covered up, and, based on what I saw on Monday night, wrestling is one of those things. I left before the first naked wrestling match finished, and I never looked back.

Of course, for those who did enjoy what they saw, my views probably won't change their minds. They'll probably order the pay-per-view when it becomes available, and maybe even go to their website and order a Naked Women Wrestling DVD or something. And to those people, I wish the best — enjoy and have fun. Maybe it's better on the screen than live. As for me, I'll be content with seeing Naked Women Not Wrestling. If there are any volunteers out there . . . call me. Just don't tell Carmen, she might get jealous.

From the writer: I probably got more emails about this story than with any other I've written. The answer:

No, sorry, I don't have any pictures that I can send you.

This was the craziest night. The building was so packed, there was barely enough room to breathe. People were standing on chairs and hanging off of walls and hooting and hollering all night. I'm too young to have experienced Beatlemania, but I imagine that this is what it would have been like . . . that is, if the Beatles fans were all drunk horny guys . . . and the Beatles were a group of naked women.

* * *

Jason Clevett

T.J. Wilson and Nattie Neidhart before they became WWE's Tyson Kidd and Natalya.

T.J. AND NATTIE: A PERFECT TEAM

By JASON CLEVETT

From the writer: I've known Nattie and T.J. since 1996, and watched them grow as both human beings and wrestlers. We've celebrated holidays and birthdays together, eaten countless meals and watched thousands of hours of tapes. That friendship, and the joy I felt in seeing two people I call friends achieve their dream of being signed by WWE, came through loud and clear in this piece. It's a great feel-good story, of which there are far too few in wrestling as of late. I've written several stories on both of them throughout their careers, but this is the one of which I am most proud.

Working for the biggest wrestling promotion in the world is the dream of any aspiring wrestler. For Calgary's Nattie Neidhart and T.J. Wilson, not only are they a step closer to achieving that dream by signing developmental deals with WWE, it is that much better because they are doing it together.

A couple since November of 2001 (Wilson was signed on November 4, 2006, five years to the exact date of them first getting together), Wilson and Neidhart have seen many parallels in their careers. Both have worked in Japan, the U.S. and England. The two never toured at the same time, but in pursuit of their dreams they knew there would be times apart. To be heading to Deep South Wrestling in Atlanta together makes their signings that much sweeter.

"It makes it a hundred times easier and better. Having people with you makes it easier. I did five tours with New Japan Pro Wrestling, but the best time I had was the last 10 days of my last tour when Harry Smith was there, I had a lot of fun," said Wilson, who along with Neidhart sat down with

SLAM! Wrestling recently for their final non-WWE-approved interview.

"Usually any of the breaks that we've gotten, it's been alone. It is hard when you have to go alone without that rock in your life. I wish I could box up my entire family and all my friends and just take them with me to Atlanta. That is the kind of girl I am," added Neidhart. "T.J. and I doing this together is really going to test us but it will also bring us closer together. I couldn't be happier that we are getting to do this together because if we weren't it could be difficult. No matter what we always know we have each other and will get through it."

The road won't always be smooth. Wrestling is a high-pressure business. Wrestling relationships, where both members of the couple are in the spotlight, often end in divorce and bitter breakups. Neidhart and Wilson are positive they will not head down the same path.

"You have to separate business from personal. In wrestling it is very hard but you have to find that line. A lot of the couples that have split up in wrestling met while wrestling. I met Nattie way before we started wrestling and that will be the difference maker," said Wilson.

Neidhart expanded on her belief. "You have to stay true to who you are. You can go and turn it on at night and be that Diva in the ring but at the end of the day you have to think about the relationships and connections you have in your life, those are the most important things that you have. At the end of the day that is all that matters, which is why my family and I are so close and why T.J. and I have such a great relationship. We've been together a long time and we have a lot of trust and communication. We have fights, we have a hard time wrestling together at times because we are so emotionally attached. It is hard to step away, but we have to. When we are in Atlanta and at work, we can't be boyfriend and girlfriend, we have to be professionals, male and female wrestler, separate entities, and then we go home later. When you are at a show or in the ring, it is like any workplace. You have to be professional and make the best of the situation. There are pros and cons, you get to be with the person that you love, but deal with the drawbacks. We take it one day at a time and do the best we can. I'm sure there are going to be times when I want to give T.J. [my finishing move] the Nattie-By-Nature."

"I'd counter it anyway," Wilson shot back.

Friends and family are very important to the couple. Neidhart is the daughter of Jim "The Anvil" Neidhart and the first third-generation female wrestler. Having the backing of the legendary Hart family has been a vital part of her success.

"They have always been very supportive. My dad was rather skeptical; he was never angry with me being in wrestling but parents always worry about their kids and pro wrestling is a very hard industry so my dad always worried about me. Now that I have made it through Japan and England and am doing well and my dad sees how much I love it and how balanced I am in my life he is so happy for me. Same with Bret — he could not be more thrilled. My uncles and aunts have all been positive influences. I wish my Grandfather Stu could be here to see this."

Another name standing in the background applauding is Tokyo Joe. The legendary Calgary-based trainer has worked extensively with Wilson, Neidhart and Harry Smith and was their link towards the opportunities to tour Japan and England. To see his charges going to the big time is all the reward he needs.

"Joe was so happy. His goal was just for us to be out there and successful. He is so proud of all of his guys," said Wilson.

Neidhart added, "Joe just wants to know not only that we are happy but that his hard work and training continues. Joe has a legacy as a trainer and his spirit is being carried on with us. Joe has never been about recognition or getting patted on the back, and he has never taken a dime from us for training. He just wants to know that he helped us for our future and made us different from other wrestlers. He knows that we have a big platform where we can display those abilities."

Being able to wrestle full-time is a big change for Nattie in that for the first time wrestling will be her sole focus. Until recently she was a server at a popular restaurant, which paid the bills, supported her and T.J.'s dreams and allowed her the flexibility to leave to wrestle. While sad to leave that part of her life, she's also eager to move on.

"Now my work is wrestling so my entire focus is on that, which is what I have always wanted it to be on since I got involved in wrestling. However, we have also had to pay the bills and it allowed T.J. and I to buy our first place together. T.J. has been very fortunate to have successful trips to Japan and England so he has been able to have more consistent work," she said.

"I am so happy for both of us that we can both focus on wrestling. We are so fortunate for this opportunity, I get to have someone say, 'We are going to focus on Nattie and make her the best Nattie Neidhart that we can make her and she is going to be ready to go.' You need someone to take you under their wing. [New DSW trainer] Tom Pritchard knows what he is doing and produces good wrestlers. The DSW trainers are going to be a great help to us. It is an exciting feeling to know you can chase your dream so hard and actually touch it and taste it. I can say when I am 80 years old I did it."

Training in Deep South means a change in style. Both Wilson, who has been wrestling for 11 years, and Neidhart, who has been wrestling for five, will have to change their approach to fit the WWE style. For now, the days of 25- to 30-minute matches are mostly in the past, but both were excited to learn new styles.

"Everywhere you go you have to adapt. Japan, England and different parts of North America are all different styles and different locker rooms. A true professional can adapt to any style and roll with the punches of that territory," said Neidhart. "Going to Deep South and working for WWE is a tremendous opportunity for myself and T.J. I don't feel that we will be compromising our work or our work ethic; I think we are just going to be stepping into different elements that we haven't focused on before. We will be working on our presence and look and wrestling — repackaging ourselves, and polishing up Nattie and T.J. and making us shinier. It's just the next step. You can go to university and work your ass off to be a teacher but once you get in there with real kids it is totally different than all the schooling you did."

It is likely only a matter of time before both wrestlers are brought up to the main roster in one of WWE's three brands. Nattie's cousin Harry Smith is already signed to the main roster but has not appeared on TV yet. A ready-made angle seems to be there for the taking involving the next generation of the Harts. With some of the best wrestlers in the world as possibilities, Wilson and Neidhart talked about whom they would like to square off against.

"Chris Benoit is number one for me because of his Dungeon history and he is such a big influence and a great wrestler," said Wilson. "Shawn Michaels is someone I would like to wrestle, and Hunter obviously. William Regal, Finlay and Dave Taylor are established guys that I could learn a lot from. Then there are newer, younger guys like Johnny Nitro and Carlito, Randy Orton. It sounds stupid but I would like to wrestle the entire roster, just for myself to see where everyone is at, how I measure up and what they can do."

Neidhart has a long history of wrestling men on the independent scene, and her list is much the same as Wilson's. It's unlikely she will be wrestling men however, and can't wait to get it on with her fellow divas. "Trish Stratus is obviously someone I really wanted to work with, and it is unfortunate that she is not wrestling anymore, but she could come back. Mickie James is so passionate and fiery about what she does, as is Victoria. These girls have characters; they have a zest about them and are so athletic. Victoria is a consummate professional and for someone who hasn't been wrestling that long she is fantastic. Some of these new girls like Maria, Candice Michelle and Ashley that have not been in the business very long at all have so much potential. When you look at Trish Stratus, when she started she was just a fitness model and she wanted to be more than that and had to take it to the next level. Trish left an impact on wrestling and will go down as one of the greatest women wrestlers of all time. She started out where these new girls are starting. Maria came to the Shimmer shows I did and was so focused and inquisitive and watched every match and was eager to learn. She is someone who is really cute and open to learning. All of those girls have potential. They just have to want to take it to the next level. As much as I have been to different countries, we can learn so much working with these new people and they can teach us so much. I am looking forward to growing with them."

Goodbyes have been said. Bags have been packed and arrangements made. After spending most of their lives and careers in Calgary, it's time to move on. While both have a great deal to be proud of from their past, the future remains wide open.

"One chapter is closing but another is open, the book is still unwritten. Truly the sky is the limit, I think it comes down to what can I do? What can I bring out of myself? What level can I go to? It is in my hands. I've wrestled in the biggest company at the time in Japan, I've wrestled for at the time the biggest company in England, I worked hard there and tried to make a name for myself. WWE is the biggest wrestling promotion in the world, it's all my accomplishments at a higher level and it is up to me if I sink or swim," said Wilson.

"As far as wrestling, I trained in Japan for several months and conquered a big life-changing experience and what I endured over there. With WWE now, Nattie, who I am, does not change. Where I am going changes but where I have been does not. It is up to me to stay positive to keep my eye on the road and keep focused. Most of all, I have to be happy," Neidhart reflected. "Wrestling makes us both happy, we are happiest in the ring or watching wrestling tapes with Harry for hours. We really do love it. As long as you can do something that you love it will never be work. I am so excited about growing and learning from WWE and so many places we haven't been yet and people we haven't met. Our job will never be boring, so this is a very exciting experience and is something I will never forget."

*   *   *

THE RICH HOBBY OF WRESTLING CARDS

By JON WALDMAN

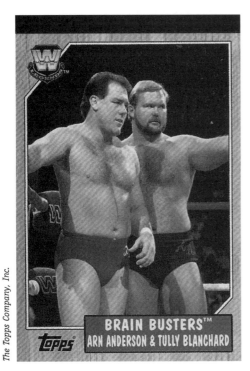

BRAIN BUSTERS™
ARN ANDERSON & TULLY BLANCHARD

The Topps Company, Inc.

Wrestling trading cards have been around for more than a century, and the recent announcement of a Topps–WWE collaboration gives collectors a new reason to celebrate.

The agreement between World Wrestling Entertainment and Topps Trading Cards, which was announced earlier this month, will see the popular sports and entertainment card company produce a variety of sets devoted to WWE's past and present stars. Prior to the agreement, Topps's United Kingdom division had been releasing WWE cards exclusively in Europe.

Topps is no stranger to the wrestling card market, having produced cards throughout the post–Second World War era.

"Topps and professional wrestling are as American as apple pie," noted Topps's Clay Luraschi. "Topps has over a half-century tradition of presenting the biggest names in professional wrestling to the North American public. Commencing with our 1951 Ringside card product, and continuing with our WWF card products in the 1980s, and our WCW card products in the 1990s."

Because of wrestling's trading card history, Luraschi believes that the new sets will be popular with the young and old alike. "Similar to our sports products and our Star Wars products, wrestling is a property that involves a multi-generational sharing of experiences, fun and collecting among children, teens, parents and grandparents," Luraschi said.

The first set under the new agreement will be Topps Heritage, a popular brand in their sports and entertainment lines. Luraschi believes that the appeal of the Heritage line will cross over well to the new WWE product. "Building on Topps's successful marketing of our Sports Heritage brand, that we successfully extended to our Star Wars Heritage product in 2004," Luraschi said, "our 2005 WWE Heritage product is going to incorporate vintage designs in showcasing a blend of current WWE Superstars, Divas and

WWE Legends from the past . . . that young and old can share the fun of collecting together."

Packs of Heritage cards are set to carry a suggested retail price of $1.99 U.S., a number that should help sales that have struggled in recent years. "Few cards sell nowadays due to the high per pack price," said Dave Gannon, organizer of the upcoming Great Canadian Wrestling Expo.

History

Prior to creating its first stand-alone wrestling set in 1951, Topps issued its first mat wars cards in 1948's Hocus Focus product. Among the cards found in that set were Stanislaus Zbyszko, the Masked Marvel, Tony Galento and others.

Since that first effort, Topps has produced cards of the greats in the wrestling industry on and off for a number of years, creating a variety of sets which children of all ages will remember vividly. Among those are WWF sets produced in the mid-1980s, which were created in Canada by sister company O-Pee-Chee.

Topps also had a licensing agreement with World Championship Wrestling in the late 1990s, which yielded a variety of cards featuring stars of WCW and the nWo. The company also produced Europe-exclusive cards featuring stars of the former company in the early 1990s.

Before Topps acquired their latest license, WWE trading cards had been produced by Fleer/Skybox International. The company had produced a wide variety of sets in the late 1990s through the summer of 2005, when it went out of business. During their run, Fleer brought a number of innovative cards to the hobby. Among these were memorabilia cards, which feature a swatch of material from a wrestling event, be it a competitor's trunks, a valet's ringside attire or the mat itself.

WWE has also had a trading card agreement with Classic Games Inc., Action Packed (which was the first company to include certified autograph cards in a wrestling product) and Comic Images, while WCW cards were produced by Impel and Cardz Distribution during the pre-nWo years. To this point, only one card set has been created that features the stars of TNA. The set, released in 2004, was created by the now-defunct Pacific Trading Cards Inc. Cards have also been produced in Japan and Mexico, featuring the top stars of puroresu and lucha libre.

Wrestling cards, in fact, date back all the way back to the early 1900s. There were a variety of pre–Second World War wrestling cards produced that were distributed in cigarette packs. These cards, however, primarily focused on amateur and Olympic wrestlers.

Among these was a 25-card set known as "Wrestling and Jiu-Jitsu." The set was created in 1913 by John Player and Sons, which was a division of the Imperial Tobacco Company of Britain and Ireland. Also popular in this era were Exhibit cards, which were produced from the 1920s through to the 1960s.

Following the cigarette card era, three companies produced wrestling card sets, including Topps, Exhibit, and Canadian company, Parkhurst. Parkhurst, a name familiar to hockey fans, is credited with creating the first "parallel" cards (cards which look similar to standard cards, but have differing elements such as color or photos or, in this case, offers for various toys) in the wrestling hobby.

A variety of other card-type collectibles have been produced over the years, including premium cards inserted in bags of chips, magazines and boxes of ice cream bars. Recently, WWE has been creating photo cards that have been inserted into their DVDs. Other collectibles include stickers and POGs.

Collectors can get a preview of the Topps Heritage set by picking up promotional cards featuring WWE champion John Cena.

* * *

ULTIMATE WARRIOR PULLS A FAST ONE

By TJ MADIGAN — *Calgary Sun*

When I heard the Ultimate Warrior was preparing to announce his return to wrestling, my reaction was a little mixed. The sports journalist side of me cringed at the idea of a retired grappler in his mid-40s — who was absolutely hideous in the ring, even in his prime — stepping back into the mix to turn exciting main events into plodding nostalgia acts.

Meanwhile, my inner 12-year-old was excited like crazy at the prospect of hearing that thumping rock riff blare over the PA system and seeing the Ultimate One running to the ring with his big '80s hair blowing in the wind, multicolored neon tassels and all.

Of course, even as a 12-year-old, I knew the Warrior sucked when it came to wrestling fundamentals but for some reason, it didn't seem to matter. I didn't care how limited his arsenal of moves was, how his matches employed virtually no psychology or how many mid-carders got buried during his push.

The Ultimate Warrior was the coolest thing since, well, Hulk Hogan, and no amount of arguing would change my pre-teen mind.

These days, my standards are a little higher but the Warrior's potential return made me wonder what reaction grown-up wrestling fans would have

Mike Lano

The one and only Ultimate Warrior . . . er, The Warrior.

to their childhood hero in the current WWE climate.

Fortunately for me (and my inner 12-year-old) the wondering didn't last long.

Tuesday morning, the Warrior clarified his plans by announcing he would indeed be returning to wrestling . . . as a pixelated character in Acclaim's upcoming Legends of Wrestling video game.

It was a bit of a letdown, even to the most closeted Warrior fans but I guess it goes to show he did learn something from his wrestling tenure after all — the art of the swerve.

He teased a return to the ring and garnered more positive press than he'd seen in years. Then he pulled the swerve by announcing he isn't really coming back but will instead be making appearances on a PlayStation or GameCube near you.

Well, he didn't "technically" lie.

Actually, I guess I shouldn't have been too surprised by the stunt. Warrior's behavior since his plunge to obscurity has been completely off-the-wall at the best of times.

Let's start with his website — Ultimatewarrior.com. This is the forum he uses to share his "Warrior Wisdom" — random threads of motivational advice, written in what I can only describe as a barely comprehensible *Lord of the Rings*–style dialect. These rants are often so incoherent they make his old nonsensical '80s promos seem as logical as Rick Bell columns. Read them if you dare.

Ramblings aside, he has legally changed his name to Warrior (he was born Jim Hellwig), so now his wrestling name appears on his driver's license, passport and all other legal documents.

On the employment front, he insists he'll never work for Vince McMahon again. These days, he earns his living preaching politics at conservative speaking engagements across the States. His mission is to educate youth and to irritate as many liberals as possible. Seriously, he said that.

Most controversially, he has been outspoken about the premature deaths of several wrestlers who have struggled with demons, insinuating they deserved to pass away. He wrote a scathing editorial on his website soon after the death of Davey Boy Smith, criticizing the former British Bulldog's lifestyle and suggesting he "chose" to die.

Overall, some pretty heavy stuff, which is sad because that's not what the Warrior character was ever about.

While researching this piece, I looked up some vintage videos of the Warrior in his prime, fully expecting to criticize his lack of ability and draw up comparisons between his kooky character and his even kookier real-life persona.

However, as soon as the entrance music started, I found myself not really caring about the politics, the work rate or the long-term ramifications of the booking.

Maybe it was nostalgia (or maybe my inner 12-year-old) but for whatever reason, I managed to suspend my disbelief for the first time in a long time and enjoy the show the way I used to when I was a kid.

Maybe that's why the Warrior had so much impact in such a relatively short career.

And why a lot of my generation will be lining up for Acclaim's Legends of Wrestling when it hits stores in April.

From the writer: To this day, I still rock out to Warrior's WWF entrance music when I need to pump myself up for a few extra minutes on the treadmill. But as a serious sports writer (well, as serious as you can be when you cover wrestling for a big Canadian daily) I tried to be objective when working on this story. A little too objective, apparently. Because not only did the Ultimate One email me a lengthy point-by-point rebuttal letter, he had his defense arguments published on SLAM! Wrestling for all to see. A lot of people think the Warrior is nuts. I personally think he's pulling a Britney. Manipulating us all with a lifelong wink-wink marketing act that always keeps us guessing — and more important, talking. Genius.

* * *

THE WARRIOR REBUTS TJ MADIGAN

By THE WARRIOR — Special to SLAM! Wrestling

TJ, hello. Warrior here.

I receive over 500 emails a day; it was natural someone would forward me your article. I appreciate parts of it and take umbrage with others.

To begin, as the creator, owner and performer of Ultimate Warrior, I find no disagreement with your pro–Ultimate Warrior points. In fact, you make my case — your article is an excellent affirmation entirely supporting the same line of defense I use for my career when others throughout the industry, pseudo-friends and foes, want to irrationally bash it as if the character wasn't

Wrestling Revue

Upset Warrior, and he might break your guitar.

an impact player or even go further and speak of his career as if it did not exist at all. Ultimate Warrior "got over" (sounds like he's still "over," even with you) and was enjoyed because he struck a chord, pure and simple.

Others — many, many others — had the same opportunity and they failed. It's the truth — take it or leave it. I realize my immodesty, confidence and self-esteem bothers people, but I'm proud of what I accomplished during my sports entertainment career and am not embarrassed to defend its worth. The critics are the ones who should be ashamed, especially those who tell untruths.

It may surprise you and those like you (part despising criticaster/part zealous fan) to hear me say it, but I've had much less to do with perpetuating the legend of the Ultimate Warrior persona than all those who keep excitedly reliving him through their remembered childhood fantasies, only later to ridicule the character now that they've "grown up" and gotten oh, so mature. I appreciate it.

Now, be honest, who's swerving who?

You haven't read anything at my site. If you had, you could not honestly make (and mean) the statements you have about the contents of my numerous posts. It would be impossible. There is a disclaimer right on the front/menu page telling that the writings are a combination of different writing voices (you're a writer, you understand that, yes? no?), all relevant to an incredible and sincere learning process I set out on and want to tell others about. The story about that, and the story behind my name change which you take a potshot at, are endearing and empowering. Only a nincompoop with a cold, cruel heart could find otherwise.

I have countless communications and professional relationships that refute every letter of every word of every sentence you write attempting to ridicule my writings. Frankly, that kind of criticism has become very worn out and boring. Blatantly absurd. Each time someone comes to my site expecting to discover the discombobulation and outer-space rhetoric they've been told they will find, they end up writing me at great length telling me the only thing they disbelieve is how well I've articulated my views and how proud they are to know they followed my career. Simply put, they tell me they are glad to now know the man behind the face paint. They get it.

When one achieves chronological maturity, it is important to think and act that way. The organizations I work with across the country are some of the most-respected organizations on the planet. Anyone who wants to know can find out for themselves; those who don't, just don't want to.

I have worked very hard to build another career, invested intellectually in myself and had to prove myself all along the way. Every speech I have ever given at conferences and forums are asked for in transcript; no others are. And they aren't asked for so they can be sleazily marked-up and used as the sick satire vulgarly displayed at abundant tasteless wrestling sites that are frequented by those, who like you, find fun in making false claims. Your vague, unsubstantiated critiques are simply another affirmation, of sorts, that we live in cultural times where virtue is reviled and vice is praised. I will, though, accept your reference to Lord of the Rings, on its success merits alone. Who's swerving who?

I will meet you halfway and acknowledge that my announcement was somewhat of a swerve, albeit creatively done — a play on words. But I will add that those who have come to know me should look at themselves for wantonly expecting that an announcement was coming that I would return to work for the McMahons.

I guess in this industry that's putridly natural, seeing how every other "shooter" went back and choked on their pride and God knows what else. I happen to have a stiffer backbone and deeper sense of pride and integrity. I happen to believe that what a man says he is, that's what he should be. That's what my word means. And not even a stroke can make me go back on it. You read that last sentence right, it's no swerve.

* * *

Despite the chaos of the weekend, Goldberg did not hit anybody — that we know of.

SF CONVENTION A COMPLETE DISASTER

By BOB KAPUR

SAN FRANCISCO — In terms of man-made disasters, Wrestle Fest 2007 can be compared to the *Hindenberg* crash-landing onto the *Titanic*.

The event, which on Thursday started off promising and on Friday managed to overcome some obstacles to entertain the fans, devolved into a fiasco of epic proportions on Saturday, culminating in the promoter skipping town, scores of unpaid talent, angry and disappointed fans, hotel fistfights and a foreboding mood for Sunday's portion of the show.

Though there was a general sense of disorganization on Friday, by Saturday, this hit an entirely new level. At 11 a.m., the area that would only an hour later host headliner Bill Goldberg for an autograph session was completely devoid of any organization. No barriers were set up to control lines, fans were confused as to where to buy the special tickets for the session and tables hadn't been set up.

And the promoter was nowhere to be seen.

The take-charge attitude of Jeremy (last name withheld on request) from Dad's Sports Emporium, onsite to help with the setup, saved the day. Giving directions to the event and building staff, the area was set up in record time. The only problem? No Goldberg.

Organizers have confirmed to SLAM! Wrestling that Goldberg was strongly considering not attending in a message of solidarity with the other workers who had not been paid and who had learned that Chris Cramer, the principal organizer of the event, was not going to be able to pay them as promised. Though SLAM! Wrestling was not on hand to see this "negotiation," apparently, Cramer refused to answer his door or his phone to avoid the confrontation. Ultimately, it seems a deal had been garnered and Goldberg and many others came to the show after all. For his part, Goldberg was a complete class act, spending time with every fan, signing whatever items they had, posing for pictures, offering some kind words and graciousness and generally making everyone feel like a champ. If not for the

Something disagreed with The Sandman.

professionalism of he and all of the other stars at Wrestle Fest — new faces to Saturday's lineup included Molly Holly, the Godfather, Ted DiBiase, Nikolai Volkoff and Christian Cage — the day would have ended up even worse of a mess, which wouldn't seem really possible. Credit has to go to the professionalism of the wrestlers involved.

And that seemed to be the position of many of the fans too. Though some had heard rumblings about the pay issues, most had not, and others didn't seem to care. Oblivious to the backstage shenanigans, they heartily enjoyed meeting legends like Harley Race, Roddy Piper (who also held his one-man show that afternoon) and Nick Bockwinkel who appeared at the Cauliflower Alley Club booth.

But those were probably the only positives of the day, and it soon took a sharp U-turn and proceeded at rocket speed to destination debacle.

The scheduled "Brawl 4 it All" mixed martial arts show was canceled by the California State Athletic Commission who cited a faulty ring setup as the reason. Fans were told of the decision at the Cow Palace shortly before the show was supposed to begin, and they were ushered back to the hotel by shuttle bus, to hang out and join several disgruntled wrestlers (those who had not left during the course of the day as a result of not being paid), mixed martial artists and their various entourages at the hotel bar. Then things got really interesting.

Short-staffing in the bar (a common gripe among many attendees) led to crowding, people being pushed out to the lobby and an overall sense of frustration/anger. As wrestlers and fans milled around to talk about the catastrophe that Wrestle Fest had become, violence erupted in the hotel entranceway, in the form of the bodyguard of Leland Chapman (from *Dog the Bounty Hunter*) running up and sucker punching and knocking out MMA legend Don Frye, then running away. Fans and wrestlers, including Scott Norton, tried to apprehend the thug but to no avail.

At this point, it is believed hotel management called the police who came into the lobby, but really didn't do anything. Rather, a fellow named Rob (last name withheld on request) assumed control. He ushered all the talent and fans that were assembled in the lobby to join him in the bar for an update. There, he

A hustling, bustling Cow Palace parking lot.

became the de facto man-in-charge, and made a series of announcements. First, he disassociated himself from Chris Cramer, then stated unequivocally that by taking charge, he would still not be accepting responsibility or accountability for paying the wrestlers. And that any checks that wrestlers had received from Cramer would "bounce like a basketball at a Lakers game."

This, as can be expected, didn't sit well with the talent on hand who had been stiffed, but there was little else that could be said.

Second, he announced that, even though he wasn't part of the organizing committee but rather contracted only to help organize the autograph sessions, he was still going to do whatever he could to ensure a positive experience for all concerned. He assured fans that Sunday's headliners, "Stone Cold" Steve Austin and Cryme Tyme, had been paid in advance, so any potential setbacks in terms of their appearing was entirely on their shoulders; and, responding to questions from some of the wrestlers that were expecting payment to pay for their transportation back to their hometowns, that he would do whatever he could to make sure that they got to wherever they needed to be, even asking for volunteers from the fan base to help drive home people like Jimmy "Superfly" Snuka, April Hunter and J.D. Michaels and the Sandman, who were scheduled to fly out from a different city. Beyond that, he said, he hopes fans enjoy themselves on Sunday, notwithstanding the circumstances.

Afterwards, SLAM! Wrestling sat down with a few of the people who had been hired as independent contractors for Sports Promotions USA, Cramer's company. Basically, they said, the problems with Wrestle Fest 2007 could be attributed to a lack of planning and organization, mismanagement of money (including funds footed by their main sponsor, Gladiator Energy Drink), and overall ineptitude in how to run an event of this magnitude.

While the event still has one day to revive itself, there is a general sense from the fans that this has been a colossal failure. Several fans expressed to SLAM! Wrestling their disappointment with the affair, including those who had traveled long distances for the weekend. "This sucks," many said. "I

Mike Mastrandrea

Mean Gene Okerlund sees a silver lining.

want a refund," cried others, commenting that the overall price for the weekend, which may have totaled $1,000 or more depending on the package purchased was not worth the experience. Or, in the words of a fan who traveled from Europe, "This was not worth it. It was so poorly disorganized. American organization is much different from European organization. . . . We expected that it would have some problems. But even in terms of American organization, this was terrible."

What this means for Sunday is still unclear. Rumors are that Austin may not attend, choosing not to associate himself with such a catastrophic failure. Though Rob claims otherwise. SLAM! Wrestling has confirmed that Cryme Tyme, one of the other headliners, is in the building, but whether they choose to appear or not remains to be seen. Speculation is abound that the scheduled Ring of Honor card may be in jeopardy as well, though the *Wrestling Observer*'s Dave Meltzer reported that it is still a go.

What is known is that Wrestle Fest 2007 has all but completely collapsed under its own weight. Despite the best intentions of the organizers (and one can only hope that they did have the best intentions when planning this, and that any "screwing over" of the talent and fans was not their intent), they essentially bit off more than they could chew. As a result, Wrestle Fest 2007 should rank up there as one of, if not the biggest failures of its kind, and will undoubtedly be spoken of for years to come . . . though, unfortunately, for all the wrong reasons.

From the writer: The funny thing about this story is that my original plan was to write a folksy, Dave Barry-esque column about attending my first wrestling convention — sometimes, though, the story just writes itself.

The weekend was surreal. Examples: Saturday night, I found myself sitting at the bar between Scott Norton and Don Frye, who, sporting a fresh black eye, didn't seem too mad — rather, we were laughing at the sheer absurdity of the whole situation. Sunday, I followed a group of Samoans as they chased an organizer backstage to "politely ask" for their owed money. . . . Scary.

Some months later, I'd heard that someone was pursuing a lawsuit against Chris Cramer (I've since learned that this was an alias), but I never heard if anything came of it.

VAINE AND O'REILLY DISCUSS THEIR SURPRISING WWE DEPARTURE

By CHRIS SCHRAMM

Chris Schramm

Krissy Vaine reads up on her profession — wrestling.

From the writer: I met Krissy when she was just breaking into the business around 2002. I saw her wrestle dozens of times, and you could see she had what it takes to be in the WWE one day, her dream. Then after just two appearances on WWE television, she quit, with boyfriend Ryan O'Reilly. It shocked many, but speaking to her for this article, I realized that fame and fortune are not worth it without happiness. If others followed this lesson, the wrestling world might not have so many tragedies.

Difficult choices come everyday, but none more so for Krissy Vaine and Ryan O'Reilly than when they asked for their release from their WWE contracts earlier this week.

The choice automatically brought up questions. Bloggers and posters on message boards called the two "morons" and their decision "stupid." Others began to speculate the reason behind them quitting what most in the industry would consider a dream job.

"There was a lot leading up to our decision," Vaine told SLAM! Wrestling in an exclusive interview. "I'm just a small-town girl with small-town values. I had my priorities messed up in the past. Being away from home [in Greensboro, North Carolina] so long and meeting Ryan [O'Reilly] really helped me realize what was important to me."

Vaine and O'Reilly began dating in 2006.

Vaine noted some family health problems as being an awakening for her. "I could hear my mother's heart breaking every time we spoke on the phone. I couldn't bear the thought that something may happen to someone while I was away and couldn't get home."

The decision to ask for her release may have come before a two-week tour of Europe, which she was supposed to attend.

Sadly, Vaine and O'Reilly have a bond brought forth by tragedy. O'Reilly told SLAM! Wrestling about his niece and cousin recently dying. He began to evaluate his life. "Just recently my father had a stroke," O'Reilly said, "and I began to really think about my family.

"A few men in my life told me that they are a strong believer that family comes first and that family values are very important."

O'Reilly recalled a story about a good friend, whom he considers like family, who recently went through a tragedy. "I had a friend whose girlfriend was in a really bad accident, and as I sat in the hospital trying to cheer him up, I began to think to myself what things could happen while you are away from home. I thought what would happen if something happened to Kristin [Krissy Vaine] or someone in my family."

Although the decision came together, they each had to ultimately make the choice on their own. "It was a big decision," O'Reilly said. "I want to give people reading this an insight on such a big decision in my and our lives."

Vaine knew she wanted to be a wrestler while in high school. She followed her dream a few years after graduating when she started attending a wrestling school near Greensboro. She made her debut in 2003, and less than three years later, she was signed by WWE to a developmental deal. She started in Deep South Wrestling out of Atlanta, and recently relocated to Florida Championship Wrestling in Tampa. Just two weeks ago, she made her debut on *Smackdown* as an unnamed person who had an issue with Torrie Wilson.

O'Reilly had been under a developmental contract for almost two and a half years, making his home in Deep South and later Florida Championship Wrestling.

Nicknamed "Roughhouse," O'Reilly would capture the Deep South heavyweight title in June 2006 and again in March 2007. O'Reilly often worked house shows and dark matches for the WWE around the country. He and partner Derrick Neikirk wrestled the FBI team of Little Guido and Tony Mamaluke throughout 2006. Recently, O'Reilly had worked numerous dark matches before *Raw* and *Smackdown* tapings. Some of his matches appeared online on WWE.com's *Heat* internet-based broadcast.

Before his release, he was expected to join the ECW brand. The two were chastised on message boards for their decision. Vaine was shown a comment calling their departure "very stupid."

"They don't know what has happened in our lives that led to us make this decision," Vaine replied. "If we are happy then that's all that matters."

O'Reilly agreed. "It sucks to hear people think badly of you for something you truly believe in. I left on good terms with my boss and all that ever mattered to me is what my boss or agent thought. Everyone has an opinion, and they are entitled to say what they want."

What is next in their plans? "I believe we can do anything we set our minds to. I think we can conquer the world," Vaine said.

O'Reilly worked for TNA in its earlier days, and Vaine likes the possibility of working there in the future.

"I hope there would be some interest," Vaine said. "A lot of my friends work there."

"Wrestling needs diversity, things that are different." O'Reilly said about TNA. "I enjoyed the work I did with them."

When asked if they had any regrets, Vaine said, "No, I don't think there will be any."

* * *

CORPORAL KIRCHNER SPEAKS: "I'M NOT DEAD!"

By GREG OLIVER

Mike Lano

Corporal Kirchner.

From the writer: WWE.com ran a story about somebody named Thomas Spear dying, who they claimed was Corporal Kirchner. Hmm, shouldn't their tax records have the proper last name on file? It didn't ring true to my memory of Kirchner, so I started digging and found his mom. She was puzzled by it all and a short while later I was talking to the truck-driving Corporal. The worst part? WWE.com, easily the wrestling website with the most traffic on the Net, didn't print a retraction.

It's been a weird couple of days for the family of Corporal Kirchner. WWE.com reported his death on Thursday, which then circulated widely through the world. But Mike Kirchner is still around.

"I'm still alive and well, and thanks for everybody's concern," he proclaimed. "I'm doing well, and I'm happy and life is good."

Kirchner was on the road when he was contacted by SLAM! Wrestling. He drives a truck now, and gets to see the world in a different way.

"I drive a big rig for a company called TMC. It's cool. It's great. I do cross-country driving now. I go all over. I've been all over the world, and it's just traveling that has been my life," he said. "You know it's great because you get to see the things that you missed from the arenas. You drive by the arenas that you used to work in, but you get to see everything else along it — the scenery, the states, the mountains. It's, 'where do I want to go this week?' and I drive where I want to go and that's where I head to, provided there's a load there. It's always interesting. I just came out of Arizona this week."

When he heard about his "death," he was actually in Connecticut, the home state of WWE. He was tempted to drive to WWE headquarters in Stamford, and say, "Guess what guys? I'm still around."

His mother, Jean Kirchner, has been suffering the most. "I have no idea where it originated or anything," she told SLAM! Wrestling. "All I know is I've been getting calls from relatives saying, 'How is Mike? Is he alright? Are you okay?' I said, 'Why?' 'Well, according to this article on the WWE website, he's dead.' It's a man named Thomas Spear, who I think might have been Leatherface in Japan, hence the confusion."

From the research SLAM! Wrestling has done, there is almost no connection with Thomas Spear to the wrestling business, and certainly not to WWE.

The Thomas Spear who died at his home in White Marsh, Maryland, on Sunday is a mystery to the Corporal. "Even back in the day, I'm thinking, 'Tom Spear, Tom Spear.' I don't recall the name Tom Spear. Them publishing my death is beyond me because I had calls from my family that notified me, asking me about it. I have no idea where this came from. This was a shocker to me. I haven't even been sick lately. It's pretty bizarre seeing your own eulogy sometimes, or hearing about. People called me all day yesterday. 'Are you alright?' I'd say, 'If I wasn't, then how could I answer the phone? What, I'm going to resurrect for you? Yeah, I'm dead but for you, I'll answer the phone.' It's pretty much that. I don't know where the story even came from."

His frequent WWF opponent Nikolai Volkoff was equally mystified. For one thing, Volkoff lives nearby where Spear died. Volkoff said a friend called after seeing the notice in the *Baltimore Sun*. "He said, 'You know Corporal Kirchner died?' I said, 'No.' I said, 'Last thing I heard, he lived in Florida, not here in Baltimore.' He said, 'No, this guy lived here in White Marsh.'"

Jean Kirchner, who wrote a fictional account of her son's career entitled, *Wrestle This . . . Corporal Punishment* under the name Genevieve O'Callaghan, called WWE to correct the mistake. "I called them [Friday], and I said, 'I'm his mother, and I'm here to tell you he's not dead.'"

The WWE's reaction? "They took it off the website yesterday."

No correction is up on the WWE website, nor has any attempt been made to retract the story and undo the damage, she said.

For a man who apparently died last Sunday, Mike Kirchner is pretty jovial about it all. "Thanks for keeping me around. It's nice being popular again. It's amazing what being dead does for you. I thought my career was dead."

* * *

BOB KAPUR'S JOURNAL FROM JAPAN

By BOB KAPUR

Bob Kapur with two Japanese fans.

Boarding the plane for Japan last week, I couldn't help but ask myself a few questions. Am I as crazy as people say, traveling halfway across the globe to go see a bunch of wrestling shows? Is it worth spending the money to fly this far for only a week? Did I remember to lock the front door? The following journal details the answers to those questions and more.

January 2–3

It's been a couple of hours since I landed in Chicago, and I still haven't seen George yet. George Mayfield has been running his Mayfield Mayhem tours to Japan for several years now. I first met him at a Ballpark Brawl show in Buffalo where he was selling custom-made wrestling DVDs. SLAM! Wrestling photographer Mike Mastrandrea had recommended going on one of George's trips, saying that he had heard great things about them. When Mayfield announced that this would be his last such journey, I couldn't pass up the opportunity.

But with less than an hour before the flight to Tokyo and still no George sighting, I have to admit I was getting a bit worried. Crisis was averted when I finally found him with about 10 minutes to go to boarding time, surrounded by my fellow travelers who were all as excited as I was to make the trip. After exchanging hellos, we boarded the plane for the 12-plus hour flight. The flight was fine and even had a bit of its own wrestling theme, the first in-flight movie being *The Game Plan*, featuring the Rock.

After landing (now January 3, since we crossed the international date line), we took the shuttle bus to the Tokyo Dome Hotel (we were staying about five minutes away). One of the guys saw TNA's Tyson Tomko — there for the next day's New Japan show — in the lobby and wanted to get a picture, so we all went inside. A TNA camera crew saw our group and interviewed us for the Dome Show special that they'll be airing on Spike TV on January 17. We then walked to our hotel, checked in and headed back to the Tokyo Dome. The week after New Year's is a huge holiday in Japan, so the area around the Dome was lit up with festive lights and decorations.

Afterwards, we headed up to the hotel bar for a drink where some of us tried sake. On the way down, we had another unique brush with greatness. One of the guys had accidentally leaned up against the buttons and we stopped at every floor. At one, the doors opened and who should be standing there but *Smackdown*'s number-one announcer, Sho Funaki, who was more than happy to pose for pictures and sign a few autographs — funny how things work out.

We went back to the hotel afterwards, where I fell asleep watching a dubbed episode of *Full House* (not funny in Japanese either).

January 4

Simply put, today was an amazing day. One of the selling points of Mayfield's trips is meet and greets with different wrestling stars — and boy, did he deliver. Today's lunch was with Hayabusa. For people who don't know, Hayabusa was a star of the FMW promotion who had a great future in front of him, until his career was cut short when he broke his neck after a failed springboard moonsault attempt and was paralyzed. He spoke with us for over two hours, talking about his career highlights and thoughts about the wrestling industry. Upbeat and positive despite his condition, when asked about his best wrestling match, it was with a smile and a twinkle in his eye that he answered, "Maybe my next one."

As Hayabusa signed the various items that everyone had brought, a couple of us noticed Scott Steiner leaving the restaurant and, despite some intimidation because of his size and crazy reputation, approached him for a photo op as well — turns out, he was a really friendly guy. Outside, Hayabusa took photos with us and judging from the crowd of fans that surrounded him, it's clear the Japanese fans haven't forgotten him, despite his not having wrestled since 2001. As we watched the throngs of fans line up for pictures with him — and he was happy to oblige them all — it dawned on me that while in North America, wrestlers may be somewhat looked down on by the general public, in Japan they are looked up to.

Bob Kapur

The Tokyo Dome.

After lunch, we went to the Tokyo Dome

Abdullah the Butcher and Bob Kapur.

for the traditional January 4 show, the 16th such event hosted by New Japan Pro Wrestling, this time featuring the stars of TNA Wrestling. The Dome was quite the sight — to think about some of the history that has taken place in that building is awe-inspiring. Our seats were fairly high up in the stands, but not too far that we couldn't see the action. And fortunately, there were mammoth video screens at the entrance ramp just in case.

Though the Dome was only about half full, with the entire stage setup and the elaborate videos and pyro effects for each wrestler, the entire presentation was akin to WrestleMania (though puroresu fans would probably cringe at the comparison) — it was really an amazing spectacle.

In watching the event, there are major differences between Japanese and American shows. While over here the crowds are generally vocal throughout the match, chanting and yelling from bell to bell, in Japan, it's quite the opposite. There, the crowd sits back, silent for the most part out of respect for the performers in the ring. Appreciating the sport more than the entertainment, they applaud politely for rope breaks, clean escapes, and after extended exchanges of punches and chops. No distracting "This is awesome!" or dueling "Let's go wrestler!" chants that tend to take away from the match; it's actually very refreshing to see and (not) hear.

The matches themselves ranged from good to excellent. The TNA guys fared very well and the crowd seemed to appreciate the international flavor they brought. Kurt Angle and Yuji Nagata stole the show with a brilliant match — probably Angle's best since his move to TNA. The last few minutes saw a series of ankle locks and reversals that was incredibly exciting. Angle retained the third IWGP heavyweight championship, setting up an inevitable unification match against Shinsuke Nakamura who won the Real IWGP championship from Hiroshi Tanahahi in the also-stellar main event. The card also featured stars from All Japan Pro Wrestling, Zero1 Max and Tradition. One standout was Brother Yashi from All Japan's Voodoo Murder faction — his pre-match promo was so entertaining, I think he would be a big star if he were to do the same on American TV. It doesn't matter that I had no idea what he was saying; it was the way he said it that really captivated. Other big names that appeared that most North American fans would know are Masato Tanaka, Jushin "Thunder" Liger and the Great Muta. I would recommend the

Bob Kapur

Bob at the Imperial Palace Garden Wall.

DVD to any fan, as it was that good of a show.

After the show, we went to Rippongi, the American section of Tokyo. There, George had set up a private meeting with Abdullah the Butcher. Abby was in a jovial mood, and he joked around with everyone, insisting on taking multiple pictures with us. In a hilarious had-to-be-there moment, he asked us to turn the tables on him and threaten him with his weapon of choice — a fork — in a group picture.

From there, a few of us were in the mood to eat, so we headed over to the Hard Rock Café. Coincidentally, many of the TNA roster were there as well, including Steiner, Christopher Daniels, A.J. Styles, Christian Cage, Jeremy Borash, Team 3-D and Jeff Jarrett himself. Once more, the wrestlers accommodated our requests for pictures and autographs, and they couldn't have been more generous with their time. Daniels was particularly excited about having wrestled at the Dome, telling me he had waited for that night for 15 years. "To be there in that building, wrestling for a title [the IWGP junior heavyweight championship], was amazing, I can't even believe it," he said.

We traveled back at the hotel, then, to see if tomorrow could even begin to compare with the events of the day. So far, the trip has exceeded expectations.

January 5

Even though it's obvious you're in a different country, walking around Tokyo, you see a lot of familiar cultural landmarks. Convenience stores like 7-Eleven are on nearly every other street corner. There are a lot of Western-style coffee and donut shops. Heck, other than the wacky burgers like the triple-decker Big Mac with a one-inch thick egg patty on it, even the McDonald's are pretty much the same.

Until you see a place like the Imperial Palace Garden.

Surrounded by a moat in the middle of the city, the garden is a remnant of the feudal days of Japan from centuries ago. The peaceful serenity of the garden is a stark contrast to the hustle and bustle of the city that surrounds the expansive area. The clash of cultures is nowhere more evident than crossing the bridge from the ancient wooden doorway to the sidewalk where, across the road, a new high-rise is in development. A similar incongruity was seen at this night's All Japan Pro Wrestling show where the traditions of Japanese wrestling were put aside for one night as the roster put

The famed Ribera Steak House.

on a show that seemed to be catered to us gaijin.

The first sense that this would be a different type of show arose in the second match, where the nWo Japan team started hurling profanities at us (we were quite prominent in the crowd, thanks to a connection of George's that got us front row seats) in English. It was actually pretty funny, their sense of how North American heels act, and they pulled no punches in insulting us, swearing, insulting our mothers and shooting us the finger and crotch chops repeatedly. The second instance was Abby taking the fight into the crowd, which I gather from the reaction of the crowd, was very uncommon. Lastly, the Voodoo Murder faction also played up to us, even grabbing my VM towel to choke out Joe Doering.

Doering's story is a great one for those who don't know him. Last year, he went to All Japan as part of a talent exchange arranged by Scott D'Amore. There, impressed by Doering's potential, Keiji Mutoh (the Great Muta) took him under his wing. Today, Doering and Mutoh are AJPW tag team champions. I had the opportunity to talk with Joe before and after the show, and he couldn't be enjoying himself more. The fans have really taken to him too, and even while we were talking, a lineup of fans formed behind me to meet the superstar. Hopefully, SLAM! Wrestling will have more time to talk with Joe when he comes home to visit later this month.

After the show, we headed back to the hotel where plans were made for the next day's festivities.

January 6

Maybe it's American — or in this case, Canadian — arrogance, but one thing that surprised me about Tokyo (other than how good Strawberry Kit Kats taste; yep, they have Strawberry Kit Kats there) is that for a major global economic center, they really don't speak a lot of English. While some of the people know a bit of the language, for the most part, we had to fake our way through it. Fortunately, most restaurants have picture menus, though it didn't help one of the guys who thought he was ordering a McChicken sandwich and ended up getting a McShrimp burger instead. Lucky for me, the local transit system has plenty of English signs. Which was helpful, since while most of the other tour members opted to stay near the Dome for a

Bob Kapur with "The Black Angel" Jaki Numazawa.

women's show, one other guy and I navigated our way across the city to go see a Big Japan show.

Big Japan Pro Wrestling is unlike other promotions in that the company specializes in hardcore death matches, as opposed to traditional pure wrestling. I got turned on to Big Japan watching death match compilation DVDs and am a huge fan of "Black Angel" Jaki Numazawa, a scary-looking guy who has turned smashing fluorescent light tubes over opponents' heads into an art form. So there was no way I was going to pass up the chance to see him in person. With directions provided by wrestling journalist Masanori Horie (a total class act who is another of George's friends), and the help of Jet Winger, a local worker who we started talking to at the subway station because he was wearing an AWA shirt, we managed to find the building with minutes to go before showtime.

To say BJPW is fan-friendly is an understatement. The show started off with the entire roster coming out with boxes of plastic balls. The roster started lobbing them into the crowd — each one was autographed by one of the wrestlers, making for an interesting souvenir — though that wasn't the only one. Indeed, the company sells the most interesting merchandise I've ever seen; things that are so weird you wonder what their marketing group was smoking when they conceived of them. You couldn't find a straight BJPW T-shirt, but if you wanted a Rubik's Cube with pictures of the roster on it, it was available. Blow-up fluorescent light tubes, BJPW tool belts, Kleenex box cozies designed to look like wrestling rings complete with plastic ring posts and elastic ropes? All for sale. Strange stuff.

As for the matches, they were incredibly fun, though not for the faint of heart. One match featured a larger guy who delivered the sickest headbutts I've ever seen. In one sequence, he thunked his opponent with a series of them that were so hard and loud, we could hear the impact in the second row. Other highlights of the undercard included 2 Tuff Tony (an American) running into the crowd during his introduction, sending the crowd scrambling while waving a barbed wire baseball bat. Numazawa's match was a hilarious blend of violence and comedy. In addition to his patented light tube smashes, other highlights included he and his partner, Abdullah Kobayahi, using a variety of sports-related items on their opponents, including kicking a barbed wire-covered soccer ball into their bodies, and a baseball spot that saw them tee off on their opponents with baseball bats, run around the ring like they were rounding the bases, and then slide into home in the form of a low dropkick to their opponents' faces. Genius.

The main event was a no rope, barbed wire, flaming board, barbed wire board, concrete block death match between Masada and Ryuji Ito for the BJPW championship. As described, you can guess this wasn't exactly a Flair-Steamboat mat classic. But then again, Flair and Steamboat didn't include craziness like a German suplex onto a pile of cinder blocks, or a Death Valley Driver through a flaming board, or whipping a guy with barbed wire, or a giant Superfly leap from a high scaffold onto an opponent covered with a barbed wire board. This match had me jumping up and down screaming like a crazy person and was one of the most insane things I have ever seen.

Bob Kapur

2 Tuff Tony.

I had introduced myself to 2 Tuff Tony during the intermission, and after the show, we hung out with him and Masada (another American). They introduced me to Jaki, who kindly presented me with a souvenir from his match — a piece of glass that they had taken out of his back. Gross, yes, but he was so sincere about giving it to me, knowing that I had come from Canada for the show, that I couldn't possibly have refused. Tony invited us to join him for dinner at Mr. Winger's Steak House, but unfortunately, we had committed to rejoin the group at Korakuen Hall for the Kaientai Dojo show that evening.

Going to Korakuen was another wrestling fan dream come true, given the history that that building has seen. It's quite an unassuming place, a small hall with quaint wood paneling and plush theater seats in the bleachers. Still, the greatness that has been showcased there adds an incomparable aura to any event.

The K-Dojo show was almost the complete opposite of BJPW, as it featured a variety of technical matches. There were a few intergender matches that were very well done and, in fact, overall the card was very solid from beginning to end. I'm not too familiar with the company, so TAKA Michinoku, Great Sasuke and Masato Tanaka were the only names I really recognized.

After the show, they and most of the other stars were at the merchandise stand to sign autographs, which was a nice touch. George used his pull to arrange us a private post-show meet and greet with Tanaka and while we were doing that, a lot of the other wrestlers came by as well, so

BJPW Light Tube Match.

we had mark-out moments aplenty.

All in all, it was a fun-filled day that ended well into the morning by the time we got back to the hotel.

January 7

Electric City in Tokyo defies description. The huge video screen storefronts, the countless electronics stores and giant video game arcades — it's like heaven for technophiles. I went there today to do some sightseeing and window-shopping. I saw some really nifty video games there; my favorite was one similar to Guitar Hero, but instead of playing a guitar along to the notes, you play the bongos with a set of clubs. I spent the morning there and at a small mall that had no less than 50 different anime stores. I'm not really a fan of anime, but I did manage to find a duty-free store where I picked up some inexpensive souvenirs, including a ninja throwing star and a sumo wrestling picture. Contrary to popular belief, the city isn't teeming with ninjas or sumos as I thought they would be; somewhat disappointed in that — ninjas and sumos rule.

What wasn't disappointing was the special lunch we had with Manami Toyota. Toyota is arguably the greatest women's wrestler of all time, with many of her matches considered classics. If you've never seen her 60-minute battle against Kyoko Inoue, I suggest you look it up on YouTube immediately. Toyota was an absolute delight, talking excitedly through her interpreter about her storied career between signing autographs and taking pictures. She was so charming that the hours with her flew by and it was nightfall when we left the restaurant.

A few of us headed to the Fighting Dojo Colosseo bar, a famous drinking hole that many wrestlers have frequented over the past few years. A couple of Sapporos was the perfect way to toast yet another day full of highlights, with one more still to go.

January 8

In Canada, when you want to buy wrestling merchandise, your options are fairly limited. You can go to a company's official site, or go to one of their shows, or go to an online store like the SLAM! Wrestling Store. In Tokyo though, they have stores devoted to wrestling merchandise. There are no less than five stores right around the Tokyo Dome devoted to selling nothing but wrestling and MMA merchandise. We spent the morning exploring every

A well-stocked wrestling store.

nook and cranny of them, looking for various goods to bring back home. Toys, clothing, magazines and other memorabilia were abundantly available. It was hard to not overspend, or worse, buy too much to fit into our suitcases for the flight back home.

After that shopping marathon, it was time to cap off the trip with dinner at the legendary Ribera Steak House. This is the place where wrestlers to go eat, and the walls and ceiling are covered with hundreds of pictures evidencing that fact. Stars from all countries representing different eras have all been there, where they have been presented with a coveted Ribera jacket (one worker I talked to said he had been in Japan for two years and was only deemed worthy enough to be given a jacket the week before we got there — that's how special it is to be given one).

The place itself is very rustic, with wooden stumps serving as stools, and the air cloudy with smoke and grease. Dinner was a choice of either a half-pound or full-pound steak, served with a side of corn and rice on a sizzling metal plate. To say the steak, which was bigger than my face, was good is an understatement — one of the group bit into his and he broke out into a goofy grin that I couldn't help breaking into a laugh. Simply delicious.

After dinner, we headed back to the hotel lobby where we talked for hours, comparing purchases from the stores, comparing photos, and not wanting the trip to end.

January 9

After one last stop at the wrestling stores to pick up the newest issue of the weekly pro wrestling magazine with the Dome Show results, we headed to the airport for our flights back home. I was offered a spot on an earlier flight, so took the opportunity to get home early.

Overall, it was a wonderful trip, a wrestling bonanza and an once-in-a-lifetime experience. . . . Though, that said, I'm already planning a return visit.

Chris Schramm gets the scoop on So Cal Val's move into TNA's X Division.

Remembering

No matter what area of journalism a young writer pursues, the unfortunate reality is that at one point or another, they will have to write an obituary, one of the hardest types of stories to write.

Whether it's a wrestler who has lived a long life, well beyond their ring years, or one who passed away before his or her time, paying tribute to a fallen hero is hard to do.

We at SLAM! Wrestling have been blessed though. For every one of these stories, we have always been fortunate to not only share our thoughts, but those of so many who have been touched by the competitor's life. Whether it's colleagues, relatives, friends or fans, it is their stories that help in the grieving process for our readers — and us.

* * *

ALLEN COAGE: MY HERO, OUR HERO

By JIM BREGMAN — Special to SLAM! Wrestling

Wrestling fans are familiar with the career of "Bad News" Allen/"Bad News" Brown. He was one tough dude. But before getting into pro wrestling late in his life, Allen Coage was a major force in judo, and was the second American to ever win a medal in the Olympics in the sport. SLAM! Wrestling turned to the first American to claim an Olympic medal (1964, bronze), Jim Bregman, to share his memories of Allen Coage.

It was an odd set of circumstances that day so long ago in Philadelphia. The venue was alive with the excitement of the Judo Trials for the 1976 Olympic Games to be held later in the year in Montreal. The event was about 90 percent complete when the tournament officials made an announcement about a late-breaking decision they had just made concerning the selection process

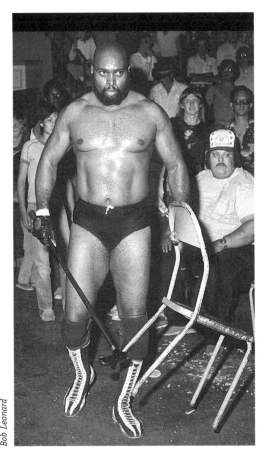

Bad News Allen takes up golf.

and the tournament. The exact details, blurred now by time, matter very little, but to these athletes who had spent their entire lives trying to make an Olympic team it was devastation — a crushing tsunami which meant that some deserving winners might indeed not be selected!

After the "official announcement," there was a long moment of stunned disbelief and silence. The ABC camera crews were baffled, as were the directors and producers. This was to be the first time the Olympic Judo Trials were to be covered live. Then the noise level rose steadily to a vibrating din and the athletes were milling around agitated, angry, hurt, confused, and astonished at this "stupid" last-minute "switch," which would completely determine their future Olympic hopes and dreams. An athletes' revolution was brewing and they were mad as hell. They were not "going to take this crap" anymore. But what on earth to do to rectify this "official blundering fiasco"? How do powerless athletes reason with unreasonable officials who are dictatorial in their edits and domineering?

Allen Coage and Jimmy Wooley were to fight next and through the confusion, milling around, athlete disgust and disappointment were being voiced now by shouting and jeering, yelling and screaming at the tournament officials, Ben Campbell and George Harris. Paul Maruyama and I were dumbfounded and, standing on the floor by the mats, completely taken aback by the announcement and the loud "revolution," which was gaining momentum.

We were approached by Allen [Coage] and Jimmy [Wooley] for advice and guidance and, as we were talking, the athletes gathered around and the boiling noise level began to simmer. Then it turned into dead silence. You could have heard a pin drop.

Allen and Jimmy asked us simply, "What would you guys do in a situation like this?" It wasn't Ben's, George's, Paul's or my Olympic birth that was on the line. It was Allen's and Jimmy's, and all the other Olympic dreamers who came to fight that day. The four of us were awestruck at the question, at the dilemma, and speechless. The six of us talked quietly and logically and explored options — all of which were, to say the least, not good.

Finally, the call came out from the announcer commanding Jimmy and Coage out to the mat for the final match. Allen and Jimmy respectfully asked one more time, "What would you guys do?" A second call to the mat came with a threat of disqualification. Time had run out.

We four told them "we" would not compete in this situation and we would demand other trials with consistent and fair selection criteria published at the start and immutable throughout the tournament. I said that the USOC/AAU will be sued by the USJA and that the four of us would work with the USJA Board to correct this mess and get a retrial under a court order if necessary! We also told Allen and Jimmy that it must be their decision and their decision alone as to what course to follow because the personal stakes were too high for us to tell them what to do — not that we ever really would have tried to do that.

Allen and Jimmy, two of the greatest American judoka of all time, had great senses of humor at this moment of "truth" and with wry, impish smiles on their faces they said, "Just watch this!"

The ABC cameras were rolling, the very nervous officials were all in their chairs and places of honor, and the venue was hushed. As they walked to the mat together, friends and competitors at the same time, they whispered quietly to each other and then took their respective places to compete opposite one another on the mat.

They stepped onto the mat and bowed to the officials. Step up to the "line" to wait for the hajime. And then, it came, loud and clear from the referee: "Hajime!" With dignified grace these two men of the mat, bowed and walked slowly to the center of the mat. They shook hands, walked back to the "line," bowed humbly and walked off of the mat.

What followed can only be described as total chaos, a loud cheer went up from the athletes and the audience, flags were waved, and cheering and yelling continued for a long time. Allen and Jimmy made their way over to the four of us and we all hugged and jumped joyously. The "athletes' revolt," which had been brewing for a long time, erupted like a volcano.

I quietly and slowly made my way through the crowded floor to an exit. I was cornered by four officials who said in essence, I was to blame for this and that I would pay for this "disrespectful behavior." I smiled and excused myself. I needed to find a pay phone.

I called Michael Rosenberg, the USJA attorney in Washington, D.C., and related all the shocking events in detail. Michael said his firm would do everything possible to see that there was a retrial. A case was filed in the Federal District Court of the District of Columbia. Short story, they settled, agreed to a retrial under consistent rules and procedures.

I was in Montreal that day and watched Allen fight and win a bronze medal. After the medal ceremony, I called Michael at the law firm from a pay phone outside the arena in the hall. I told him Allen had won and let him listen to the applause. We, American judo athletes, had won, and Allen and Jimmy showed the way with dignity and courage at a time of high crisis.

I can hear my youngest son, Matthew, calling me, as he often did as a child: "Hey Dad, come on down and watch wrestling with me! 'Bad News Brown' is wrestling tonight. Hurry, you don't want to miss it!"

This was a ritual on wrestling night and I would sit with Matthew and we'd watch the latest saga of "Bad News" Brown unfold week after week.

After the wrestling was over, I would tell Matthew many stories about the Olympic Trials events, the Montreal Olympics, the Camp Olympus stories, training trips to Europe with Allen and the trips to South Africa to have team judo matches with the South Africans during Apartheid. Allen was the captain of all of those teams. The South Africans loved him.

We all loved him. We will all miss him.

He was a courageous and honorable man, dignified, steady and had a great sense of humor. He was a tremendous *dancer*.

Matthew and I, like many millions of children and parents around the world, mourn the passing of the one and only Allen Coage, Olympian, and our hero. Our regrets and sympathy are with his loved ones.

Respectfully,
Jim Bregman
Olympic and World Medallist
Dancer

* * *

BULLDOG STILL IN FAMILY'S HEARTS

By JASON CLEVETT

James Oliver

Davey Boy Smith signs autographs at a corporate meet and greet in 1987.

It was a year ago this weekend that Davey Boy Smith died of a heart attack in Fairmont, British Columbia, while vacationing with girlfriend Andrea Hart.

After an outpouring of respect, tributes and stories from fans and wrestlers a year ago, Davey's name slipped into the background as just another sad statistic of the wrestling business. But to those who knew him, and his family, his loss is still deeply felt.

"Some days are hard and some days are fine. It has been a lot tougher lately as it approaches the one-year anniversary. I've been okay for the most part, but right now it is hard," said Davey Boy's son, Harry Smith, in an exclusive SLAM! Wrestling interview.

Davey Boy Smith's life had many different levels. In the last years of his life, his battles with drugs, a near-fatal motorcycle accident, a highly publicized split with wife Diana and confrontations with family members Bruce Hart and Ellie Niedhart overshadowed the real Davey Boy, who was a kind, gentle soul.

"He was very sensitive, and people thought because he was such a big guy he was a bully. He wasn't, we had a few disagreements that got a little rough but Davey was not a bully," Diana Hart said of her ex-husband, whom she first met when she was 17 and he was 18. "Everyone remembers Davey in my family very fondly and what a good sense of humor he had. He was so funny."

Stampede star T.J. Wilson lived with Davey for a number of years and brought up the side of Davey that those who knew him, even briefly, got to see the most. "Anybody that Davey ever met liked him. He was always laughing, smiling, and up to no good with ribbing and pranks."

It was that Davey who gave a 17-year-old kid a thrill of a lifetime when he would take the time to sit down and talk to me, which he did frequently. He was the first wrestling star that I met, and he made an impression on me that will last my whole life. The Bulldog also regularly attended Stampede Wrestling shows, often cheering his young son from the stands. He was always mobbed for pictures and autographs, but he never had a problem with it, doing so gladly and smiling and joking with fans.

But the other side to Davey was a long history of drug abuse, starting young with steroids but moving in later years to a variety of painkillers to try and block the pain stemming from a series of injuries, including a staph infection resulting from being slammed on a steel trap door in the ring at Fall Brawl 1997 in WCW and a near-fatal motorcycle accident 16 months before his death.

"Right now, there are all these wrestlers having neck surgeries in the WWE. Davey had the same injuries as Kurt Angle, and didn't get surgery, he took three months off and went back to Japan," said Wilson. "He had three discs missing in his back and two degenerating. In the end there were five disks missing in his back and a screwed-up neck and he fought through it, you can't take anything away from him for that."

Losing Smith so young did have an effect on Wilson's decision-making. "I've never been interested in drinking or doing drugs, but [his death] contributed to me not doing drugs. But it isn't the sole reason."

"I hate to borrow a line from the Dynamite Kid, but he is right in saying, 'in the end there is a big price to pay,'" said Harry. According to the third-generation grappler, "They [Davey, Hennig, Pillman, etc.] did what they had to do to succeed."

"It wasn't just a pain issue, but he did suffer a lot of pain," explained Diana. As much as she misses Davey, she does try to see some positive from his death. "I am not blind to drug use at all, I saw it firsthand. I don't have that worry about this generation of wrestlers. Maybe they [Davey and other wrestlers] were sacrifices for this generation of new stars to learn from. It's possible Davey was a sacrifice so that Harry will never, ever touch drugs.

"Everything happens for a reason, you just don't see it at the time."

Davey was trying to get his life back on track before he died, working on his relationships with his children, Harry and Georgia, as well as Diana. Although Hart's controversial book, Under the Mat, shed a negative light on her husband, Diana doesn't regret the book. "Everything that was in the book were things that happened to me."

She is glad that she had the chance to bury the hatchet before he died. "We were working on getting back together; I feel we would have gotten back together again." Things seemed to be going well, she went on to explain. "It was a year ago for my dad's birthday that Davey was here. We had such a good time that night. Davey and Harry were planning their trip to

Winnipeg to do a wrestling show out there — and then he wasn't here any-more."

Diana feels that Davey's legacy has been passed on to their son. "I felt like Davey was there in the ring with Harry [at Stu's birthday show]. I see a lot of Davey in Harry."

Although Davey is not with them physically, in spirit he can be felt — and seen — in 17-year-old Harry, whose style is reminiscent of his father's. This is no accident, as the Bulldog had a huge impact on both Harry and T.J., as well as many young stars.

"He taught me a lot about life, and my wrestling basics and wrestling altogether. He told me . . . there are times when you're on top of the world and times when you are on the bottom. The business sometimes chews you up and spits you out and sometimes you are world champion," said Harry. "He was a very big star in the '80s and '90s, and paved the pathway to me."

Davey and Harry were planning to try to go to the WWF together as a father–son tandem. A meeting had been planned with Vince McMahon at the Smackdown tapings in Calgary the week after Davey's death. They had the chance to realize their dream to a small degree, teaming on a tour of Manitoba days before he died.

"That was my favorite match, for obvious reasons," Harry said.

Harry hopes to carry on the legacy of his father, without the difficulties that plagued him. Stepping into the ring is his tribute to a loving father and hero. "I wouldn't have had another father. One, it was cool to have a dad who was a professional wrestler, that brought us closer together. He was a very special person to me, my biggest influence in wrestling."

From the writer: This was my first big SLAM! Wrestling piece, and one that hit close to home. Harry and I lost our fathers, mine to cancer, within seven months of each other and shared that common bond of loss. Having been friends with Harry and T.J. for years, it was important to me to balance a professional story with my relationship with them. Harry especially is often guarded about his personal life, so it meant a lot that he opened up to me for this story. This was the first time that I really felt I had written some-thing special and it really helped launch my SLAM! Wrestling career.

* * *

END OF AN ERA ON TBS

Solie, Georgia and "Black Saturday"
By JOHN MOLINARO

I was a gawky 10-year-old in July of 1984.

Having just finished the fifth grade, I was looking forward to a summer of afternoons spent at the Centennial Community Swimming Pool, house league soccer games and wading knee-high in a creek by Sherwood Forest with the Middleton brothers searching for minnows.

I ran home every day for lunch, checking the mailbox to see if "it" had arrived. I was waiting on a letter from school that would have my class assignment for the following year. I was praying that I wouldn't get Mrs. Gowan for homeroom. A middle-aged woman with a quick temper, she had terrorized my two older brothers when they attended Ascension Primary School. My brothers, the louts that they were, had terrorized me with exaggerated stories of how she grabbed students up from their desks by the ear and marched them out into the hall where she smacked them across the knuckles with a ruler.

The letter arrived about a week after school let out and, as luck would have it, I was assigned to Mr. Rzepa's class. Whew! I rejoiced. I was in the clear. I could relax and turn my attention to what mattered most to me that summer: street hockey games, trading baseball cards and wrestling. Nothing could possibly ruin this summer, I thought.

And then it happened.

July 14, 1984.

Black Saturday.

After 12 years of airing in the 6 p.m. time slot on SuperStation TBS, *Georgia Championship Wrestling* was replaced with WWF programming.

Instead of Gordon Solie and Freddy Miller talking about this Sunday's card at Atlanta's Omni, there was Vince McMahon Jr. and Gorilla Monsoon engaging in some inane banter before throwing to some "jobber" matches. Instead of the NWA's brand of hard-hitting wrestling, there was the WWF's circus sideshow.

Georgia Championship Wrestling was an institution on WTBS ever since Ted Turner launched Atlanta UHF television station WTCG (TBS'S predecessor) in 1972. Taped on Saturday mornings in the WTBS-TV studios in downtown Atlanta, each week Gordon Solie, God rest his soul, opened the program and welcomed millions of wrestling fans with his famous refrain:

"When you see this symbol (pointing to an NWA emblem), you are assured of the optimum in professional wrestling."

Good ol' Gordon wasn't lying. *Georgia Championship Wrestling* was the Holy Grail of wrestling TV programs. The first nationally broadcasted wrestling program in the U.S., it revolutionized how wrestling was presented on television and laid the groundwork for shows like *Nitro*, *Raw* and *Smackdown* to follow: the two-hour format, episodic formatting, well-timed commercial breaks, cliff-hanger endings, ring entrances accompanied by rock music, strong main events, major angles that led to the big payoff matches down the road.

A small TV studio. A handful of fans. Three cameras. One ring. One microphone. That brown backdrop with the TBS call letters and the NWA symbol on it that stood behind the interview podium. Gordon Solie.

It may sound like just another wrestling show, but to many of us, *Georgia Championship Wrestling* was more. Much more.

A generation of wrestling fans grew up and lost our innocence watching *Georgia Championship Wrestling*. It was a part of our lives. To many, the stately Gordon Solie was like a favorite uncle, heels such as Masked Superstar and the Freebirds like annoying cousins we loved to hate. Every Saturday evening we invited them into our home. Every Saturday, they brought us a little bit of magic.

Bill Watts. Ole and Gene Anderson. The Assassins. Mr. Wrestling II. Dory and Terry Funk. Stan Hansen. Tommy Rich. Austin Idol. Kevin Sullivan. Thunderbolt Patterson. The Fabulous Freebirds. Masked Superstar. Ernie Ladd. Dusty Rhodes. Ivan Koloff. The Samoans. The Super Destroyer. Bob Armstrong. Buzz Sawyer. Roddy Piper. They were all there. At one time or another, every major star in the NWA, regardless if he worked for the Georgia territory or not, appeared on *Georgia Championship Wrestling*.

Even a young upstart from Jim Crockett's Mid-Atlantic Wrestling promotion by the name of Ric Flair. Flair, who in 1978 was being considered by the NWA Board of Directors to be made NWA world champion, knew the importance of appearing regularly on *Georgia Championship Wrestling*. Being seen on a TV program viewed by millions of fans, not to mention every other NWA promoter, helped Flair fulfill his dream of becoming NWA world champion three years later.

In 1976, a second show was added to WTCG's lineup as *Best of Georgia Championship Wrestling* started airing on Sunday afternoons. In the fall of 1979, *Georgia Championship Wrestling* became the first wrestling television show to be broadcast across the country on cable as SuperStation TBS, the flagship station of media tycoon Ted Turner, was born.

The program became such a cult favorite that no matter where they were, wrestling fans made sure they were in front of a TV set at 6:05 every Saturday for two hours of *Georgia Championship Wrestling*. Everybody watched the show.

"I used to drive 60 miles over to the nearest town because we didn't have cable where we grew up," WWF senior vice president Jim Ross told Dave Meltzer, editor of the *Wrestling Observer* newsletter in July 2000. "No matter where I was on Saturday, I tried to watch that show."

Like I said . . . everybody.

By 1981 the show, then renamed *World Championship Wrestling*, was drawing an average 6.4 rating on Saturday nights, making it the most-watched show at that time on cable television.

But just as *Georgia Championship Wrestling* reached incredible levels of popularity, it started to slide. The promotion struggled the next few years as booker and part-owner Ole Anderson, mismanaged the company by booking the territory's top stars on other NWA shows around the country as opposed to having them appear on shows in cities like Atlanta, Macon and Savannah that made up the Georgia territory. They started running shows in states like Michigan, Ohio, Pennsylvania and West Virginia and in the process skipped going to cities that had been a part of their house show circuit for years.

At the urging of local Georgia promoters who were growing frustrated with Ole, majority stockholders Jim Barnett, and Jack and Jerry Brisco sold controlling interest in the company to Vince McMahon Jr. McMahon had visions of taking the WWF, a regional promotion based in the Northeast he had purchased from his dad, to a national level. McMahon closed Georgia Championship Wrestling down and assumed the company's TV contract, bringing the WWF to Ted Turner's TBS.

And so, on Saturday, July 14, 1984, the WWF debuted on TBS, thus pulling a death shroud over *Georgia Championship Wrestling* and putting an end to what was an institution to millions of wrestling fans. In one fell swoop, 12 years of quality wrestling on TBS went straight down the drain and McMahon, with TV clearances on TBS and the USA Network, suddenly seemed poised to dominate the wrestling world.

No wonder so many of us back then dubbed it "Black Saturday."

Within days after the WWF first aired on TBS, thousands of phone calls jammed the station's switchboards from irate viewers demanding that *Georgia Championship Wrestling* be brought back. Fans started a national campaign to get *Georgia Championship Wrestling* back on the air as thousands of cards and letters flooded into TBS, telling them to kick the WWF off the air.

McMahon got word of the complaints and in an *Atlanta Journal Constitution* news article responded by saying, "We'll show those complainers the difference between a major league and a minor league production, given time."

Instead, it was "those complainers" who trumped McMahon.

As the complaints kept pouring in, TBS decided to listen to its viewers. Two weeks after the WWF debuted, the station granted a 7:30 a.m. time slot to Ole Anderson's upstart *Championship Wrestling from Georgia* outfit. Solie was back as the lead play-by-play man, quality wrestling was back on TBS and everybody seemed at peace.

All except for McMahon.

Outraged, he reneged on the deal he had with Turner to produce a separate weekly TV program for TBS that was to be taped at TBS's studios. Instead, McMahon aired tapes of his other syndicated WWF programs. The relationship between Turner and McMahon began to further fall apart when Turner, upset over the WWF's low ratings on TBS, gave a one-hour, Sunday evening time slot to Bill Watts's *Mid South Wrestling*. Hosted by a much younger Jim Ross, *Mid South Wrestling* drew better ratings than the WWF by its second week on TBS.

Realizing they could no longer work together, McMahon and Turner came to an agreement as McMahon sold the right to his time slots on TBS to Jim Crockett Jr. for $1 million, thus ending one of the most tumultuous business relationships in wrestling lore and laying the foundation for the bitter WCW vs. WWF promotional war that followed years later.

McMahon, Hulk Hogan, Randy Savage, Hillbilly Jim, the British Bulldogs and Gene Okerlund were out. Crockett, Ric Flair, Dusty Rhodes, the Four Horsemen, the Road Warriors, the Midnight Express and Tony Schiavone were in.

And so began a new era on TBS: the Crockett Years.

Looking back at the era of *Georgia Championship Wrestling* on TBS, so many fond memories come to mind:

Gordon Solie and his trademark phrases ("Indeed," "We've got to get some order restored," "Oh my word," "pier-sixer" and "crimson mask"); Freddy Miller hyping the upcoming shows at Atlanta's Omni, punctuating his pitch with his famous, "don't-ya-dare-miss-it"-like tagline, Roddy Piper revolutionizing the concept of the heel color commentator, long before Jesse Ventura was credited for it; Ole Anderson turning on Dusty Rhodes during a steel cage match — the culmination of an angle that played out for a year where Ole tried to convince Dusty to team with him so that he could then backstab him; Flair cutting his first interview as NWA world champion in 1981 two days after beating Rhodes for the title; Don Muraco shoving a beleaguered Solie to the ground, only to have Piper turn babyface and come to his rescue; Buzz Sawyer battling Tommy Rich in the Omni in a bloody, steel cage match that was dubbed "The Last Battle of Atlanta" by the local media; the infamous four flat car tires angle with Austin Idol and the Freebirds.

So many memories.

* * *

Bob Leonard

Helen Hart, Bob Leonard and Stu Hart.

HELEN HART: A FRIEND'S RECOLLECTION

By BOB LEONARD — Special to SLAM! Wrestling

On the evening of December 15, 1995, I stood beside Helen Hart in a place where she had virtually never been: inside the ropes of the Stampede Wrestling ring. We listened together as more than 5,000 Calgarians rocked the storied Stampede Corral with waves of cheers. And we watched from just a few feet away as a rich sampling of Stampede's greater and lesser lights from years past — Dory and Terry Funk, Leo Burke, Moose Morowski, Angelo Mosca, Gil Hayes, Tor Kamata, Brian Pillman, John Helton, Dan Kroffat and more — streamed into the ring to add their best wishes to Stu Hart at the huge wrestling event that officially marked his 80th birthday on that night.

"Helen, when we first met going on 40 years ago, did you ever imagine you and I would end up in a wrestling ring together?" I jokingly queried, as the cheers and the handshakes washed over Stu.

And in the delightfully nonplussed manner that she often exhibited, Helen allowed that she certainly hadn't imagined any such thing, adding, ". . . And I'm still not sure just what I should do in here, even after all these years!"

The quiet sense of humor, the gentle wit and self-deprecating manner, were so typical of the true heart of the Hart household. Helen's innate dignity, her warm and effusive personality, exerted its gentle charm and persuasion equally on legendary boxing champions, ruggedly individualistic wrestlers, businesses seeking trade or pressing for payment, jaded sports editors, and the wide range of others who crossed her path.

Her genuine graciousness to all who entered her home — and there were so many, for Hart House has for 50 years been a people place — or whom she met in Calgary or on visits to some of North America's premier wrestling venues with Stu, sticks vividly in many minds and hearts. Helen had a wonderful ability to make old friends or new acquaintances feel "special." She combined attentiveness in conversation, sincerity in her gaze and a small gesture or a few well-chosen words to make each meeting with her that extra bit more memorable.

To remember Helen is to recall as well her deft handling of many major and minor problems of the sometimes abrasive personalities on Stu's talent roster. To marvel at her solo juggling act in running the business end of Stampede for some 40 years: payrolls, taxes and accounts, immigration clearances, talent scheduling, publicity and advertising, arena rentals, commission problems, complaints and concerns and a myriad of secretarial duties, along with an occasional frantic long-distance call from a local promoter demanding, "where are the wrestlers, it's 7:15 and nobody's here yet!" and to be amazed at her ability to lovingly raise a dozen children in the midst of ever-ringing phones. Helen handled it all, and more often than not transformed potential chaos to a semblance of order.

And there are the special personal recollections. Helen's wonderful New York accent, still present after more than 50 years so far from the place of her upbringing, and the precise diction of her speech. Her loving touch on the arm of her burly "Buff" or her fingers gently patting down a stray cowlick of his hair — so spontaneous and un-self-conscious as we reminisce about the people of the old Stampede days. Her companionable presence during those early-morning Calgary Stampede breakfasts of the 1960s and 1970s, where Stu's and Helen's introduction to the crowds prompted cheers equaling those for Hollywood celebrities and world champion cowboys. And her trips to the kitchen at 2:30 in the morning, to bake up just one more tray of chocolate chip cookies to crown an after-show Hart House buffet for the whole Stampede Wrestling crew, at the promotion's relaunch in April 1999.

That warm, wonderful voice is stilled. That loving touch is gone. But the memories will keep Helen Hart forever in so many hearts and minds.

Rest well, dear friend.

* * *

STU HART: A DUNGEON PERSPECTIVE

By "HOTSHOT" JOHNNY DEVINE

Bruno Silveira

"Hotshot" strikes a pose.

It was always a treat to see Stu at the Stampede shows as you could see him perk up when bell time hit. Afterward he would always have kind things to say and make you feel like you were doing really well even if your match sucked.

At his 88th birthday show in May, all the guys on the card pulled out all the stops because we all wanted to make Stu proud of us; and I think we put on one of the best indie wrestling cards of all time that night. Everyone wanted to impress Stu, no matter if it was in or out of the ring. He was just one of those remarkable people that draw folks to them like moths to a flame. And still he always had time for everyone. Young, old, rich, poor it didn't matter, Stu would always give his time.

Time. It's such a precious commodity. You never have enough to do the things you need or want to do. Whenever someone is taken from you some of your first words are invariably, "I wish I had spent more time with . . ." On the night before Stu died I asked Nattie Niedhart how he was doing and she told me not too good. So I made a promise to go and visit him the next day.

I woke up Thursday morning and had some errands to run and to hit the gym. I thought to myself, "I'll do my running around and hit the gym, then get cleaned up and make myself presentable and go to the hospital."

At around 3:30, I finished at the gym and when I turned on my phone I had two messages telling me the news.

I wish I had gone to the hospital first.

I wish I had been able to say goodbye.

I wish I had more time to spend with him.

Most of all I wish Stu peace and a safe journey.

God Bless you Stu, you were my hero and a tremendous role model. I will miss you.

Wrestling Revue

Bob Orton Sr.

THE BIG "O" STOOD FOR "ORIGINAL"

Friends recall Bob Orton Sr.

By GREG OLIVER

Bob Orton Sr. touched a lot of lives in pro wrestling. His friends recalled many things over the past few days — his tremendous in-ring talent, his quirkiness, his pride over his family, and, over the last few years, his phone calls.

Danny Miller used to get a call a couple of times a month from Orton on the weekend. "I'm going to miss that," said Miller, who battled Orton many times around the rings of Florida. "The first thing he'd say was, 'Hey, kid, do you know who this is?' How could you help but know?"

Orton loved to talk wrestling, said Miller. "He'd talk about what's going to happen to the world. He was very high on Vince McMahon because of his grandson Randy."

He loved conspiracy theories and ranting on any number of subjects. "International bankers, they run the central banks of the major countries, are the ones running the show. They create and promote the wars, finance both sides and everything. They've made puppets out of all the so-called leaders and politicians," he once told this writer.

His friend of more than 50 years, Sonny Myers, laughed when once asked about Orton's calls. "He's told me so much I don't believe goddamn nothing."

After hearing of Orton's death, Myers reflected on their time together. "He was a good friend of mine. He was a happy-go-lucky boy. Hell, I don't know of anybody who ever said he was a bad guy or nothing. He just was a good guy. He was just a nice fella."

And Myers, with his 84 years of wisdom, is correct. No one had anything negative to say about Orton's in-ring abilities.

"I always thought that Bob's problem was he didn't know how good he was," chuckled Dick Brown, the son of the great Orville Brown, who Orton worshipped. "He was really better than maybe he thought he was. I considered Bob to be very good. . . . I think he was maybe a little underrated."

Brown wrestled Orton a handful of times, and worked out with him for a couple of years. Perennial babyface Sandy Scott, meanwhile, was often on the other end of Orton's blows.

"He was a heck of a heel, a very serious heel. His work was excellent. He was very convincing, very convincing," said Scott. "Whatever he did, he did it right, and it was slow. Nothing was hurried up with Bob. What he did, though, was serious and very convincing."

Scott recalled going to visit Orton Sr. in Kansas City, who was doing work around his home. Orton stepped on a nail. "It was no big deal to him. 'I'll take care of it. Don't worry about. Nice seeing you guys,'" said Scott.

Manager Sir Oliver Humperdink, who first met Orton Sr. and his rookie son Bob Jr. in 1976, concurred. "I think what got him over with the fans was his straight ahead, grinding wrestling style that wasn't fancy but was believable and effective. By that, I mean with Bob there was no wasted motion. Everything he did made 'sense.' In short, he wrestled you but when you thought you had the best of him, he would do a single heel move to get the advantage again."

At six-foot-three, 235 pounds, he could match up with just about anyone. The December 1954 edition of Boxing and Wrestling magazine explored Orton's rougher side. "When Bashin' Bob started to break about every rule of civilized conduct in the ring, he started to break into the magic circle of big-time money makers," wrote Joe Weider. "His fuzzy apple cheeks give him an appearance of angelic temperament that he immediately starts to destroy once he swings into action. He combines a rapid succession of stomps, hair pulls, eye gouges and other variations of pier-six tactics to break down an opponent's defense as soon as possible. When his man is weakened sufficiently, he will use a pile driver, body slam, or flying dropkick to get his fall."

The toughness was bred in Orton from the start, with his parents running a bar. When he became a wrestler, it became a favorite haunt for his colleagues. "We used to go down to Bob Orton's mom's tavern, called Mary's Tavern, in Kansas City, Kansas. We used to go there after the matches on Thursday night religiously," recalled Kansas City announcer Bill Kersten.

"Mary was a beautiful lady, well liked by everybody in there. When we'd go in there, we'd always keep the trouble away."

Perhaps some of Orton's quirkiness was brought to the forefront with his donning of a mask as the mysterious Zodiac in Florida. In a June 1972 newsletter, correspondent Hal Habib talked about his first impressions of the Zodiac. "The weirdest thing I have ever seen in wrestling has come to Florida last week. He is a masked guy called Zodiac. His is a tough one, but dirty. That is not the odd part. The odd part about him is his interviews. He refuses to talk to Gordon Solie on TV so instead he sends him film. See if you can picture this: On the old thrillers, they all have the boss but all you can see is his head's shadow against a white screen. His voice is taped through an amplifier with the treble on all the way, so his voice is heard about three or four times. . . . He has a new friend called (you guessed) Taurus."

One of the youngsters influenced by Orton Sr. during the twilight of his career in Florida was Randy Colley, who would go on to be Moondog Rex and the creator of Demolition, among countless other personas. "You had to get to know him. We got to be good friends. He rode with me just about all the time," said Colley. "A lot of people couldn't stand him and tried to pack him off to ride with somebody else. He was just somebody you'd have to try to get to know."

Humperdink also learned in the car with Orton Sr. "We would travel together back then, and I learned a lot from him by simply listening," SOH said. "I am so happy to have been able to spend some time with him in Vegas over the last few years at Cauliflower Alley [Club]."

We'll leave the last word with Danny Miller, who praised Orton Sr.'s in-ring ability and explained that Orton had more wrestling skills than was immediately apparent. "He was very defensive, very, very defensive. He knew how to protect himself at all times," concluded Miller. "One of the tougher opponents I ever had, equal with Lou Thesz."

— With files from Steven Johnson

* * *

MISS ELIZABETH DIES
By JOHN POWELL

Elizabeth Hulette, known as Miss Elizabeth to wrestling fans, was pronounced dead at the Kennestone Hospital in Cobb County, Georgia, at 5:45 Thursday morning. Hulette was 42.

WBS-TV in Atlanta reported that emergency workers were called to a town-

Elizabeth pre-signs autographs backstage in WCW.

house owned by Lawrence Pfohl (pro wrestler Lex Luger). Pfohl then accompanied the medical personnel as they transported Hulette to hospital. Hulette died shortly after she arrived.

Pfohl was questioned about the death and initially released. He has since been charged by Cobb County for possession of a controlled substance and is in custody.

"At this point, we don't know if it's a suicide, we don't know if it's a natural death [and] we don't know if it's a homicide," Cobb police spokesman Corporal Brody Staud told WBS-TV.

Local police confirm that they responded to a domestic disturbance call at the location on Easter Sunday. WSB-TV reported that the police report said that Pfohl was arrested for allegedly beating Hulette, and that he was out on a $2,500 bond in connection with that incident.

It could be over a month until toxicology reports reveal what killed Hulette. Foul play has been ruled out.

Described by many as the "First Lady" of professional wrestling, Hulette was a major name in the WWF (now WWE) during the 1980s as the manager of her real-life husband at the time, Randy "Macho Man" Savage. Savage and Hulette joined the WWF in 1985.

On his website, Savage posted a short message. "I am deeply saddened by this news, and our thoughts and prayers are with Elizabeth's family," he wrote.

The Kentucky-born Hulette met Savage in a gym, and worked with the Poffo family's International Championship Wrestling for a time. The family patriarch, Angelo Poffo, shared a quick memory with SLAM! Wrestling. "She was a hard worker, she worked hard," said Poffo. "She took a lot of chances in the ring and a lot of dangerous bumps." He hasn't spoken with her since her divorce from Randy.

At her peak in the WWF, Hulette was so recognizable and popular that she was the focus of many major WWF storylines during the wrestling boom.

Many of the angles revolved around the pair's off-again, on-again love affair. Savage even proposed to Hulette on a WWE television broadcast in 1992 and married her at the SummerSlam pay-per-view, even though the pair was really married in 1984. An episode of *Lifestyles of the Rich and Famous* was even filmed about the pair.

James Myers, known better to fans as the wrestler George "The Animal" Steele, was saddened to hear the news of Hulette's death when contacted by SLAM! Wrestling. Myers, who worked an unforgettable "crush" angle with Savage and Hulette in the '80s, remembered her as wonderful woman and hoped that her death would bring about some positive change.

"I had nothing but respect for her. I think she carried herself in a very respectful way during the years I knew her," he said. "It's sad to see a person that young die," Myers continued. "It's such a waste. Maybe these [recent wrestling-related] deaths start opening some eyes and change some lifestyles. Maybe it's not all in vain."

James Harris worked as Kamala in the WWF, and knew Hulette there. "She was always nice and quiet," said Harris. "She stayed to herself, I guess it was because she was with Randy all of the time. I never saw her take a drink, so it's all pretty shocking to me. I could never say a bad thing about her."

Hulette divorced Savage in 1992. After leaving the WWE and disappearing from the wrestling scene, Hulette returned briefly to World Championship Wrestling in 1995 to join the red-hot nWo and worked with Savage once again.

She even worked a wrestling match in WCW, a brief encounter with the late Rhonda Sing.

Luger had a decent football career, including time under coach Marv Levy with the Montreal Alouettes of the late 1970s. He got involved in pro wrestling in the mid-1980s in Florida and rose to prominence in Florida Championship Wrestling.

A hot, young prospect, he was brought into World Championship Wrestling and quickly made a part of the heel stable, the Four Horsemen. He jumped to the WWF and Vince McMahon's World Bodybuilding Federation. At first he was a narcissistic heel, but surprised many by turning good and feuding with Yokozuna.

He was one of the early big names to jump back to WCW during the peak of the Monday night wars, and was with the company until its purchase by WWE.

Pfohl owns the Main Event gym in Cobb County.

— With files from Greg Oliver, Stephen Laroche and
SLAM! Wrestling news sources

From the staff: It's a testament to both her fame and to the staying power of SLAM! Wrestling — and therefore its deep indexing by search engines — that her obituary continually ranks within our top 300 page views each month, years after her death.

* * *

MOTHER'S DAY SPECIAL:
REMEMBERING CHRISTINE JARRETT

By RYAN NATION

Long before her son and grandson laced up their first pair of boots, the late Christine "Teeny" Jarrett was becoming a pioneer in professional wrestling.

Nick Gulas began promoting wrestling in Tennessee during the late 1940s and early 1950s in conjunction his promoting partner Roy Welch. Gulas and Welch owned pro wrestling's Tennessee territory. Early in his career, Gulas hired Christine Jarrett to sell tickets to the weekly wrestling show.

SLAM! Wrestling recently caught up with both her son (Jerry Jarrett) and grandson (Jeff Jarrett) to discuss the matriarch of their family.

"My mother and father divorced in 1945. I was three years old, and my sister was about six months old. My mother, Teeny, was already working at Woolworth's five-and-ten in downtown Nashville," recalled Jerry Jarrett. "We were living with my grandparents because my father was in the army. Prior to the divorce, my father was sending money home. While it was a meager standard of living, we were surviving. After the divorce, my father never sent one dollar. So in desperation, Teeny had to find another job. She went to work selling tickets for the Gulas-Welch wrestling matches held at the Hippodrome in Nashville.

"She later took a full-time job selling tickets during the week for the wrestling matches at Jarman's shoe store," Jerry continued. "I'm not sure of the exact date, but sometime in the late 1940s or early 1950s she moved into their office in the Maxwell House Hotel, which at the time was on Church Street. She loved her job and, as little it paid, it was a big promotion from her ticket selling job and her clerk job at Woolworth's. I remember that she was making $26 per week in 1964 when I went to work full-time at the wrestling office. One day she showed me her First American Bank savings book. It was filled, page after page, with 50-cent deposits. On her meager salary and the financial pressure she was under she had managed to save 50 cents per week since the day she began her job with Gulas and Welch."

"She literally came from a very poor upbringing and broke out of that mold," added Jeff. "She was one of five kids and helped all of her siblings.

Honestly, she was a real trendsetter and groundbreaker for our family."

Jerry Jarrett also recalled how compassionate his mother was when it came to family.

"Teeny took care of my invalid aunt. Teeny bought a house across the street from her, so she could take her meals and see to her needs," Jerry said. "You might say that Teeny's hobby was looking after the needs of a great many of our family members. She saw not only to their material needs, but she was 'mother' to my aunts, uncles and cousins."

She moved up the ranks while working for Gulas and Welch. In the early 1970s, she ran shows for the promotion in Louisville and Lexington, and Evansville, Indiana. With the addition of these towns, the territory continued to grow. Prior to the expansion into Kentucky and Indiana, she had been able to witness her son debut in-ring as a professional wrestler in the late 1960s.

"During my days as a wrestler, she would get as nervous watching my matches as if they were a shoot," recalled Jerry. "Teeny was very old-school and would come down really hard on the wrestlers if she caught one of them breaking kayfabe. The wrestlers feared her wrath and many times they would say to me, 'Damn, Jerry, how did you survive under her roof as a child?' I'd answer, 'I didn't get out of line often.' The truth was Teeny never one time gave me a spanking as a child. Her little talks were quite enough. Teeny had what I call presence. It was if she could look through you, and this is what the wrestlers hated when she would correct them.

"She was the angel of encouragement in whatever I was trying to do," Jerry continued. "Teeny gave the same encouragement to my ability at a game of marbles as she did when I bought the wrestling business from Roy Welch and later from Nick Gulas. She was a great believer in positive reinforcement. She would always say, 'Jerry, God has blessed you with a good mind, and I'm sure you can do anything that you set your mind to.' If I got distracted from any project as a child or as an adult, she would use positive reinforcement as a tool to get me back on track instead of a negative butt chewing or punishment. I can remember wishing for a spanking instead of a talk. Her talks always made me feel so guilty from letting her down. As an adult, I saw the wisdom in her style and tried to do the same with my children."

Christine Jarrett would remain involved in the wrestling business in various roles for many years to arguably become the longest running female associated with a professional wrestling promotion. When her son opened up his own promotion in 1977, she became his partner. She also continued to nurture some of the cities she and Jerry opened up for Gulas and Welch, particularly Louisville, Lexington and Evansville. She also worked for years on Saturday nights at the box office at the weekly Nashville card. Her wrestling career truly came full circle.

"Honestly, there's no one I really respect more because of what she accomplished in the business at the time she did it," said Jeff. "That covers quite a bit of ground. On the surface, she made it in a man's world when it was really a man's world. Everyone she worked for and everybody that worked for her respected her. Over the years, I've heard some marvelous stories about guys that would come through this area that didn't particularly care for her at the time. As the years went by, they respected her so much for what she tried to get them to do and accomplish. She generally cared for the guys as people. She wanted them to save their money. Back in that day, it was much more cash business than it is now. She really set up savings plans and accounts for guys."

In 1995, Louisville's A Night to Remember card honored Christine Jarrett, a longtime unsung hero for the promotion and a major reason wrestling flourished over the years in Louisville and in the territory. In November 1998, she passed away at the age of 75.

Jeff Jarrett, executive vice president of TNA Entertainment, LLC, would go on to follow the footsteps of both his grandmother and father when he co-founded NWA-TNA in 2002.

According to his father, Jerry, "Teeny was a bit reserved in her excitement about Jeff being in the wrestling business because his only involvement while she was alive was as a wrestler. Of course she knew that the wrestling business has a short shelf life for wrestlers and she was concerned that Jeff had no interest in the promotion end of the business."

When asked what his grandmother would think of TNA, Jeff Jarrett answered: "She was a hard-charging, hard-driving woman. She'd always say we could do better. She was also so proud of my dad and his accomplishments. I know she would get real nervous when he would wrestle, and she would get real nervous when I would wrestle. She was a worrywart at times, but I think that went with her caring nature. I think she would be very pleased and proud."

Both Jerry and Jeff expounded upon the advice and wisdom she bestowed to them.

"My mother had a huge bag full of wisdom," recalled Jerry. "She would say things such as, 'Treat people the way you want to be treated.'"

"Obviously, save your money because it won't last forever," chuckled Jeff. "Coming up third-generation in this business, you really have to know who your fan base is and who your paying customers are. Back in those days, it was knowing who came to the shows and bought souvenir pictures. Today, I can translate that into who is the fan base that buys the pay-per-views, watches the television shows and buys the video games, dolls and DVDs. Above anything, she said learn your trade. If you're going to be a carpenter, electrician or lawyer, learn it better than anybody. If you work harder than anybody, you're guaranteed success.

"I've tried to prepare myself for the road ahead of me," continued the former NWA world champion. "She's instilled in our family such a strong work ethic. If you outwork everybody — literally putting in the man hours and necessary efforts — that will put you so far in front of the pack. It reminds me of the old adage 'Luck is when preparation meets opportunity.' There really aren't a lot of lucky people. It's people that work hard and have the opportunity to present it. If there wasn't a Christine Jarrett, there would be no Jeff Jarrett in the wrestling business.

"She instilled the principles and values that still work today," Jeff added. "Work hard and you will reap the fruits of your labor. You've got to be patient and continue to learn your craft. With the wrestling business today, everybody thinks they can do it. People also think it's easy to become a wrestler and a promoter. If she was alive today and was to walk into a dressing room, I know she would tell the guys to learn every aspect of this business. You may never have to run a camera or promote a show but try to learn about it. It gives you different perspectives on just how this business is indeed a business. It's not always glamorous. That's the wisdom she passed on to me, and I think that's exactly what she would try to pass on today.

"Her legacy will be that she treated this wrestling business like a business," continued Double J. "That's always been very hard to do for many, many guys. She wanted the guys to have something when their wrestling days were over. I learned basic simple principles from her that I carry on and will take to my grave just because they're sound and true. They're pretty simple. If you follow a few simple rules in business, it's really hard to go wrong."

From the writer:While Jerry and Jeff have conflicting professional and personal views, they share an admiration for their late matriarch. During our conversations, both lit up with exuberance when recalling memories of her. After reading the story, Jim Cornette explained to me how Christine Jarrett gave him his first break into the wrestling world.

From the staff: James E. wasn't the only one who enjoyed Ryan Nation's tribute to Christine Jarrett. Jerry Jarrett said the following after seeing Nation's story: "When Ryan did the Mother's Day article on my mother, he was able somehow to capture the passion my mother had for this business. Teeny would have been so proud of Ryan's article."

* * *

SAMMARTINO ADMIRED MONSOON

By JOHN MOLINARO

Bruno Sammartino rips into Gorilla Monsoon.

Bruno Sammartino turned 64 years old on Wednesday. The former two-time WWF world heavyweight champion had plans to go out with his wife and visit his grandchildren. It was going to be a birthday he would never forget.

And it was, but for all the wrong reasons. Sammartino received a phone call on his birthday that Gorilla Monsoon had passed away. Sammartino was devastated over the passing of one of his contemporaries.

"Getting the call put a real big lump in my throat," Sammartino told SLAM! Wrestling from his home in Pittsburgh, Pennsylvania. "Knowing how sick he was, having received that call, I still couldn't believe it. I couldn't accept it. To me it was a real shocker."

A younger and healthier Monsoon is the one that Sammartino chooses to remember. He was very disturbed over the image of an aging Monsoon the past few years. "To have seen him deteriorate to what he had become, it was mind-boggling," admitted Sammartino.

Sammartino had a long and storied history with Monsoon. During his first reign as WWF champion between 1963 and 1971, the two wrestled against each other over a hundred times, selling out major arenas through out the northeastern U.S. and Canada.

"We wrestled in Madison Square Garden 12 or 13 times through the years," recalled Sammartino. "All the times I wrestled him, we sold it out. We packed the arenas."

As champion, Sammartino wrestled every major star that passed through the Northeast. Looking back at all his opponents, he ranks Monsoon as one of the best.

"When people would ask me through the years who some of the people that amazed were, guys like Don Leo Jonathan and [Killer] Kowalski and Big

Bill Miller, I always mentioned Monsoon. For a guy at 420 pounds it was rare a man that size could do what he did."

Sammartino was in awe of Monsoon. He was amazed that a man of his size had such agility, speed and stamina.

"One time I wrestled him in Madison Square Garden for one hour and twenty minutes," remembered Sammartino. "I always had great respect for that because people that big run out of gas, but he didn't. He stayed in there with me for the duration. That's the kind of guy he was."

Sammartino was also impressed with Monsoon's mat wrestling skills. "He had a very good amateur background," stated Sammartino. "He was a terrific wrestler. He knew good maneuvers from his experience in amateur wrestling. He was amazing."

New York City fans came out in droves to see Sammartino square off against Monsoon in one of their epic battles. One of the major reasons why it was such a big draw was because people considered Monsoon a legitimate contender for the world title.

"All the times I wrestled him, we always sold out the Garden," said Sammartino. "That in itself will tell you how people viewed him. They saw him as a great challenge to me. He was someone the fans saw as an awesome talent and people believed in wrestling back then."

Despite the respect he has for Monsoon, Sammartino won't be attending the funeral. After wrestling 25 years for the McMahon family, Sammartino had a falling out with Vince McMahon Jr. over the direction the company was taking wrestling. The two have legitimate hard feelings towards each other. As a result, he has lost touch with some of his old adversaries and friends.

"Monsoon and I were never close," admitted Sammartino. "I haven't seen or spoken to him in 12 or 13 years. Last time I saw him, I was doing color commentary for the WWF. WWF people will be [at the funeral] and I don't particularly want to see any of those people."

* * *

"THE BIG CAT" WAS SELDOM TAMED

Ernie Ladd, dead at 68, remembered by friends and fans
By STEVEN JOHNSON and GREG OLIVER

It almost didn't happen. All the honor, fame and glory bestowed on Ernie Ladd during his career on the gridiron and in the ring almost went up in a puff of smoke early in his football career.

Ladd was having one of his frequent spats with the San Diego Chargers' front office in the early 1960s, even before he started wrestling seriously, and he was ready to bag the whole endeavor. His wife, Roslyn, had a good job, and if the Chargers of the old American Football League were not going to treat him with due respect, he'd use that fine Grambling College education in some other form.

"I was serious," he said in an interview with SLAM! Wrestling in 2006. "I had other things that I could do. To me, it was a matter of principle and a matter of the proper way in which someone should be treated."

Chris Swisher Collection

Ernie Ladd chokes Bobo Brazil.

Ladd and the Chargers eventually reached an uneasy accommodation — he later played out his option to jump to the Houston Oilers and Kansas City Chiefs and never had much love for the San Diego brass that chose him in the 15th round of the 1961 college draft.

But in understanding the phenomenon that was "The Big Cat," the incident speaks volumes. Ladd was a proud man from humble beginnings, not afraid in the least to stand up for what he believed was right, whether it was instigating a walkout of an AFL All-Star game because of racial injustice, or pulling rank on mat promoters who salivated for his services.

"At first, I disliked him strongly, enough that I wanted to beat the heck out of him," said Johnny Powers, who had a memorable feud with Ladd in promoter Pedro Martinez's National Wrestling Federation in the early 1970s. "But Pedro said, 'We making money?' 'Yes.' 'Don't hit him, then, with the bat.' I ended up totally respecting him because he was very unique, very creative, would give to the business and would put people over. He actually had his ego under management very well."

Born in Rayville, Louisiana, in 1938, and raised in Orange, Texas, Ladd was a football and basketball star in high school. At six-foot-nine and 300 pounds, he was simply bigger and quicker than anyone of his era, earning the nickname "Little Samson." As a star for the Chargers, "he was so big and strong, he didn't have to be mean," Buffalo Bills guard Billy Shaw said in Jeff Miller's AFL remembrance, *Going Long*. "I'm six-foot-three, but Ladd is six-foot-fantastic," sportswriter Kent Nixon once famously cracked.

Ladd played in four AFL All-Star games, though a series of devastating knee injuries dating back to his college days probably prevented him from becoming as dominant as he might have been. But his biggest all-star role came after the 1964 season, when he couldn't even get a cab ride during the All-Star game prelude in New Orleans. After talking with other discrimination victims, Ladd explained of the decision of 22 black players, "We chose to go."

The league hastily arranged a substitute game in Houston, but Ladd had become known for his willingness to take a stand. When AFL officials pressured Ladd to cut off his trademark goatee, you had another case of respect splashed across the sports pages. "I was going to cut it off a long time ago, but when they started talking about it, and ordered me to take it off, I purposely didn't," he told the Associated Press in 1966. "I could care less. The commissioner can't tell me how to do my face."

Yet, as Powers suggested, Ladd was more measured than militant, and he exemplified that in his wrestling career, launched during his tenure with the Chargers after the 1961 season with Fred Blassie's help. His close friend Bill Watts recounted a time in the mid-1960s when he and Ladd were in the World Wide Wrestling Federation, and Don McClarity, Watts's tag team partner, aimed a series of racial taunts at Ladd, then a fan favorite.

As Watts recalled McClarity's words: "'I want you to tell you one thing, to me you're a nigger, you're still a nigger and you'll always be a nigger." Ladd's reaction? To pay no mind and continue a card game with Bobo Brazil.

"In my mind, in my heart of hearts back then, in my total ignorance of the situation and the times, I thought, 'Gee, Ernie, you're not too tough,'" Watts said. "I didn't realize that it took so much more courage on his part just to take that, to sit there at the table and continue playing cards with Bobo."

Ladd entered the business full-time in 1969 after his knees gave out — he missed out on the Chiefs' win in Super Bowl IV. His great motivation was still to make a good living for his wife and family and he never regretted it. "This is a great business. You can earn a fantastic dollar in it. And because you can, and I have, it's made me a complete man. Football isn't like that. The money is just fair,

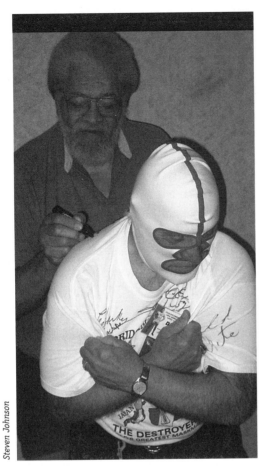

Steven Johnson

Ernie Ladd signs the T-shirt of The Destroyer (Dick Beyer) at the 2005 Cauliflower Alley Club reunion.

and for six months out of the year, you're not your own man," he said, though acknowledging he'd be worth a lot more in today's NFL.

Still, you never found Ladd taking wild broadsides at football — after all, it was his gateway to the manic world of wrestling. "The value of playing professional sports is what you can do after," he said. "Pro sports should be a stepping stone to security, a better job. I have the greatest admiration for someone who does that."

Though he initially worked mostly as a good guy — Cowboy Bob Kelly booked him as the first black man to wrestle white men in a tag bout in Louisiana — Ladd always credited Martinez with allowing him to use his monstrous size as a heel. "That's where the money was," he said.

An attraction from coast to coast in the 1970s, Ladd had huge runs in Japan, California, Indiana, Georgia, the Northeast, the Buffalo-Cleveland territory, Florida, and the Mid-South area around his adopted home of Franklin, Louisiana. He held more than two dozen titles, including the NWF world title, the Southern title, the Florida belt and assorted tag championships. Less important than gold though was his role as a unique ex-football crossover star who could put fannies in the seats.

"He always called me 'Ace.' He dressed the part and he had everything going for him. He was really the first big man in the business," said manager Bobby Heenan, who worked with him a lot in Dick the Bruiser's Indianapolis-area promotion.

Jake "The Snake" Roberts knew him well towards the end of Ladd's run in the Mid-South promotion in the late 1970s and early 1980s, and was entranced with the way such a big man could plead for mercy as a way of incensing a crowd. "The Cat, he was too much, man. I got him at the end of his career. But still, he had that sneaky . . . I mean it's hard not to hate a big man that begs off. 'You big, sorry shit, how dare you beg off, after you just kicked the shit out of this guy for 20 minutes. Now that the tables are turned, you beg and ask for mercy?' God, you've got to hate that guy. How could you not? Everyone in the building wanted to kill that bastard."

As a wrestler, Ladd was never considered a great and fluid worker, but he never pretended that was his strength. A nonstop talker, he invariably referred to microphone holders as "Mr. TV Announcer," and launched his verbal bombs regardless of race, color or creed. "He was not seen as black. He was seen as Ernie Ladd," said Tony Atlas, whom Ladd helped bring into the WWF.

The Cat demeaned every aspect of what he called Dominic Denucci's "spaghetti-bending" Italian heritage, though he said Denucci was probably his favorite opponent. He did most of his damage with a taped thumb he lifted from Luke Graham, his massive boots — billed as size 18 — and his ability to sell even to smaller opponents. Powers called him "maybe the smartest heel," in the sense that he mastered a sport that did not come naturally to him.

"He was a smart man. He'd be on the mat thinking right there, adjusting," Powers said. "Some people are naturally weird . . . like [Abdullah the] Butcher is, kind of, and Sheik was and all that. Ladd was thought-out weird. In other words, he thought it out first and then executed. In my opinion, that's tougher to do than if it's naturally you."

Case in point — to convince Los Angeles fans that diminutive Ruben Juarez was his equal, Ladd popped Alka-Seltzer tablets into his mouth before a fracas to convince fans Juarez had so battered him that he was foaming at the mouth.

Sir Oliver Humperdink managed Ladd in Florida on several occasions during the 1970s and visited again with him at the 2005 Cauliflower Alley Club reunion. Humperdink called his old friend, "a manager's dream."

"By that, I mean he could talk on promos, and I never had to worry about his performance in the ring. I could go out there and do my thing knowing that Big Cat was doing his. Sometimes a manager had to worry about his protégé 'hitting all his marks.' Not so with Ernie," said Humperdink. "I don't know anyone who didn't love Ernie. . . . It was a pure pleasure to accompany him into battle. I will miss him greatly."

In addition to being the first truly nationally recognized black heel, Ladd became the first man of color to walk into a front office as a booker working for Watts and Carolina promoter Jim Crockett. "I broke a lot of color barriers, particularly in the Deep South," Ladd said. "It was important to end that injustice so other wrestlers could come in and earn a livelihood."

In recent years, Ladd continued his work with a variety of charitable causes and his beloved Grambling. He also had a close relationship with former U.S. president George H.W. Bush, the product of a meeting 40 years ago when Bush was trying to round up support for a U.S. Senate bid. In 2005, he accompanied Bush on a visit to see victims of Hurricane Katrina.

A member of the WWE Hall of Fame, the Louisiana Sports Hall of Fame and the San Diego Hall of Champions, Ladd was beset by colon cancer during the winter of 2003–04. But, displaying both the faith and the conviction for which he was so well known, he refused to meet his maker on anything other than his own terms. "The doctor told me I had three to six months to live," he told SLAM! Wrestling in a 2004 interview. "I told the doctor that he's a liar and that Dr. Jesus has got the verdict on me! I also told him, 'You're working with a miracle when you work with me.'"

His condition worsened in recent months and his last major appearance was at promoter Greg Price's fan festival in Rockville, Maryland, last August, when friends were disturbed at his loss of weight and mobility.

"The Big Cat answered my first phone call with, 'Jesus loves you,' which I'd later discover was his standard telephone greeting instead of 'Hello.' In my phone conversations that followed, I would have never known that he was losing his battle with cancer. He was always very positive and upbeat," said Price, who said his time with Ladd created memories for a lifetime.

Ladd had been booked to appear at a fan show in New Jersey next month, but his family reported that the cancer, which had spread to his bones, claimed him overnight on March 10. Pedro Martinez's son Ron, a booker and announcer who also worked with Ladd in the International Wrestling Association, called his passing "a tremendous loss for both the wrestling business and for his family as well. He was a true prince of the business. I am sure that he and my father are shooting the breeze in the dressing room right next to heaven."

Ladd is survived by his wife of more than 45 years, Roslyn, and four children. Funeral arrangements were pending.

* * *

THE LEGEND OF EL SANTO

Who was that masked man?
By JOHN MOLINARO

On July 26, 1942, Rodolfo Guzman Huerta made his pro wrestling debut, winning an eight-man battle royal in Mexico City. At the time, very little was made of the event. After all, wrestling's popularity in Mexico was exploding and Huerta was just another green, awkward rookie.

El Santo.

Nobody could have imagined that Huerta would go on to enjoy a 40-year career and capture the hearts of the nation of Mexico as the masked El Santo (translated into English as The Saint), the most beloved wrestler in lucha libre history.

This past Saturday marked the anniversary of Santo's death in 1984. Sixteen years after passing away, the people of Mexico have not forgotten the indelible mark El Santo made on the nation. Although not an official holiday, the day is marked by nationwide celebrations, memorials and wrestling cards honoring his memory. Fans from all across Mexico make a pilgrimage to his mausoleum site in Mexico City, paying homage to the man affectionately nicknamed "El Enmascarado de Plata" (The Man in the Silver Mask).

It seems odd that a masked wrestler could have such a lasting effect on an entire country, but then, El Santo was far from your average wrestler.

The story of El Santo's incredible career is directly tied to lucha libre's earliest days. In 1933, a Mexican promoter by the name of Salvador Lutteroth brought pro wrestling to Mexico after seeing it while on a trip to Texas. With its fast-paced, athletic style, Mexican pro wrestling became one of biggest attractions in Mexico. Lucha libre (the Spanish word for pro wrestling, which translates into *free fighting* in English) was born.

Huerta moved to Mexico City and became enthralled and captivated by lucha libre. He trained to become a pro wrestler at a local gym and made his debut under the name Rudy Guzman. Guzman competed as a *rudo* (Spanish word for heel wrestler) but never gained any measure of notoriety.

In 1934, an American wrestler debuted in Mexico under a black, leather mask. Lutteroth dubbed him El Enmascarado, "The Masked Man." Soon, Lutteroth incorporated the use of other masked wrestlers into lucha libre, creating superheroes and villains for the audience to identify with. The move was a huge success and the modern era of Mexican wrestling was born.

This trend towards masked heroes was not lost on Huerta. He put on a mask and called himself Murcielago II (The Bat) but quickly dropped the name when the wrestler playing the original Bat character complained. Needing a new name and gimmick, Guzman took the name El Santo from a character from Alexandre Dumas's novel *The Man in the Iron Mask*, donned a long flowing silver cape and what would become his trademark silver mask. And with that, a career was born that would see El Santo become embedded in Mexican popular culture and become a national treasure for over four decades.

"He totally transcended wrestling," states Dave Meltzer, editor of the *Wrestling Observer* newsletter. "He was much bigger than just a wrestling star. I think there have been wresters as big as him and as popular as him but none for 40 years where everybody in the country knows him. Santo was more than just a wrestler. Nobody had the enduring popularity he had."

"He was a such a phenomenon because he touched so many people," comments Mike Tenay, WCW broadcaster and noted lucha libre expert. "There were so many people who identified with Santo and I think that was one of the things that made him the cultural icon he was.

"He was among the first to take the persona of the masked wrestler and to really gain an identity with it," continues Tenay. "He was among the first wave of the masked wrestlers. He was the first that really made it big."

Masked wrestlers are not all that uncommon in American wrestling. There have been a host of them over the years; but when they leave the arena after the matches are over, they slip out of their character and assume their real identities.

As soon as Huerta put on that silver mask his life literally changed. He was no longer Rudolfo Guzman Huerta; he was El Santo.

"He didn't have a secret identity. He was always El Santo," offers David Wilt, a Santo expert who runs the Santo, el Enmascarado de Plata website, celebrating the career of El Santo. "He wasn't just a fictional character, he was an actual person. He wasn't like George Reeves playing Superman and making a few public appearances, he was actually El Santo."

As he grew in popularity as a wrestler, Santo quickly went from a cult figure to a national hero who crossed over into every imaginable form of Mexican culture. In 1951, a weekly comic book was created based on El Santo. The comic was a million-dollar seller as the people of Mexico followed the superhero exploits of El Santo each and every week.

And then the film industry came calling. Mexican cinema was looking for a new film formula to bank on. Producers saw the popularity of lucha libre and its masked wrestlers and wanted to capitalize. Santo was immediately cast and the lucha libre horror genre was born.

The memorial marker for a legend.

"In the 1940s and 1950s he was really popular with the wrestling and the comic book," explains Wilt. "But film really brought it to a whole new level for fans who were not wrestling fans and who didn't read comic books. Now, he's reached the level where he really was a major figure in Mexican popular culture."

As lucha libre enjoyed its golden years in the 1940s and 1950s, the basic struggle in the matches was defined by the battle between the *technicos* (Spanish term for babyfaces) and the *rudos*. More and more lucha libre story-lines mirrored the real-life corruption, hardship and the struggles on the streets of Mexico City. Wrestlers like Santo, who were portrayed as law-abiding, honest citizens fighting the evil, corrupt *rudos* filled the void, balancing the laws of justice in favor of the working man.

"There are few figures like El Santo who have historically dominated the most popular end of the popular culture spectrum," says David William Foster, a Spanish language professor at the University of Arizona and an expert on Mexican cinema and literature. "In a society like Mexico there is the need for cultural heroes.

"The idea of someone who is going to avenge the wrongs of the world; there's a lack of sense of justice, order and in society. El Santo caught on and he was absolutely venerated in Mexico for decades."

Between 1958 up until his last movie in 1982, Santo starred in 54 films. Fighting for justice and the forces of good, these campy movies saw Santo battle vampires, aliens, zombies and Martians. He was often joined by Mil Máscaras and Blue Demon, two other lucha stars that had big film careers, battling his real-life wrestling opponents. Sequences from Santo's pro wrestling matches were often used in the films.

"The formula for classic lucha libre films have the hero who is an active wrestler and at the same time he's also a costumed crime fighter," explains Wilt. "What really distinguishes it from run-of-the-mill superhero films is that instead of having a secret identity, his other identity is as a pro wrestler. The plot spills over into the arena matches. You have this dichotomy between pro wrestling and crime fighting."

As the legend of El Santo grew, so did the lengths he went to to protect his identity. Whenever he went out in public, he always wore his mask.

"El Santo really guarded his secret identity," states Wilt. "Whenever he was in public he always wore his mask. He had different masks for different occasions. When he had to eat he had a mask with a chin cut away, you couldn't eat with a small hole in his mask. He would make public appearances at bullfights and with politicians in his mask."

"Everything he would do to protect his identity, that for me is one of the most amazing aspects about him," exclaims Tenay. "That mask was omnipresent at every public appearance he made. In today's wrestling time that's just nonexistent, that anybody would care to that degree, but I think you could tell he took that care in protecting his identity. I think that was also part of that package that made him larger than life."

"Without the mask he was just Rudolfo," says Rogelio Agrasanchez Jr., whose father helped produce two of El Santo's most popular movies in the 1970s. "But when he put that mask and costume on he was El Santo."

"He was in Misterio en las Bermudas [Mystery in Bermuda], which my dad was filming in Texas," recalls Agrasanchez. "My brother was driving him and Mil Máscaras up from Mexico into Texas. As they were approaching the Texas border, my brother told them they had to take off their masks when they went through customs. Santo was very leery and told my brother, 'Okay, but don't look back.' That's how secretive he was."

Santo was so protective of concealing his identity that he would often

take a different flight from the production crew to film locations because he didn't want them to see him go through customs without his mask for fear of being identified later on the set.

While El Santo was unquestionably the most popular and recognizable lucha star, he was not as good of a worker as Gory Guerrero, Eddie Guerrero's father, who was considered by many as the best wrestler in the history of Mexico.

Guerrero and Santo teamed in the 1960s as La Pareja Atómica (The Atomic Pair) and set Mexico on fire. And although Santo was more popular, Guerrero was by far the better wrestler.

"They grew a really special relationship," says WWF star Eddie Guerrero. "They were real good buddies and my dad had nothing but respect for him. When Santo made his name for himself it was a real pleasure for my dad to be a part of it in some way. They went out there and busted their butts and made names for themselves into something big."

"The reputation Santo had was he was good, not great," says Mike Tenay. "I think it's very similar to Hulk Hogan where that ability to work in the ring was secondary due to that larger than life presence."

Through the 1960s and 1970s, Santo would split his time between wrestling and movies. And so the legend continued to grow.

Finally, cracks in the lucha libre horror film genre began to appear. In 1976, a new president was elected in Mexico and a new agency was formed dedicated to Mexican film. The government, not impressed with the genre, quickly pulled all funding for the films, making it impossible for producers to finance their movies. This move combined with the import of foreign kung fu movies into Mexico, spelled the end for the film genre.

"One of his last films, *Misterio en las Bermudas*, marks the end of the genre," explains Wilt. "Santo made four more films and there was a brief revival in the early 1990s [without Santo] but it was pretty much over."

As Santo continued to wrestle his body began to break down. He was no longer as effective in the ring as he once was and on September 12, 1982, he retired from active competition. For Santo, the pain of retiring was made easier when his son debuted shortly after carrying on in his footsteps as El Hijo del Santo (the son of the Saint).

Even in retirement, El Santo protected his identity. He wore the mask on several TV appearances and as he entered a new career as an escape artist.

On January 26, 1984, El Santo appeared on a Mexican talk show and without previous warning he publicly unmasked for the first time in his career. Underneath the legendary silver mask was an old, battered face.

Days later he was performing in a skit at a theater when he complained of a pain in his arm. He was rushed to the hospital. But it was no use. He passed away that evening in his hospital bed. He was 68.

Santo's funeral was among the largest in the history of Mexico. Thousands flooded the streets of Mexico City outside the funeral parlor, wanting to catch a glimpse of their fallen hero. Masked wrestlers Mil Máscaras and Blue Demon attended the funeral, breaking down in front of the coffin as they paid their final respects.

It took hours for Santo's coffin to make it from the funeral parlor into the hearse. He was placed in a mausoleum in Mexico City with a simple plaque bearing a likeness of his silver mask. And of course he was buried with the mask on. The wrestling storyline goes that on his deathbed Santo told his son El Hijo del Santo to carry on the tradition and to never lose the mask as part of match stipulation.

El Santo remains embedded in Mexican popular culture. His likeness was recently printed on a series of national lottery tickets in Mexico.

And even in death there is a concerted effort to respect his memory by protecting his identity. In November 1999, SOMOS, a Mexican film-nostalgia magazine, published photos of El Santo without his mask. El Hijo del Santo was outraged and threatened to sue the publication. As it turned out, one of El Santo's other sons provided the magazine with the photos, and the lawsuit was quickly forgotten.

Looking back, several experts try to contextualize Santo's popularity and explain his popularity.

"He was one of the biggest stars in Mexico even before he made his first movie," explains Meltzer. "I've read it where he's been compared to Babe Ruth or John Wayne in American publications trying to put him in a context for Americans."

So why was he such a cultural phenomenon?

"He was a real person," Wilt remarks. "Here was someone who was not an actor. You see him in the movies and then you could watch him on TV and go to your local arena and see him wrestle in person, and go to your newsstand every week and buy a comic book that had his adventures in it. He's not just a fictional character, he's an actual person.

"El Santo is one of the maximum idols in Mexico," continues Wilt. "He's different in that he's not someone playing a role, he lived his entire life almost unable to show his face. His impact on Mexican culture and society was huge."

* * *

"WAY TOO MANY GUYS HAVE DIED": JBL

By TIM BAINES — *Ottawa Sun*

Unlike the title of his book, Eddie Guerrero couldn't cheat death.

Last Sunday, Guerrero woke up and brushed his teeth, knowing another milestone in his storied wrestling career was on the horizon — a triple threat match for the world heavyweight championship against Batista and Randy Orton that night in Minneapolis. The match wouldn't happen. Guerrero was found dead by his nephew, Chavo — killed by heart failure.

Yet another wrestling death. Just 38 years old. A shame. A tragedy. Joining others like Road Warrior Hawk (age 45), Davey Boy Smith (39), Brian Pillman (36), Big Boss Man Ray Traylor (42), "Mr. Perfect" Curt Hennig (44), "Ravishing" Rick Rude (41), Terry "Bam Bam" Gordy (40), Hercules Hernandez (46), "Hot Stuff" Eddie Gilbert (33), Chris Candido (33), Crash Holly (34) . . . death under peculiar circumstances. The list goes on. And so does the mourning.

"Way too many guys have died," John "Bradshaw" Layfield (JBL) said over the phone earlier this week. "The culture 10 to 15 years ago was guys were making a lot of money — it was a sex, drugs and rock and roll mindset. And a lot of deaths we've seen came from that. We've really tried to establish a new culture, a corporate mindset. The biggest risk the guys are at now is carpal tunnel syndrome from playing too many video games."

JBL knew Guerrero. He knew him well. Eddie stood beside him as a groomsmen at his wedding.

The loss and void are huge. It was JBL who battled Eddie's nephew Chavo on *Smackdown*. Chavo, thankfully, wrestled as himself, tossing away his Kerwin White character for good.

JBL has never been shy about voicing his opinion.

"Eddie was one of my very best friends," said JBL. "In the ring, he was my arch-nemesis. Out of the ring, he was a friend.

"There are not a lot of better people on this planet. He had such a connection with the fans. It was like being in a ring with an ungrounded electric cord."

On Sunday night, good guys and bad guys stood side by side — guys we love to hate — Triple H and Kurt Angle gushed tears. So did others, like Chris Benoit, Rey Mysterio Jr., Shelton Benjamin and the Big Show. Guerrero was an inspiration to some, a hero to others.

It's not surprising, in life, that Guerrero looked every bit 38 years old . . . and then some. Drugs, alcohol and a separation from wife and family will do that to you.

In an interview earlier this year, Guerrero told me: "There was a time when I didn't want to live anymore. I was in utter despair. I believe in God . . . but I was having a hard time. I wanted to give up."

He reconciled with his wife, but continued to battle the demons.

"Every day is a battle," he said. "Some days are easy, some aren't. Some days you just want the night to come. You want to go to bed and get the day over with. I'm not perfect. I was a trash can. But I can say I haven't drank in three years. I haven't gotten high in three years. The positives outweigh the negatives. It feels good to wake up."

"Eddie had so many obstacles to overcome. He lost his family and the road to getting them back meant he had to beat his addiction," said JBL. "This is really a tragic story."

Eddie is survived by his wife, Vickie, and daughters Shaul, 14, Sherilyn, nine, and Kaylie Marie, three.

"It was heart failure," Vickie told WWE.com. "It was from his past — the drinking and the drug abuse. They found signs of heart disease. [The examiner] said that the blood vessels were very worn and narrow, and that just showed all the abuse from the scheduling of work and his past.

"We just celebrated his four-year sobriety last Thursday. We just thought we had life by the handful. We thought we had it all figured out. He worked so hard to make a better life for us."

Vaya con dios, mi amigo!

* * *

From the staff: The outpour of emotion following Eddie Guerrero's passing was understandably huge. Guerrero touched many lives during his time in and out of the squared circle. JBL's comments about his friend are matched by an unexpected submission SLAM! Wrestling received from one person whose life was influenced by the Latino wrestling legend.

MEETING EDDIE: A SOLDIER'S STORY

By STAFF SERGEANT PAUL H. MODESTO — Special to SLAM! Wrestling

CAMP VICTORY, IRAQ — I really hope that this letter will make it back to the Guerrero family.

I would like to start by expressing my deepest sympathy to the Guerrero family, especially to Mr. Eddie Guerrero's wife and children. I want the Guerrero family to know something about Eddie Guerrero as they know he is and was a great dad, husband and professional man.

First off, my name is Staff Sergeant Paul H. Modesto Sr. I am a soldier currently deployed in Iraq for my second tour. What I would like the family members to know is that I have been watching wrestling since I was a child and even today I am still a big fan. I happened to meet Eddie Guerrero in Sacramento, California, while heading back to Fort Hood, Texas. I was getting ready to deploy again and was on emergency leave for a few days. The night I left just happened to be the midnight flight or red eye flight on the Fourth of July this year. I have more to say about that night but first . . .

As I read about the passing of Eddie Guerrero, I thought about the importance of how special that day was for me. You see, I wrestled throughout middle school, high school and then for USA Wrestling. It was then when I put in an application for Ted Turner's Power Plant and wanted to wrestle for WCW. I became a huge fan, trained harder than ever and was dedicated to eating right and working out. I have always seen Eddie Guerrero and many other superstars. I must admit I was not the biggest Guerrero fan right away. Then one day, Eddie came out with the LWO [Latino World Order] T-shirt. I was so proud to see that. I was a proud Mexican American, so I ran out to get me my own LWO T-shirt. I have worn that shirt out, to the point I made it a muscle shirt as a matter of fact. I have the Mexican flag and that very shirt here with me in Iraq.

I happened to be living in Lodi, California, at the time of all the training. I was working for COCO's family restaurant as a line cook; my wife happened to be a waitress there as well. It was there at COCO's where Ken Shamrock and his father, Bob Shamrock, ate breakfast just about every day. It was an honor at the time to know I cooked Ken Shamrock's breakfast.

I talked to him about wresting and how I wanted to wrestle for WCW in the lightweight competition. It drove me to train harder and I got some tips from Ken Shamrock about training. After saving my money and getting ready to submit my application to WCW, I realized that you had to be five feet, nine inches tall to go to the Power Plant. I was devastated. I ended up finding a different job and realized that I had to change my goals. With wresting now no longer being my passion, I had to set new goals. I decided to join the California Army National Guard.

Just as I spoke earlier, this is my second trip to Iraq. As I stood in line at the airport waiting to check in on that Fourth of July night, I looked in front of me and I said to myself, "That looks like Christian." I thought it was just me, when I turned around and saw Orlando Jordan standing right behind me. I couldn't believe I was in line with WWE superstars.

I was not flying in my uniform because I didn't want to draw attention to myself. It is for security purposes. As I looked towards the counter, I noticed Eddie Guerrero standing in front of me with a straw in his mouth, in his black sportscoat and jeans. Next to Eddie was Chris Benoit. I was like a little kid on Christmas Day standing in front of the Christmas tree. You should have seen the gleam in my eyes.

As I got closer to the counter I said hello to Eddie Guerrero. He looked at me and said, "Hello." To me, that was a big moment. I finally met the man that made me proud of my heritage and he was all I ever wanted to be.

At first he didn't say much. I figured it was just about midnight and he was tired, probably from a show and didn't want to be bothered by a fan.

I then told him how I am looking forward to seeing him in Iraq and that I had just left Iraq when they showed up. He looked at me and said, "What is your name again?" As he reached his hand out, I told him my name again and he then told me how proud of us soldiers he was, that us soldiers were true heroes in his eyes.

I told him it's ironic, but I have felt like that about him for many years. I can only begin to tell you how proud Eddie talked about us troops and then he went on about his trip to Iraq and how he felt about being there for the two weeks.

I had forgotten that I had my camera with me, and at that time his cell phone rang and I called my wife right away to tell her who I was standing there talking to for the past 20 minutes. As Eddie hung up his phone, he still stood next to me. I felt like, "Wow, here is my favorite WWE superstar waiting to continue his conversation with me." I asked Eddie to say hello to my wife and he was more than happy to. I hung up the phone with my wife so I could talk to Eddie more. A few minutes later the plane started to board.

I asked Eddie if I could get a picture of us and when I saw him in Iraq he could sign it. He said for a soldier he would be honored to take a picture with me. I didn't know he had a seat in the front of the cabin as I made my way through the cabin. I saw Booker T, J.R., Kurt Angle, Hardcore Holly and many others. As we arrived in Texas, I could not find Eddie Guerrero, but I knew I would see him again in Iraq.

Now that will never happen.

I now realize that we shared a moment on that Fourth of July. I realize that no matter how long the hour, how long the day or how long this tour will last, I met a man and a legend who was proud of me and the service I do for my country, his country, our country. I will never forget the day I met Eddie Guerrero and how much it meant to me. I will continue to train hard, train my troops and be even that much more proud as a Mexican American that a superstar like Eddie Guerrero cares about us soldiers.

My prayers go out to the Guerrero family.

Sincerely,
SSG Paul H. Modesto
Camp Victory, Iraq

*   *   *

From the staff: In stark contrast to the death of Eddie Guerrero is the story of Chris Benoit. On the day the world learned of Chris, Nancy and Daniel's deaths, emails flew back and forth between our writers. How do we pay tribute to a man who, in one way or another, we all idolized? Do we do a group tribute, talking about our favorite matches? Do we open up the email bag and invite fans share their memories?

All such conversation, however, ceased, as the chilling tale of what happened soon changed the tones of our discussion. What was sadness and mourning turned to anger and shock, and later pure bewilderment. Those sentiments have been echoed countless times since then by wrestlers, fans and everyone else tied to the wrestling business.

Even today, Benoit's name is still a sensitive subject in conversation.

*   *   *

Greg Oliver

Trevor Murdoch with his title belt.

TREVOR MURDOCH "CONFUSED" BY BENOIT TRAGEDY

By GREG OLIVER

From the writer: Trevor was a cool interview, but because the interview was so fresh after the Benoit double-murder suicide, I didn't bring it up early in the conversation. But then, as I was getting ready to go, I mentioned something and he said he was eager to talk about it.

WATERLOO, IOWA — It was obvious once he started talking that Trevor Murdoch wanted to talk about Chris Benoit. The topic is a delicate one in the industry. Some refuse to talk about Benoit, and others seem to be on every talk show.

With their star status and built-in entourage of public relations soldiers, WWE wrestlers don't always get to speak their minds like they might like; and sometimes when they do, it can be to a general assignment reporter on a small-town paper who knows little about what they do to make a living.

After some insightful conversation about the joys of working in front of small crowds and the trials of being a tag champion, Murdoch (real name Bill Mueller) insisted to SLAM! Wrestling that he was cool to talk about what happened with Benoit the weekend of June 22–24, 2007, when he is alleged to have murdered his wife, Nancy, and son, Daniel, before hanging himself in their home outside Atlanta.

Chris and Nancy Benoit listen to Melanie Pillman speak at a Brian Pillman Memorial Show.

It turns out that Benoit was one of Murdoch's supporters. Through his trainer Harley Race, Murdoch had gotten a chance to go to Japan for six months, where he learned a lot of the unique Japanese style.

When Murdoch got a WWE tryout, Benoit saw him in the ring, liked what he saw of the Japanese influence and encouraged WWE talent relations honcho John Laurinaitas to keep an eye on Murdoch.

Once he was hired, Benoit kept up his interest in Murdoch.

"Every time I'd seen Chris, he was asking me how I was doing, if I needed help with anything. Just generally, if everything was okay," Murdoch told SLAM! Wrestling. "He seemed to always be concerned that my well-being was okay. And we're on two different programs, he's on *Smackdown* and I'm on *Raw*."

From there, Murdoch is rolling.

"He was a guy that had an immense drive and desire to be number one and to be the best in this business. That drive and desire made him who he was — the best in the business. It sucks the way things turned out. That person I don't know. I don't know the Chris Benoit that committed this insane tragedy. But the guy that I knew, I never would have assumed, or put two and two together, and if you ever spoke to him, or spent any time with him, you'd know that Chris was not the guy that would ever have been associated with this. And the media is just burying us. I'm just being honest. They're all extremely easy and eager to point the finger at steroids and to make it sensational. I don't. It's easy to point the finger at steroids. This whole thing went over three days. There's just no way that 'roid rage can last that long. And if people would just listen to the facts, they could put two and two together."

Murdoch will admit that painkillers are a fact of life on the WWE circuit. It's a tough business. "I'm not saying the guys on the road don't take painkillers. I'm not saying that average people that are sitting at home reading this don't take painkillers. Just because right now we're in the spotlight, it's a bad thing. We're in a business where our bodies get beat up. We go through, on an average, if you say on average, we get knocked five, six times, at the very minimum, a night. Imagine standing up there, throwing yourself back down six or seven times, five or six times; after a while, after a time period, you're going to hurt. And you need stuff, not all the time, but just to make you sleep so your legs quit hurting, or your hips quit hurting, so your back quits hurting. There are times that guys get dependent on them. It happens. It's called addiction. Everybody has a weakness. And granted, it may have been a combination of painkillers, steroids, alcohol, I don't know. We may never know. But I know Chris was, bottom line, a good-hearted man that loved wrestling. That's the only person that I'm ever going to remember."

Like fans, Murdoch also feels a sense of betrayal at what Benoit did and how it will affect his legacy, which will be forever "tarnished" with the "horrible, horrible tragedy."

"What sucks is that Chris will never go down in a Hall of Fame. He'll never, from this point, be remembered for being the wrestler that he was. He's always going to be remembered for his last actions, his last three days. It's horrible that one man's life can be summed up in three days, but that's exactly what happened. It's human nature to remember the bad instead of the good."

In the WWE locker room, Murdoch said that wrestlers are dealing with the situation in their own way.

"It is what it is, and we all have to deal with it today. In the locker room, it's a little shocked and stunned. We all loved Chris, so we're all at a serious crossroads in our feelings. Some guys are extremely upset, some guys are holding their feelings in and it doesn't bother them at all," he said.

"It can be an extremely cold business, because you've got so many different guys, so many different personalities, so many different backgrounds.

Some guys hear this, and they're like, 'To hell with him. If that's what he's going to do, then I have no respect for him.' Other guys, like me, I'm just confused. Bottom line, that's the only answer I have, I'm confused."

* * *

ONE OF HELEN'S DOZEN MISSING THIS YEAR

By RICK BELL — *Calgary Sun*

Bob Leonard

Owen Hart poses with the Stampede Wrestling British Commonwealth and North American titles.

From the staff: Undeniably, Owen Hart's tragic death was the one that hit SLAM! Wrestling's family the hardest. Following the fatal accident, SLAM! Wrestling's readers were invited to leave tributes for the "King of Harts" on the website. The messages and memories of Owen were some of the most heartfelt words that we've ever read.

Nearly one year after Owen's passing, his mother, Helen Hart, spoke with Calgary Sun columnist Rick Bell to share her own stories.

He won't be there when they gather later today at the big house on the hill.

He won't be there with the kids, the grandkids, the family, the friends, the dogs, the cats and whoever else shows up.

He won't be there on this special Sunday, this Mother's Day. A fall from the heights of a Kansas City arena into a wrestling ring ended all that for Owen Hart, one of the best guys you could ever meet.

Owen died just after last year's Mother's Day.

"I don't know what to say," says Helen Hart, who raised 12 kids, has 34 grandchildren and handles the death of the youngest of her own with a grace many can only imagine and few can explain.

"You don't get over it. It was Owen's birthday last Sunday and it is Mother's Day this Sunday. The anniversary coming up. You just don't get over it.

"Owen wrote me a card once. It was so touching. I still have it. Owen wrote: 'Thanks for having me. I love life.'

"Owen was the baby. We could've stopped at 10 kids or 11. But we didn't. We had Owen."

Helen's mind goes back to her Austrian doctor telling her she couldn't have more kids after Owen. Helen cried. She wanted a family of 15.

"The doctor told me: You are no shicken," says Helen, imitating the doctor's German accent. "He was right. I was no shicken."

Then Helen mentions her children. A lot. She mentions her husband Stu, the legend of wrestling and one of the best guys you could ever meet. She mentions him a lot too. She talks a lot about family.

"When you have all the other children, it helps at times like this. And Stu is a rock."

Helen laughs, explaining why she had so many children. "We had a lot of cold winter nights," explains Helen, and you can already hear the punch line through her New York City accent.

"On Saturday night they would have a wrestling show in Edmonton. About four in the morning I could see the headlights of Stu's car as it chugged up the road. I was so glad to see him back home I jumped in bed and warmed it up and there was Stu. One thing led to another."

Helen pauses, then laughs. "I don't think Stu ever knew what was happening."

Yes, Helen was born in the Bronx, a premature baby in a shoebox with two water bottles, in the days before incubators.

The doctors told Helen's folks two things. "They said I'd never be normal, and they might have been right. And they said I'd never be a mother. I think there they might have been wrong."

Helen, who says she's still 38 years old, met Stu through a friend when the grappler was in the Big Apple.

"I loved his blue eyes. I've always been weak for blue eyes. He was shy. He wouldn't say anything. Now I can't get him to stop talking." She laughs.

Helen's mom didn't go for the marriage but the couple got hitched on New Year's Eve, back in 1947.

Their first child, Smith, was born in New York while Bruce and Keith saw the light of day in Montana and the other kids drew their first breath here.

"You need a strong husband and both of you must have a sense of humor," advises Helen. "There was no job too big or too small for Stu. He could diaper a baby and put you in a wrestling hold at the same time. He never thought certain things were woman's work.

"Sometimes I compare the life I might have had in New York City — the Broadway plays, the glamorous cafés."

But Helen thinks of those times all 12 kids would be at home, watching TV or playing ball. The family.

"This has been a wonderful life. I really wouldn't have traded it for the world. I know it's not original, but if you take the word Mom and turn it upside down it spells the word Wow," says Helen Hart, one very original mom.

Epilogue
The Stories Continue

Picking articles that represent the best of a dozen years in publication is no easy task.

Obviously, you want to have as many parts of your history represented as possible, with the highest quality pieces appearing. Certainly, we all have favourites that we feel should belong on these pages, while others are so outwardly horrid that you can't help but want to re-live them (sort of like a WCW object on a pole match).

To break kayfabe and give you an idea of how the book was formed, we can tell you that the selection process wasn't an easy one — some articles were picked because of the quality of the writing. Others were picked because we needed to have x wrestler be a part of the book. Others, still, were simply staff favourites that may be more of an insider selection than one that got huge traffic.

The good news is this —the articles you don't see here are all available on the SLAM! Wrestling website. We're still going strong, producing the best stories about pro wrestling that can be found anywhere. Whether it's interviews, reviews, opinions or predictions, we're hard at work covering the world in and around the squared circle. And our archives, with stories dating back to 1997, are unequaled.

As is the case with our online work, we love to hear back from our readers. Please email us and let us know what you thought of *SLAM! Wrestling: Shocking Stories from the Squared Circle*   or, better yet, email ECW Press and tell them you loved the book, so they will want to do a second volume!

Thanks for reading and be sure to keep your browser clicked on to SLAM! Wrestling.

— Greg Oliver (goliver@canoemail.com)
& Jon Waldman (jonathanwaldman@hotmail.com)

NOTES ON THE PHOTOS

We'd like you to make note of some of the talented men and women who have helped bring some flair to SLAM! Wrestling. (We also lament the fact that the photos from the site's early days, taken with an Apple QuickTake, just don't hold up to high-quality reproduction.)

Photographers

Mike Mastrandrea is the SLAM! Wrestling staff photographer. The Toronto-based lensman has been shooting wrestling for over 15 years. His work has been seen in publications across North America, Europe and Asia. The cover image was shot by Mike at WrestleMania 24 in Orlando, Florida, at the Citrus Bowl while on assignment for the website. (http://slam.canoe.ca/Slam/Wrestling/Gallery/mastrandrea.html)

Andrea Kellaway is a Toronto-based photographer who captures witty and powerful portraits. (www.andreakellaway.com)

Bob Leonard was a promoter and photographer for Calgary's Stampede Wrestling from 1963 to 1989, and is the Director of Canadian Affairs for the Cauliflower Alley Club. (bob.leonard@accesscomm.ca)

Bruno Silveira covers the scene from his New England home, and runs the website www.TopRopePhotography.com.

Christine Coons travels to many area fan fests from her home in Connecticut. (www.studio11b.com)

Roger Baker shot for magazines like The Wrestler, Inside Wrestling, Wrestling Revue, and Boxing Illustrated from 1958 to 1973.

Terry Dart is a long-time fan from London, Ontario, who has probably been to more wrestling shows than the entire SLAM! Wrestling staff combined.

Mike Lano has covered wrestling, boxing, mixed martial arts and TV/movie celebrities around the world since 1966, and has many radio projects on the go. He is the official photographer for the Cauliflower Alley Club. (wrealano@aol.com)

Collections

Chris Swisher Collection (www.csclassicwrphotos.com) — Includes the Lil' Al collection of negatives and photos, negatives from part of the Early Yetter collection, the Detroit area from the '60s & '70s, negatives taken by Scott Teal from the '70s, the collection of photos and items from promoter Fred Ward of Columbus, Georgia.

Wrestling Revue Archives (www.wrestleprints.com) — Brian Bukantis is publisher of *Wrestling Revue* and curator of the Wrestling Revue Archives, which has continued to grow with new acquisitions.

The SPORT Collection (www.thesportgallery.com), based in Toronto, is one of the largest and most significant collections of 20th century sports photography in the world.

Sun Media (www.torontosun.com/buy/) — The collection includes not only Sun Media photographs but also *Toronto Telegram* images dating back to the 1900s.

Mike Mastrandrea

Matt Mackinder, Jason Clevett, Mike Mastrandrea, and Ryan Nation are not mistaken for the Four Horsemen at a Ring of Honor show in Detroit before WrestleMania 23.

JBL has trouble with Steven Johnson's politics.

John Cena and his new bud Jason Clevett.

Jon Waldman gets down with the Hardys.

Kenai Andrews dares to ask Batista about haircuts.